Introduction to Buddhist East Asia

SUNY series in Asian Studies Development

Roger T. Ames and Peter D. Hershock, editors

Introduction to Buddhist East Asia

Edited by

ROBERT H. SCOTT AND JAMES McRAE

Cover: Bodhisattva Avalokiteshvara in Water Moon Form (Shuiyue Guanyin). 11th Century, China. Metropolitan Museum of Art. Fletcher Fund, 1928. 28.56

Published by State University of New York Press, Albany

For information, contact State University of New York Press, Albany, NY
www.sunypress.edu

Library of Congress Cataloging-in-Publication Data

Names: Scott, Robert H., (Assistant Professor of Philosophy), editor. |
  McRae, James, 1976– editor.
Title: Introduction to Buddhist East Asia / edited by Robert H. Scott and
  James McRae.
Description: Albany : State University of New York Press, 2023. | Series:
  SUNY series in Asian studies development | Includes bibliographical
  references and index.
Identifiers: LCCN 2022030251 | ISBN 9781438492414 (hardcover : alk. paper) |
  ISBN 9781438492438 (ebook) | ISBN 9781438492421 (pbk. : alk. paper)
Subjects: LCSH: Buddhism—Study and teaching—East Asia. | Buddhism—East
  Asia. | Buddhism—Study and teaching.
Classification: LCC BQ614 .I586 2023 | DDC 294.309095—dc23/eng/20220709
LC record available at https://lccn.loc.gov/2022030251

10 9 8 7 6 5 4 3 2 1

We dedicate this book to undergraduate teachers who are devoted to diversifying the humanities curriculum and to the staff of the East-West Center in Honolulu, Hawaiʻi, who worked tirelessly to make the 2018 NEH Buddhist East Asia Summer Institute a reality, and without whom this book would never have been possible. Mahalo nui loa.

Contents

Acknowledgments

Robert H. Scott: I would like to thank the University of North Georgia for its Presidential Summer Incentive Award program and the National Endowment for the Humanities for providing generous support for my work on this project. It has been a pleasure to work with James McRae, and I want to thank him for his tireless work on this project. Special thanks to Peter Hershock for his excellent leadership in organizing the 2018 Summer Institute, *Buddhist East Asia: The Interplay of Religion, the Arts, and Politics* from which this work grew. I am also grateful to Robert E. Buswell Jr., John Russon, and Jin Y. Park for their insights on various themes related to this project. Finally, I would like to thank my family, especially Elizabeth, Emma, Henry, and Julieta, for their love and support.

James McRae: I would like to thank Peter Hershock, Meiko Arai, Audrey Minei, Nathan Lancaster, June Kuramoto, and all the staff at the East-West Center for putting together the NEH Buddhist East Asia Summer Institute (2018), which planted the "karmic seeds" for this book. I would also like to gratefully acknowledge the National Endowment for the Humanities, whose support made the Summer Institute possible. I offer sincere gratitude to Pepper Davis and to the Buschman family for their generous support of my research. Many thanks to my family—especially my wife Heather Thornton McRae, my son Jack McRae, my parents John and Derrill McRae, my wife's parents John and Catherine Thornton, and my brother Andrew—for their love and support (and patience). Thanks very much to Robert H. Scott, who envisioned this project while we were in Hawai'i and invited me to join him as co-editor, and with whom it has been a great pleasure to work. Thanks to Sujung Kim for helping with the Korean glossary terms. Finally, I offer my heartfelt gratitude to the staff at SUNY Press—especially James Peltz and our series editors, Roger T. Ames and Peter D. Hershock—with whom it is always a great pleasure to work. Mahalo and aloha!

Foreword

PETER D. HERSHOCK

This collection of essays, edited and written by and for undergraduate educators, marks a deeply welcomed turning point in the scholarly study and presentation of Buddhism. Academic studies of Buddhism in the West can be dated back at least to Michel-Jean-François Ozeray's *Recherches sur Buddou ou Bouddou*, published in Paris in 1817. For much of the two centuries since then, academic investigations of Buddhism remained a fringe pursuit undertaken by small numbers of religious studies specialists.

For a host of reasons, this began to change midway through the twentieth century. Interest in Buddhism blossomed, and original research on Buddhism is now mainstream and stretches across a range of humanities disciplines, including history, literature, art history, anthropology, philosophy, and religious studies, but also extends into such social science disciplines as political science and economics, and increasingly into the sciences, most notably psychology and neuroscience. This blossoming of scholarly commitment to the study of Buddhism has had the happy consequence of vastly expanding the number of expert academics ready to introduce Buddhism to their students, both graduate and undergraduate. Interest in Buddhism has also blossomed among students, however, and it is no longer uncommon for college and university teachers without graduate training in Buddhist studies to include Buddhism in their courses.

This collection of essays emerged out of a multidisciplinary, four-week summer residential institute on *Buddhist East Asia: The Interplay of Religion, the Arts and Politics* that was hosted in 2018 at the East-West Center in

Honolulu and funded by the National Endowment for the Humanities. That program was designed to strike a pedagogically useful balance between the needs for both breadth and depth in undergraduate teaching and learning and was structured both geographically and historically to afford participants with an understanding of how Buddhism functioned in East Asia as a new "total care system" that addressed both personal and social needs in ways that were inseparable from the dynamics of cultural interaction, artistic production, trade, and politics. The aim of the institute was to provide undergraduate educators with the resources to infuse content on East Asian Buddhism into a range of humanities courses.

The eleven essays included in the volume, along with its substantive introduction, offer readers a topical introduction to the history and dynamics of Buddhism in Chinese, Japanese, and Korean social and cultural contexts. Reflecting the diversity of Buddhist traditions and the complexity of their societal ramifications in East Asia, the contributing authors represent fields ranging from philosophy to religion, film studies, gender studies, and literature. Distinctively, the volume also affords readers with profound and practical insights into the challenges of teaching American undergraduates about Buddhism and how most effectively and creatively to meet them. The intended peer audience of undergraduate educators will find the teaching strategies presented admirably concrete and readily actionable. Yet, specialists whose research focuses on Buddhism will also find value in seeing how their colleagues in the humanities sample the fruits of their specialist labor and with them compose compelling learning opportunities—object lessons in blending content with clarity.

College and university professors are often accused of living in "ivory towers," their heads deep in clouds of arcane and hotly debated minutiae. The contributors to this volume invalidate the caricature. Manifestly evident in their essays are passionate commitments to working with their students to realize the conditions for critically-informed, difference-appreciating, and deeply caring communication and shared deliberation—conditions that are needed now, perhaps more than ever, and not only on our college and university campuses.

Introduction to Buddhist East Asia

Origins, Core Doctrines, Transmission, and Schools

ROBERT H. SCOTT AND JAMES MCRAE

The purpose of this volume is to provide an introduction to the development of Buddhism[1] in East Asia—particularly China, Korea, and Japan—along with practical pedagogical resources for teaching East Asian Buddhism in the undergraduate classroom.[2] Wherever Buddhism germinates throughout the world, it not only changes the culture into which it assimilates, it is also changed by each culture in which it takes root.[3] Each chapter in this volume, including the opening chapters that focus on pedagogy, provides a view onto a significant aspect of Buddhism in its dynamic interplay with culture over the course of two thousand years in East Asia. This introduction is divided into five sections: The first section provides a general historical overview of the origins and development of Buddhism in India; the second section offers a brief summary of core Buddhist doctrines; the third section provides a historical overview of the transmission of Buddhism to East Asia beginning in the 1st century CE in China; the fourth section outlines the principal schools of Buddhism that have arisen in East Asia, several of which continue to flourish to this day; and the final section offers synopses of the following chapters in this anthology.

The Origins of Buddhism

The origins of Buddhism in East Asia trace back to Siddhartha Gautama (San.; Pli. Siddhattha Gotama), who was a prince of the small republic of the Śākya people of the Ganges basin in what now forms the border between Nepal and Northeast India. Generally known as "the historical Buddha," in Mahāyāna Buddhist tradition Gautama is known as Śākyamuni ("the Śākyan sage").[4] The story of his spiritual awakening is probably apocryphal and meant to serve as a spiritual lesson more than as a historical record. Siddhartha was born in 563 BCE in Kapilavastu in an area that is now part of southern Nepal. The son of a king, he lived a life of sheltered luxury until the age of twenty-nine. At that time, while riding outside the palace in his chariot, he witnessed four signs: an elderly man whose body was crippled by advanced age, a man ravaged by disease, a funeral procession, and a recluse sitting in peace. The first three signs made him aware of the existence of suffering in the world, while the fourth sign made him realize that it is possible to transcend suffering through diligent training. Siddhartha left the palace and began to study yoga, first under Arāḍa Kālāma and later under Udraka Rāmaputra. Though he mastered both systems of yoga, Siddhartha found that neither provided a way to eliminate suffering in the world. He then tried asceticism, including extreme bodily mortification, but again found that his questions about the elimination of suffering remained unanswered. Disappointed by available systems of spiritual care, he decided to create his own "middle way" between the self-indulgence of his youth and the self-denial of his life as a recluse. He sat beneath a tree in tranquil meditation until he became enlightened to the nature of suffering, its causes, and the ways to remove these causes.[5] Following his enlightenment, Gautama traveled the region for more than forty years, gathering a cohort of followers who embraced his teachings.

Buddhism arose within the religious context of Brahmanism, which later (around 200 BCE) became known as Hinduism.[6] Brahmanism took root in the region at the twilight of the Indus Valley Civilization (2500–1500 BCE) with the arrival of Aryan people from Central Asia. Along with Brahmanic religion, the Aryans brought the Sanskrit language to the region as well as a four-tier, hierarchical class structure in which the priestly class (brahmin) were set at the top. Central to Brahmanic doctrine and practice is belief in thirty-three gods (Devas), each representing natural forces, along with rites that included hymns and sacrifices performed by priests.[7] Brahmanism was originally based on oral teachings and hymns that were codified in the Vedas sometime between 1000 and 800 BCE. In the Vedas, the ideal of liberation (mokṣa) is conceptualized in terms of gaining an understanding of the unity between one's true self (ātman) and the underlying substance of Ultimate Reality (Brahman). The doctrine of reincarnation (the development of which was likely influenced by non-Aryan sources) arose in close connection with the idea of *karma,* which refers to the moral quality of one's *ātman,* which can be improved through ethical action and the fulfillment of one's social duties in life as defined by one's place in the social hierarchy.

The period in which the Buddha lived (during the 5th century BCE) was characterized by dramatic social and economic change. An increasingly urban, money-based trade economy was rapidly displacing the small, kin-based agrarian communities of the previous millennium, and the expansion of large urban centers of trade in the regional kingdoms of Magadha and Kosala facilitated the ongoing discussion and dissemination of new and diverse ideas and ways of life. Within this dynamic cultural context, a growing number of groups of wandering ascetics, known as *Śramanas,* began to question the Vedic tradition and develop new ways of responding to the rapidly changing social realities. Gautama, upon renouncing his position as a Sakyan prince, joined a group of *Śramanas* and later, following his enlightenment experience, established his own *Śramana* movement that included close followers who would become the first Buddhist monks. That is to say, Buddhism was, at first, a *Śramana* movement, but it soon set itself apart from other such movements including Jainism, the *Ájīvaka* movement, the materialists, and the Skeptics. The Jainists emphasized extreme self-denial and total nonviolence (*ahiṃsā*) as the means to freeing oneself from *karmic* residues; the *Ájīvakas* affirmed a kind of *karmic* fatalism (*niyati*) according to which one could not change one's *karmic* destiny; the materialists rejected the idea of reincarnation, embracing "annihilationism," and the distinguishing mark of the Skeptics was to be critical of all points of view.[8] While the Buddha agreed to some extent with some of the ideas put forward by other *Śramana* movements, such as the shared sense that the *Vedic* understanding of *karma* and rebirth called for some kind of revision, he thought these groups to be too extreme either in terms of their way of life (as with extreme self-denial, promoted by Jainism) or their doctrine (as with the materialist view of extreme annihilationism). Two of the Buddha's closest disciples, Sāriputta and Moggallāna, were at first Skeptics, a movement whose critical approach to all doctrine resonates to some extent with the Buddhist idea of the emptiness of all things (*śūnyatā*).[9] However, in contrast to the extreme tendencies of these other *Śramana* movements, the Buddha developed the broadly applicable idea of the "middle way." For instance, in response to the extreme asceticism embraced by Jainism, the Buddha called for moderation of appetites. In response to the fatalism of the *Ájīvakas,* while the Buddha upheld the power of *karma* to affect the opportunities and outcomes one experiences, he argued just as strongly in favor of the ability to change one's *karma* by altering one's values, intentions, and the relational dynamics one has with others and with one's surroundings.[10] In response to annihilationism put forward by the materialists, the Buddha's response was to not take a stance on the afterlife but, rather, to redirect attention to the central point of his teaching, that the way to end suffering is to end craving.[11] Finally, in relation to Skepticism, while the Buddha's affirmation of *śūnyatā* aligns with a generally skeptical metaphysical understanding of things as empty, the Buddha departs from Skepticism in affirming a few basic doctrines, including the four noble truths, as fundamental guides to enlightenment.

While there is some scholarly disagreement on the precise dates of the Buddha's death as well as the time and place of the subsequent "community councils" that were held to establish the core teachings (*Dhamma*) and monastic codes of conduct (*Vinaya*), many scholars agree that the first community council took place in 400 BCE at Rájagaha in what is now Northeast India. The second and third community councils (estimated to have taken place in 330 BCE at Vesāli and 314 BCE at Pātaliputta) involved heated debates on the monastic codes of conduct and discipline (*Vinaya*) which led to a schism among Buddhist monastics into two fraternities, the *Sthaviravāda* (San.; Pli. *Theravāda*—meaning "ancient teachings") and *Mahāsānghika* (meaning "Belonging to the Universal Sangha"), which later subdivided even further.[12] In total, eighteen or more different fraternities developed in early Buddhism, but the doctrinal differences among the various fraternities, in retrospect, appear to have been relatively minor, and only three primary branches continue today: *Theravāda, Mahāyāna,* and *Vajrayāna.* *Mahāyāna* (literally "the greater vehicle") stemmed from the *Mahāsānghika* fraternity and began to thrive as a separate tradition sometime between 100 BCE and 100 CE in the Kusān empire in Northwest India.[13] *Mahāyāna* is the primary branch of Buddhism that went on to thrive in East Asia. The third branch of Buddhism, *Vajrayāna* (Tantric or Esoteric Buddhism), developed as an offshoot of *Mahāyāna* and has flourished in Tibet and in Japan (as Shingon Buddhism).

It was during the reign of the Magadhan King, Aśoka (268–239 BCE) that the spread of Buddhism accelerated throughout the Indian subcontinent. In the early years of his reign, King Aśoka expanded his empire through bloody conquests; however, following the violent subjugation of the Kalinga region in 259 BCE, Aśoka, having embraced Buddhism a year earlier, felt great remorse for the bloodshed and violence and decided to end the kingdom's policy of violent aggression. Following this turn away from violence, subsequent edicts issued by King Aśoka show that he promptly committed to ruling his kingdom according to the Buddhist *dhamma* and gave up aggressive military conquest.[14] For the remainder of his reign, Aśoka demonstrated the ideal virtues of a *Cakkavatti*, a Buddhist "wheel-turning king," setting up generous public works including widely accessible medical aid, prioritizing education in Buddhist virtues, and advocating for religious freedom and mutual respect among religions.[15] Such was Aśoka's dedication to *Dhamma* that he sent aid and missionaries beyond the borders of his empire, including sending his son Mahinda south to Sri Lanka to establish *Theravāda* Buddhism there, where it continues to thrive to this day. From Sri Lanka, *Theravāda* spread east across the Bay of Bengal to Southeast Asia, where it continues to flourish in Myanmar/Burma, Thailand, Laos, Cambodia, and Malaysia.

Core Doctrines of Buddhism

This section offers a brief overview of the basic tenets of Buddhism in terms of the original teachings of the historical Buddha. While several schools of Buddhism developed in East Asia (discussed in the fourth section below), the core doctrines are shared by all schools.

The central teachings of Buddhism were summarized by Siddhartha Gautama, the historical Buddha, in the first sermon he delivered in Deer Park just after his awakening.[16] The Buddha presented these teachings in the form of the Four Noble Truths (Pli. *cattāri*[17] *ariyasaccāni*; San. *catvāri āryasatyāni*; Chi. 四聖諦 *sìshèngdì*; Kor. *sa-seong-je*; Jpn. 四諦 *shitai*).[18] The First Noble Truth states that all life is characterized by *dukkha* (San. *duḥkha*; Chi. 苦 *kǔ*; Kor. *ko*; Jpn. *ku*), which can be translated as "suffering," "sorrow," or "unsatisfactoriness." *Dukkha* refers to physical pain, psychological distress, and the general sense of dissatisfaction that accompanies everyday living. At its worst, *dukkha* is epitomized by things such as infirmity, sickness, poverty, famine, death (via natural causes or violence), warfare, racism, and genocide. *Dukkha* is made worse by the fact that human beings are trapped within *saṃsāra* (San. *saṃsāra*; Chi. 輪迴 *lúnhuí*; Kor. *ryunhoe*; Jpn. *rinne*), the cycle of rebirth. A person's actions build up karma (Pli. *kamma*; San. *karma*; Chi. 業 *yè*; Kor. *eop*; Jpn. *gō*), which is a kind of metaphysical record of a person's moral worth. Morally significant actions accrue karma, which determines the type of rebirth that a person gets after death. Immoral humans with a great deal of negative karma might be born as nonhuman animals or into a different realm of existence (e.g., one of many hells). Moral humans who have built up karmic merit will return in a more favorable rebirth, for example, as a human being of favored social status with the means to focus on spiritual cultivation. Because life is characterized by *dukkha,* rebirth is not a blessing, so the goal of Buddhism is to permanently exit the cycle of *saṃsāra.*[19]

The Second Noble Truth is that *dukkha* comes as a result of *taṇhā* (San. *tṛṣṇā,* Chi. 貪愛 *tānài,* Kor. *gal-ae,* Jpn. 渴愛 *katsuai*), which literally means "thirst," though it is often translated as "craving." Because of our ignorant attachment to false ideals, we crave things that we cannot or should not have, which causes us to act in ways that promote suffering. This is related to the Buddhist notion of *paṭiccasamuppāda* (San. *pratītyasamutpāda;* Chi. 緣起 *yuánqǐ;* Kor. *yeongi;* Jpn. 緣起*engi*), which can be translated as "interdependent arising," "dependent co-arising," or "dependent origination." The true nature of reality is that all things exist as part of an interdependent process in which all things are impermanent (Pli. *anicca;* San. *anitya;* Chi. 無常 *wúcháng;* Kor. *musang;* Jpn. *mujō*), coming into being, persisting for a finite period, and decaying into oblivion. Contrary to the Hindu notion that human beings have an *ātman,* or true self that is one with Brahman (unchanging Ultimate Reality), Buddhism asserts the idea of no-self or non-self (Pāli *anatta;* San. *anātman;* Chi. 無我 *wúwǒ;* Kor. *mua;* Jpn. *muga*). What I call my "self" exists only as a temporary aggregate of matter that is a function of a continual process of interchange with the world around it. Craving comes when I attach myself to notions of ego and permanence.[20] For example, if I'm attached to the false idea that I'll never get old, I will go to great lengths to preserve a youthful appearance (e.g., comb-overs, liposuction, Botox, face-lifts, etc.) rather than aging gracefully and enjoying each of life's stages as they come. If I'm attached to wealth, I will harm my employees, customers, and other stakeholders to maximize personal profit. If I'm attached to the illusion of white supremacy and the unjust privileges it accrues, I will cause immeasurable harm to members of my community to promote my misguided racist attitudes. In general, if we persist in our ignorant attachment to false ideals, we will always suffer.

The Third Noble Truth says that if we eliminate our ignorant attachment to false ideals, we can eliminate the craving that causes suffering. This is Buddhism's optimistic solution to the reality of *dukkha:* most of our suffering is self-inflicted because of our attachments, and we can alleviate suffering by reshaping the way that we view and experience the world.[21]

The Fourth Noble Truth is the Eightfold Path, which outlines the method of practice that must be used to eliminate ignorance, craving, and suffering. It consists of three categories of cultivation: wisdom (right views and intentions), ethics (right speech, actions, and livelihood), and meditation (right effort, mindfulness, and concentration). All three categories are complementary: meditation promotes wisdom about the true nature of reality as nonsubstantial and dynamically relational interdependent arising; wisdom, in turn, promotes compassion for all beings (who are part of the same interrelated process); compassion encourages one to diligently meditate and pursue wisdom. One who has diligently followed the Eightfold Path can attain *nibbana* (San. *nirvāṇa*; Chi. 涅槃 *nièpán*; Kor. *yeolban*; Jpn. *nehan*), the extinguishing of one's karma that will lead to release from *saṃsāra*. In Theravāda Buddhism, one who has attained *nibbana* is known as an *arahant* (San. *arhat*; Chi. 阿羅漢 *āluóhàn*; Kor. *arahan*; Jpn. *arakan*), and attaining this state is the ultimate goal of one's training. In Mahāyāna Buddhism, one who realizes *nibbana* will vow to become a *bodhisatta* (San. *bodhisattva*; Chi. 菩薩 *púsà*; Kor. *bosal*; Jpn. *bosatsu*), a buddha who chooses to remain in *saṃsāra* until all sentient beings have become awakened.[22]

The Transmission of Buddhism to East Asia

THE TRANSMISSION OF BUDDHISM TO CHINA

Buddhism arrived in China from Central Asia sometime during the first century CE, entering by way of trade routes ("silk roads") that extended from the Chinese Capital Chang'an (now Xi'an) through Central Asia to the Indian subcontinent. According to legend, Emperor Ming of China (58–75 CE) dreamed of "a mystifying foreign deity with golden hue," foretelling the arrival of Buddhism in China.[23] In the context of the decline of the Han Dynasty (200 BCE–220 CE) and throughout the ensuing 360 years of divided kingdoms, Buddhism took root in China. While some Buddhist ideas and practices, such as the doctrine of emptiness (Pli. *suññatā*; San. *śūnyatā*), were entirely new to the region, others resonated with indigenous Confucian and Daoist beliefs. For instance, the high importance given to written texts by Buddhist monks and the Buddhist idea of no-self were values compatible with Chinese literary culture and the Confucian understanding of identity as defined in terms of a relational harmony of differences.

By the first century CE, Buddhist teachings and practices were being transmitted, little by little, into China via the "silk road" from the Kusān empire in Northwest India through Central Asia. By the third century CE, Kuchean monks were regularly transmitting both *Theravāda* and *Mahāyāna* texts along this route.[24] The divided kingdoms period in China (220–589 CE) proved conducive to the reception of new ideas, as no state religion was enforced. During this period, many in the educated elite in China turned to Buddhist texts and practices. The growth of Buddhism in China was further facilitated by the steady translation of several *Mahāyāna* texts by Lokaksema (born circa 147 CE, known by the Chinese name Zhī Lóujiāchèn), a missionary from Central Asia, and Kumārajīva (344–413 CE, aka Jiūmóluóshí) a Kuchean monk and founder of the Old Sanlun school (see the first part of the following section below) who translated more than three hundred *Mahāyāna* Sutras. While some early Chinese Buddhist scholastics followed the highly formalized Yogācāra approach to Buddhist textual analysis, which emphasized the ideas of "three natures" and eight levels of consciousness, culminating in "appropriating" or "storehouse" consciousness (Pli. *ālayavijñāna*; San. *Ālāyavijñāna*), Kumārajīva was strongly influenced by the Madhyamaka school, which emphasized the doctrines of emptiness (San. *śūnyatā*), two truths (conventional and ultimate), and conditioned origination. Another important figure during this time was Daosheng (360–434 CE), a Sanlun Buddhist monk who was instrumental in popularizing the central East Asian Buddhist doctrine of Buddha-nature, the idea that all sentient beings have the potential for enlightenment. The doctrine of emptiness, by contrast, met with some resistance in China due to its perceived negative connotations, but the monk Dushun (557–640 CE) was able to draw out the positive significance of the doctrine of emptiness by linking it with the Confucian principle of *li* (禮, the underlying principle of reality, tied to ritual practices), thereby bringing a central Buddhist concept into attunement with Chinese cultural sensibilities.[25]

As access to Buddhist texts and translations increased from the third to fifth centuries CE, a rigorous tradition of Chinese Buddhist scholasticism grew that placed particular emphasis on the study of *Mahāyāna* texts, especially the *Lotus Sūtra*, which rose in importance as the focal text of the Tiantai school (see the following section). Other texts that became central to Buddhist practice as it began to flourish in China during the divided kingdoms period included the *Nirvana Sūtra*, the *Prajñāpāramīta Sūtras*, and the *Vimalakīrti-Nirdēśā Sūtra*.[26] Tensions arose, however, in the fifth century CE in the Northern states between monastics and rulers due to the independence of the monasteries from the states. In addition to the independence of monasteries from the government, another point of contention involved the requirement for monks to take a vow of celibacy, which was seen as conflicting with the central Confucian virtue of filial piety that placed family relationships at the center of virtuous living. Such tensions culminated in state-led persecutions of Buddhism in the Northern states from 446–451 CE (in the Wei kingdom) and 574–577 CE (in the Zhou kingdom).

In 581 CE, following the reunification of China under the Sui Dynasty, Buddhism returned to favor as the state-sponsored religion, and it was embraced by all sectors of Chinese society throughout the Sui (581–618 CE) and Tang (618–907 CE) Dynasties, except for a three-year period of persecution from 842–845 CE under the Emperor Wuzang.[27] From the late sixth to seventh century CE, support for Buddhist institutions from the state as well as from private donors rapidly increased, enabling the widespread construction of Buddhist temples, monasteries, and shrines, the crafting of ritual objects, and the casting of Buddhist statues. By the eighth century CE, 70 to 80 percent of the total wealth of the empire was in Buddhist hands, but these days of overflowing abundance for Buddhist institutions in China were short lived, as public criticism of the economic privileges of monasteries increased in the ninth century, leading to imperial proscriptions that placed limits on donations to Buddhist institutions.[28] In spite of these setbacks, Buddhism remained the dominant religion in China throughout the Tang, through the subsequent warring period (907–960 CE), and into the Song dynasty (960–1279 CE).

During the Sui and Tang dynasties, four primary Chinese Buddhist schools emerged: Chan (founded, according to legend, by Bodhidharma in the sixth century), Huayan (founded by Dushun in the early seventh century), Tiantai (founded by Zhiyi in the sixth century), and Pure Land (founded by Tanluan in the early sixth century—see the following section for more on these schools of Buddhism). Despite the variety of schools, there was a fluid interchange among monks of different schools, and monks of all schools shared monastic institutions and resided together in "public monasteries." In most cases the differences among schools were more a matter of emphases on focal texts or practices than stark divisions.[29]

The immense impact of Buddhism on Chinese society and culture remained largely intact during the Song Dynasty (960–1279 CE), though its cultural influence was moderated by the rise of Neo-Confucianism in the late twelfth century. Buddhist practice and monastic life remained an important part of Chinese culture and society throughout the Ming (1368–1644 CE) and Qing (1644–1911 CE) dynasties all the way up to the Cultural Revolution of 1966–1976, which had a devastating effect on all religious practice in China. Since 1976, however, religious tolerance has improved in China, and Buddhism has been experiencing a restoration and resurgence.[30]

The Transmission of Buddhism to Korea

The transmission of Buddhism from China to the Korean peninsula began in the late fourth century CE. In 372 CE, Fujuan, a former king of the Qin dynasty in the Northern kingdom of China, sent the Sanlun (三論; Kor. Samnon; Jpn. Sanron) monk Shundao to Koguryeo, one of the three kingdoms on the peninsula (Paekche and Silla were the other two). The king of Koguryeo welcomed the monks and commissioned the building of the first two Buddhist monasteries on the peninsula in their honor.[31] Twelve years later, in 384 CE, Buddhism was conveyed to the Paekche kingdom by monks sent from the southern Chinese state of Eastern Jin. Among the monks in the convoy was the Central Asian monk Mālānanda who led the way in introducing Buddhism to the Paekche court. The Paekche court readily embraced the new teachings, and in the first half of the sixth century CE, the Paekche King Seong (523–554 CE) commissioned the construction of the first Buddhist temple complex in the region, Taet'ong-sa. King Seong also sent monks to Japan, introducing Buddhism there (see below).

The third kingdom on the peninsula, the Silla, was resistant to Buddhism until (according to tradition) a miraculous event occurred in 527 CE in which a courtier named Ichadon, who advocated for the construction of a Buddhist temple, was beheaded. According to tradition, when Ichadon was beheaded a white liquid flowed from his neck, and his head immediately flew away to a nearby mountain. News of this event led to the Silla court embracing Buddhism as the state religion, and the first Buddhist temple was built in the region in 535 CE.[32] State-sponsored Buddhism in the Silla kingdom proved instrumental to military recruitment leading up to the Silla victory in the battle for unification of the three kingdoms. A Silla government-sponsored institution called *hwarang* gathered youth for education in native traditions, military training, and Buddhist religious practice devoted to the worship of Maitreya, the Buddha of the future. The *hwarang* institution effectively promoted a patriotic spirit and prepared young military leaders who fought in the war for unification in 668 CE.[33]

As Buddhism developed and spread across the Korean peninsula, it combined in a pluralistic fashion with indigenous shamanic traditions as well as with Confucian and Daoist beliefs. In the late seventh century, the Korean monk Weonhyo's classic text *Ten Approaches to the Pacification of Disputes* became very influential in promoting an ecumenical spirit among these traditions, and the peninsula also proved receptive to a plurality of schools of Buddhism arriving from China during the unified Silla. In the early unification period, the monk Uisang (625–702 CE), having studied with the Huayan master Zhiyan (602–668 CE) in China, transmitted Huayan (華嚴; Kor. Hwaeom; Jpn. Kegon) Buddhism to the peninsula and was a founder of the *Paseok-sa* temple.[34] Hwaeom remained an important Buddhist tradition on the peninsula throughout the unified Silla well into the Goryeo dynasty (918–1392 CE).

Chan Buddhism (禪; Kor. Seon; Jpn. Zen) arrived on the peninsula in 821 CE through the monk Doeui, who had received mind-to-mind transmission from the Chan master Xitang Zhizang (735–814 CE) in Hongzhou in Southeastern China. The third disciple of Doeui, Ch'ejing (804–880 CE), was able to secure state recognition for Seon. In 858 CE, with the backing of the state, Ch'ejing helped to establish the first temple for the Kaji-Seon school (on Mt. Kaji), which grew into the "nine mountains of Seon" community and continues to thrive up to the present day.[35]

During the Goryeo dynasty (918–1392 CE) Buddhism became the state sponsored religion on the peninsula, and state-administered monastic exams were put in place as a system of rank for both monastic and secular offices. While this situation facilitated the growth of Buddhist practices and institutions, tensions began to rise among Buddhist schools during the Goryeo. In the twelfth century the Cheontae (Chi. Tiāntāi) and the Hwaeom (Chi. Huáyán) schools accused the Seon school, which emphasized meditation and mind-to-mind transmission of enlightenment, of departing too far from the authority of Buddhist texts. A key figure in diffusing these tensions was the Seon monk Chinul. Chinul affirmed the importance of both sudden (mind-to-mind) awakening and gradual cultivation (which involved the careful study of texts), a doctrinal view that diverged from the Chinese Linji school of Chan, which affirmed sudden awakening and sudden cultivation. Chinul's influence was crucial to restoring the ecumenical spirit of Korean Buddhism as well as in validating Seon practice in Korea, which remains the most active school of Buddhism in Korea today.[36]

During the Cheoson dynasty (1392–1910), Buddhism lost state sponsorship, as Neo-Confucianism gained favor with the state. Despite the lack of state support, Buddhism continued to be practiced throughout the Cheoson period and formed an important part of the social fabric in Korea, where it maintains a vital presence today.[37]

THE TRANSMISSION OF BUDDHISM TO JAPAN

In 538 CE, King Seong of the Paekche court sent Samnon (Chi. Sānlùn) Buddhist monks across the sea to introduce Buddhism to Japan. However, Buddhism initially met with resistance from the Japanese nobility, who considered it a foreign religion that would anger the *kami* (indigenous Shintō gods).[38] By the seventh century, however, Buddhism was embraced by Japan nobility and a productive, pluralistic relationship between indigenous Shintō practices, Confucianism, and Buddhism rapidly took root and flourished. By 692 CE there were more than five hundred Buddhist Temples in Japan,[39] and the expansion of Buddhism continued during the Nara period (710–784 CE), during which Kegon (Chi. Huáyán) Buddhism became the most prevalent school (see the following section for more on Kegon Buddhism). One distinguishing characteristic of the Nara period was its emphasis on gender equity, especially during the reign of Emperor Shōmu (720–749 CE) and his consort Kōmyō (701–760 CE). Shōmu founded a network of official temples that included at least one temple for monks and another for nuns in each province.[40] The strong emphasis on gender equity in Japan was short-lived, however, as the ordination of female monks declined during the Heian period (794–1185 CE). During the Heian period, there was a sharp increase in "household nuns," that is, women who were ordained but who stayed at home in family life rather than living in celibacy in a monastery, which might have been viewed as a way of resolving the tension between filial values and monastic vows.[41]

From the eighth to the thirteenth centuries, several other schools of Buddhism arrived in Japan. In the late eighth century, the monk Saichō (767–822 CE), having travelled to China, brought Tendai (Chi. Tiāntái) Buddhism to Japan. In the early ninth century, the charismatic monk Kūkai, having studied Vajrayāna Buddhism under the monk Huiguo in China, introduced esoteric Shingon Buddhism in Japan and founded the Kangōbuji monastery on Mt. Kōya. In the tenth century, the monk Kūya helped transmit Pure Land Buddhism to Japan, later advocates of which include the very influential monks Hōnen (1133–1212 CE) and Shinran (1173–1263 CE). Pure Land Buddhism flourished and remains the most popular form of Buddhism in Japan to this day. During the Kamakura period (1185–1333 CE), a military government (the Shogunate) came to power and remained in place up to the modern period (1868 CE). Early in the Kamakura period, the monk Yōsai (1141–1215 CE), having traveled to China, founded Rinzai Zen in Japan. In 1227 CE, the monk Eihei Dōgen

(1200–1253 CE), after receiving transmission from the master Tiantong Rujing of the Caodong School of Chan in China, founded the Sōtō Zen school in Japan.[42] While all schools of Buddhism in Japan share a few core doctrines, significant differences in the practices and focal texts of the various schools remain, as will be discussed below in the following section.

In the modern period (1868–1945), in an effort to restore indigenous traditions and promote patriotism, Shintō was embraced as the state religion and separation edicts required kami deities to be removed from Buddhist temples. Such measures curtailed the pluralistic spirit of Buddhism in Japan and relegated the influence of Buddhism to the private sphere.[43] In the early twentieth century, however, discourse about Buddhism expanded in the public sphere through scholars at Kyoto University such as Nishida Kitarō (1870–1945) and Nishitani Keiji (1900–1990), who drew out the metaphysical implications of Zen Buddhism in relation to contemporary European philosophy. Known as the "Kyoto School," this academic movement drew a great deal of scholarly attention to Japanese Buddhism and highlighted to a global audience the universal relevance of Buddhist doctrine to the human condition. In postwar Japan, there has been an increased spirit of ecumenism among Shintō, Christian, and Buddhist practices; however, while Buddhist monasteries and several Buddhist schools remain active, including Zen, Shingon, Kegon, and Pure Land, religious life in Japan has become increasingly privatized.[44]

Major Schools of East Asian Buddhism

SĀNLÙN[45] (三論; KOR. SAMNON; JPN. SANRON)

"Sanlun" means "three treatises" and refers to the three major texts that the tradition views as authoritative: Nāgārjuna's *Fundamental Verses on the Middle Way* (San. *Mūlamadhyamaka-kārikā*; Chi. 中論 *Zhōng Lùn*) and *Twelve Gate Treatise* (San. *Dvādaśadvāra-śāstra*; Chi. 十二門 *Shíèr Mén Lùn*), along with his disciple Aryadeva's *One Hundred Verses Treatise* (San. *Śata-śāstra*; Chi. 百論 *Bǎi Lùn*). "Old Sanlun" was founded by Kumārajīva (344–413 CE), who translated all three texts into Chinese, while "New Sanlun" appeared later when the monk Jizang (549–623 CE) gave a systematic account of its philosophy.[46]

Sanlun developed from Indian Mādhyamaka philosophy. It adopts Nāgārjuna's two-truth theory, which argues that there are both conventional truths about reality that are useful for daily life and ultimate truths that can be discovered through meditation, the latter of which often differ from our everyday understanding of the world. Wisdom also has two levels: ordinary wisdom, which draws a distinction between subject (the knower) and object (what is known), and extraordinary wisdom (Pli. *paññā*; San. *prajñā*; Chi. 智慧 *zhīhuì*; Kor. *jihye*; Jpn. *chie*), which realizes the emptiness of such distinctions.[47]

Sanlun argues that suffering comes from attachment to objects and false ideals. Nonattachment can be achieved by cultivating "no mind" (Chi. 無心 *wúxīn*; Kor. *musim*; Jpn. *mushin*) in which ordinary conceptions of self and mind fall away, and all things are perceived as interrelated and in possession of Buddha-nature. Growing away from its Mādhyamaka roots, Sanlun stresses the ethical implications of dependent co-arising (San. *pratītyasamutpāda*) and Buddha-nature more than the theoretical logic of emptiness. This emphasis upon Buddhism as a practical philosophy had an enormous influence on Chinese culture, particularly the development of Tiantai Buddhism (see below for more on Tiantai Buddhism).[48] The Sanlun monk Daosheng (c. 360–434 CE) was the first to popularize the idea that all beings possess Buddha-nature and are thus capable of enlightenment. Though he was initially criticized by senior monks for this view due to its apparent contradiction of the *Nirvana Sutra*, Buddha-nature ultimately became one of the most important concepts for virtually all schools of East Asian Buddhism.[49]

FĂXIÀNG (法相; KOR. BEOPSANG; JPN. HOSSŌ)

Făxiàng was founded in 645 CE by the Chinese monk Xuanzang (600–664 CE), who traveled to India in 629 CE to study Yogācāra Buddhism. It was later imported into Korea as Beopsang Buddhism by Woncheuk (613–696 CE) and into Japan as Hossō Buddhism by Dōshō (629–700 CE).[50] The names *Faxiang, Beopsang*, and *Hossō* are translations of the Sanskrit term *dharma lakṣaṇa*, which means "dharma marks" or "dharma characteristics." The term *dharma*, in this context, refers to the constituents of phenomenal reality, the things that make up the world around us. Yogācāra argues that our consciousness (Pli. *viññāṇa*; San. *vijñāna*; Chi. 識 *shí*; Kor. *sik*; Jpn. *shiki*) influences our experience of reality. There is a "storehouse consciousness" (Pli. *ālayaviññāna*; San. *ālāyavijñāna*; Chi. 阿賴耶識 *ālàiyēshí*; Kor. *aroeyasik*; Jpn. *Araya-shiki*) that is a repository of our karma based upon our past actions. This storehouse consciousness conditions our perceptions of the world. Because unenlightened people experience the world through the lens of karma, the world as they know it is a mental fabrication.[51]

Fǎxiàng diverges from traditional Yogācāra philosophy on the issue of *gotra* theory, which argues that human beings are born with an innate potential for spiritual achievement based upon their karma. *Gotra* theory claims that some people are *icchantikas*, deluded beings who can never reach enlightenment. While early Fǎxiàng endorsed *gotra* theory, Woncheuk rejected it because it contradicted the idea that all beings manifest Buddha-nature (innate enlightenment). Woncheuk's interpretation of Fǎxiàng became the orthodox view in China, Korea, and Japan, and reflects the positive world-view that came to characterize East Asian Buddhism.[52]

Tiāntāi (天台; Kor. Cheontae; Jpn. Tendai)

One of the most prominent East Asian schools of Buddhism, Tiantai takes its name from the mountain where Zhiyi (538–597 CE), the third patriarch of the tradition, trained and taught.[53] Tiantai philosophy is grounded in the notion that the *tathatā*—the "suchness" (San. *tathātā*; Chi. 真如 *zhēnrú*; Kor. *jinyeo*; Jpn. *shinnyo*) or fundamental nature of reality—is Buddha-nature. Insight into dependent co-arising yields knowledge of the emptiness of distinctions and an awareness that all beings are interdependent, which in turn generates compassion for all sentient beings. Tiantai asserts that both meditation and doctrinal study are equally important for awakening.[54]

The central doctrine of Tiantai is the notion of "3,000 realms in an instant of thought" (Chi. 一念三千 *yī niàn sān qiān*; Kor. *ilnyeom samcheon*; Jpn. *ichinen sanzen*), which refers to the interdependent nature of all things in the universe. This can be experienced via "the threefold contemplation in a single mind" (Chi. 一心三観 *yīxīn sān guān*; Kor. *ilsim samgwan*; Jpn. *isshin sangan*) in which one realizes the provisional truth that all things are impermanent, the ultimate truth that all things are empty, and the middle truth that all things are a mean between impermanence and emptiness. These three should not be viewed oppositionally, but rather as a "round threefold truth" of mutual complementarity.[55]

The proliferation of Buddhist schools in China caused many people to question why there were so many conflicting doctrines. Zhiyi argued that the historical Buddha revealed his teachings progressively based on his audience's capacity for understanding. His first twenty years of teachings were simple and foundational, forming the core components of the "lesser vehicle." The second period introduced the basic Mahāyāna concepts associated with the Yogācāra and Madhyamaka schools. The third teaching period offered advanced Mahāyāna teachings. In his final days, the Buddha gave his most advanced teachings in the form of the *Huayan* and *Lotus Sutras*. Because Zhiyi believed the *Huayan Sutra* to be too esoteric to be understood by everyone, he chose the *Lotus Sutra* as the foundational text of Tiantai Buddhism.[56]

The *Lotus Sutra* explains how the Buddha used "skillful means" (Pli. *upaya*; San. *upāya*; Chi. 方便*fāngbiàn*; Kor. *bangpyeon*; Jpn. *hōben*) to present his teaching at his students' level of understanding in order to progressively lead them from lower, partial truths to higher, complete truth. Following this, Tiantai describes its teachings as "Round Teachings" because they encircle everything. Other schools of Buddhism are not wrong, but they offer simpler, more limited visions of the truth. The example of a chariot can be used to illustrate the Tiantai school's doctrine of three truths (provisional, empty, and middle). A chariot can be provisionally called "chariot" because it came into existence as a result of specific causes and conditions that shaped it in a particular way; that is, when I say "chariot," I mean "a two-wheeled vehicle that is pulled by a horse." The concept *chariot* is also empty because there is no intrinsic, universal thing to which it corresponds (a "form" as Plato would have it). *Chariot* is just a linguistic handle that we use to refer to a temporary aggregate of matter that performs a certain function. There is also a nondualistic, middle truth between these: a chariot can be aptly described as both provisional and empty and, at the same time, as neither provisional nor empty. A chariot exists in the tension between the extremes of the provisional and the empty. Zhiyi uses this nondualistic three truth theory to understand enlightenment. The deluded mind and the pure mind are not separate, but rather part of the same interconnected process.[57]

Saichō (767–822 CE), also known as Dengyō Daishi, founded the Tendai school at Mount Hiei near Kyoto, Japan, after studying for a year at Mount Tiantai in China. Tendai became the most influential school of Japanese Buddhism. It emphasized the doctrine of original enlightenment (Chi. 本覺 *běnjué*; Kor. *bongak*; Jpn. *hongaku*), the idea that since everything possesses Buddha-nature, all beings are inherently enlightened and can thus attain immediate awakening once we eschew the delusions that mask our true nature. Tendai also emphasized the interconnection of all things: every person constantly affects and is affected by the world around them.[58] Saichō emphasizes *shikan* (Chi. 止観 *zhǐguān*) meditation as the method through which one can realize the truth of the Middle Way that all things are both empty and provisionally existing. Originally developed by Zhiyi, *shikan* involves seated meditation in which one calms one's mind to directly experience the world. Saichō also emphasizes socially engaged Buddhism with his philosophy of *ichigu wo terasu* (一隅を照らす), or "light up one corner [of the world]." In this way, Saichō emphasized that Buddhists have the responsibility to devote their time, money, and effort to the betterment of the world around them.[59]

Huáyán (華嚴; Kor. Hwaeom; Jpn. Kegon)

Huayan was founded by Dushun (557–640 CE) and significantly expanded by its third partriach, Fazang (643–712 CE). It takes its name from the *Flower Garland Sutra* (San. *Avataṃsaka Sūtra*; Chi. 華嚴經 *Huáyán Jīng*), which it considers to be the highest teaching of the historical Buddha.[60] Huayan was imported into Japan as the Kegon school in the eighth century CE.[61] It was the most dominant Buddhist school of the Nara Period (710–794 CE). Imported into Korea as Hwaeom, it has remained one of the most influential Buddhist traditions in East Asia.[62]

According to Huayan, because all things are interdependent, there are no fundamental differences between things, only conventional distinctions that we draw for the sake of convenience. All things exist only as a function of their relationships to other things. This interdependence is described through the metaphor of Indra's Jewel Net. The universe is like an infinite net made of shining jewels interconnected by strings. Each jewel perfectly reflects the other jewels and is in turn reflected by them. Just as every jewel in Indra's net is connected to and reflects every other jewel, everything in the universe is interconnected with every other thing through interdependent arising.[63] This idea of interconnectedness is also described in "The Treatise on the Golden Lion," which Fazang wrote for Empress Wu to explain the complexities of Huayan in plain language using the metaphor of a golden lion figure at the palace. Just as the lion only exists because a skilled artist shaped it from gold, all things exist only because of their relationships with other things. While the gold that makes up the lion is real, the lion itself is empty because it is only a temporary manifestation of the matter that makes it up.[64]

The Huayan Sutra reflects the ideas expressed by the Buddha during the first seven days of his enlightenment. During this time, the Buddha entered "sea-state *samādhi*" (Pli. *Sāgara-mudrā samādhi*; San. *Sāgara-mudrā samādhi*; Chi. 海印三昧 *hǎi yìn sān mèi*; Kor. *haeinsammae*; Jpn. *kaiin sanmai*), "a condition wherein one experiences reality directly, without interpretation and evaluation."[65] Here the metaphor of an ocean is used to illustrate four patterns of thinking that characterize the stages of cultivation as one progresses from ignorance to enlightenment. In the lowest stage, one views each wave in the ocean as a separate, unconnected entity. This is the everyday worldview endorsed by most people, a sort of naive realism that considers things to be real and independent. In the second stage, one is able to perceive the water of the ocean without seeing the waves. One understands that all things are empty and undifferentiated. In the third stage, one sees the interdependence of the water and waves. Awakened beings understand that phenomena and emptiness are identical. In the final stage, one sees the waves interacting with one another as well as with the ocean. All phenomena are mutually interdependent.[66]

Zhēnyán (真言; Jpn. Shingon)[67]

Zhenyan is the Chinese version of Vajrayāna Buddhism (also known as Mantrayāna, Guhyamantrayāna, or Tantrayāna). It was imported into Japan by Kūkai (aka Kōbō Daishi, 774–835 CE), under whom it quickly became one of the most prominent schools of Japanese Buddhism, leaving a lasting impression on Japanese art. The term "tantra" is typically avoided in East Asia due to its association with sexual practices, so the term *mikkyō* (密教) is used, which refers to mysterious or esoteric teachings.[68] "Zhenyan" literally means "true word," which refers to mantras, sounds used to focus consciousness during meditation. The goal of Zhenyan is to realize oneness with the universe through the practice of the "three mysteries": *mantras* (vocal sounds), *mudrās* (hand gestures), and *maṇḍalas* (visual symbols). These three practices help one to focus body, speech, and mind on the Buddha Mahāvairocana (also known as Vairocana Buddha), who symbolizes the perfect cosmic being. The Japanese Shingon patriarch Kūkai claims that they allow one to "become the Buddha in this body" (即身成佛 *sokushin jōbutsu*), simultaneously realizing the world as *saṃsāra* and coming to dwell in the *dharmadhātu* (Ultimate Reality).[69]

Zhenyan emphasizes the idea that sentient beings share *bodhicitta*—the buddha-mind or potential for Buddhahood—with Mahāvairocana. Unlike the Huayan tradition, which argues that practice allows one to realize buddha-potential, Zhenyan/Shingon claims that buddha-potential itself has the ability to destroy delusion, so practice (*mantras, mudrās,* and *maṇḍalas*) is merely the means through which buddha-body (*sokushin jōbutsu*) becomes manifest. Zhenyan uses two *maṇḍalas* to focus meditation. The Womb Maṇḍala (sometimes called the Truth Maṇḍala) is female and represents the first five elements that comprise the universe: space, air, fire, water, and earth. The Diamond Maṇḍala (also known as the Wisdom Mandala) is male and represents the last of the six elements, mind.[70]

Pure Land (Chi. 淨土宗 Jìngtǔzōng; Kor. Jeongtojong; Jpn. Jōdo Shū)

Pure Land Buddhism represents a significant philosophical departure from the other types of Buddhism that preceded it in India and China.[71] According to Pure Land, the historical Buddha emphasized awakening through "self-power" (Chi. 自力 zìlì; Kor. jaryeok; Jpn. jiriki), which is one's own concentrated effort to realize nirvāṇa. While self-power might have worked in the Buddha's time, we now live in a degenerate age (Chi. 末法 mòfǎ; Jpn. mappō) in which realization of enlightenment through one's own efforts is impossible because of the inordinate amount of suffering and ignorance in the world. Rather than trying to reach enlightenment on one's own, one should abandon the futility of jiriki and instead embrace the "other power" (Chi. 他力 tālì; Kor. taryeok; Jpn. tariki) of the Buddha Amitābha, who will transport the practitioner at the moment of death to the Pure Land (or Western Paradise), an idyllic realm in which one can realize enlightenment without distraction. While early incarnations of Pure Land Buddhism view Amithāba's Western Paradise as a place where one can realize nirvāṇa without interference from the degenerate world, later Pure Land describes it as a final heavenly realm in which the faithful will dwell for eternity. Tanlun (476–542 CE) encouraged the chanting of the niànfó (念佛; Kor. yeombul; Jpn. nembutsu), a short phrase that literally means "Praise to Amitābha Buddha" (Chi. 南無阿彌陀佛 Nāmó Ēmítuófó; Kor. Namu Amita Bul; Jpn. Namu Amida Butsu). In Japan, Hōnen (1133–1212 CE), founder of the Jōdo school, promoted the chanting of the nembutsu among lay Buddhists, and Pure Land quickly gained popularity (and remains to this day the most popular form of Buddhism in Japan).[72]

Chán (禪 Kor. Seon; Jpn. Zen)

Chan is one of the most influential traditions of East Asian Buddhism, leaving an indelible impression on the arts of China, Korea, and Japan.[73] "Chan" is short for channa, the Chinese translation of dhyāna, which is the Sanskrit word for "meditation." The Chan tradition emphasizes meditation as the primary method of training as opposed to the intensive academic study that is considered essential by most other traditions. The First Patriarch of

Chan was Bodhidharma (c. fifth to sixth century CE) who is said to have brought the tradition from India around 520 CE (though, like the historical Buddha, his origins are somewhat apocryphal). He emphasized direct transmission from mind to mind, where understanding is passed from teacher to student without the use of language or discursive reasoning. Though Chan training includes some *sūtra* study, true insight will always come as "a special transmission outside the scriptures" (Chi. 教外別傳 *jiào wài bié zhuàn*; Kor. *kyooe pyolchon*; Jpn. *kyōge betsuden*). Most of our everyday experience of the world involves mental evaluation, a type of internal dialogue Chan identifies as our sense of self, which is responsible for our ignorant attachment to false ideals. Meditation allows us to disengage from this self-reflection and directly experience reality as it truly is, which will bring an end to the dualistic thinking that causes suffering.[74]

For Chan, there is no fundamental distinction between enlightenment and nonenlightenment because all things have Buddha-nature (and the Zen philosopher Dōgen goes so far as to say all things *are* Buddha-nature). Chan practitioners seek understanding (Chi. 悟 *wù*; Kor. *o*; Jpn. *satori*) of their own nature (Chi. 見性 *jiàn xìng*; Kor. *gyeon seong*; Jpn. *kenshō*) as buddhas through direct experience of reality as it truly is. This is accomplished primarily through the practice of seated meditation (Chi. 座禅 *zuòchán*, Kor. *jwaseon*; Jpn. *zazen*) while focusing on breathing and concentrating on a point below the navel called the *dantian* (丹田; Kor. *danjeon*; Jpn. *tanden*).[75] Because all things are Buddha-nature, meditation is not a means to achieving enlightenment, but rather the practice of enlightenment itself. As a result, the Chan tradition emphasizes sudden enlightenment: awakening is not the product of many lifetimes of study, but can instead happen at any moment of one's training.[76]

In addition to seated meditation, many Chan schools also practice *gōng'àn* (公案 Kor. *gong-an*; Jpn. *kōan*), which are puzzling statements or records of encounters between teacher and student that can act as a focus during meditation. Developed originally by Linji (d. 867 CE), *gōng'àn* were meant to disrupt the rationalistic thinking of the everyday mind and thereby create opportunities for awakening.[77]

Chapter Summaries

This volume consists of eleven chapters and is divided into two parts. Part 1 of the volume, entitled "Creative Pedagogies for Teaching Buddhist East

Asia," includes five chapters that present ideas on pedagogy for undergraduate teaching on Buddhism and/or East Asian culture as it relates to Buddhism. A reasonable concern that nonspecialists of East Asian Buddhism may have in considering teaching East Asian Buddhism is that of inadvertently misrepresenting material to students. In chapter 1, Sarah Mattice addresses three common misconceptions about East Asian Buddhism that teachers new to the topic should be careful to avoid and should bring to the attention of their classes in order to clarify them. The first is the common misunderstanding that Buddhism is characterized, generally, by gender equity. In East Asia, Mattice points out, the treatment of women in Buddhism has been mixed, and largely dependent on preexisting cultural attitudes. Moreover, Buddhist studies have largely focused on the contributions of male monks, overlooking the contributions of women. To counter this tendency, Mattice briefly highlights the outstanding contributions of seven Buddhist women, and she provides resources for showing students ways in which Buddhist women have made important, yet often overlooked, contributions throughout history. Second, Mattice addresses the idea that Buddhism in East Asia (and elsewhere) may be characterized as nonviolent, and she clarifies ways in which East Asian Buddhism bears associations with violence and/or the use of force through imagery, texts, and conflicts involving monks. Finally, Mattice addresses the problems behind the common view that Buddhism might be considered more of a philosophy than a religion. She notes that both concepts, philosophy and religion, are sedimented with Western Enlightenment assumptions, and she offers helpful strategies for helping students see the problematic cultural assumptions inherent in this debate.

In chapters 2 and 3, Elizabeth Schiltz and Mark Wells argue in support of both the educational value and pedagogical feasibility of teaching Buddhism and East Asian culture in undergraduate courses in the United States and other Western countries. In chapter 2, Schiltz provides support for the value and feasibility of teaching non-Anglo-European philosophy to undergraduates by bringing into focus the unique way in which such material facilitates the development of crucial philosophical skills and dispositions such as open-mindedness, creativity, and critical thinking. Drawing on several years of experience teaching comparative philosophy to undergraduates, Schiltz offers hard-won pedagogical advice on course design, effective learning goals, and how to include meditative practice and other embodied forms of learning in course content on East Asian Buddhism.

In chapter 3, Wells addresses potential concerns or doubts a nonspecialist might have about including content on Buddhism and East Asian philosophy in their syllabus. Drawing from his own experience as someone who does not have graduate specialization in Chinese Philosophy yet has been able to successfully teach a course on the subject, Wells provides a compelling case for the feasibility of including content on Buddhism and other traditions of East Asia, with the proviso that extra preparation is necessary for doing so. While Wells acknowledges there are some personal costs involved, such as attending available workshops on Chinese or East Asian studies prior to teaching (when possible) and time devoted to preparing new teaching material which may cut into research work time, he considers the personal and professional benefits, as well as the benefit to students, to far outweigh the costs.

In chapter 4, Jesús Ilundáin-Agurruza shares creative pedagogical insights developed through several years of teaching an upper-level philosophy of mind class that focuses on embodied cognition. Similar to Schiltz and others who include meditation practice as part of their pedagogical toolkit for teaching East Asian Buddhism, Ilundáin-Agurruza includes a swordsmanship "lab" practicum (using wooden swords or *bokken*) which allows students to experience an active, embodied Buddhist practice common in Japanese *dō* practice. Ilundáin shows how this "lab" exercise, in tandem with readings in cognitive science, embodied cognition, phenomenology, and East Asian Buddhism, facilitates student understanding of the East Asian embodied notion of mind as "heartmind," which stands in contrast with dualistic Cartesian conceptions of mind. Ilundáin-Agurruza goes on to highlight ways in which the active component of the course facilitates a learning experience that is not only intellectually engaging but can also be personally transformative for students.

In chapter 5, the final chapter of Part 1, George Wrisley offers a creative pedagogy for introducing students to Dōgen's Sōtō Zen. This chapter begins with a concise introduction to the life and work of Dōgen, founder of the Sōtō Zen school in Japan, and then goes on to detail central aspects of Dōgen's deeply philosophical approach to Zen, centered as it is around an uncompromising application of emptiness (*śūnyata*) to all aspects of life and practice. A central issue for Dōgen is his distinctive approach to language and his creative interpretation of familiar Zen literature, including kōans. In his writings, Dōgen often makes these texts new and vibrant while drawing out important insights about Zen practice and thought. The chapter ends with a class exercise that provides students the opportunity to experience this revitalization of familiar texts, asking them to grapple with a Dōgen-esque commentary on a familiar nursery rhyme, the objective of which is to enable students to apply the content of the chapter to interpreting the commentary on the kōan-like verse.

Part 2 of the volume, entitled "East Asian Buddhisms and the Humanities: Ethics, Art, and Politics," includes six chapters, each of which focuses on a theme, figure, or work of art as a window onto interactions between Buddhism and the broader culture in East Asia. Chapters 6 and 7 focus on the theme of the relation between East Asian Buddhism and attitudes toward the natural environment. The current environmental crisis represents a serious existential threat to human beings, as well as to all other sentient beings, and these two chapters are devoted to exploring different aspects of this issue. In chapter 6, James McRae considers the conceptual resources possessed by East Asian Buddhism for developing a strong environmental ethic. He discusses the Japanese ethical paradigm of *kyōsei* (symbiosis), which developed from the Buddhist concept of *tomoiki* (living together), as a valuable concept for the ongoing development of a global culture of ecological responsibility that would rein in consumerism and promote a more mutualistic, symbiotic way of life. He argues that Buddhism can be best understood as a type of environmental virtue ethic that advocates an ecocentric perspective that can help us to reconceptualize the problematic worldviews that are damaging our environment. In chapter 7, Jesse Butler develops the idea of ecological self-understanding as it relates to the Buddhist concept of no-self. Butler takes ecological self-understanding to be a normative epistemic virtue, and he considers the extent to which East Asian Buddhist doctrine and practice align with and reinforce this virtue. As a complement to McRae's chapter on environmental virtues, Butler points to the value of the Chan Buddhist ideas of karma and *upāya* ("skillful means") as well aligned with the epistemic virtue of ecological self-understanding. Butler also considers some East Asian Buddhist practices and doctrines such as *fangsheng*, the catching and releasing of fish to gain karmic merit, which seem to conflict with ecological self-understanding. He concludes with a critical reflection on the extent to which East Asian Buddhist practices and doctrines possess the internal resources to fully align with the virtue of ecological self-understanding.

Chapters 8 and 9 delve into medieval Korean (Silla/Goryeo) Buddhism, with chapter 9 drawing connections between Chinese, Korean, and Japanese Buddhism. In chapter 8, Robert H. Scott provides a window onto the life and influence of the twelfth century Seon monk Chinul. In this chapter, Scott discusses the key role Chinul played in diffusing tensions, in the twelfth-century Goryeo dynasty, between Seon Buddhism (Chi., Chan;

Jpn., Zen) and the scholastic schools of Buddhism in Korea, and how the influence of Chinul continues to impact Korean Buddhist practice today. Scott further shows how Chinul's life and work emphasize the dynamic relationship between wisdom and compassion and point to an ethic of responsive virtuosity which resonates in many ways with ethical thinking developed by contemporary postmodern philosophers such as John Russon.

In chapter 9, Sujung Kim presents an object study of the *Kegon Engi Emaki*, a thirteenth-century picture scroll by the Japanese Kegon monk Myōe (1173–1232) which portrays the seventh-century story of unrequited love between the Chinese lady Shanmiao (Jpn. Zenmyō) and the Silla monk Ŭisang (625–702). In the story, Ŭisang rejects Shanmiao's declaration of love due to his vow of celibacy and commitment to study. Despite being rejected, Shanmiao continues to support Ŭisang, and she turns into a dragon to protect the monk on his return trip from China to Korea. Myōe, the illustrator of the picture scroll, was deeply inspired by the story, and he named a monastery he founded for nuns Zenmyō. In addition to recounting a fascinating love story, this chapter provides a window onto several important issues in East Asian Buddhism including the storytelling role of picture scrolls, monastic views on women, gender, and sexuality, and the close interrelationship between Chinese, Japanese, and Korean Buddhism.

Chapter 10 takes a look at ways in which the popular kung fu film *Shaolin* (2011), directed by Hong Kong director Benny Chan, reflects perceptions of both Buddhism and cultural politics in contemporary China. In this co-authored piece, Melissa Croteau and Xin Zhang offer insights on the religious and political messaging of *Shaolin* in a way that will facilitate classroom discussion on the message of the film as well as on the relation between the film, Buddhism, and politics in China and Hong Kong, the latter having become increasingly troubled in the years since the film was released. The authors highlight ways in which the film conveys a message of increased openness to religion in post-Mao China, but they question the authenticity of this message. Through critical reflection on the message of the film, its portrayal of Buddhist doctrine, and possible political influences on the film, the authors provide a window onto the significance of popular film in understanding Buddhism and cultural politics in China today.

In chapter 11, James Mark Shields presents a historical and philosophical study of "Critical Buddhism," a movement among scholars in Japan that arose in the early 1990s in response to the problematic convergence between Zen Buddhism and Japanese militaristic imperialism. Critical Buddhists boldly questioned cherished ideas, doctrines, and figures associated with

East Asian Buddhism, especially Zen and the Kyoto School, and called for the integration of Buddhist ideals with modern, liberal ideals of rationality, justice, and human rights. Through an analysis of historical precedents for Critical Buddhism in the New Buddhist movements of the early twentieth century, Shields argues that the movement has deep historical roots and continues to have relevance for Buddhist ethics and politics today.

Notes

1. The term *Buddhism* represents a dynamic tradition that has developed for thousands of years across the Asian continent and beyond. In reality, there is not just one Buddhism with a homogeneous set of beliefs and practices, but rather many Buddhisms that share common origins and themes. This introduction traces the development of some of these Buddhist traditions from their inception in India to their transmission to China, Korea, and Japan. Throughout this volume, Buddhism will be referred to interchangeably as a "philosophy" and as a "religion" because there is not a sharp distinction between these disciplines in the Asian traditions of thought. In Indian Buddhism, the term *dharma* (San.; Pli. *dhamma*) is often used to refer to the teachings of Buddhism. In China, the term *fójiào* 佛教 refers to "Buddhist teachings" (*bulgyo* in Korea and *bukkyō* in Japan). In the West, there has traditionally been a distinction drawn between philosophy (grounded in rational argumentation) and religion (based on lived experience in a faith tradition). In Asia, this distinction is much blurrier. In Japan for example, there was not a clear discrepancy between *shūgyō* (religion) and *tetsugaku* (philosophy) until scholars such as Nishida Kitarō started studying Western philosophy in the late nineteenth century. Buddhism has historically considered lived experience, ritual practice, and scholarly argumentation to all play some role in spiritual cultivation, so it makes sense to consider it both a philosophical and religious tradition. For more discussion of the applicability of the labels of philosophy and religion to Buddhism, see chapter 1 of this volume.

2. For suggestions about how to incorporate Buddhist traditions from other parts of Asia into a liberal arts curriculum, see Andy Alexander Davis, "The Buddhist Canon and the Liberal Arts Classroom," in *Buddhisms in Asia: Traditions, Transmissions, and Transformations*, ed. Nicholas S. Brasovan and Micheline M. Soong (Albany: State University of New York Press, 2019), 1–18. See also Jane Collins, "Not Knowing Is Most Intimate: Introducing Buddhism into a Humanities Course," in the same volume (165–72).

3. Peter Hershock, *Chan Buddhism* (Honolulu: University of Hawai'i Press, 2005), 27.

4. Peter Harvey, *An Introduction to Buddhism: Teachings, History, and Practices*, 2nd edition (Cambridge: Cambridge University Press, 2013), 14. The

term *Buddha* means the "Awakened" or "Enlightened One" and is a descriptive title, which Buddhists apply to anyone who is considered to have attained perfect Buddhist enlightenment.

5. Carl Olson, ed., *Original Buddhist Sources: A Reader* (New Brunswick: Rutgers University Press, 2005), 29–34. See also John M. Koller, *Asian Philosophies*, 7th edition (New York: Routledge, 2018), 47–51, and Harvey, *An Introduction to Buddhism*, 13–14 and 17–22.

6. Harvey, *An Introduction to Buddhism*, 9.

7. Harvey, *An Introduction to Buddhism*, 9.

8. Harvey, *An Introduction to Buddhism*, 14.

9. Harvey, *An Introduction to Buddhism*, 14. See also Olson 131–33 ("Story of Śāriputra").

10. Hershock, *Chan Buddhism*, 21–24.

11. *Sabbāsava Sutta* (MN 2).

12. Hershock, *Chan Buddhism*, 74–75.

13. Hershock, *Chan Buddhism*, 27, and Mariko Namba Walter, "Buddhism in Central Asian History," in *The Wiley Blackwell Companion to East and Inner Asian Buddhism*, ed. Mario Poceski (Chichester: John Wiley & Son, 2014), 25.

14. Harvey, *An Introduction to Buddhism*, 101.

15. Harvey, *An Introduction to Buddhism*, 101.

16. This summary of the Four Noble Truths is drawn from the Buddha's first sermon, translated with commentary by John M. Koller and Patricia Koller, *A Sourcebook in Asian Philosophy* (New York: Macmillan, 1991), 195–96. See also Olson, 46–54 and David J. Kalupahana, *Buddhist Philosophy: A Historical Analysis* (Honolulu: University of Hawai'i Press, 1976).

17. For Buddhist terms used in this section of the Introduction, the Pāli (Pli.) is typically given first with Sanskrit, Chinese, Korean, and Japanese equivalents afterward (San., Chi., Kor., and Jpn., respectively), unless otherwise indicated. Chinese characters are provided only once if the same characters are used by the Korean and Japanese traditions. Please see also the glossary at the end of this anthology.

18. While "Four Noble Truths" is the most common translation (e.g., Olson, 46), Koller prefers "Fourfold Noble Truth" while Harvey uses "The Four True Realities for the Spiritually Ennobled." See Koller, *Asian Philosophies* and Harvey, *An Introduction to Buddhism*, 50–52.

19. Koller and Koller, 195–96. See also, Olson, 47–49 ("Selections from the *Saccamyuttasutta*"); Koller, *Asian Philosophies*, 53–56; Peter Harvey's "Dukkha, Non-Self, and the Teaching on the Four 'Noble Truths,'" in *A Companion to Buddhist Philosophy*, ed. Steven M. Emmanuel (Malden, MA: Wiley-Blackwell, 2013), 26–37; and Harvey, *An Introduction to Buddhism* (2013), 52–62. For an exploration of the relationship between ignorance, racism, and suffering (and how to overcome them), see Jan Willis, "Spirituality and Resistance: How We Wake Up to Racism," *Journal of Feminist Studies in Religion* 36, no. 1 (2020): 85–97.

20. Koller and Koller, 195–96. See also Olson, 47–49 ("Selections from the *Saccamyuttasutta*"); Koller, *Asian Philosophies*, 56–57 and 65–88; Harvey, *An Introduction to Buddhism* (2013), 62–73; and Harvey, "Dukkha, Non-self, and the Teaching on the Four 'Noble Truths,'" 37–39.

21. Koller and Koller, 195–96. See also Olson, 47–49 ("Selections from the *Saccamyuttasutta*"); Koller, *Asian Philosophies*, 56–58; Harvey, *An Introduction to Buddhism* (2013), 73–81; and Harvey, "Dukkha, Non-self, and the Teaching on the Four 'Noble Truths,'" 39–44.

22. Koller and Koller, 195–96. See also Olson, 47–49 ("Selections from the *Saccamyuttasutta*"); Koller, *Asian Philosophies*, 58–62; Harvey, *An Introduction to Buddhism* (2013), 79–87; and Harvey, "Dukkha, Non-self, and the Teaching on the Four 'Noble Truths,'" 39–44.

23. Mario Poceski, "Buddhism in Chinese History," in Poceski, ed., *The Wiley Blackwell Companion to East and Inner Asian Buddhism*, 41.

24. Walter, "Buddhism in Central Asian History," 34.

25. Peter Gregory, *Tsung-mi and the Sinification of Buddhism* (Princeton: Princeton University Press, 1991), 6–7.

26. Hershock, *Chan Buddhism*, 30, and Walter, "Buddhism in Central Asia," 34.

27. Poceski, "Buddhism in Chinese History," 43.

28. Hershock, *Chan Buddhism*, 33.

29. Poceski, "Buddhism in Chinese History," 52.

30. Poceski, "Buddhism in Chinese History," 56–61.

31. Sem Vermeersch, "Buddhism in Korean History," in Poceski, ed., *The Wiley Blackwell Companion to East and Inner Asian Buddhism*, 66.

32. Vermeersch, "Buddhism in Korean History," 67.

33. Vermeersch, "Buddhism in Korean History," 68.

34. Vermeersch, "Buddhism in Korean History," 70. For more on Ŭisang, see chapter 9 of this volume.

35. Vermeersch, "Buddhism in Korean History," 74.

36. For more on Chinul, see chapter 8 of this volume.

37. Vermeersch, "Buddhism in Korean History," 75–79.

38. Heather Blair, "Buddhism in Japanese History," in Poceski, ed., *The Wiley Blackwell Companion to East and Inner Asian Buddhism*, 86.

39. Blair, "Buddhism in Japanese History," 87.

40. Blair, "Buddhism in Japanese History," 89.

41. Blair, "Buddhism in Japanese History," 90.

42. Blair, "Buddhism in Japanese History," 87–97. For more on Dōgen, see chapter 5 of this volume.

43. Blair, "Buddhism in Japanese History," 100–101.

44. Blair, "Buddhism in Japanese History," 101.

45. For each of the major schools of East Asian Buddhism, the Chinese name is given first followed by the Korean and Japanese names. The names are presented

in this order because these schools were typically founded in China (sometimes after being imported from India) and then moved first to Korea and then to Japan.

46. Ronald S. Green, "East Asian Buddhism," in Emmanuel, ed., *A Companion to Buddhist Philosophy*, 114. See also Harvey, *An Introduction to Buddhism* (2013), 214.

47. Green, "East Asian Buddhism," 114–15. See also Poceski's "Buddhism in Chinese History," 53.

48. Green, "East Asian Buddhism," 115.

49. Koller, *Asian Philosophies*, 290–91.

50. Green, "East Asian Buddhism," 112. See also Poceski, "Buddhism in Chinese History," 53, Koller, *Asian Philosophies*, 212–14, and Harvey, *An Introduction to Buddhism* (2013), 128, 214.

51. Green, "East Asian Buddhism," 112–13. See also Harvey, *An Introduction to Buddhism* (2013), 132.

52. Green, "East Asian Buddhism," 113–14. See also Vermeersch, "Buddhism in Korean History," 71, and Harvey, *An Introduction to Buddhism* (2013), 141.

53. Green, "East Asian Buddhism," 115.

54. Green, "East Asian Buddhism," 115. See also Harvey, *An Introduction to Buddhism* (2013), 215. For a detailed exposition of Tiantai thought, see Haiyan Shen's "Tiantai Integrations of Doctrine and Practice" in Poceski, *The Wiley Blackwell Companion to East and Inner Asian Buddhism*, 127–44.

55. Green, "East Asian Buddhism," 116–17, 193. See also Brook Ziporyn's "The Three Truths in Tiantai Buddhism," in Emmanuel, ed., *A Companion to Buddhist Philosophy*, 256–69.

56. Koller, *Asian Philosophies*, 293. See also Poceski, "Buddhism in Chinese History," 48–49.

57. Koller, *Asian Philosophies*, 294.

58. Koller, *Asian Philosophies*, 225.

59. Koller, *Asian Philosophies*, 335. Socially engaged Buddhists, including many outside the Tendai tradition, have had a transformative influence around the world. See Christopher S. Queen and Sallie B. King, *Engaged Buddhism: Buddhist Liberation Movements in Asia* (Albany: State University of New York Press, 1996), Pamela A. Yetunde, Cheryl A. Giles, and Gaylon J. Ferguson, eds. *Black and Buddhist: What Buddhism Can Teach Us about Race, Resilience, Transformation, and Freedom* (Boulder: Shambhala, 2020), and Rima Vesely-Flad, *Black Buddhists and the Black Radical Tradition: The Practice of Stillness in the Movement for Liberation* (New York: New York University Press, 2022).

60. Koller, *Asian Philosophies*, 295. See also Harvey, *An Introduction to Buddhism* (2013), 215.

61. Koller, *Asian Philosophies*, 214.

62. Green, "East Asian Buddhism," 117.

63. Koller, *Asian Philosophies*, 295–96.

64. Koller, 295, 296–97.

65. Green, "East Asian Buddhism," 117–18.

66. Green, "East Asian Buddhism," 118–19.

67. Though esoteric Buddhism has been practiced in Korea in various forms (typically referred to as *milgyo*), there is no direct Korean equivalent to the Zhen-yan school.

68. Koller, *Asian Philosophies*, 334. See also Green, "East Asian Buddhism," 119–20, and Beata Grant, "Buddhism and Poetry in East Asia," in Poceski, ed., *The Wiley Blackwell Companion to East and Inner Asian Buddhism*.

69. Green, "East Asian Buddhism," 119–20. See also Harvey, *An Introduction to Buddhism* (2013), 214, 228.

70. Green, "East Asian Buddhism," 120–21.

71. Kendall Marchman, "Seeking the Pure Land (in the Classroom)," in *Buddhisms in Asia: Traditions, Transmissions, and Transformations*, ed. Nicholas S. Brasovan and Micheline M. Soong (Albany: State University of New York Press, 2019), 37–56.

72. Green, "East Asian Buddhism," 121–22. See also Harvey, *An Introduction to Buddhism* (2013), 216–17 and Koller, *Asian Philosophies*, 299–300 and 336–37.

73. Green, "East Asian Buddhism," 124.

74. Green, "East Asian Buddhism," 123. See also Harvey, *An Introduction to Buddhism* (2013), 217–18.

75. Green, "East Asian Buddhism," 123–24.

76. Koller, *Asian Philosophies*, 297–98. See also Harvey, *An Introduction to Buddhism* (2013), 218.

77. Koller, *Asian Philosophies*, 298–99. See also Ann Pirruccello, "Awakening in the Hongzhou School of Chan Buddhism," in *Buddhisms in Asia: Traditions, Transmissions, and Transformations*, ed. Nicholas S. Brasovan and Micheline M. Soong (Albany: State University of New York Press, 2019), 19–36.

Bibliography

Blair, Heather. "Buddhism in Japanese History." In *The Wiley Blackwell Companion to East and Inner Asian Buddhism*, edited by Mario Poceski, 84–103. Chichester, West Sussex, UK: John Wiley & Son, 2014.

Brasovan, Nicholas S., and Micheline M. Soong, eds. *Buddhisms in Asia: Traditions, Transmissions, and Transformations*. Albany: State University of New York Press, 2019.

Emmanuel, Steven M., ed. *A Companion to Buddhist Philosophy*. Malden, MA: Wiley-Blackwell, 2013.

Grant, Beata. "Buddhism and Poetry in East Asia." In *The Wiley Blackwell Companion to East and Inner Asian Buddhism*, edited by Mario Poceski, 408–23. Chichester: John Wiley & Son, 2014.

Green, Ronald S. "East Asian Buddhism." In *A Companion to Buddhist Philosophy*, edited by Steven M. Emmanuel, 110–25. Malden, MA: Wiley-Blackwell, 2013.

Gregory, Peter. *Tsung-mi and the Sinification of Buddhism*. Princeton: Princeton University Press, 1991.

Harvey, Peter. *An Introduction to Buddhism: Teachings, History, and Practices*. 2nd edition. Cambridge: Cambridge University Press, 2013.

———. "Dukkha, Non-Self, and the Teaching on the Four 'Noble Truths.'" In *A Companion to Buddhist Philosophy*, edited by Steven M. Emmanuel, 26–45. Malden, MA: Wiley-Blackwell, 2013.

Hershock, Peter. *Chan Buddhism*. Honolulu: University of Hawai'i Press, 2005.

Kalupahana, David J. *Buddhist Philosophy: A Historical Analysis*. Honolulu: University of Hawai'i Press, 1976.

Koller, John M. *Asian Philosophies*. 7th edition. New York: Routledge, 2018.

———, and Patricia Koller. *A Sourcebook in Asian Philosophy*. New York: Macmillan, 1991.

Olson, Carl, ed. *Original Buddhist Sources: A Reader*. New Brunswick: Rutgers University Press, 2005.

Poceski, Mario. "Buddhism in Chinese History." In *The Wiley Blackwell Companion to East and Inner Asian Buddhism*, edited by Mario Poceski, 40–62. Chichester: John Wiley & Son, 2014.

———, ed. *The Wiley Blackwell Companion to East and Inner Asian Buddhism*. Chichester: John Wiley & Son, 2014.

Queen, Christopher S., and Sallie B. King. *Engaged Buddhism: Buddhist Liberation Movements in Asia*. Albany: State University of New York Press, 1996.

Shen, Haiyan. "Tiantai Integrations of Doctrine and Practice." In *The Wiley Blackwell Companion to East and Inner Asian Buddhism*, edited by Mario Poceski, 127–44. Chichester: John Wiley & Son, 2014.

Vermeersch, Sem. "Buddhism in Korean History." In *The Wiley Blackwell Companion to East and Inner Asian Buddhism*, edited by Mario Poceski, 63–83. Chichester: John Wiley & Son, 2014.

Vesely-Flad, Rima. *Black Buddhists and the Black Radical Tradition: The Practice of Stillness in the Movement for Liberation*. New York: New York University Press, 2022.

Walter, Mariko Namba. "Buddhism in Central Asian History." In *The Wiley Blackwell Companion to East and Inner Asian Buddhism*, edited by Mario Poceski, 21–39. Chichester: John Wiley & Son, 2014.

Willis, Jan. "Spirituality and Resistance: How We Wake Up to Racism." *Journal of Feminist Studies in Religion* 36, no. 1 (2020): 85–97.

Yetunde, Pamela A., Cheryl A. Giles, and Gaylon J. Ferguson, eds. *Black & Buddhist: What Buddhism Can Teach Us about Race, Resilience, Transformation, and Freedom*. Boulder: Shambhala, 2020.

Ziporyn, Brook. "The Three Truths in Tiantai Buddhism." In *A Companion to Buddhist* Philosophy, edited by Steven M. Emmanuel, 256–69. Malden: Wiley-Blackwell, 2013.

Part 1

Creative Pedagogies for
Teaching Buddhist East Asia

Chapter 1

Three Common Misconceptions about East Asian Buddhisms

On Women and Gender, Violence and Nonviolence, and Philosophy and Religion

SARAH A. MATTICE

Who is misconceiving what? According to basic Buddhist principles, most of us are misconceiving the true nature of reality. Ignorance, after all, is one of the three poisons, and Buddhist doctrine and practice are often understood as remedies for our fundamental ignorance of our own nature and situation. In addition to these misconceptions, however, there are a number of misconceptions in today's world about Buddhism, and contemporary scholars and practitioners work hard to address these. In a 2014 article in *Tricycle* magazine, scholars Robert E. Buswell Jr. and Donald Lopez Jr. briefly address common misconceptions about Buddhism, including the mistaken beliefs that all Buddhists meditate, that mindfulness is the main form of meditation, that all Buddhists are vegetarians, that Buddhism does not involve deities, that Zen rejects conventional Buddhism, and that Buddhism has the same spiritual goals as all other traditions, to name a few.[1] Some of these mistaken beliefs are easy to correct—no, not all Buddhists are vegetarian, not even all ordained Buddhists! It's very difficult to be vegetarian in a climate like Tibet's, or in a case where you take most of your food in alms rounds as in South Asia, and most lay Buddhists even in East Asia eat meat except on certain holidays.[2] Some can be corrected by simply resisting the urge to think of Buddhism as a single, monolithic tradition, and instead foregrounding a conception of diverse Buddhism*s*: Buddhist traditions, communities, and practitioners that really do differ. But some misconceptions about Buddhism are very pervasive, and may require us as educators to be particularly thoughtful in remedying mistaken beliefs in the context of our pedagogy. In this chapter, I consider three such misconceptions about East Asian Buddhisms that seem to be common in both the general public and in at least some contexts where Buddhism is taught at the undergraduate level.

These three misconceptions concern the way that narratives about East Asian Buddhism and Buddhist philosophy have tended:

1. to foreground men, especially ordained monks, and to ignore the roles of lay and ordained women;

2. to take at face value ideals of nonviolence, and to ignore or cover over instances of violence connected to Buddhist theorizing and/or lived Buddhist communities; and

3. to perpetuate the claim that Buddhism is "really" a philosophy or way of life, but not a religion, and so to value certain forms of theory and practice over others.[3]

The aim of this chapter is to provide resources for teachers, students, and interested parties to delve deeper into these aspects of East Asian Buddhisms.[4] My comfort zone as a philosopher is with explicitly philosophical texts, but I have found the opportunity for interdisciplinary or cross-disciplinary work and for using material that challenges the bounds of our current disciplinary structures to be engaging and exciting, for myself and hopefully my students as well. Thus, many of the texts I recommend here do not fit neatly into one discipline or another, but I have found them all to be relevant to teaching about East Asian Buddhism in the context of philosophy and religious studies, and I hope that this will also be of use to others.[5]

Women and Gender

The "story" of Buddhism tends to begin with Siddhārtha Gautama and, for East Asian traditions, continue through generations of lineage holders (real and imagined) from bridge figures such as Bodhidharma (ca. 6th c.), to indigenous Chinese Masters such as Zhiyi (538–597), Huineng (638–713),

Fazang (643–712), Zongmi (780–841), and Dahui (1089–1163), to major Korean and Japanese thinkers such as Wŏnhyo (617–686), Ŭisang (625–702), Chinul (1158–1210), Kūkai (774–835), Dōgen (1200–1253), Hōnen (1133–1212), Shinran (1173–1263), Nichiren (1222–1282), Hakuin Ekaku (1686–1769), and many, many more. However, until relatively recently, it has been rare for this story to spend significant time on any women—monastic or lay. Yet we know that not only were women not absent from this story, they were key participants in its development, from the very earliest times to the present. Beginning with Mahāprajāpatī and Yaśodharā, the founders of the women's order (Siddhartha's aunt/stepmother and wife, respectively) and continuing through to Jingjian[6] (ca. 292–361), who founded the women's order in China, and Zenshin, Zenzo, and Kenzen,[7] the three nuns who were the first Japanese persons, male or female, to be ordained, there have been women involved in the historical development of Buddhism as both monastics and lay supporters, from its early transmission.[8]

Although female monastics were subjected to the eight special rules, this did not stop large numbers of women from practicing or from being ordained.[9] In China, for instance, in the centuries after the women's order was established, by the year 1021 CE, a Chinese census reported 61,240 nuns, and by the 1200s, Miriam Levering estimates that women were about 13-percent of the ordained Buddhist population.[10] And in Korea, the only place where the word for monk/nun—*Sunim*—is gender neutral, "when the monks' order was formed upon the transmission of Buddhism to Korea, a nuns' order was established at almost the same time. This leaves Korean nuns with a long history of some 1,600 years, a rare and remarkable feat that stands out in the history of world religion. This achievement runs contrary to the dominant narrative of a long moribund female Buddhist tradition."[11] Not only is there a long narrative of a "moribund" female Buddhist tradition, but there has often been extensive emphasis on the eight special rules, the five hindrances, the issue of the controversy over the need for transformation to a (sexed) male body for enlightenment, and the realities of on-the-ground patriarchy in Buddhist majority Asian locations that have led some to incorrectly assume that women have not been active participants in Buddhist traditions.[12] As scholarship catches up on these issues, we must make sure that our pedagogical practices keep pace. In this section, I describe several selections of texts relevant to gender and kōans by or about women that I often use, before moving to share seven historical women figures I often incorporate into my courses on Buddhism. There are obviously many figures left out of this brief section, and it is my hope that you might find here, or in the references given in the notes, figures whose work will make sense to incorporate into your courses.

Although there are many texts that might be relevant to this discussion, four are consistently part of my repertoire: selections from *Vimalakīrti Nirdeśa*, the *Heart Sutra*, selections from Dōgen's *Shōbōgenzō*, and the *Blood Bowl Sutra*.[13] From *Vimalakīrti*, we often read chapter 6, with its playful body-switching Goddess who teaches monk Śariputra a lesson, about both his own attachment to dualistic sex/gender identity and about the greater capaciousness of Mahāyāna thinking, using impossible-to-remove flower petals. The *Heart Sutra* is a personal favorite of mine, and in this context we read and discuss its ideas and main speaker, Guanyin, one of the most important Buddhist figures in East Asia.[14] After the Tang Dynasty (618–907 CE), in most East Asian contexts she takes on a plethora of roles (Guanyin has thirty-three different manifestations in the *Lotus Sutra*), but she is popularly understood through her female guises, especially Princess Miaoshan, child-giving Guanyin, thousand-arm/eye Guanyin, fish-basket Guanyin, etc.[15] The two selections on women and gender from Dōgen that I often use in this context are his discussion of Bodhidharma's succession in "Katto" and the early fascicle on women as teachers in "Raihaitokuzui."[16] Finally, I am fascinated by the *Blood Bowl Sutra*, an indigenous Chinese sutra that gained a cult following in China and Japan in the sixteenth and seventeenth centuries. According to this text, because women pollute the earth with menstrual/childbearing blood, they are destined for a special hell, but the sutra promises clear ways to fulfill these karmic debts, for oneself or one's relatives.[17] These pieces, along with additional lecture materials, help students to keep in mind that East Asian Buddhisms do not have one easy account of women and gender.

Kōans can be a great way to incorporate more women's voices into coursework. For those who might not be familiar, kōans (Chi. *gong'an*) or "public cases" are sometimes strange or paradoxical statements taken as objects of contemplation and interpretation in some Buddhist practices from perhaps the mid-ninth century onward. As T. Griffith Foulk explains, they are "brief sayings, dialogues, or anecdotes that have been excerpted from the biographies and discourse records of Ch'an/Sŏn/Zen patriarchs and held up for some sort of special scrutiny . . . the sayings, dialogues, or anecdotes that are selected for use as koans frequently comprise elements that render them difficult to understand at first glance."[18] Even this short explanation of kōans implicitly imports the erasure of women from the history by suggesting that the sayings that have been excerpted are from the "patriarchs" only. When making decisions about which kōans to teach (assuming some are part of the course material), any number of kōans and/or commentaries by classical Buddhist women—old and young, monastic and lay—can serve just as pedagogically valuable a role as the traditionally all-male collection.[19] Consider including "Miaoxin's Banner,"[20] "The Old Woman Burns Down the Hermitage,"[21] "Eshun's Deep Thing,"[22] "Ganji's Family,"[23] "The Old Woman's Rice Cakes,"[24] "Satsujo Sits on the Lotus Sutra,"[25] "Yoshihime and the Gate Through Which All Buddhas Enter The World,"[26] "Songyong Doesn't Undress,"[27] or perhaps even one of my favorites, a story about Ohashi, a filial daughter-turned-prostitute who became a student of Hakuin, who gave her the kōan phrase that ultimately led to her awakening, "Who is it that does this work?"[28] One of the reasons students see Buddhism as a generally male institution is that they do not see women in what they read, so even something as small as adding in some kōans that involve women as authors and/or characters helps to change that, especially in the cases where women in the kōans are explicitly teaching male monastics.[29] These kōans provide pedagogical opportunities for the same connections to larger Buddhist concepts and themes, as well as some additional themes not present in the classical set.[30]

In what follows, I give brief descriptions of seven women whose stories and texts have become woven into how I tell students the small parts of the story of the history of East Asian Buddhist philosophy that we have time for together in one or two semesters. Although we do not have a lot of information about her, Moshan Liaoran (ca. 800, China), Abbess of Moshan Monastery, is the only woman to have a full record of her own in the *Transmission of the Lamp*. Moshan's story is of her dharma encounter with Guanxi Zhixian (d. 895), who was initially very skeptical of a woman as a teacher. The depth of her understanding and immediacy of her practice so impressed Guanxi that he became her gardener for three years after their exchange.[31] Her story is referenced by many later thinkers, including Dōgen, as "evidence of women's religious potential. . . . Indeed, one of the highest compliments that most male Chan masters could think to pay a Chan nun was either to refer to her as a reincarnation of Moshan or, at the very least, to assure her that she was worthy of carrying on the Moshan lineage."[32]

Like Moshan, Miaozong (1095–1170, China), was an influential figure in the tradition—so influential that later Masters not only reference her and her work, but they built matching kōan commentary sets, choosing to comment on the same passages as Miaozong (including later women masters

Baochi and Zukui).[33] Miaozong lived most of her life as a lay practitioner, a wife and mother, and an elite and well-educated member of upper-class society. She was student and dharma heir of Dahui, and was ordained after her husband's death. One of the most well-known stories about Miaozong concerns her encounter with the head monk, Wan'an, who was skeptical of the close relationship between her and Dahui, which included his allowing her to stay in the abbot's guest quarters. As Schireson explains, "In her most famous teaching encounter she vindicates the vagina: she extracts it from the Buddha's 'blazing hot charcoal pit' and 'mouth of a poisonous black snake' and transforms it into the passageway and birthplace of all Buddhas and practitioners."[34] Wan'an requested a dharma interview with Wuzhuo (Miaozong's lay name prior to ordination), and when he came to meet with her he found her in her quarters without any clothes on.

He pointed at her [genitals] and said, "What kind of place is this?"

Wuzhuo replied, "All of the buddhas of the three worlds and the six patriarchs and all of the great monks everywhere—they all came out from within this."[35]

We are lucky to have many of Miaozong's teachings, including her commentaries on classical kōans and some of her dharma talks.

Turning from China to Japan, Mugai Nyodai (1223–1298), was one of the first Japanese women to receive transmission in the Rinzai Zen lineage (from Chinese master Wuxue Zuyuan, aka Mugaku Sogen, 1226–1286), and the first woman to be recognized as a Rinzai Zen Master.[36] She founded Keiaiji temple, and is credited with organizing the Rinzai system of convents.[37] Her enlightenment story was preserved through a poem she wrote to her master about her awakening experience, and was reproduced not only for Dharma talks in convents and monasteries but also for gazetteers and kōan collections across Japan.[38]

Her enlightenment story is only five or six pages long, and yet it contains many central Rinzai Zen themes—Chiyono (Mugai Nyodai's secular name) is from a well-off family, but she is a servant at the convent because of her spiritual aspirations.[39] She feels an urgent drive to practice, and that urgency is seen by an elderly nun, who advises her on how to sit *zazen*, not to pay too much attention to words and scriptures but to attend to her own mind and body, and to cultivate a heart of compassion with the intention to save all sentient beings. The piece discusses sudden enlightenment, buddha nature, delusional thinking, fathoming the source, practice in all actions—key philosophical themes that can be explored in detail from this selection—and her experience of enlightenment, which occurs when the bottom falls out of a bucket of water she was carrying, and with it, the reflection of the evening's full moon. Her enlightenment poem reads:

> With this and that I contrived
> And then the bottom fell out of the bucket.
> Where water does not collect,
> The moon does not dwell.[40]

The story of her enlightenment experience is not the only story of her life that was famous, however. In some circles, perhaps equally famous was the story of the lengths she had to go to in order to practice with the eminent Japanese Rinzai teacher, Enni Ben'en (1202–1280), at Tofukuji. Although he accepted her as a student, his male disciples were not as accepting, and even though she offered to sponsor the construction of a convent (she was from a wealthy family and so could pay for such a solution), the monks were still unhappy at having a woman in their midst. To deal with this problem, she scarred her face with a hot iron, mutilating her face to indicate her sincerity to practice and her rejection of her femininity as an obstacle to practice.

Mugai Nyodai may have influenced many other Buddhist women, including perhaps Abbess Ryonen Genso[41] (1646–1711, Japan) and Abbess Kakuzan Shido (1252–1305, Japan), the founding Abbess of Tokeiji.[42] Tokeiji was established initially as a place of refuge for women, and later became known as a "divorce temple"—a temple where women could go if they had no other legal way to leave a bad marriage. There, women could ordain and practice for several years, and then legally become a candidate for a new marriage: "After serving their time as Tokeiji nuns, they could respectably reenter society."[43] Kakuzan also initiated several unique practices at Tokeiji, including a "mirror zen" practice. In this practice, married women—who had previously been taught to view themselves as valuable only because of their appearance—were encouraged "to see through their feelings and attachments to physical form by meditating in front of a mirror. Instructions were to look deeply into one's nature and to ask, 'Where is a single feeling, a single thought, in the mirror image in which I gaze?'"[44] In my course on Zen, there is a weekly meditation component, and when we read about Kakuzan and Tokeiji, we also do a version of this exercise—not limited by gender. At home, each of us (I do all of the exercises the students do) does this exercise in front of a mirror, and I ask students to focus on a feature of their face and reflect on what that feature will be like in twenty years. This is a little softer version of the exercise than Kakuzan's, but it is often very powerful, and the students' responses are usually quite intense.

While most of the figures mentioned to this point are centrally located within Chan or Zen traditions, Pure Land Buddhist groups are among the largest and most popular in Japan, and Pure Land traditions are hugely important and influential across East Asia. While most scholarship has tended to focus on Hōnen and Shinran as founding figures, Eshinni (1182–1268, Shinran's wife) and her daughter Kakushinni (1224–1283) were nuns in the Shinshū tradition, and they were largely responsible for perpetuating Shinran's vision of Pure Land Buddhism.[45] Eshinni wrote letters to Kakushinni that were discovered in 1921, and these letters, along with James Dobbins's commentary and explication, are amazing resources for teaching about medieval Japanese Buddhism and the history and philosophy of Pure Land traditions in Japan.[46] Eshinni's letters have not only the kind of religious instruction or information that is found in letters from other religious figures of the time, including Shinran, Hōnen, and later Nichiren, but they also include personal reflections, although not the kind of refined or urbane aesthetic consciousness found in other letters or diaries from Japanese women of the time. According to Dobbins, "One . . . significant feature of the letters is that they provide an image, fleeting though it is, of what religion was like in ordinary life. . . . The views and practices described in her letters thus reveal the actual religion that underlay Shinran's abstract ideal."[47] Using Eshinni's letters, together with Shinran's materials, then, makes for an especially rich opportunity to delve into different kinds of primary source material with students.

Getting closer to the modern and contemporary world, I regularly teach pieces by and about early-twentieth-century figures Kim Iryŏp (1896–1971, Korea) and Raichō Hiratsuka (1886–1971, Japan). Iryŏp was a Korean "new woman," a feminist writer, a Zen nun, a philosopher, and a public intellectual in the mid-twentieth century in Korea.[48] As Jin Park explains, for Iryŏp, "Her creative activities as a writer, social rebellion as a new woman, and religious practice as a Zen Buddhist nun were paths toward the single goal of how to be fully human and thus how to live as an absolutely free being with unlimited capacity."[49] Where Iryŏp's life seems at times neatly divided in two—her years as a feminist writer who had wild public love affairs and her years as a Zen nun—for Japanese lay Buddhist Raichō Hiratsuka, there are both striking parallels and major divergences. Like Iryŏp, Raichō was of the "new woman" generation—Raichō founded Japan's first all-women's literary magazine, *Seitō*, lived an unconventional, explicitly feminist life-style, and practiced Zen Buddhism. Unlike Iryŏp, however, Raichō never ordained but did continue her social activism, and perhaps because of that her writings don't have quite the same dramatic changes as Iryŏp's.[50] Iryŏp and Raichō's work is wonderful to pair for students, as, while both are strongly influenced by early twentieth century feminism and by Zen, and both are interested in questions of embodiment and liberation, they take these interests in different directions—stylistically and philosophically.

Finally, although all of the women mentioned to this point have been historical figures, I also think it is important for students to see Buddhist traditions as living traditions, and ethnographies are a great way for students to engage contemporary women Buddhists.[51] In particular, I often use selections from Paula Arai's ethnographic work on Sōtō Zen nuns.[52] In my Zen course, because we spend a lot of time reading Dōgen, and then reading Kaoru Nonomura's memoir, *Eat Sleep Sit: My Year in Zen's Most Rigorous Training Temple* (which is fantastic but very intense and at times, very "macho" Zen), I like to have students see how Arai's nuns think about, talk about, and put Dōgen into practice in their lives. This helps us compare, reflect, and dig deeper into both Dōgen's texts and into what lived Buddhist experience means in ways that often directly challenge students' preconceptions: it is Japanese Zen nuns, not monks, who are celibate; nuns had to fight for the equality they have, even in the twentieth century in a Buddhist context; nuns have to work much harder to keep their temples going than monks, but most temples struggle if they are not especially famous; not all nuns chose to be nuns for the same reason, or for one reason, or stay nuns for their whole lives; some nuns are mean sometimes!

This last point carries across the previous examples; there is a gen-dered dimension that is often underrepresented in courses on Buddhism, but which is deeply relevant for understanding both theoretical and lived aspects of Buddhist traditions.[53]

Violence and Nonviolence

Misconceptions about Buddhism and violence tend to be pretty straightfor-ward: Aren't Buddhists pacifists? Don't Buddhists all commit to nonviolence? The first of the five precepts, after all, is the precept against intentional killing! And what about karma, compassion, suffering, and the call for all sentient beings to be liberated? How could these be consistent with any sort of violence, against human or nonhuman animals? The account of East Asian Buddhists as fundamentally nonviolent is a deeply embedded view held by many Americans and Europeans, and it is perpetuated in stereotypes and caricatures across a variety of platforms. It is also the misconception that is the most challenging for students to let go of. The idea—and ideal—of a truly nonviolent religion or lived tradition is one that many are reluctant to reconsider, even in light of extensive evidence to the contrary.

While a number of features of Buddhist thought and practice suggest the importance of nonviolence—the early emphasis on *ahiṃsā* (non-harm), the first precept against intentional killing, the doctrine of karma, the central role of compassion for all sentient beings, and the nature of anger as one of the three poisons—when we examine Buddhist traditions carefully we find not only combative rhetoric or violent deities and imagery; we also find Buddhist leaders and regimes—from Aśoka to the present—that waged war, kept active militaries, supported the death penalty, and more. There were monk-warriors and military monks, explicitly Buddhist armies dedicated to sectarian or millenarian violence, and contemporary genocidal violence. Both laypersons and monastics have been and are involved in violence of many different kinds, and knowing this does not require us to denounce those as "inauthentic" Buddhists. Buddhists, like Christians and Muslims and atheists and so on, are people, and people live their traditions in complex and sometimes contradictory ways. While religious insiders have specific commitments to their traditions and so can make judgments about who legitimate members are or are not, this is not the role of scholars.

When I teach or lecture about Buddhist violence, I often break the discussion up into three categories: violence in Buddhist imagery, violence in lay and monastic communities, and textual justifications for violence.[54] While much scholarly attention has been drawn to violence in early South Asian Buddhism and on the contemporary case of the Rohingya genocide and "radical Buddhists" such as Burmese monk Ashin Wirathu, I will focus my attention here on primarily East Asian examples.[55]

In thinking about violence in Buddhist imagery, I take "imagery" to be both visual and linguistic. In visual terms, I often show students images of Mañjuśrī, the bodhisattva of wisdom, and his flaming sword that cuts through delusion, and Fudō Myōō, a wrathful deity popular in esoteric Buddhism and especially Shingon Buddhism in Japan, usually depicted with a blue or black body, fierce or monstrous face, holding a sword in his right hand and a rope in his left hand, surrounded by flames. His sword is said to cut through our ignorance and his rope can bind our violent passions and emotions, leading us to a path of self-control. So, although these images contain some elements of violence, their ultimate purpose is compassion and service.

Miyamoto Musashi's painting "Shrike on a Dead Tree (*Koboku-meigekizu*)" is a useful comparison to these images, as unlike the flames and swords of Mañjuśrī and Fudō Myōō, "Shrike on a Dead Tree" appears to be a lovely monochromatic ink painting of a bird on a branch above a lake or river. Musashi (c. 1584–1645) was a Japanese swordsman (a *kensei*, or sword-saint undefeated in sixty matches), philosopher, strategist, *rōnin* (samurai without a master), *sumi-e* painter, and author of *The Book of Five Rings*, a text on his martial arts that is popular today in many circles. In this painting Musashi's sword and brush skills collide—the branch that the shrike rests on is indicative of a focused and confident hand. The painting *seems* very "Zen"—calm, serene, natural. But as those familiar with the shrike might be anticipating, the image is actually suggesting something different. There is a small worm on the branch, and the shrike is waiting, perfectly still, perhaps for the worm to crawl all the way up to it in order to strike with immediacy for its next meal. This lovely "Zen" painting is a painting about swordsmanship, fighting, and killing. And when we learn about the sociohistorical context of the time, this is not a surprise, as Zen and the samurai class were closely linked.

In literary terms, we see violence in East Asian Buddhist literature in a number of different contexts,[56] beginning with the combative metaphors of the *Sutra of 42 Sections*: "A man practicing the Way is like a lone man in combat against ten thousand. Bearing armor and brandishing weapons, he charges through the gate eager to do battle, but if he is weak-hearted and cowardly he will withdraw and flee."[57] This is a far cry from the stereotypical image of a pacifistic monk—here the sutra is suggesting that engaging in Buddhist practice requires one to view oneself as a brave (if massively outnumbered) soldier in a battle against one's own habituations, passions, and mental formations. We also see literary violence all over the place in Zen encounter dialogues and kōans. In some Zen literary contexts, the association between violence and enlightenment is so strong that it can seem as if one might require a knock upside the head or a kick down the stairs to gain enlightenment, and you should be so lucky as to have the teaching moment of Linji (Jpn. Rinzai) hauling you up and slamming you against the wall by your throat, calling you a used shit-wiping stick.[58]

In terms of violence among lay communities in East Asia, it is impossible to avoid discussing Samurai in this context. Students are often fascinated by the ideals of *bushido,* the way of the warrior (also reflected in Musashi's work above), and because of the tight historical connections between Zen and samurai training, this is a very important topic to consider.[59] Equally important although less well known, however, in the context of historical lay violence, are examples of fierce fighting between sixteenth-century Japanese *ikki,* locally based leagues of support that "sought to assert their interests, often by force. In these struggles, different social groups often had different religious affiliations: the Ikkō (Jōdo Shinshū or True Pure Land) forces represented farmers, the Tendai stronghold on Mount Hiei represented the old landed aristocracy, and the Nichiren Hokkeshū ('Lotus Sect') represented the city's merchant class."[60] Taking as an example the *Ikko-ikki,* these groups began as small peasant and landowning groups organized for mutual defense, but developed into serious and significant forces behind numerous uprisings in the Muromachi period (14–16th centuries). They were largely members of an offshoot group of the Jōdo Shinshū (True Pure Land) sect, and would go into battle chanting the *nembutsu* (*Namu Amida Butsu,* Hail Amida Buddha). These groups were eventually supported by the Jōdo Shinshū institutional clergy, and Shōnyo (1516–1554) was the first Jōdo Shinshū patriarch who explicitly justified religious violence; he said that his followers who died in battle in the Tembun War (1532–36) would achieve rebirth in the Pure Land.[61]

The Tembun War, also called the Tenbun Hokke Disturbance, started when Tendai Buddhist monks from Enryakuji attacked and burned down a number of Nichiren Buddhist temples. Nichiren Buddhists of the time were commonly engaged in violent means of conversion, as directed by Nichiren's writings on the need for extreme methods in the time of *mappō* (the third age of the decline of the *dharma*).[62] Because students are often not familiar with many of the different sects of Japanese Buddhism that were feuding during these periods, having them read primary source material from founding figures, along with historical material contextualizing the time period, can be very effective. The Tendai monks who burned the Nichiren temples were also called *sōhei,* warrior-monks initially dedicated to temple defense, and *sōhei* of various denominations became extremely powerful during this period.[63] Many became specialized in different weapons—some were specialists in a pole-arm called a *naginata,* a spear, and an iron club called a *kanabo*—and many wore their armor under their monastic robes.[64]

Another example of historic monastic violence is the Faqing Revolt, which happened around 515 CE in China. This was a millenarian rebellion focused on the idea that the time of Maitreya (Chi. Milefo), the Buddha of the Future, was coming soon.[65] Led by the monk Faqing, more than fifty thousand people were convinced that the earth needed to be cleansed of demons in order for Maitreya to arrive. In particular, they believed that the current clergy and religious administration were full of demons. Killing those demons would be an especially pious act of karmic merit-making, securing promotion on the ladder of bodhisattva-hood: for every demon (monk/nun/person) killed, you ascend one stage. Killing ten people takes you to the tenth stage of bodhisattva-hood, the stage just prior to buddha-hood.[66] The age of the new Buddha would bring with it a new, true *dharma*, so actions that seemed unacceptable under a previous morality would make sense once Maitreya arrived. The government at the time had to mobilize an army of around one hundred thousand to subdue this rebellion.[67] This was not an isolated incident—groups dedicated to the coming of Maitreya, both militant and not, recurred throughout East Asian history.

In the twentieth and twenty-first centuries, there have unfortunately been many examples of violence involving lay and monastic Buddhists in East Asia. Buddhists were involved in all of the major conflicts in East Asia in the twentieth century, from the Chinese civil war to the Pacific War and Japan's Imperial military projects, from Vietnam's fight for independence to the Korean War and beyond.[68] There is a great deal of scholarship on the relationship between Zen communities and Imperial Japan before and during the Pacific War, for instance, and Brian Victoria's *Zen at War* is a good starting point to use with students on this issue.[69]

Michael Jerryson argues that for Mahāyāna traditions, justifications for exceptions to general commitments to nonviolence derive primarily from *upāya* (expedient/skillful means) and *śūnyatā* (emptiness).[70] Because the Buddha needs to tailor his teachings to the specific liberatory needs of the audience, the teachings will vary. This is part of how Mahāyāna thinkers account for new texts, ideas, and practices, and also how some Mahāyānists justify the use of violence—as an expedient means for the liberation of sentient beings.[71] The other key concept used in justifying violence is emptiness, specifically the emptiness of own-being, or the fact that persons (and all things) are empty of isolated, independent, or unconditioned essences or selves. Normally, this is taken to be an insight into the dependent, contingent, impermanent, and relational nature of our existence, but taken to the extreme, emptiness and the corresponding idea of no-self (*an-ātman*) have been used to justify violence. After all, if there is no self, then who is there to hurt anyway? What is being killed, and who does the killing? The Zen saying, "It is the sword that kills," is a feature of this logic.[72]

All of this is not to suggest that there are not extensive and sophisticated East Asian Buddhist discourses on nonviolence, or that many or most Buddhists have not practiced nonviolence, but rather to provide resources for the start of a conversation with students about the mythos of Buddhists as perfect pacifists and Buddhism as a philosophy that could not support violence in any form. As educators we do a disservice to a rich and complex tradition when we gloss over or ignore the ways in which the tradition has had to deal with its own internal tensions and challenges.[73]

Philosophy and Religion

It is not uncommon for me to hear students say that Buddhism is "really more a philosophy, or way of life, than a religion." This way of characterizing Buddhism has its roots in European colonial philology and the early construction of the idea of a Buddhist "religion," and flourished in the United States with the work of figures such as D. T. Suzuki, Alan Watts, and beat Zen figures of the mid-twentieth century. For some practicing Buddhists, this might accurately capture how they understand their tradition. In the classroom, however, I want my students to approach that claim with some skepticism, and to try to unpack the assumptions that might be driving the way that these two categories—philosophy and religion—are being used in this claim.[74] Whose definitions of "philosophy," "religion," and "Buddhism" are at play here, for what audience, and whose purposes are being served by this claim? Who is accurately represented, and who is left out, and why? How do we know? Does it matter, and if so, why, and to whom?

The short answer to these questions, I think, is that in this claim—that Buddhism is really more philosophy than religion—"philosophy" seems to mean something like no ritual, no devotional activity, no "deities," no violence, no identity politics, just rationally justified beliefs and one's own (rational) effort to gain enlightenment.[75] But, as Tomoko Masuzawa has shown, that way of thinking about "philosophy" and "religion" is much more about what was happening in Europe in the nineteenth century than what Buddhist traditions really involve.[76]

To illustrate this, I want to use an example from how East Asian Buddhist philosophy tends to be taught. It is not uncommon for Buddhist philosophy courses to discuss meditation in some form or another, as students often think that meditation is *a* if not *the* defining Buddhist practice. In an East Asian context, however, seated meditation (Chi. *zuochan*; Jpn. *zazen*) is practiced much less often and by significantly fewer Buddhists—monastic or lay—than Pure Land practices of recollecting the Buddha or calling the name of the Buddha (Chi. *nianfo*; Jpn. *nembutsu*).[77] The Buddha in this case is Amituofo/Amidabutsu (Amida Buddha), not the historical Buddha.[78]

Pure Land imagery can be found very early in Buddhist teachings, but began to coalesce in China after the second-century translation of the three *Pure Land Sutras*,[79] with several figures who were later, somewhat anachronistically, described as "Pure Land Patriarchs," including Tanluan (476–542), Daochuo (562–645), and Shandao (613–681).[80] These figures focused on visualization and chanting practices, distinguished between easy and difficult paths to awakening, emphasized the need for sincere entrustment in the "other power" of Amituofo, and came to describe the recitation of the name of Amituofo as a primary practice—the goal of practice was rebirth in Amituofo's western Pure Land, where the karmic conditions were more favorable for the possibility of awakening than here on earth in this age of decline. As a group, Pure Land Buddhists are by far the largest single group in East Asia, though separating them out as a distinct sect is really a Japanese phenomenon, as Pure Land practices and beliefs are commonly intertwined with other Buddhist traditions—including Chan/Zen—elsewhere in East Asia.[81] As Robert Sharf explains, "Chinese Buddhists, both monastic and lay, have, throughout their history, aspired to rebirth in the Pure Land, whether conceived of in metaphorical or in literal terms. The Pure Land is both a world of "ease and bliss" as well as a place wherein one may easily progress along the Buddhist path unencumbered by physical and mental impurities. To those born in the Pure Land, final liberation is assured."[82] A number of Chinese Buddhists who engaged in Pure Land and other practices came to be identified with "mind-only" pure land thinking; as the fourth Pure Land Patriarch, Daoxin (580–651) wrote, "Contemplate [*nian*] the Buddha continuously in each moment of thought. . . . Apart from mind there is no buddha, apart from buddha there is no mind."[83] This is related to the later, widespread use of the kōan: "Who is reciting the name of the Buddha?"[84] This kōan shows clearly the intertwining of Chan/Zen and Pure Land practices: the Chan/Zen inquiry into the nature of the self, combined with the practice of recitation.

While it may be common for seated meditation to have a place in philosophy courses, at least to some extent, discussions of *nianfo/nembutsu* are extraordinarily rare. Chan/Zen and Pure Land are often described as opposite ends of the Buddhism spectrum, and *zazen* and *nembutsu* as poles of the practice continuum: from the philosophical to the devotional.[85] If "devotional" means that it is religious, and if it is religious then it is not philosophical, then a central Pure Land activity is not philosophical. But if Buddhism is really more a philosophy than a religion . . . what sense do we make of chanting the name of the Buddha or visualizing the Pure Land—which more Buddhists do than sit in silent meditation? There are (at least) two problems here. First, philosophers have failed to consider the philosophical significance of *nianfo* practice specifically and Pure Land traditions generally.[86] Second, and more to the point here, it hardly makes sense that "Buddhism" could "really" be anything that excludes most of the people the category is designed to include. That should tell us that something is not working well with the way that the categorization of "philosophy" and "religion" is working in the claim, and that we need to be more careful about how we make these kinds of claims, more nuanced about who is included, and more explicit about the definitions we are employing. After all, both "philosophy" and "religion" are categories that come out of Enlightenment Europe, not Buddhist East Asia, so it should come as no surprise that they don't always have an easy and obvious fit.[87] This is especially pronounced in trying to define American Buddhism.[88] In teaching about these complicated and multifaceted traditions, as instructors we can help students avoid the trap of thinking that they ought to make claims about "Buddhism" being either "philosophy" or "religion" without keeping some of these larger issues in mind.

In conclusion, these misconceptions—that East Asian Buddhists were/ are mostly nonviolent male monastics practicing (philosophical, not religious) *zazen*—are pervasive, and yet remedying them is not too difficult. Doing so will provide you with numerous opportunities to enrich and enliven your undergraduate classes, and perhaps to push the boundaries of what you think of as philosophically relevant in ways that might enhance your and your students' experiences.

Notes

1. Robert E. Buswell Jr. and Donald Lopez Jr. "10 Misconceptions about Buddhism," *Tricycle*, Summer 2014, https://tricycle.org/magazine/10-misconceptions-about-buddhism/.

2. For more on vegetarianism, see Geoffrey Barstow, *Food of Sinful Demons: Meat, Vegetarianism, and the Limits of Buddhism in Tibet* (New York: Columbia University Press, 2017); James Stewart, "The Question of Vegetarianism and Diet in Pali Buddhism," *Journal of Buddhist Ethics* 17 (2010): 110–40.

3. Two of these three are included in Buswell and Lopez's list of misconceptions: all Buddhists are pacifists, and Buddhism is a philosophy and not a religion. But their answers are barely a paragraph long, and do not suffice to the complexity of the issue nor the depth to which these misconceptions are grounded in many people's minds. See Buswell and Lopez, "10 Misconceptions." The third, misconceptions about women and gender, is not mentioned by Buswell and Lopez.

4. This chapter was inspired by research conducted during and after the 2018 NEH summer program East Asian Buddhism: Religion, Politics, and the Arts. I would like to extend my gratitude to the program organizer, Dr. Peter Hershock, as well as to the seminar leaders and participants. Parts of this work were also presented at the Zen Buddhism: Roots and Branches Conference at the Center for Mind, Body, and Culture at Florida Atlantic University in 2018 and at the Central Meeting of the American Philosophical Association in 2019.

5. For readers new to Buddhism or to teaching about Buddhism, there are many excellent textbooks to consider. I often use selections from Donald Mitchell and Sarah Jacoby's 2013 text, *Buddhism: Introducing the Buddhist Experience* (3rd edition, Oxford University Press). For a text more narrowly focused on Zen, some faculty choose *Zen: Tradition and Transition: A Sourcebook by Contemporary Zen Masters and Scholars*, ed. Kenneth Kraft (New York: Grove Press, 1994).

6. For more on Jingjian and other early Chinese nuns, see Kathryn Tsai's *Lives of the Nuns: Biographies of Buddhist Nuns from the Fourth to Sixth Centuries* (Honolulu: University of Hawai'i Press, 1994). Jingjian was a widow who left home to pursue formal Buddhist training, eventually found a teacher, and had a profound awakening experience. Although there was at that point no nuns order in China, she took the ten precepts that were available for monks, studied to learn about the historical role of *bhikṣuṇī* (fully ordained nuns), and established an independent convent for nuns. Then, she found a foreign monk, Tanmo Jieduo, who was willing to support her quest for full ordination; he ordained her and three of her students, over the objections of some Chinese monks. See also Grace Schireson, *Zen Women: Beyond Tea Ladies, Iron Maidens, and Macho Masters* (Boston: Wisdom Publications, 2009), 51–53.

7. Also spelled Zenso and Ezen. They were fully ordained in Paekche (Korea) around 590 CE, after earlier ordinations in Japan. They did not initiate an ordination lineage of nuns in Japan. See Akira Hirakawa, "The History of Buddhist Nuns in Japan," *Buddhist Christian Studies* 12 (1992): 143–58.

8. There are a number of works that might be helpful to those just becoming familiar with these issues more broadly in Buddhist traditions, or looking for more depth. Consider, for instance: Schireson, *Zen Women*; Karma Lekshe Tsomo, *Women in Buddhist Traditions* (New York: NYU Press, 2020); *Zen Sourcebook: Traditional Documents from China, Korea, and Japan*, ed. Stephen Addiss, Stanley Lombardo, and Judith Roltmann (Indianapolis: Hackett, 2008); *The Hidden Lamp: Stories from Twenty-Five Centuries of Awakened Women*, ed. Zenshin Florence Caplow and Reigetsu Susan Moon (Boston: Wisdom Publications, 2013); *Buddhist Feminisms*

and Femininities, ed. Karma Lekshe Tsomo (Albany: State University of New York Press, 2019); *Buddhist Women Across Cultures,* ed. Karma Lekshe Tsomo (Albany: State University of New York Press, 1999); *Eminent Buddhist Women,* ed. Karma Lekshe Tsomo (Albany: Srare University of New York Press, 2014); *Women's Buddhism, Buddhism's Women: Tradition, Revision, Renewal,* ed. Ellison Banks Findley (Boston: Wisdom Publications, 2000); Rita Gross, *Buddhism beyond Gender: Liberation from Attachment to Identity: Buddhism After Patriarchy* (Berkeley: Shambhala Publications, 2018).

9. The *garudhammas,* eight special or heavy rules for fully ordained nuns that subjugate them to even the most junior male monastics. See Schireson, 5–6.

10. Miriam Levering, "Miao-tao and her Teacher Dahui," in *Buddhism in the Sung,* ed. Peter Gregory and Daniel Getz (Honolulu: University of Hawai'i Press, 2002), 188.

11. Eun-su Cho, "Introduction," *Korean Buddhist Nuns and Laywomen: Hidden Histories, Enduring Vitality,* ed. Eun-su Cho (Albany: State University of New York Press, 2011), 1.

12. In the *Bahudhātuka Sutta (Majjhima Nikāya* 115), for instance, the Buddha asserts that although women can become awakened *arhats,* they cannot (as such) become bodhisattvas or fully awakened buddhas. See Naomi Appleton, "In the Footsteps of the Buddha? Women and the *Bodhisatta* Path in Theravāda Buddhism," *Journal of Feminist Studies in Religion* 27, no. 1 (2011): 33–51. For more on sexual transformation and the five hindrances, see Hae-ju Sunim (Ho-Ryeon Jeon), "Can Women Achieve Enlightenment? A Critique of Sexual Transformation for Enlightenment," in Tsomo, *Buddhist Women Across Cultures,* and Anālayo, "The Bahudhātuka-sutta and Its Parallels on Women's Inabilities," *Journal of Buddhist Ethics* 16 (2009): 136–90. For more on the contemporary state of ordained women's affairs, see Karma Lekshe Tsomo, "Mahaprajapati's Legacy: The Buddhist Women's Movement: An Introduction," in *Buddhist Women across Cultures.* For more on how nuns in medieval Japan dealt with these issues, see Lori Meeks, *Hokkeji and the Reemergence of Female Monastic Orders in Premodern Japan* (Honolulu: University of Hawai'i Press, 2010); for a discussion of gender in Tibetan Buddhism that involves some of these questions, see Michelle J. Sorensen, "Feminine Identities in Buddhist Chöd," in *Buddhist Feminisms and Femininities,* ed. Karma Lekshe Tsomo (Albany: State University of New York Press, 2019).

13. The story of the Nāga Princess (Dragon Princess) from the twelfth chapter of the *Lotus Sutra* is also commonly included in discussions of gender, although like the story of the Goddess from *Vimalakīrti,* while some take these stories to demonstrate that Buddhist texts can justify women's enlightenment, the texts do not clearly do this—they more straightforwardly justify the enlightenment of those who go beyond all dualisms, including sex/gender. This is a complex issue that is a rich topic for discussion with students. See also Miriam L. Levering, "Dōgen and the Dragon Princess," *Japan Mission Journal,* Autumn 2014, 166–80.

14. Although most English translations render the main speaker with the Sanskrit name and pronouns Avalokiteshvara (him/his), when discussing the text in an East Asian context I translate the speaker in the vernacular: Guanyin (Guanshiyin, Guanzizai), Kannon (Kanzeon), and with the more common female pronouns (she/they). For more on the *Heart Sutra*, see my recent book, *Exploring the Heart Sutra* (Lanham, MD: Lexington Books, 2021); in it, I explore not only issues relating to Guanyin and gender, but also the history of women's practice in China, and contemporary ethnographic research with Buddhist women in the United States, Taiwan, and China.

15. For more on Guanyin, see the groundbreaking work by Chün-fang Yü, *Kuanyin: The Chinese Transformation of Avalokitesvara* (New York: Columbia University Press, 2000). The story of Miaoshan can be a good one to read with students, and I sometimes use this in my Chinese philosophy course to talk about filiality in the context of Chinese Buddhism.

16. See *Treasury of the True Dharma Eye: Zen Master Dōgen's Shobo Genzo*, trans. Kazuaki Tanahashi (Boston: Shambala Press, 2013). The Sōtō Zen Translation Project also has a new complete translation underway (2020). See also Miriam L. Levering, "'Raihaitokuzui' and Dōgen's Views of Gender and Women: A Reconsideration," in *Dōgen and Sōtō Zen*, ed. Steven Heine (Oxford: Oxford University Press, 2015).

17. See Lori Meeks, "Women and Buddhism in East Asian History: The Case of the Blood Bowl Sutra: Part I: China," in *Religion Compass* (2020);14:e12336. https://doi.org/10/1111/rec3.12336, and "Women and Buddhism in East Asian History: The Case of the Blood Bowl Sutra: Part II: Japan" in *Religion Compass* (2020);14:e12335. https://doi.org/10/1111/rec3.12335.

18. T. Griffith Foulk, "The Form and Function of Koan Literature: A Historical Overview" in *The Koan: Texts and Contexts in Zen Buddhism*, ed. Steven Heine and Dale S. Wright (Oxford: Oxford University Press, 2000), 16.

19. These kōans can be separated pedagogically into those that are by and feature women but do not thematize women or gender and those that do. The brief recommendations I've given here are mostly kōans that do thematize gender in some respect. Schireson's *Zen Women* has many more stories throughout the text, and the entire text of *The Hidden Lamp* is women's kōans, including commentary from contemporary Western women Zen teachers. Beata Grant's *Zen Echoes: Classic Kōans with Verse Commentaries by Three Female Zen Masters* (Boston: Wisdom Publications, 2017) has forty-two traditional kōan cases with commentaries by three women masters, including classics such as Nanchuan Kills the Cat.

20. Caplow and Moon, *Hidden Lamp*, 286; Schireson, *Zen Women*, 19–20.

21. Caplow and Moon, *Hidden Lamp*, 101.

22. Caplow and Moon, *Hidden Lamp*, 114.

23. Caplow and Moon, *Hidden Lamp*, 59.

24. Caplow and Moon, *Hidden Lamp*, 256.

25. Caplow and Moon, *Hidden Lamp*, 253.

26. Schireson, *Zen Women*, 203–205; Caplow and Moon, *Hidden Lamp*, 131.

27. Caplow and Moon, *Hidden Lamp*, 332.

28. Caplow and Moon, *Hidden Lamp*, 41.

29. In my Spring 2020 and Spring 2022 Zen courses, I required students to write one of their three main essays engaging primary source material written from one of the women we read. By not only including women as part of the reading, but focusing an assignment on that material, I communicated to students (implicitly and explicitly) that this material is important—not a "nice addition" but a crucial component of our inquiry together.

30. In the preface to *Hidden Lamp*, Norman Fischer writes about the classical distinction in kōans between the "grasping way" and the "granting way" (xi–xii). This classical distinction between the grasping and the granting ways is pedagogically very useful, and I ask students in their responses to various kōans to identify which way(s) they think the kōan is using and give reasons. This helps them to think of the kōan as a teaching tool, and to connect individual kōans with other material we read about the use of language in Zen traditions.

31. Beata Grant's account of the story: "Guanxi Zhixian asks Moshan, whose name means 'Summit Mountain,' what this summit is like, to which Moshan Liaoran replies that it 'does not reveal its peak.' The monk persists, asking who the owner of Summit Mountain is, to which Moshan Liaoran replies, 'Its appearance is not male or female.' At this point, Guanxi Zhixian changes direction and asks, 'Why doesn't it transform itself?' Moshan Liaoran's response is immediate: 'It is not a god and it is not ghost, What should it transform itself into?' Her reply echoes that of the nameless nun who was a discipline of Linji Yixuan's and, when challenged by the monk Tankong to manifest at least one transformation retorted, 'I am not a wild fox spirit. What should I change into?' The point, of course, was that 'maleness' and 'femaleness' are not essential attributes—indeed Buddhism denies any such unchanging essence or 'own-being.' In the end, Guanxi Zhixian has the grace and wisdom to recognize Moshan Liaoran's superior wisdom and even goes so far as to work as her gardener for three years" (Grant, *Eminent Nuns: Women Chan Masters of Seventeenth-Century China*, 14–15). Moshan's story is also found in Caplow and Moon, *Hidden Lamp*, 231, and Schireson, *Zen Women*, 11–14.

32. Beata Grant, "Introduction," *Zen Echoes*, 14–15.

33. See Grant, *Zen Echoes*. In this book, Grant translates the kōans and Miaozong's commentaries, along with commentaries by Baochi and Zukui, two seventeenth-century female Chan masters. Miaozong can also be found in Caplow and Moon, *Zen Women*, ch 9; *Zen Sourcebook*, ed. Stephen Addiss, Stanley Lombardo, and Judith Roitman (Indianapolis: Hackett, 2008), ch 15; and in Schireson, *Hidden Lamp*, 107 and 234.

34. Schireson, *Zen Women*, 187.

35. Miriam Levering, "Stories of Enlightened Women in Ch'an," in *Women and Goddess Traditions: In Antiquity and Today*, ed. Karen King (Georgia: Trinity

Press International, 1997) 152. Quoted in Schireson, *Zen Women*, 192–93. In this encounter, Miaozong turns Wan'an's interrogation on its head—he points directly to his problem with her—her sex, gender, and different embodiment in his mono-gendered world—and she returns his question with one of her own—how do you think you or any monks, or buddhas or bodhisattvas or anyone got here, were it not for "this" that you are so judgmental of? She draws his attention to the immediacy of his failure to live his nondual theoretical commitments, the fact of his deep attachment to sexed and gendered norms when his practice ought to be aiding him with releasing those attachments, and so on.

36. For more on Mugai Nyodai, see Barbara Ruch, *Engendering Faith: Women and Buddhism in Premodern Japan* (Ann Arbor: University of Michigan Center for Japanese Studies, 2003). It is due to Ruch's groundbreaking scholarship that we know what we do about Mugai Nyodai. Passages on Mugai Nyodai can also be found in Schireson, *Zen Women*, ch 5; Addiss et al., *Zen Sourcebook*, ch 18; Caplow and Moon, *Hidden Lamp* 37 and 96, the latter of which shows how important and influential her enlightenment poem was for later monastics. Although women had initially had full ordination in Japan, this practice stopped for several hundred years and was only restarted in the late 1200s.

37. For more on Japanese convents outside of a Rinzai context, see Meeks (2010).

38. See "The Awakening of Mugai Nyodai," trans. Anne Dutton, Addiss et al., *Zen Sourcebook*, ch 18. In Buddhist history, gazetteers are historical accounts, similar to a magazine or newspaper, that record the development of both human and geographical contexts of Buddhist practice. They often serve as compendiums of Buddhist history and geography local to a particular region.

39. According to Dutton, there are a number of inconsistencies in the longer versions of her enlightenment story, and some of these contradict some aspects of her general biography.

40. Mugai Nyodai, trans. Anne Dutton, in Addiss et al., *Zen Sourcebook*, 179.

41. For more on Ryonen, see Ruch, *Engendering Faith*; Stephen Addiss, *The Art of Zen: Paintings and Calligraphy by Japanese Monks 1600–1925* (Vermont: Echo Point Books, 2018); Stephen Addiss, "The Zen Nun Ryonen Genso," *Spring Wind* (1986): 180–87; Schireson, *Zen Women*, ch 7; and Caplow and Moon, *Hidden Lamp*, 117. Like Mugai Nyodai, Ryonen was well off and well educated, and she demonstrated her sincerity and commitment to practice by burning her face in order to become a student of Obaku Master Hakuo Dotai. Many of Ryonen's poems and calligraphic works have been preserved in Addiss, *The Art of Zen*.

42. Caplow and Moon, *Hidden Lamp*, 128 and 263.

43. Schireson, *Zen Women*, 114.

44. Schireson, *Zen Women*, 112. For more on Tokeiji, see Sachiko Kaneko Morell and Robert Morell, *Zen Sanctuary of Purple Robes: Japan's Tokeiji Convent Since 1285* (Albany: State University of New York Press, 2012).

45. Another Pure Land figure that would be a great addition to a course would be Chin'ichibō (?–1344), a nun who was a follower of the movement founded by Ippen (1239–1289). For more on her, including primary source materials, see Cailtin Griffiths, *Tracing the Itinerant Path: Jishu Nuns of Medieval Japan* (Honolulu: University of Hawai'i Press, 2016). For more on women in early Pure Land Buddhism in Japan, see also Paul Harrison, "Women in the Pure Land: Some Reflections on the Textual Sources," *Journal of Indian Philosophy* 26, no. 6 (1998): 553–72.

46. James Dobbins, *Letters of the Nun Eshinni: Images of Pure Land Buddhism in Medieval Japan* (Honolulu: University of Hawai'i Press, 2004).

47. Dobbins, 21.

48. For more on Iryŏp, see Kim Iryŏp, *Reflections of a Zen Buddhist Nun: Essays by Zen Master Kim Iryŏp*, trans. Jin Park (Honolulu: University of Hawai'i Press, 2014); Jin Park, *Women and Buddhist Philosophy: Engaging Zen Master Kim Iryŏp* (Honolulu: University of Hawai'i Press, 2017); Jin Park, "Gendered Response to Modernity: Kim Iryŏp and Buddhism," in *Makers of Modern Korean Buddhism*, ed. Jin Y. Park (Albany: State University of New York Press, 2018); and Schireson, *Zen Women*, ch 9.

49. Jin Park, "Translator's Introduction," *Reflections of a Zen Buddhist Nun*, 2.

50. For more on Raichō, see *Japanese Philosophy: A Sourcebook.* ed. James Heisig, Thomas Kasulis, and John Maraldo (Honolulu: University of Hawai'i Press, 2011); Christine James, "Raicho Hiratsuka and Socially Engaged Buddhism," in *Buddhist Feminisms and Femininities*; Raichō Hiratsuka and Teruko Craig, *In the Beginning, Woman Was the Sun: The Autobiography of a Japanese Feminist*, trans. Teruko Craig (New York: Columbia University Press, 2006); and Michiko Yusa and Leah Kalmanson, "Raicho: Zen and the Female Body in the Development of Japanese Feminist Philosophy," in *The Oxford Handbook of Japanese Philosophy*, ed. Bret W. Davis (Oxford: Oxford University Press, 2019).

51. See for instance Matthew Mitchell, "Conflicts and Compromises: The Relationship between the Nuns of Daihongan and the Monks of Daokanjin within the Zenkoji Temple Complex," in Tsomo, *Buddhist Feminisms and Femininities*; Taiwan has a fascinating situation with women, and Elise Anne Devido's *Taiwan's Buddhist Nuns* gives an excellent account of the history and contemporary situation of the major groups of monastic nuns in Taiwan, many of whom have extensive power in Taiwan's monastic community. See Elise Anne Devido, *Taiwan's Buddhist Nuns* (Albany: State University of New York Press, 2010). Gesshin Claire Greenwood gives an autobiographical look from a Western perspective into Japanese Zen in *Bow First, Ask Questions Later: Ordination, Love, and Monastic Zen in Japan* (Boston: Wisdom Publications, 2018), and Martine Batchelor does something similar, along with translating autobiographical material from twentieth-century nun Son'Gyong Sunim, in *Women in Korean Zen: Lives and Practices* (New York: Syracuse University Press, 2006); in chapter 4 of my recent book *Exploring the* Heart Sutra, and in my essay "Menstruation, Gender Segregation, and a Kōan Concerning Miscarriage: On Gender and Embodiment in Contemporary Buddhist Practices," forthcoming in an

edited volume on Buddhist embodiment and somaesthetics (ed. Kenneth Holloway), I draw on ethnographic work with women Buddhists from the United States and East Asia, and I argue that in some cases, especially concerning feminist reconstruction, we ought to think of ethnography as a philosophical method.

52. Paula Kane Robinson Arai, *Women Living Zen: Japanese Sōtō Buddhist Nuns* (Oxford: Oxford University Press, 2012). Arai has also written a number of articles and chapters that work very well for classroom use.

53. In addition to sources already mentioned, see also Beata Grant, *Daughters of Emptiness: Poems by Buddhist Nuns of China* (Boston: Wisdom, 2012); Beata Grant, "The Red Cord Untied: Buddhist Nuns in Eighteenth-Century China," in Tsomo, *Buddhist Women Across Cultures*; Paula K. R. Arai, "Japanese Buddhist Nuns: Innovators for the Sake of Tradition," in Tsomo, *Buddhist Women Across Cultures*; Eun-su Cho, "The Religious Life of Buddhist Women in Choson Korea," in Tsomo, *Buddhist Feminisms and Femininities*; and Ching-ning Wang, "A 'Great Man' is No Longer Gendered: The Gender Identity and Practice of Chan Nuns in Contemporary Taiwan," in Tsomo, *Buddhist Feminisms and Femininities*.

54. Following Michael Jerryson in "Buddhist Traditions and Violence," in *The Oxford Handbook of Religion and Violence*, ed. Mark Juergensmeyer, Margo Kitts, and Michael Jerryson (Oxford: Oxford University Press, 2013). There is sometimes overlap between the first and third categories. See also Michael Jerryson and Mark Juergensmeyer, eds., *Buddhist Warfare* (New York: Oxford University Press, 2010).

55. For a broader discussion of violence in traditional Chinese culture, see Barend ter Haar, *Religious Culture and Violence in Traditional China* (Cambridge: Cambridge University Press, 2019). For more on the contemporary situation in Burma/Myanmar, see Francis Wade, *Myanmar's Enemy Within: Buddhist Violence and the Making of a Muslim "Other"* (London: Zed Books, 2019); for more popular accounts of Buddhist violence, see Emmanuel Stoakes, "Monks, PowerPoint Presentations, and Ethnic Cleansing," *Foreign Policy* October 26, 2015, https://foreignpolicy.com/2015/10/26/evidence-links-myanmar-government-monks-ethnic-cleansing-rohingya/; Randy Rosenthal, "What's the Connection between Buddhism and Ethnic Cleansing in Myanmar?" *Lion's Roar*, November 13, 2018, https://www.lionsroar.com/what-does-buddhism-have-to-do-with-the-ethnic-cleansing-in-myanmar/; Dan Arnold and Alicia Turner, "Why Are We Surprised When Buddhists Are Violent?" *New York Times, The Stone*, March 5, 2018, https://www.nytimes.com/2018/03/05/opinion/buddhists-violence-tolerance.html; Michael Jerryson, "Monks with Guns" *Aeon*, April 26, 2017, https://aeon.co/essays/buddhism-can-be-as-violent-as-any-other-religion.

56. Consider, for instance, Frederick P. Brandauer, "Violence and Buddhist Idealism in the *Xiyou* Novels," in *Violence in China: Essays in Culture and Counterculture*, ed. Jonathan N. Lipman and Stevan Harrell (Albany: State University of New York Press, 1990).

57. Robert Sharf, "The Scripture in Forty-Two Sections," in *Religions of China in Practice*, ed. Donald S. Lopez Jr. (Princeton: Princeton University Press, 1996), 370. I have a longstanding interest in combat metaphors, as seen in my book,

Metaphor and Metaphilosophy: Philosophy as Combat, Play, and Aesthetic Experience (Lanham, MD: Lexington Books, 2014).

58. For an interesting reading of this story, see Peter D. Hershock, *Chan Buddhism* (Honolulu: University of Hawai'i Press, 2004). This kind of "dharma encounter" or "dharma combat" has a number of violent connotations, in both Zen and Tibetan contexts. In a Japanese literary context, for a discussion of violence and nonviolence in Shinran's work, see Dennis Hirota, "Violence and Nonviolence in Shinran" *Religions* 9, no. 6 (2018).

59. See G. Cameron Hurst III, "Death, Honor, and Loyality: The Bushidō Ideal," *Philosophy East and West* 40, no. 4 (1990): 511–27; Samurai entry in Heisig et al., *Japanese Philosophy: A Sourcebook*.

60. Donald S. Lopez, *The Lotus Sutra: A Biography* (Princeton: Princeton University Press, 2016), 106.

61. Carol Richmond Tsang, *War and Faith—Ikkō Ikki in Late Muromachi Japan* (Boston: Harvard University Asia Center, 2007), 191. See also William Deal and Brian Ruppert, *A Cultural History of Japanese Buddhism* (New Jersey: Wiley-Blackwell, 2015).

62. See Nichiren entry in Heisig et al., *Japanese Philosophy: A Sourcebook*.

63. The Chinese analog for *sōhei* can be found in Shaolin monks—monastics who trained in martial arts, for the purposes of defending their temples (and the temple treasuries) against thieves. For more on Shaolin monks and the Shaolin monastery, see chapter 10 by Croteau and Zhang in this volume.

64. For more on *sōhei*, see Mikael Adolphson, *The Teeth and Claws of the Buddha: Monastic Warriors and Sōhei in Japanese History* (Honolulu: University of Hawai'i Press, 2007).

65. "Millenarian" in this context refers to the belief in the coming massive transformation of society, often after a major natural disaster or other transformative event. They often claim that the current society is corrupt and that those who are not part of the group will be destroyed in the coming transformation. Millenarian movements have been and can be found in many different cultures and societies.

66. Mahāyāna texts often refer to various levels of progression for bodhisattvas (persons/figures who stay in the cycle of birth and death out of compassion for others). One common account has it that there are ten levels, beginning with the arising of *bodhicitta* (aspiration to help others) and insight into emptiness, and progressing until the tenth stage, where figures such as Guanyin wait to become future Buddhas.

67. Hubert Michael Seiwert, *Popular Religious Movements and Heterodox Sects in Chinese History* (Leiden: Brill, 2003).

68. Consider for instance Xue Yu, *Buddhism, War, and Nationalism: Chinese Monks in the Struggle against Japanese Aggression 1931–1945* (Abingdon: Routledge, 2013).

69. Brian Daizen Victoria, *Zen at War* (Lanham, MD: Rowman and Littlefield, 2006). See also Christopher Ives, *Imperial-Way Zen: Ichikawa Hakugen's Critique and Lingering Questions for Buddhist Ethics* (Honolulu: University of Hawai'i Press, 2009).

70. Jerryson, "Buddhist Traditions and Violence," 49. Jerryson argues that in general, exceptions to commitments to nonviolence are organized around issues of intent, nature of the actor, and nature of the victim.

71. Tibetan liberation killings are one example of this. For more on that, see Jacob Dalton, *The Taming of the Demons: Violence and Liberation in Tibetan Buddhism* (New Haven: Yale University Press, 2011).

72. There are Zen counterpoints to this idea, as seen, for instance, in Yagyu Munenori's *The Life-Giving Sword: Secret Teachings from the House of the Shogun*, trans. William Scott Wilson (Boston: Shambala Press, 2012). Munenori was a contemporary of Musashi, but advocated very different ideas.

73. In addition to sources already mentioned, see also Nicolas Gier, ed., *The Origins of Religious Violence: An Asian Perspective* (Lanham: Lexington Books, 2014) and Mariam Kurtz and Lester Kurtz, eds., *Women, War, and Violence: Topography, Resistance, and Hope* (Santa Barbara: Praeger Press, 2015).

74. To see more on how I approach this problem of categorization with the tradition of Confucianism/Ruism, see the co-authored (with Paul Carelli) chapter, "Ruism and the Category of Religion: Or, What to Do about the Confucians?" in *Asian Philosophies and the Idea of Religion: Beyond Faith and Reason*, ed. Ashwani Peetush and Sonia Sikka (Routledge, 2020).

75. I am not saying this is what I think philosophy is, but rather that this seems to be what is implied by "philosophy" in this claim.

76. Tomoko Masuzawa, *The Invention of World Religions: Or, How European Universalism Was Preserved in the Language of Pluralism* (Chicago: University of Chicago Press, 2005).

77. *Nianfo/nembutsu* practices range from calling the name of the buddha, out loud or internally, visualizing the buddha or buddha-field, the pure land, pure land sutras, and other practices of recollecting the buddha. While Japanese pure land practices narrowed in on "exclusive" *nembutsu*, or sole-recitation of the name of the buddha, other pure land recollection practices were and are still popular elsewhere. For more on this in the historical Chinese context, see Robert H. Sharf, "On Pure Land Buddhism and Ch'an/Pure Land Syncretism in Medieval China," in *T'oung Pao* LXXXVIII (Leiden: Brill, 2002).

78. In China the Buddhas Amitayus and Amitabha are combined into Amituofo, and in Japanese this is Amida Butsu (Amida Buddha). See Galen Amstutz, *Interpreting Amida: History and Orientalism in the Study of Pure Land Buddhism* (Albany: State University of New York Press, 1997).

79. The three Pure Land Sutras are the *Longer* and *Shorter Sukhāvatīvyūha Sutras* and the *Amitayurdhyana* (Contemplation) *Sutra*. These sutras describe Amito/

Amida Buddha, who as a bodhisattva made a vow that when he was a Buddha he would help anyone gain access to his Buddha field (the Western Pure Land), as long as they called his name. They also describe *Sukhavati*, his Pure Land of Bliss, and visualization practices given to Queen Vaidehi.

80. For more on Chinese Pure Land Buddhism, see Charles B. Jones, *Chinese Pure Land Buddhism: Understanding a Tradition of Practice* (Honolulu: University of Hawai'i Press, 2019). For more on Pure Lands in a wider context, see, Georgios T. Halkias and Richard K. Payne, eds., *Pure Lands in Asian Texts and Contexts: An Anthology* (Honolulu: University of Hawai'i Press, 2019).

81. See Sharf, "On Pure Land Buddhism." Also Miriam L. Levering, "The *Huatou* Revolution, Pure Land Practices, and Dahui's Chan Discourse on the Moment of Death," *Frontiers of History in China* 8, no. 3 (2013). See also Natasha Heller, "Buddha in a Box: The Materiality of Recitation in Contemporary Chinese Buddhism," *Material Religion* 10, no. 3 (2014).

82. Sharf, "On Pure Land Buddhism," 286.

83. Daoxin, T. 2837: 85.1287a9–15: Yanagida 1971: 192. Quoted in Sharf, "On Pure Land Buddhism," 304.

84. Morten Schlütter, " 'Who Is Reciting the Name of the Buddha' as *Gongan* in Chinese Chan Buddhism," *Frontiers of History in China* 8, no. 3 (2013).

85. Karyn Lai expresses this common view when she notes that Pure Land Buddhism in China is a "practice" sect, while Tiantai, Huayan, Weishi, and Chan are "doctrinal," and so relevant for philosophical consideration, in Lai, *Introduction to Chinese Philosophy* (Cambridge: Cambridge University Press, 2017), 282–303.

86. For more on this, see Mattice, "Shinran as Global Philosopher," *Religions* 13, no. 105 (2022).

87. For more on the history of the term *religion* in the context of Japan, see Jason Ananda Josephson, *The Invention of Religion in Japan* (Chicago: University of Chicago Press, 2012). See also Leah Kalmanson, "*Dharma* and *Dao*: Key Terms in the Comparative Philosophy of Religion," in *Ineffability: An Exercise in Comparative Philosophy of Religion*, ed. Timothy Knepper and Leah Kalmanson (Switzerland: Springer, 2017).

88. See for instance Jan Nattier, "Who Is a Buddhist? Charting the Landscape of Buddhist America," in *The Faces of Buddhism in America*, ed. Charles Prebish (Berkeley: University of California Press, 1998); Ann Gleig, *American Dharma: Buddhism Beyond Modernity* (New Haven: Yale University Press, 2019). For those whose courses focus more on American Buddhisms, you might consider work by contemporary scholars and teachers who highlight the diversity in American Buddhist communities, including Ruth King's *Mindful of Race* (Boulder: Sounds True, 2018); Pamela Ayo Yetunde and Cheryl A. Giles, eds., *Black and Buddhist: What Buddhism Can Teach Us About Race, Resilience, Transformation, and Freedom* (Boston: Shambala, 2020); George Yancy and Emily McRae, eds., *Buddhism and Whiteness: Critical Reflections* (Lanham, MD: Lexington Books, 2021); Rev. Angel

Kyodo Williams and Lama Rod Owens, *Radical Dharma: Talking Race, Love, and Liberation* (Berkeley: North Atlantic Books, 2016); Jan Willis, ed., *Dharma Matters: Women, Race, and Tantra* (Boston: Wisdom Publications, 2020); Zenju Earthlyn Manuel, *The Way of Tenderness: Awakening Through Race, Sexuality, and Gender* (Boston: Wisdom Publications, 2016); Charles S. Prebish and Kenneth K. Tanaka, eds., *The Faces of Buddhism in America* (Berkeley: University of California Press, 1998); Duncan Ryūken Williams, *American Sutra: A Story of Freedom in the Second World War* (Boston: Belknap Press, 2020); and Chenxing Han, *Be The Refuge: Raising the Voices of Asian American Buddhists* (Berkeley: North Atlantic Books, 2021).

Bibliography

Addiss, Stephen. "The Zen Nun Ryonen Genso," *Spring Wind* (1986): 180–87.

———. *The Art of Zen: Paintings and Calligraphy by Japanese Monks 1600–1925.* Vermont: Echo Point Books, 2018.

———, Stanley Lombardo, and Judith Roltmann, eds. *Zen Sourcebook: Traditional Documents from China, Korea, and Japan.* Indianapolis: Hackett, 2008.

Adolphson, Mikael. *The Teeth and Claws of the Buddha: Monastic Warriors and Sōhei in Japanese History.* Honolulu: University of Hawai'i Press, 2007.

Amstutz, Galen. *Interpreting Amida: History and Orientalism in the Study of Pure Land Buddhism.* Albany: State University of New York Press, 1997.

Anālayo, "The Bahudhātuka-sutta and Its Parallels on Women's Inabilities." *Journal of Buddhist Ethics*, 16 (2009): 136–90.

Appleton, Naomi. "In the Footsteps of the Buddha? Women and the *Bodhisatta* Path in Theravāda Buddhism." *Journal of Feminist Studies in Religion* 27, no. 1 (2011): 33–51.

Arai, Paula Kane Robinson. *Women Living Zen: Japanese Sōtō Buddhist Nuns.* Oxford: Oxford University Press, 2012.

Arnold, Dan and Alicia Turner. "Why Are We Surprised When Buddhists Are Violent?" *New York Times, The Stone*, March 5, 2018, https://www. nytimes. com/2018/03/05/opinion/buddhists-violence-tolerance. html.

Ayo Yetunde, Pamela, and Cheryl A. Giles, eds. *Black and Buddhist: What Buddhism Can Teach Us About Race, Resilience, Transformation, and Freedom.* Boston: Shambala, 2020.

Barstow, Geoffrey. *Food of Sinful Demons: Meat, Vegetarianism, and the Limits of Buddhism in Tibet.* New York: Columbia University Press, 2017.

Batchelor, Martine, and Son'Gyong Sunim. *Women in Korean Zen: Lives and Practices.* New York: Syracuse University Press, 2006.

Brandauer, Frederick P. "Violence and Buddhist Idealism in the *Xiyou* Novels." In *Violence in China: Essays in Culture and Counterculture*, edited by Jonathan

N. Lipman and Stevan Harrell, 115–48. Albany: State University of New York Press, 1990.

Buswell, Jr., Robert E., and Donald Lopez Jr. "10 Misconceptions about Buddhism." *Tricycle*, Summer 2014, https://tricycle. org/magazine/10-misconceptions-about-buddhism/.

Caplow, Florence, and Susan Moon, eds. *The Hidden Lamp: Stories from Twenty-Five Centuries of Awakened Women*. Boston: Wisdom Publications, 2013.

Cho, Eun-su. "The Religious Life of Buddhist Women in Choson Korea." In *Buddhist Feminisms and Femininities*, edited by Karma Lekshe Tsomo, 67–84. Albany: State University of New York Press, 2019.

———, ed. *Korean Buddhist Nuns and Laywomen: Hidden Histories, Enduring Vitality*. Albany: State University of New York Press, 2011.

Dalton, Jacob. *The Taming of the Demons: Violence and Liberation in Tibetan Buddhism*. New Haven: Yale University Press, 2011.

Deal, William, and Brian Ruppert. *A Cultural History of Japanese Buddhism*. New Jersey: Wiley-Blackwell, 2015.

Devido, Elise Anne. *Taiwan's Buddhist Nuns*. Albany: State Unoversoty of New York Press, 2010.

Dobbins, James. *Letters of the Nun Eshinni: Images of Pure Land Buddhism in Medieval Japan*. Honolulu: University of Hawai'i Press, 2004.

Dōgen. *Treasury of the True Dharma Eye: Zen Master Dōgen's Shobo Genzo*. Translated by Kazuaki Tanahashi. Boulder: Shambala Press, 2013.

Findley, Ellison Banks, ed. *Women's Buddhism, Buddhism's Women: Tradition, Revision, Renewal*. Boston: Wisdom Publications, 2000.

Foulk, T. Griffith. "The Form and Function of Koan Literature: A Historical Overview." In *The Koan: Texts and Contexts in Zen Buddhism*, edited by Steven Heine and Dale S. Wright, 15–45. Oxford: Oxford University Press, 2000.

Gier, Nicholas, ed. *The Origins of Religious Violence: An Asian Perspective*. Lanham, MD: Lexington Books, 2014.

Gleig, Ann. *American Dharma: Buddhism beyond Modernity*. New Haven: Yale University Press, 2019.

Grant, Beata. "The Red Cord Untied: Buddhist Nuns in Eighteenth-Century China." In *Buddhist Women Across Cultures*, edited by Karma Lekshe Tsomo, 91–104. Albany: State University of New York Press, 1999.

———. *Eminent Nuns: Women Chan Masters of Seventeenth-Century China*. Honolulu: University of Hawai'i Press, 2009.

———. *Daughters of Emptiness: Poems by Buddhist Nuns of China*. Boston: Wisdom Publications, 2012.

———. *Zen Echoes: Classic Kōans with Verse Commentaries by Three Female Zen Masters*. Boston: Wisdom Publications, 2017.

Greenwood, Claire. *Bow First, Ask Questions Later: Ordination, Love, and Monastic Zen in Japan*. Boston: Wisdom Publications, 2018.

Griffiths, Caitlin. *Tracing the Itinerant Path: Jishu Nuns of Medieval Japan*. Honolulu: University of Hawai'i Press, 2016.

Gross, Rita. *Buddhism beyond Gender: Liberation from Attachment to Identity: Buddhism After Patriarchy.* Berkeley: Shambhala, 2018.

Haar, Barend ter. *Religious Culture and Violence in Traditional China*. Cambridge: Cambridge University Press, 2019.

Halkias, Georgios T., and Richard K. Payne, eds. *Pure Lands in Asian Texts and Contexts: An Anthology*. Honolulu: University of Hawai'i Press, 2019.

Han, Chenxing. *Be the Refuge: Raising the Voices of Asian American Buddhists*. Berkeley: North Atlantic Books, 2021.

Harrison, Paul. "Women in the Pure Land: Some Reflections on the Textual Sources." *Journal of Indian Philosophy* 26, no. 6 (1998): 553–72.

Heisig, James, Thomas Kasulis and John Maraldo, eds. *Japanese Philosophy: A Sourcebook*. Honolulu: University of Hawai'i Press, 2011.

Heller, Natasha. "Buddha in a Box: The Materiality of Recitation in Contemporary Chinese Buddhism." *Material Religion* 10, no. 3 (2014).

Hershock, Peter D. *Chan Buddhism*. Honolulu: University of Hawai'i Press, 2004.

Hirakawa, Akira. "The History of Buddhist Nuns in Japan." *Buddhist Christian Studies* 12 (1992): 143–58.

Hirota, Dennis. "Violence and Nonviolence in Shinran." *Religions* 9, no. 6: 2018.

Hurst III, G. Cameron. "Death, Honor, and Loyality: The Bushidō Ideal." *Philosophy East and West* 40, no. 4 (1990): 511–27.

Ives, Christopher. *Imperial-Way Zen: Ichikawa Hakugen's Critique and Lingering Questions for Buddhist Ethics*. Honolulu: University of Hawai'i Press, 2009.

James, Christine "Raicho Hiratsuka and Socially Engaged Buddhism." In *Buddhist Feminisms and Femininities* edited by Karma Lekshe Tsomo, 85–106. Albany: State University of New York Press, 2019.

Jones, Charles B. *Chinese Pure Land Buddhism: Understanding a Tradition of Practice*. Honolulu: University of Hawai'i Press, 2019.

Jerryson, Michael. *Buddhist Warfare*. Edited by Michael Jerryson and Mark Juergensmeyer. New York: Oxford University Press, 2010.

———. "Buddhist Traditions and Violence." In *The Oxford Handbook of Religion and Violence*, edited by Mark Juergensmeyer, Margo Kitts, and Michael Jerryson. Oxford: Oxford University Press, 2013.

———. "Monks with Guns" *Aeon*, April 26, 2017, https://aeon.co/essays/buddhism-can-be-as-violent-as-any-other-religion.

Josephson, Jason Ananda. *The Invention of Religion in Japan*. Chicago: University of Chicago Press, 2012.

Kalmanson, Leah. "*Dharma* and *Dao*: Key Terms in the Comparative Philosophy of Religion." In *Ineffability: An Exercise in Comparative Philosophy of Religion*, edited by Timothy Knepper and Leah Kalmanson. Switzerland: Springer, 2017.

Kim Iryŏp, *Reflections of a Zen Buddhist Nun: Essays by Zen Master Kim Iryŏp*. Translated by Jin Park. Honolulu: University of Hawai'i Press, 2014.

King, Ruth. *Mindful of Race: Transforming Racism from the Inside Out*. Boulder: Sounds True, 2018.

Kraft, Kenneth, ed. *Zen: Tradition and Transition: A Sourcebook by Contemporary Zen Masters and Scholars*. New York: Grove Press, 1994.

Kurtz, Mariam, and Lester Kurtz, eds. *Women, War, and Violence: Topography, Resistance, and Hope*. Santa Barbara: Praeger Press, 2015.

Lai, Karyn. *Introduction to Chinese Philosophy*. Cambridge: Cambridge University Press, 2017.

Levering, Miriam. "Stories of Enlightened Women in Ch'an," in *Women and Goddess Traditions: In Antiquity and Today*, ed. Karen King. Georgia: Trinity Press International, 1997.

Levering, Miriam. "Miao-tao and her Teacher Dahui." In *Buddhism in the Sung*, edited by Peter Gregory and Daniel Getz, 188–219. Honolulu: University of Hawai'i Press, 2002.

———. "The *Huatou* Revolution, Pure Land Practices, and Dahui's Chan Discourse on the Moment of Death." *Frontiers of History in China* 8, no. 3 (2013): 342–65.

———. "Dōgen and the Dragon Princess." *Japan Mission Journal* (Autumn 2014): 166–80.

———. "'Raihaitokuzui' and Dōgen's Views of Gender and Women: A Reconsideration." *Dōgen and Sōtō Zen*, edited by Steven Heine, 46–73. Oxford: Oxford University Press, 2015.

Lopez, Donald S. *The Lotus Sutra: A Biography*. Princeton: Princeton University Press, 2016.

Manuel, Zenju Earthyln. *The Way of Tenderness: Awakening Through Race, Sexuality, and Gender*. Boston: Wisdom Publications, 2016.

Masuzawa, Tomoko. *The Invention of World Religions: Or, How European Universalism Was Preserved in the Language of Pluralism*. Chicago: University of Chicago Press, 2005.

Mattice, Sarah. *Metaphor and Metaphilosophy: Philosophy as Combat, Play, and Aesthetic Experience*. Lanham, MD: Lexington Books, 2014.

———. *Exploring the* Heart Sutra. Lanham, MD: Lexington Books, 2021.

———. "Shinran as Global Philosopher." *Religions* 13, no. 105(2022).

———, and Paul Carelli. "Ruism and the Category of Religion: Or, What to Do about the Confucians?" In *Asian Philosophies and the Idea of Religion: Beyond Faith and Reason*, edited by Ashwani Peetush and Sonia Sikka, 106–24. Abingdon: Routledge, 2020.

Morell, Sachiko Kaneko, and Robert Morell. *Zen Sanctuary of Purple Robes: Japan's Tokeiji Convent Since 1285*. Albany: State University of New York Press, 2012.

Meeks, Lori. *Hokkeji and the Reemergence of Female Monastic Orders in Premodern Japan*. Honolulu: University of Hawai'i Press, 2010.

————. "Women and Buddhism in East Asian History: The Case of the Blood Bowl Sutra: Part I: China." *Religion Compass* (2020), https://doi. org/10/1111/ rec3. 12336.

————. "Women and Buddhism in East Asian History: The Case of the Blood Bowl Sutra: Part II: Japan." *Religion Compass* (2020), https://doi. org/10/1111/ rec3. 12335.

Mitchell, Donald, and Sarah Jacoby. *Buddhism: Introducing the Buddhist Experience.* 3d edition. Oxford: Oxford University Press, 2013.

Mitchell, Matthew. "Conflicts and Compromises: The Relationship between the Nuns of Daihongan and the Monks of Daokanjin within the Zenkoji Temple Complex." In *Buddhist Feminisms and Femininities*, edited by Karma Lekshe Tsomo, 219–36. Albany: State University of New York Press, 2019.

Munenori, Yagyu. *The Life-Giving Sword: Secret Teachings from the House of the Shogun.* Translated by William Scott Wilson. Boston: Shambala Press, 2012.

Nattier, Jan. "Who Is a Buddhist? Charting the Landscape of Buddhist America." In *The Faces of Buddhism in America*, edited by Charles Prebish, 183–95. Berkeley: University of California Press, 1998.

Park, Jin. *Women and Buddhist Philosophy: Engaging Zen Master Kim Iryŏp.* Honolulu: University of Hawai'i Press, 2017.

————. "Gendered Response to Modernity: Kim Iryŏp and Buddhism." In *Makers of Modern Korean Buddhism*, edited by Jin Park, 109–27. Albany: State University of New York Press, 2018.

Prebish, Charles S., and Kenneth T. Tanaka, eds. *The Faces of Buddhism in America.* Berkeley: University of California Press, 1998.

Raichō Hiratsuka. *In the Beginning, Woman Was the Sun: The Autobiography of a Japanese Feminist.* Translated by Teruko Craig. New York: Columbia University Press, 2006.

Rosenthal, Randy. "What's the Connection between Buddhism and Ethnic Cleansing in Myanmar?" *Lion's Roar*, November 13, 2018, https://www. lionsroar. com/what-does-buddhism-have-to-do-with-the-ethnic-cleansing-in-myanmar/.

Ruch, Barbara. *Engendering Faith: Women and Buddhism in Premodern Japan.* Ann Arbor: University of Michigan Center for Japanese Studies, 2003.

Schireson, Grace. *Zen Women: Beyond Tea Ladies, Iron Maidens, and Macho Masters.* Boston: Wisdom Publications, 2009.

Schlütter, Morten. "'Who Is Reciting the Name of the Buddha' as *Gongan* in Chinese Chan Buddhism." *Frontiers of History in China* 8 no. 3 (2013): 366–88.

Seiwert, Hubert Michael. *Popular Religious Movements and Heterodox Sects in Chinese History.* Leiden: Brill, 2003.

Sharf, Robert H. "The Scripture in Forty-Two Sections." In *Religions of China in Practice*, edited by Donald S. Lopez Jr., 360–71. Princeton: Princeton University Press, 1996.

————. "On Pure Land Buddhism and Ch'an/Pure Land Syncretism in Medieval China." In *T'oung Pao* LXXXVIII, 282–331. Leiden: Brill, 2002.

Sorensen, Michelle J. "Feminine Identities in Buddhist Chöd." In *Buddhist Feminisms and Femininities*, edited by Karma Lekshe Tsomo, 271–84. Albany: State University of New York Press, 2019.

Stewart, James. "The Question of Vegetarianism and Diet in Pali Buddhism." *Journal of Buddhist Ethics*, 17 (2010): 110–40.

Stoakes, Emmanuel. "Monks, PowerPoint Presentations, and Ethnic Cleansing." *Foreign Policy* October 26, 2015, https://foreignpolicy.com/2015/10/26/evidence-links-myanmar-government-monks-ethnic-cleansing-rohingya/.

Sutra of Queen Rimala of the Lion's Roar/The Vimalakirti Sutra. Translated by John R. McRae and Diana Y. Paul. Moraga, CA: BDK America, 2006.

Tsai, Kathryn. *Lives of the Nuns: Biographies of Buddhist Nuns from the Fourth to Sixth Centuries*. Honolulu: University of Hawai'i Press, 1994.

Tsang, Carol Richmond. *War and Faith—Ikkō Ikki in Late Muromachi Japan*. Boston: Harvard University Asia Center, 2007.

Tsomo, Karma Lekshe. *Buddhist Women across Cultures*, ed. Karma Lekshe Tsomo. Albany: State University of New York Press, 1999.

———. *Women in Buddhist Traditions*. New York: New York University Press, 2020.

———, ed. *Eminent Buddhist Women*. Albany: State University of New York Press, 2014.

———, ed. *Buddhist Feminisms and Femininities*. Albany: State University of New York Press, 2019.

Victoria, Brian Daizen. *Zen at War*. Lanham, MD: Rowman and Littlefield, 2006.

Wade, Francis. *Myanmar's Enemy Within: Buddhist Violence and the Making of a Muslim "Other."* London: Zed Books, 2019.

Wang, Ching-ning. "A 'Great Man' Is No Longer Gendered: The Gender Identity and Practice of Chan Nuns in Contemporary Taiwan." In *Buddhist Feminisms and Femininities* edited by Karma Lekshe Tsomo, 17–136. Albany: State Univeristy of New York Press, 2019.

Williams, Rev. Angel Kyodo, and Lama Rod Owens. *Radical Dharma: Talking Race, Love, and Liberation*. Berkeley: North Atlantic Books, 2016.

Williams, Duncan Ryūken. *American Sutra: A Story of Freedom in the Second World War*. Boston: Belknap Press, 2020.

Willis, Jan, ed. *Dharma Matters: Women, Race, and Tantra*. Boston: Wisdom Publications, 2020.

Yancy, George, and Emily McRae, eds. *Buddhism and Whiteness: Critical Reflections*. Lanham, MD: Lexington Books, 2021.

Yu, Xue. *Buddhism, War, and Nationalism: Chinese Monks in the Struggle against Japanese Aggression 1931–1945*. Abingdon: Routledge, 2013.

Yü, Chün-Fang. *Chinese Buddhism: A Thematic History*. Honolulu: University of Hawai'i Press, 2020.

———. *Kuanyin: The Chinese Transformation of Avalokitesvara*. New York: Columbia University Press, 2000.

Yusa, Michiko, and Leah Kalmanson. "Raicho: Zen and the Female Body in the Development of Japanese Feminist Philosophy." In *The Oxford Handbook of Japanese Philosophy*, edited by Bret W. Davis. Oxford: Oxford University Press, 2019.

Chapter 2

"Meditation Is the Embodiment of Wisdom"

Chan and Zen Buddhism in the Philosophy Classroom

ELIZABETH SCHILTZ

While the word *philosophy* is indeed derived from the Greek for the "love of wisdom," the early Greek thinkers were certainly not alone in engaging in its practice. Contemporary philosophers now have access to a rich array of rigorous thought-traditions from disparate parts of the world that aim at the development of wisdom. As such, it is notable that most American colleges and universities continue to offer their students a philosophy curriculum that is largely—if not wholly—focused on what is often called the "Western" tradition of philosophical inquiry.[1] As Joseph Prabhu noted: "One would have to say that news of the much touted multiculturalism, supposedly a feature of our globalized world, has not reached the profession of philosophy in the U.S., which remains sublimely provincial and insular."[2]

Even the most cursory reflection reveals that this "resolutely Eurocentric" approach is counterproductive to the philosophical pursuit of wisdom in several ways.[3] If we seek to interpret the texts themselves, it is simply foolish to cling to a version of the story that excludes many traditions that the thinkers themselves deemed important.[4] If we seek to attain philosophical insight, it is disadvantageous to stubbornly exclude the wide range of well-considered, well-argued, and well-respected analyses of global thinkers that might inform our understanding of and engagement with philosophical problems.[5] Finally, and perhaps most importantly, if we seek to interpret and flourish in our increasingly interdependent world, it is shockingly short-sighted to ignore the philosophical systems that influence its development and functioning. Van Norden makes the case: "China is an increasingly important geopolitical power, and President Xi Jinping routinely praises Confucian philosophers. In India, the dominant political party espouses a version of Hindu nationalism, grounded in classical Vedanta philosophy. The US population is increasingly ethnically diverse, and within a few decades whites of European descent will be a minority. Can we afford *not* to learn about philosophy outside the European tradition?"[6] Whereas engaging with global philosophy would facilitate an understanding of crucially significant systems of thought, our failure to do so reduces the contemporary practical relevance of our discipline and work.

In this chapter, I argue that the value of engaging with global philosophical traditions transcends even these crucial considerations—that it has value not only for us as practitioners of philosophy, but also as teachers of the discipline. To that end, I consider several foundational questions about our roles as philosophy teachers: How should we think about the goals of the teaching of philosophy? What sorts of texts and methodologies are effective in achieving these goals? I conclude that the teaching of philosophy ought to aim at the development of philosophical persons—and that insightful analyses and practices from global traditions in general, and the Chan and Zen Buddhist traditions in particular, can make enormously valuable contributions to that end.[7]

How Should We Think about the Goals of the Teaching of Philosophy?

I begin by suggesting that we reconsider many of the traditional descriptions of the goals of teaching philosophy. In particular, I suggest that, as Garrett Thomson asserts, approaching our philosophy classes only in terms of the study of what past philosophers have said, as the analysis of concepts, or even as the attempt to find answers to critical questions, is in an important sense, "incomplete." As he continues, taking one of these approaches as comprehensive "leaves out the most important aspect of philosophy, which is the practice. The point of studying philosophy is to actually engage in doing it."[8]

On the reading I am suggesting, philosophy is an activity—a kind of skillful reflection on the way we address the world. We as philosophy teachers, then, try to develop our students' abilities to engage in this process—we guide them to examine presuppositions, analyze concepts, and evaluate both claims and the reasons that support them, often with respect to a traditional set of questions to be answered, and a canonical set of texts to be considered. This project is not as dull as I am afraid I have made it sound here—this critical thinking is powerful stuff! To get the students in our classes to carefully and rigorously engage with, say, Aristotelian teleology, Cartesian dualism, or Hobbesian social contract theory is a significant and important achievement in our students' development as independent and sophisticated thinkers. As most philosophy professors will affirm, it is also a daunting challenge. As Mary Midgley asserts, "Bending thought round to look critically at itself is quite hard."[9]

Yet, however important philosophy classes under this description are, I argue that the goals of teaching them may go even farther than this. It is not merely the case that we should aim at developing the kind of students who have the ability to analyze arguments about major philosophical issues in traditional philosophical texts upon request. Rather, it must also be that we aim at inspiring and encouraging the development of a certain kind of person—one who engages in and values this philosophical activity. Sharon Bailin and Harvey Siegel describe this second requirement as the need to develop certain dispositions in our students. As they assert: "Having the ability to determine the goodness, or probative force, of candidate reasons for belief, judgement, or action may be necessary, but cannot be sufficient, for critical thinking, since a given thinker may have the ability but not (or not systematically or routinely) use it."[10] John Rudisill characterizes this in terms of a transition from *studying* philosophy to *doing* philosophy: "A student who 'does philosophy' is a student who, in a self-directed way, exercises a set of intellectual skills in the service of reaching greater clarity with respect to a broad range of issues."[11]

Whereas teaching philosophical methodology is challenging, this inculcation of dispositions is even more so. We need to do more than just teach skills to get "at" this—we need to help students develop into the kind of people who value this kind of reflection and are disposed to exercise it in their daily lives. As Thomson describes it: "Guiding one's attention is governed not only by the intellect, but also by our feelings. Hence philosophy is a personal struggle, requiring the development of attitudes as well as skills."[12] For his part, Bertrand Russell argues that this "enlargement of the Self" "makes us citizens of the universe, not only of one walled city at war with the rest. . . . In this consists man's true freedom, and his liberation from the thralldom of narrow hopes and fears."[13]

Mary Midgley has usefully compared philosophy to plumbing: "Plumbing and philosophy are both activities that arise because elaborate cultures like ours have, beneath their surface, a fairly complex system which is usually unnoted, but which sometimes goes wrong. In both cases, this can have serious consequences."[14] Whereas problems with plumbing systems are surely noticed, problems with our philosophical frameworks are not as readily recognized; "When the concepts we are living by work badly, they don't usually drip audibly through the ceiling or swamp the kitchen floor. They just quietly distort and obstruct our thinking."[15] Performing the job of the philosophical plumber allows our students to recognize, evaluate, and revise the seemingly 'given' notions of the world. To quote Midgley one more time: "The alternative to getting a proper philosophy is not avoiding philosophy altogether, which cannot be done, but continuing to use a bad one."[16] Guiding students to develop philosophical dispositions encourages them to become the kind of open-minded and sophisticated thinkers who deliberately and critically engage with the ways they address the world.

Thus, I argue that upon reflection, we may realize that we should aim to use our philosophy classes to develop the kind of students who are not only able to participate in the activity of philosophical analysis, but who are also motivated to continue its practice and to become independent philosophical persons themselves. We can try to help our students become "philosophical plumbers"—and thus reflective members of our moral, academic, social, and political communities.

What Texts Promote the Development
of Philosophical Persons?

If my description of at least some of the goals of teaching philosophy in general is apt, we can now consider various approaches in terms of their efficacy at achieving these aims.

Approaching philosophy in our classes through what is often called "the Western canon" might well serve to advance some of the goals of the teaching of philosophy that I have outlined above. Identifying and critically considering the frameworks through which many of our students experience the world can help them to develop skills in, and see the need for, critical thinking. It can also go farther—it can inspire them to evaluate and accept, amend, or reject the claims they themselves make. Given that this is in fact the training that many contemporary philosophers themselves received, it has surely been shown to be capable of turning at least some students into philosophical plumbers.

Still, the use of this "canonical" approach to the teaching of philosophy suffers from the same limitations as the "Eurocentric" approach to the project of doing philosophy noted above. It limits our student's understanding by presenting a circumscribed—and often inaccurate—picture of both the historical texts and the modern world. Further, it excludes a huge range of possible questions and answers—some of which are foundational to the worldviews of members of our global community. As Bryan Van Norden asserts: "Education must become multicultural in order to maintain its contemporary relevance."[17]

Finally, and most to the point here, it excludes powerful pedagogical tools for truly getting students to "bend thought around." These canonical texts are indeed tried and true models of critical thinking. However, if the positions being analyzed are those very ones that are providing the framework, they may not challenge the students and their beliefs seriously enough to inspire the development of the kind of dispositions I identified as a key goal of teaching philosophy. As long as some students, for example, cannot even fully conceive of an alternative to understanding the divine in terms of a transcendent, "maximal" being, raising worries about the nature and implications of omniscience, omnipotence, and omnibenevolence may turn out to be more like an exercise in troubleshooting than a deep reflection on the merits of conceiving of the divine in this way. As long as our students take for granted an atomistic view of the individual, a consideration of social contract theory may turn on the details of Hobbesian and Lockean theory, rather than bringing up a rigorous evaluation of those presuppositions and their deep implications for our ways of being in the world.

Serious and careful consideration of global philosophical traditions can illuminate and challenge these presuppositions—and study of Chan and Zen Buddhist traditions can do this particularly well. To take just one example: personal identity is both a central and contested concept in canonical philosophy. As Derek Parfit famously notes, there is a widespread view about the "special nature" and importance of personal identity—many think both that questions about personal identity must have an answer, and that "unless the question about identity has an answer, we cannot answer other important questions (questions about such matters as survival, memory, and responsibility)."[18] However, the criterion of personal identity is, to put it mildly, disputed. While it is generally the case that the students in my classes begin by being tremendously engaged in debates between and among proponents of various proposals, it is just as often the case that they end up in a completely frustrated state of *aporia*.

Fortunately, there is a long and fruitful discussion of extraordinarily rich ideas in the East Asian Buddhist traditions, which might serve not just to multiply our options, but to highlight for our students the assumptions that lead them to this place. Consideration of the rich history of challenges to the very idea and importance of personal identity in the Chan and Zen traditions can effectively show how to not only challenge the underlying presuppositions—but also how to reconceive the world in light of those challenges.

Consider, for example, the pedagogical value of introducing students to the view of the sixteenth-century warrior-turned-Zen-monk Suzuki Shōsan:

> Although all things are distinct from one another, the original mind is one. What are we to call "self" and "other"? For the ignorant person, individual selves are separate from one another. For the accomplished person, there is no distinction between "self" and "other." . . . The undivided waters flow along and part into myriad waves. The one moon in heaven is reflected in countless ponds and pools, and human nature is in no way different. Thus there is nothing to be despised, nothing to be held at a distance.[19]

Engaging with such a passage can spur our students to not only evaluate the claim, but also, importantly, to reconsider their initial commitments. Shōsan's thinking highlights the ontological presuppositions that ground the contemporary debate about personal identity—and, by extension, so many of our contemporary ideas and practices with respect to agency, ethics, and politics. Consideration of this kind of Zen approach calls on our students to rethink our most basic ideas of ourselves, our actions, and our world—and, happily, then goes on to provide both an attractive and alternate conceptual scheme, and myriad more challenging ideas with which to engage critically.

Consideration of East Asian Buddhist ideas can help us guide our students not just to more effective engagement in philosophical evaluation, but also toward seeing that this project is genuinely necessary and productive. Our students can consider their plumbing system in light of others, recognize that at least their initial acceptance of their own is, in some sense, contingent, move at least a little bit toward developing an understanding of the perspectives of others, and come to value not only the various systems, but also the expertise that helps them sort the possibilities. It can inspire an intellectual tension that inspires our students to a reconsideration of even their most basic presuppositions, and move them toward becoming philosophical persons.

What Methodologies Help Us to
Develop as Philosophical Persons?

I have been here arguing that, insofar as the teaching of philosophy aims at helping our students to develop into people who engage in the practice of philosophy, our courses can be effectively improved by the inclusion of global—and especially Chan and Zen Buddhist—philosophers. The texts themselves raise a further opportunity: to think carefully about the means by which we understand, undertake, and teach the project of philosophy itself. If we are asking our students to consider their own plumbing—and here I am perhaps pushing Midgley's metaphor far beyond where it ought to go—we do well to also raise questions about the project of plumbing itself. If we seek to help our students become the kind of people who reflect deeply on the concepts with which they understand the world, we should also challenge the concepts with which we understand our own methods.

One promising option is to do what I have suggested above: bring a diverse array of texts to bear on attempts to answer seminal philosophical questions, and use a conventional philosophical methodology to analyze these texts. In our classes, we might, for example, focus on a text's ability to clarify concepts, solve philosophical problems, and support its claims with rigorous argumentation. This process will help our students not only identify alternative answers, but also reconceive their questions. As J. N. Mohanty suggests, we can employ comparative philosophy both "for the purpose of freeing philosophers from their dogmatic inhabiting of their own traditions" and "for the purpose of bringing to the attention of thinkers other possibilities."[20]

Importantly, this method of teaching can also do much to push us, as practitioners of philosophy, to reflect on the methods by which we interpret and evaluate these texts and ideas. To take just one example: in "Helping Western Readers Understand Japanese Philosophy," Thomas Kasulis articulates the standard of "argument by relegation." Contrary to the way many of us describe a canonical approach, on which one attempts to refute and replace opposing arguments, this approach responds to them by "accepting them as true, but only true of a part of the full picture. That is, rather than denying the opposing position, one compartmentalizes or marginalizes it as part of a more complete point of view; the argument relegates rather than rejects." As Kasulis explains, this argumentative style has important strengths:

> First, there is a logical point behind it. Suppose you and I have philosophic positions that are in fundamental disagreement. If my view of reality is comprehensive, I should be able to account not only for how my position is correct, but also how it is possible for someone to hold your view. Your view, even if it is false in some respect, is nevertheless a real point of view and my theory of reality must be able to account for its existence. . . . Second . . . an argument by relegation has the appearance of being irenic or conciliatory rather than agonistic or adversarial. If we disagree, in the relegation form of argument, I am not saying you are wrong. Quite the opposite, I am agreeing that your position is correct but limited.[21]

While many count differences in expository and argumentative approaches as a mark against including global thought in our philosophical classes, reading it with our students represents a unique opportunity to reconsider and revise even our own presuppositions about what constitutes philosophical success.

Another option, however, might represent an opportunity to go even farther toward challenging the philosophically taken-for-granted. While much of contemporary, "Eurocentric" philosophy understands its pursuit of wisdom in terms of employing rational tools in order to achieve intellectual insight, many global traditions challenge even those assumptions about the appropriate method and goals for our engagement with the concepts by which we approach the world. A great many East Asian Buddhist texts, in particular, are clear that wisdom is cultivated, at least in part, through action- and life-transforming practices that go beyond strictly discursive reasoning. If, in our classes, we focus exclusively on the analysis of arguments, we may miss the opportunity presented by some of the texts' own insistence on the centrality and value of contemplative, meditative, and/or bodily practices.

Many Chan and Zen accounts, for example, provide an account on which the attainment of philosophical understanding is closely tied to meditative practices. (The term "*chan* 禅" is, in fact, derived from the Sanskrit term "*dhyāna*," which we frequently translate as "meditation.") As Peter Hershock explains, Chan is a "practice lineage," rather than a "doctrinal school": "As encapsulated in slogans repeated throughout East Asia by the middle of the Song dynasty, Chan was a 'special transmission, beyond words and letters,' that was based on 'directly pointing toward the human mind, seeing one's nature, and becoming a Buddha.' "[22] This is indeed a very different model from one on which discursive reasoning serves as the method to attain the goal of intellectual apprehension!

The early *Record II* of the *Bodhidharma Anthology*, for example, explicitly warns against reliance on the traditional tools of philosophical analysis: "It comes down to this: If there are terms and written words, all of it will deceive you."[23] Instead, many Chan and Zen practitioners seek the unmediated perception of the original mind—the underlying buddha-nature that our engagement with concepts can obscure. As Huang Po has it:

> This pure Mind, the source of everything, shines forever and on all with the brilliance of its own perfection. But the people of the world do not awake to it, regarding only that which sees, hears, feels and knows as mind. Blinded by their own sight, hearing, feeling and knowing, they do not perceive the spiritual brilliance of the source-substance. If they would only eliminate all conceptual thought in a flash, that source-substance would manifest itself like the sun ascending through the void and illuminating the whole universe without hindrance or bounds.[24]

Many Chan and Zen adepts aim at insight, but emphasize practices such as seated meditation over the tools familiar from the "canonical" approach. Hui-neng, for example, tightly links the practice of meditation and the attainment of wisdom: "They are like the lamp and the light it gives forth. If there is a lamp there is light; if there is no lamp there is no light."[25] In a similar way, Dōgen asserts that "the established means of investigation is pursuing the way in seated meditation."[26]

Interestingly, however, this does not necessarily indicate a simple substitution of one kind of process over another; many Chan and Zen adepts work to subvert even the idea that we should think of these practices in terms of a means to an end at all. Thus, Dōgen stresses, as Masao Abe has it, "the oneness of practice and attainment."[27] Dōgen's *Shōbōgenzō* asserts: "To think practice and realization are not one is a heretical view. In the Buddha Dharma, practice and realization are identical. Because one's present practice is practice in realization, one's initial negotiation of the Way in itself is the whole of original realization."[28] Hui-neng's *Platform Sutra* explains further: "Students, be careful not to say that meditation gives rise to wisdom, or that wisdom gives rise to meditation, or that meditation and wisdom are

different from each other. To hold this view implies that things have duality. Meditation itself is the embodiment of wisdom; wisdom itself is the
function of meditation. . . . The practice of self-awakening does not lie in
verbal arguments. If you argue which comes first, meditation or wisdom,
you are deluded people."[29] The study of Chan and Zen Buddhism, then,
allows our students to reconsider even their most basic assumptions about
philosophical methodology.

It is, of course, one thing to read and analyze the texts' claims about
the value of practices—it is another to experience and reflect on the practices
themselves. I have found that my attempts to facilitate an expanded range
of practices in my classes have greatly enriched my students' reflection,
and I have experimented with a number of methods to this end.[30] I have
had the great fortune to be able to use grants—often, for "Experiential
Learning"—both to take students to engage with cultural sites, and, more
frequently, to bring skilled practitioners to my classes. In general, incorporating three sessions involving experiential learning, each of which involves
both discussion of and experience with a particular set of practices, has
been especially fruitful.

Most recently, I have fruitfully paired these activities with a "Live Like
a Philosopher" assignment inspired by the Mellon Philosophy as a Way of
Life project.[31] This project takes its cue from Pierre Hadot's argument that
it is actually a modern "prejudice" to think of philosophy as wholly con-
sisting of discourse—that, for ancient thinkers, philosophy was a way of life
"both in its exercise and effort to achieve wisdom, and in its goal, wisdom
itself. For real wisdom does not merely cause us to know: it makes us 'be'
in a different way."[32] As such, this assignment invites students to carefully
research and then attempt to engage in a set of philosophical practices as
described in a specific text for five days. (I ask them to keep a journal,
and then work with other students who have chosen to study the same
text to create a presentation that introduces the practices to the rest of the
class.)

Of course, facilitating these experiences must be approached with great
care. As the only-recently-lifted, twenty-eight-year total ban on "any techniques
that involve the induction of hypnotic states, guided imagery, meditation
or yoga" in K-12 public schools in Alabama demonstrates, participation
in practices is not without controversy.[33] For my part, I have been guided
by Steve Geisz's tremendously thoughtful discussion of ways to respond to
worries about, on the one hand, *exclusion*, "in the sense that the practices
might improperly marginalize certain students from full participation," and,

on the other hand, *advocacy*, "in the sense that the very act of including these practices as part of an undergraduate course might make a teacher cross a line from critically engaged pedagogy to problematic advocacy of a particular substantive set of values."[34] In my classes, I am sure to include alternative options, stress student safety, and encourage careful discussion about respectful engagement.

The student responses to these activities have been, quite frankly, remarkable. This is, of course, a tremendously difficult interpretive challenge. On the one hand, the students are required to think in terms of particular practices in individual schools—to see intricate differences where one might be inclined to see sameness. On the other hand, they need to reflect deeply to interpret practices from which they are often "doubly distanced"—"not only are they products of a different time and culture, they are also based on a world view that is fundamentally different from ours in its structure and orientation."[35] These activities have done a great deal to inform the way my students approach these traditions.

At the same time, my students often report that engaging in practices stimulates them to reconsider the ways they themselves understand the world. To return to our personal identity example above, engaging with a broader range of philosophical practices may go even farther toward helping our students develop a deeper grasp of the challenges to the idea of identity itself. This is, of course, well in keeping with at least one of the traditional roles of many of the meditative and contemplative practices. As Suzuki Shōsan has it: "What should your practice be? Simply to rid yourself of your self."[36] Charles Goodman elaborates:

> Powerful and persuasive arguments can be given for the absence of any real, substantial self. Yet the innate tendency to believe in a self is so strong that even someone who has been convinced by the arguments is likely still to feel the nagging question "But must not I, somehow, really exist as a thing? Must not there be something that is me, after all?" A direct experience of being no one can accomplish what intellectual arguments cannot: it can bring about genuine confidence in the view of non-self and the actual abandonment of the false view of a real self. Since you cannot know what you do not even believe, this represents an advance in knowledge for someone who finds the view of non-self to be utterly persuasive intellectually and yet impossible to believe on an emotional level.[37]

Finally, and perhaps most significantly, my students might at least begin to think of doing philosophy as a life-transforming endeavor. They are generally quite surprised by the effects of incorporating seemingly small practices into their days, and they are often moved to reflect quite deeply on how these practices reorient their thinking about their activities and interactions with others, and what it would be to live in accord with the thought-systems. This, perhaps, is at least a step toward an appreciation for the kind of wisdom that Peter Hershock describes as at play in Chan thought: "Buddhist wisdom does not simply consist in seeing what Buddha-nature is, but also means realizing in direct social demonstration what Buddha-nature does."[38]

Ultimately, incorporating an expanded range of philosophical practices can inspire our students to a reconsideration of even their most fundamental presuppositions, and move them toward becoming philosophical persons. It has left my students better able and more inspired to wrestle with deep questions not only about the texts' ideas, but also about the methodologies we bring to the very project of doing philosophy.

Engaging in the study I have described above will push our students to truly "[bend] thought round to look critically at itself." If, as I have here argued, the teaching of philosophy aims at helping our students to develop into people who engage in the practice of philosophy, then our courses can be effectively improved by the inclusion of global, and especially Chan and Zen Buddhist, philosophical texts, ideas, and practices.[39]

Bibliography

Abe, Masao. "Zen Is Not a Philosophy, but . . ." In *Zen and Western Thought*. Honolulu: University of Hawai'i Press, 1985.

———. *A Study of Dōgen*. Edited by Steven Heine. Albany: State University of New York Press, 1992.

Bailin, Sharon, and Harvey Siegal. "Critical Thinking." In *The Blackwell Guide to the Philosophy of Education*. Malden, MA: Blackwell, 2003.

Balslev, Anindita N. "Philosophy and Cross-cultural Conversation: Some Comments on the Project of Comparative Philosophy." *Metaphilosophy* 28, no. 4 (Oct. 1997), 359–70.

Chappel, Bill. "Alabama Will Now Allow Yoga in Its Public Schools (But Students Can't Say 'Namaste')." May 21, 2021. https://www.npr.org/2021/05/21/999020140/ its-now-legal-to-practice-yoga-in-alabamas-public-schools.

Dōgen. In *Japanese Philosophy: A Sourcebook*. Edited by James W. Heisig, Thomas P. Kasulis, and John C. Maraldo. Manoa: University of Hawai'i Press, 2011.

Dotson, Kristie. "How Is This Paper Philosophy?" *Comparative Philosophy* 3, no. 1 (2012): 3–29.

Garfield, Jay L., and Bryan W. Van Norden. "If Philosophy Won't Diversify, Let's Call It What It Really Is." *The New York Times*, May 11, 2016.

Geisz, Steven. "Body Practice and Meditation as Philosophy: Teaching Qigong, Taijiquan, and Yoga in College Courses." *Teaching Philosophy* 39, no. 2 (June 2016): 115–35.

Goodman, Charles. "Buddhist Meditation Theory and Practice." In *A Companion to Buddhist Philosophy*, edited by Steven M. Emmanuel. Oxford: Blackwell, 2013.

Gopnik, Alison, "Could David Hume Have Known about Buddhism? Charles Francois Dolu, the Royal College of La Fleche, and the Global Jesuit Intellectual Network." *Hume Studies* 35, no. 1–2.

Gregory, Peter N. Introduction to Alan Sponberg's "Meditation in Fa-hsiang Buddhism." In *Traditions of Meditation in Chinese Buddhism*, edited by Peter N. Gregory. Honolulu: University of Hawai'i Press, 1986.

Hadot, Pierre. *Philosophy as a Way of Life*. Edited with an Introduction by Arnold I. Davidson and translated by Michael Chase. Oxford: Blackwell, 1995.

Hershock, Peter D. *Chan Buddhism*. Edited with an Introduction by Henry Rosemont Jr. Honolulu: University of Hawai'i Press, 2005.

———. "Chan Buddhism." In *The Stanford Encyclopedia of* Philosophy, edited by Edward N. Zalta. Accessed Spring 2019.

Huang Po. *The Zen Teaching of Huang Po on the Transmission of Mind*. Translated and edited by John Blofeld. London: The Buddhist Society, 1958.

Hui-neng. *The Platform Sutra of the Sixth Patriarch*. Translated with notes by Philip B. Yampolsky. New York City: Columbia University Press, 1967.

Kasulis, Thomas P. "Helping Western Readers Understand Japanese Philosophy." In *Frontiers of Japanese Philosophy 6: Confluences and Cross-Currents*, edited by Raquel Bouso and James W. Heisig. Nanzan Institute for Religion & Culture, 2009.

Midgley, Mary. "Philosophical Plumbing." In *Utopias, Dolphins, and Computers*. New York: Routledge, 2000.

Mohanty, J. N. "What the East and West Can Learn from Each Other in Philosophy." Reprinted in *Explorations in Philosophy*, edited by Bina Gupta. Oxford: Oxford University Press, 2001.

Parfit, Derek. "Personal Identity." *The Philosophical Review* 80, no. 1 (Jan. 1971): 3–27.

Park, Peter K. J. *Africa, Asia, and the History of Philosophy*. Albany: State University of New York Press, 2013.

Prabhu, Joseph. "Philosophy in an Age of Global Encounter." *Newsletter on Asian and Asian-American Philosophers and Philosophies* I, no. 1 (Fall 2001): 29–31.

Raju, P. T. "Educational Significance of Indian and Comparative Philosophy." *Forum* 3 (1971).

Record II of the *Bodhidharma Anthology*. In *The Bodhidharma Anthology: The Earliest Records of* Zen, edited and translated by Jeffrey L. Broughton. Berkeley: University of California Press, 1999.

Rudisill, John. "The Transition from Studying Philosophy to Doing Philosophy." *Teaching Philosophy* 34, no. 3 (Sept. 2011): 241–71.

Russell, Bertrand. *The Problems of Philosophy*. London: Williams and Norgate, 1912.

Shōsan, Suzuki. In *Japanese Philosophy: A Sourcebook*, edited by James W. Heisig, Thomas P. Kasulis, and John C. Maraldo. Manoa: University of Hawai'i Press, 2011.

Suzuki, Shunryu. *Zen Mind, Beginner's Mind*. New York: Weatherhill, 1970.

Thomson, Garrett. *On Philosophy*. London: Thomson Learning, 2003.

Van Norden, Bryan W. "On His Book *On Taking Back Philosophy: A Multicultural Manifesto*." *Rorotoko*, December 10, 2017.

———. *Taking Back Philosophy*, New York: Columbia University Press, 2017.

———. "Western Philosophy is Racist." *Aeon*, October 31, 2017.

Notes

Chapter title from Peter Hershock, "Chan Buddhism," in *The Stanford Encyclopedia of Philosophy* (Spring 2019 Edition), ed. Edward N. Zalta, https://plato.stanford.edu/archives/spr2019/entries/buddhism-chan/. See also Huineng, *The Platform Sutra of the Sixth Patriarch*, trans. and ed. Philip Yampolsky (New York: Columbia University Press, 1969), 13.

1. Sadly, this rather bald statement is, if anything, too generous. Jay Garfield and Bryan Van Norden lay out the statistics: "The vast majority of philosophy departments in the United States offer courses only on philosophy derived from Europe and the English-speaking world. For example, of the 118 doctoral programs in philosophy in the United States and Canada, only 10 percent have a specialist in Chinese philosophy as part of their regular faculty. Most philosophy departments also offer no courses on Africana, Indian, Islamic, Jewish, Latin American, Native American or other non-European traditions. Indeed, of the top 50 philosophy doctoral programs in the English-speaking world, only 15 percent have *any* regular faculty members who teach *any* non-Western philosophy." Jay L. Garfield and Bryan W. Van Norden, "If Philosophy Won't Diversify, Let's Call It What It Really Is," *The New York Times*, May 11, 2016, https://www.nytimes.com/2016/05/11/opinion/if-philosophy-wont-diversify-lets-call-it-what-it-really-is.html.

2. Joseph Prabhu, "Philosophy in an Age of Global Encounter," *Newsletter on Asian and Asian-American Philosophers and Philosophies* I, no. 1 (Fall 2001): 29.

3. Garfield and Van Norden, "If Philosophy Won't Diversify."

4. See, for instance, the repeated references to Indian and Egyptian origins in Greek philosophy, and the clear influence of Islamic thinkers on Medieval texts.

P. T. Raju goes farther, arguing that, insofar as the study of philosophy "reveals what elements of outlook my personality . . . has inherited," and the *Vedas* are the earliest book composed by the Aryans, that "a study of Indian philosophy is nearly as useful for understanding the nature of the Western mind, and so the American, as the study of Greek philosophy." P. T. Raju, "Educational Significance of Indian and Comparative Philosophy," *Forum* 3 (1971): 72. Some have also recently explored the possibility of connections between Enlightenment thinkers and East Asian ideas. See, for example, Alison Gopnik, "Could David Hume Have Known about Buddhism? Charles Francois Dolu, the Royal College of La Fleche, and the Global Jesuit Intellectual network," *Hume Studies* 35, no. 1–2: 5.

5. Bryan Van Norden provides a compelling case that there's more to it than simple foolishness: "The exclusion of non-European philosophy from the canon was a decision, not something that people have always believed, and it was a decision based not on a reasoned argument, but rather on polemical considerations involving the pro-Kantian faction in European philosophy, as well as views about race that are both unscientific and morally heinous." Bryan Van Norden, *Taking Back Philosophy* (New York: Columbia University Press, 2017), 21. See, for example, Peter K. J. Park's *Africa, Asia, and the History of Philosophy* (Albany: State University of New York Press, 2013), for an enormously careful examination of the formation of an "exclusionary, Eurocentric canon of philosophy" in eighteenth- and nineteenth-century German philosophy.

6, Bryan Van Norden, "Western Philosophy Is Racist," *Aeon*, October 31, 2017. Anindita Balslev suggests that engaging in world philosophy can go even farther: "its value for promoting inter-cultural understanding is evident. How could we otherwise identify traditional mistakes that perpetuate prejudices? Who can do that job but those who know more than one tradition?" Anindita N. Balslev, "Philosophy and Cross-cultural Conversation: Some Comments on the Project of Comparative Philosophy," *Metaphilosophy* 28, no. 4 (Oct. 1997), 359–70.

7. This suggestion, of course, reflects a challenge to what Kristie Dotson calls the "justifying norms" of "proper philosophical conduct and investigation." As Dotson persuasively argues, however, the "culture of justification" of professional philosophy "creates a difficult working environment for many diverse practitioners." While her focus in "How Is This paper philosophy?" is on the culture of professional philosophy, I am hopeful that my suggestion for philosophical pedagogy is in accord with the shift she advocates to a culture of praxis, on which value is "placed on seeking issues and circumstances pertinent to our living, where one maintains a healthy appreciation for the differing issues that will emerge as pertinent among different populations," and we emphasize "recognition and encouragement of multiple canons and multiple ways of understanding disciplinary validation." Kristie Dotson, "How Is This Paper Philosophy?" *Comparative Philosophy* 3, no. 1 (2012): 6, 17.

8. Garrett Thomson, *On Philosophy* (London: Thomson Learning, 2003), 4.

9. Mary Midgley, "Philosophical Plumbing," in *Utopias, Dolphins, and Computers* (New York: Routledge, 2000), 2.

10. Sharon Bailin and Harvey Siegal, "Critical Thinking," in *The Blackwell Guide to the Philosophy of Education*, ed. Nigel Blake, Paul Smeyers, Richard D. Smith, and Paul Standish (Malden, MA: Blackwell, 2003), 183.

11. John Rudisill, "The Transition from Studying Philosophy to Doing Philosophy," *Teaching Philosophy* 34, no. 3: 243.

12. Thomson, 143.

13. Bertrand Russell, *The Problems of Philosophy* (London: Williams and Norgate, 1912), 249.

14. Midgley, 1.

15. Midgley, 1–2.

16. Midgley, 10.

17. Bryan Van Norden, "Western Philosophy Is Racist," 2017.

18. Derek Parfit, "Personal Identity," *The Philosophical Review* 80, no. 1 (Jan. 1971): 4.

19. Suzuki Shōsan, in *Japanese Philosophy: A Sourcebook*, ed. James W. Heisig, Thomas P. Kasulis, and John C. Maraldo (Manoa: University of Hawai'i Press, 2011), 185.

20. J. N. Mohanty, "What the East and West Can Learn from Each Other in Philosophy," in *Explorations in Philosophy*, ed. Bina Gupta (Oxford: Oxford University Press, 2001), 85.

21. Thomas Kasulis, "Helping Western Readers Understand Japanese Philosophy," in *Frontiers of Japanese Philosophy 6: Confluences and Cross-Currents*, ed. Raquel Bouso and James W. Heisig *(Nanzan Institute for Religion and Culture, 2009), 229–30*. Many thanks to Peter Hershock for bringing my attention to this interesting passage! As Shunryu Suzuki notes, Zen may point to practices even farther beyond the contemporary conventions of philosophical engagement: "Usually when we say something, we are apt to try to sell our teaching or force our idea. But between Zen students there is no special purpose in speaking or listening. Sometimes we listen, sometimes we talk; that is all. It is like a greeting: 'Good morning!' Through this kind of communication we can develop our way." Shunryu Suzuki, *Zen Mind, Beginner's Mind* (New York: Weatherhill, 1970), 91.

22. Peter D. Hershock, *Chan Buddhism* (Honolulu: University of Hawai'i Press, 2005), 66. "In part, this trend seems to have been a function of prevalent Chinese convictions that purely intellectual knowledge is at best incomplete. Any true understanding is necessarily embodied and practically demonstrated."

23. *Record II*, in *The Bodhidharma Anthology: The Earliest Records of Zen*, trans. and ed. Jeffrey L. Broughton (Berkeley: University of California Press, 1999), 54.

24. Huang Po, *The Zen Teaching of Huang Po On the Transmission of Mind*, trans. and ed. John Blofeld (London: The Buddhist Society, 1958), I.9.

25. Hui-neng, *The Platform Sutra of the Sixth Patriarch*, trans. Philip B. Yampolsky (New York: Columbia University Press, 1967), 15.

26. Dōgen, *Shōbōgenzō* 88–94, in *Japanese Philosophy: A Sourcebook*, ed. James W. Heisig, Thomas P. Kasulis, and John C. Maraldo (Manoa: University of Hawai'i Press, 2011), 144.

27. Maseo Abe, *A Study of Dōgen*, ed. Steven Heine (Albany: State University of New York Press, 1992), 23.

28, Dōgen, *Shōbōgenzō Bendōwa EB 144, in Abe*, 24.

29. Hui-neng, *The Platform Sutra of the Sixth Patriarch*, trans. and ed. Philip Yampolsky (New York: Columbia University Press, 1969), 13. I have substituted Peter Hershock's felicitous "embodiment" for Yampolsky's "substance" here. Peter Hershock, "Chan Buddhism," in *The Stanford Encyclopedia of Philosophy* (Spring 2019 Edition), ed. Edward N. Zalta, https://plato.stanford.edu/archives/spr2019/entries/buddhism-chan/.

30. "Experimented" is the correct word here—various attempts have been more or less successful! However, even those that have gone in unexpected directions (e.g., the guest speaker on Zen who refused to speak about Zen) have represented wonderful opportunities for reflection.

31. While I was introduced to the assignment in 2019 at a Mellon Philosophy as a Way of Life Project meeting led by Stephen Grimm, Steve Angle, and Meghan Sullivan, the originator of the project is apparently Amy Olberding. Sample assignments are available at the project's homepage: https://philife.nd.edu/. See also Tushar Irani's helpful discussion of his development and implementation of exercises for his ancient philosophy courses: https://endoxa.blog/2019/02/20/interview-with-tushar-irani-wesleyan-on-exercises-for-teaching-ancient-schools-as-ways-of-life/.

32. Pierre Hadot, *Philosophy as a Way of Life*, ed. with an Introduction by Arnold I. Davidson and translated by Michael Chase (Oxford: Blackwell, 1995), 265, 269. Hellenistic and Roman philosophy "was a way of life . . . philosophy was a mode of existing-in-the-world, which had to be practiced at each instance, and the goal of which was to transform the whole of the individual's life" (265). For his part, Hadot traces our limited, contemporary view of philosophical method to our discipline's medieval ensconcement in university structures, where the emphasis was on training specialists (270).

33. Bill Chappell, "Alabama Will Now Allow Yoga in Its Public Schools (But Students Can't Say 'Namaste')," May 21, 2021, https://www.npr.org/2021/05/21/999020140/its-now-legal-to-practice-yoga-in-alabamas-public-schools.

34. Steven Geisz, "Body Practice and Meditation as Philosophy: Teaching Qigong, Taijiquan, and Yoga in College Courses," *Teaching Philosophy* 39, no. 2 (June 2016): 117.

35. Peter N. Gregory's introduction to Alan Sponberg, "Meditation in Fa-hsiang Buddhism," in *Traditions of Meditation in Chinese Buddhism*, ed. Peter N. Gregory (Honolulu: University of Hawai'i Press, 1986), 4.

36. Suzuki Shōsan, in *Japanese Philosophy: A Sourcebook*, ed. James W. Heisig, Thomas P. Kasulis, and John C. Maraldo (Manoa: University of Hawai'i Press, 2011), 184.

37. Charles Goodman, "Buddhist Meditation: Theory and Practice," in *A Companion to Buddhist Philosophy*, ed. Steven M. Emmanuel (Oxford: Blackwell, 2013), 569. A tremendously helpful articulation of the process at play can be found in Masao Abe, "Zen Is Not a Philosophy, but . . . ," in *Zen and Western Thought* (Honolulu: University of Hawai'i Press, 1985), 3–24.

38. Hershock, *Chan Buddhism*, 68.

39. The classes discussed in this chapter are the result of years of rich discussion, patient guidance, and enthusiastic support from faculty, staff, and students at the College of Wooster, the Asian Studies Development Program, the Japan Studies Association, and the Mellon Philosophy as a Way of Life project, for which I am deeply grateful. Thanks also to Robert Scott, James McRae, and Mark Wells for enormously helpful comments on an earlier draft of this chapter.

Chapter 3

The Possibility and Costs of Responsibly Teaching East Asian and Buddhist Philosophy

Mark Wells

In *Taking Back Philosophy*, Bryan Van Norden argues that members of philosophy departments in the United States should diversify their curricula to include more than just Anglo-European thought.[1] I concur with Van Norden that such diversification is a good worth realizing. Nonetheless, more needs to be said to derive substantive normative conclusions from this evaluative presupposition. The purpose of this chapter is to make progress toward some of those conclusions. Specifically, I argue for the feasibility of responsibly teaching a more diverse philosophy curriculum, especially for those philosophy instructors who teach the bulk of philosophy in undergraduate classrooms.

In particular, I have in mind those who teach at community colleges, small liberal arts institutions, and non-flagship state schools including adjuncts and temporary faculty.[2] Many—and I speculate most—such instructors teaching at the undergraduate level in the United States have no graduate preparation in non-Anglo-European philosophy. I focus on those teaching at these schools on the assumption that such schools have fewer, if any, opportunities to hire a person with graduate equivalent training in non-Anglo-European philosophy.[3] Absent such opportunities, the curriculum at such schools can only be diversified by the teachers there.

Without such graduate preparation (or some equivalent) these philosophers might infer that they cannot responsibly teach such philosophy in their undergraduate classes. And, given the cost of receiving such training,

their lack of formal training in the area might seem to justify their choice
not to teach it. I presume that Van Norden would be sympathetic to these
concerns, as he himself justifies his focus on Chinese philosophy in *Taking
Back Philosophy* as follows: "I can only responsibly discuss the areas in which
I claim competence."[4]

Though sympathetic to this line of reasoning, I think it rests on dubitable
premises. That is, even without graduate-equivalent preparation many such
philosophers *can* responsibly teach non-Anglo-European philosophy in their
undergraduate classes. And the sort of preparation that *is* required can be
done by many (though not all) without compromising professional success.

Before proceeding to the argument, a few remarks on the scope of the
chapter are in order. First, whereas non-Anglo-European philosophy includes
a wide variety of traditions, I will primarily speak to the feasibility of responsibly teaching philosophy from ancient and imperial China and, to a lesser
extent, the broader Sinosphere.[5] This is due to my comparative unfamiliarity
with other parts of philosophy and the learning opportunities that exist for
them. Nonetheless, if my arguments in this chapter are successful, readers
who are familiar with other philosophical traditions (such as traditions of
the Indian subcontinent) may substitute in, *mutatis mutandis*, details about
those traditions into the remarks that follow and see what results. Though I
am optimistic they will succeed, optimism is a poor substitute for evidence.

Here's a brief overview of what is to come. In the first section, I
introduce some principled reasons we might think graduate-equivalent
preparation is required to teach some non-Anglo-European philosophy. In
section two, I argue that none of these considered reasons obtain in general
for those who teach philosophy yet lack graduate-equivalent preparation in
non-Anglo-European philosophy. Finally, in the third section, I conclude
with a discussion of some of the costs and benefits for individuals seeking
to diversify their own teaching.

Why Graduate Equivalent Preparation
Might Be Required for Responsible Teaching

Again, I reject the inference from a person's lack of graduate-equivalent
preparation in East Asian or Buddhist philosophy to the thought that such
a person cannot responsibly teach such philosophy to undergraduates. But
what might justify such an inference? Perhaps a principle like:

GENERAL: No one can responsibly teach philosophical material for which they have not completed graduate-equivalent preparation.

But, if our everyday practices are any indication, such a principle is clearly false. Many departments have graduate students teach introductory material without having completed the course work for their graduate program. These departments, and these students, are not acting irresponsibly in doing so. Similarly, as happens at many small departments with long-serving or adjunct faculty, philosopher's interests shift over time or in response to contemporary events. Such philosophers end up teaching a course for which they have no graduate training, for instance, on philosophy of law or sport, the ethics of climate change or social media, or the meaning of life. And, again, such philosophers are not irresponsible for doing so.

Instead of a broad principle, we might claim something narrower:

EXCEPTIONAL: No one can responsibly teach East Asian or Buddhist philosophy for which they have not completed graduate-equivalent preparation.

This principle avoids dubious implications for everyday practice which GENERAL did not. But isn't it ad hoc? Only if there is no independent reason for accepting it. And comparative philosophers have pointed out significant methodological differences between Chinese and contemporary Anglo-European philosophy. Henry Rosemont Jr. raises doubts that the methods of the Western intellectual tradition (e.g., philosophical analysis, hermeneutics, or phenomenology) are appropriate for many Chinese philosophical texts.[6] Leah Kalmanson argues that "East Asian traditions are rarely confined" to the intellectual activities of Western philosophy such as "identifying premises, defining terms, making arguments, evaluating evidence, and drawing out conclusions or implications."[7] They additionally include rote memorization, meditation, and a diverse array of ritual practices.[8] Such considerations provide independent reason for EXCEPTIONAL. Someone trained in Anglo-European ethics or philosophy of language can read a canonical text of philosophy of law, such as H. L. A. Hart's *The Concept of Law*, and immediately begin fully engaging with the text by identifying premises and arguments. But not so for Confucius' *Analects* or the *Record of Linji*. Though these texts certainly do contain arguments with premises and terms, full engagement requires more. Further, well-meaning philosophers of the

Anglo-European tradition who try to adopt Chinese textual strategies risk doing so in a piecemeal fashion and, per Kalmanson, becoming part of the problem of colonialization.[9]

Why Graduate Equivalent Preparation
Is Not Required for Responsible Teaching

I find EXCEPTIONAL reasonable. Yet, I also think it is false. There are plenty of classic texts in Chinese philosophy that can be engaged in an introductory class using the same methods of Anglo-European philosophy. As Van Norden points out, selections from the *Mozi* are well suited for a course unit on political philosophy.[10] And readings from Mengzi and Xunzi could enhance a course unit on human nature.[11] I may add that excerpts from Śāntideva's *A Guide to the Bodhisattva's Way of Life* would fit equally well. It would not be irresponsible to engage with such philosophy by looking for premises, identifying key terms, and reconstructing arguments.

Perhaps, however, this argument misunderstands the comparative philosophers' warnings. Namely, adding readings from East Asian and Buddhist philosophers as above fails to realize the value in studying those traditions of philosophy. It is to turn creative and insightful philosophical traditions into Anglo-European philosophy with Chinese (or Buddhist) characteristics. The curriculum is only worth diversifying insofar as that diversity includes methods beyond those found in Anglo-European philosophy. To fail to include a diversification of methods that correlate with diverse texts is not just to miss out on the value of these texts but to distort them as well. This concern is made clear when it comes to the role of meditation in Buddhism. Despite heterogeneous approaches to meditative practices across various Buddhist traditions, all take meditation as an important method involved in realizing the nature of things. If such a position is correct, then we cannot see a major line of support for Buddhist philosophical claims without meditation. As such, to teach Buddhist philosophy without teaching meditation is to present caricatured arguments. And it is irresponsible of philosophy instructors to caricature the arguments of those we teach. Even if Buddhist philosophers are incorrect about the evidentiary role of meditation, we beg an important philosophical question by not taking that position seriously.

I am unpersuaded by this objection. First, while methodological differences between Anglo-European and Chinese or Buddhist philosophy contribute to the value of diversifying the curriculum, they do not exhaust it. I think the aforementioned non-Anglo-European philosophers are also worth studying in virtue of the content of their ideas, the scope of their philosophical projects, and the truths they reveal. Students have something to learn about language from Gongsun Long's "A White Horse Is Not a Horse" or metaphysics from Fazang's "Essay on the Golden Lion." And few, if any, texts match the inner chapters of the *Zhuangzi* for synthesizing argumentation with style and imagination. Using methods dominant in contemporary Anglo-European philosophy to engage with these texts may not completely realize their value, but it does realize some. Second, even if this were not so, there would remain an instrumental value to so engaging with these texts. If the intellectually curious first come to read the second chapter of the *Zhuangzi* or sections of Zhiyi's *Profound Meaning of the Lotus Sutra* via such methods, they will afterward be better positioned to go farther. Indeed, the nagging feeling that the standard methods of contemporary Anglo-European philosophy are inadequate to realizing the value of such texts may even motivate some students to do so. Third, in pedagogy, we can differentiate between distorting the value of a text by begging important philosophical questions or simplifying it to the point of caricature on the one hand and bracketing important philosophical questions for the sake of learning on the other. While the first *is* irresponsible (at least in most contexts), the second is responsible as it is necessary. To illustrate this point, consider any introductory course covering ethics. Such a course cannot begin without bracketing substantive questions in metanormative theory, for example, about normative semantics, epistemology, and metaphysics. Yet, so long as one is appropriately honest with students, doing so is not irresponsible. Fourth, this concern might not support EXCEPTIONAL. Pierre Hadot suggests that Ancient Greek philosophy involved spiritual exercises that went beyond looking for premises, identifying key terms, and reconstructing arguments.[12] If we allow that people can responsibly teach texts by philosophers from Ancient Greece, then we once again need to specify what makes Chinese and Buddhist philosophy a special case. If we deny that people can responsibly teach Ancient Greek philosophy without such exercises, then we indict nearly every philosophy instructor and, it seems, the entire system by which we train graduate students to teach academic philosophy. This might be correct. A number of philosophy instructors have begun incorporating philosophical exercises that go beyond the standard intellectual activities of Western philosophy.[13] However, if this sweeping indictment is correct, then EXCEPTIONAL once again follows as an unexceptional entailment.

Of course, the issue might not be whether diversifying the curriculum *has* a plurality of values to be realized, but whether those without graduate-equivalent training are up to the task of realizing that value. Without such preparation, instructors run a much greater risk of—even inadvertently—disrespecting or otherwise failing to do justice to the material. How so? One way has to do with the social meaning of using East Asian or Buddhist philosophy in this way within our context of Anglo-European dominance.

As I take it, this objection runs as follows: Our actions can have meaning just as much as our language. And the meaning of our actions isn't simply a matter of our intentions. For example, a guest in an unfamiliar culture might inadvertently make a hand gesture that disrespects their host. Even if the host excuses the guest due to their ignorance, the guest's action still had a disrespectful social meaning and the guest should be on guard against a repeat offense in the future. Furthermore, as Sally Haslanger notes, our actions have such meaning in virtue of their social context as part of our "culturally shared concepts, beliefs, and other attitudes"[14] by which we "interpret resources and guide our interactions with each other and the material world."[15] The context in which U.S. philosophy instructors attempt to diversify the curriculum by teaching East Asian or Buddhist philosophy is one with a legacy of colonialism and racism giving rise to a host of stereotypes, many disrespectful, about the peoples of Asia and their intellectual traditions. As such, without extensive preparation, an attempt to introduce philosophy from such traditions into the curriculum runs too great a risk of expressing these disrespectful stereotypes.

I do not challenge the conception of social meaning or interpretation of history on which this objection relies. Nor do I deny the normative import of respect. But while this objection applies to some modes of presenting East Asian or Buddhist philosophy, I do not think it holds for all those who lack graduate-equivalent preparation. That is, graduate-equivalent preparation is not necessary to identify and avoid the disrespectful modes of presenting (e.g., promoting disrespectful stereotypes or denigrating students who identify with an East Asian or Buddhist culture). Such stereotypes and possibilities for denigrating students exists within Western philosophy as well. All responsible instruction requires careful attention to the manner and context in which we present material. In support, I appeal to our shared experience as philosophy instructors. Consider the care that needs to be taken in discussing abortion, euthanasia, disability, or gender in a course covering issues in applied ethics, or slavery in the teaching of Aristotle and Locke. But these are challenges that apply to teaching *in general* and not to diversifying the curriculum per se. And, so, such attention and care in presenting East Asian or Buddhist philosophical material does not require graduate-equivalent preparation in non-Anglo-European philosophy. Moreover, if we are considering the social meaning of our actions, we should pay special attention to the meaning of our individual *silence* on non-Anglo-European philosophy and its now conspicuous absence from our curriculum.[16] If we are concerned about the risk of expressing disrespect, instructors may need to bear the risk of the occasional moral failure as the cost of correcting a greater historical and habitual failure.[17]

How do the preceding remarks apply to instructors in disciplines outside of philosophy?[18] After all, the texts of Confucians, Mohists, Daoists, Legalists, and Buddhists are also of interest to historians, literary theorists, social scientists, and religious studies scholars. These instructors teach philosophy too, even if they do not teach it using the same methods, or with the same interests, as philosophers. So, if EXCEPTIONAL is true, then it would apply to them as well.

So much the worse for EXCEPTIONAL. To start, notice that some of the concerns that motivated EXCEPTIONAL simply do not apply to instructors in disciplines other than philosophy. Comparative philosophers point out that the methods of Western philosophy fail to realize the philosophical value of many Chinese and Buddhist texts. But instructors in other disciplines do not share the responsibility of philosophy instructors to realize the philosophical value of these texts. Rather, their responsibility is to realize the value of the text relevant to their discipline, that is to say, its historical, literary, religious, sociological, or cultural value. In demonstrating such value, an instructor need not demonstrate the text's philosophical value (though they may).[19]

Furthermore, most of my remarks above generalize to those other disciplines as well. In their courses, these instructors outside of philosophy can realize (at least some of) the historical, literary, and cultural value of these texts and, with proper attention and care, can do so without distortion or disrespect. As I noted, teaching material respectfully is a challenge that applies to teaching in general and not just teaching as a philosopher. And the conspicuous absence of these texts from our curricula has social meaning, whether that curriculum belong to philosophy, history, social science, or literature.

With this, I rest my case against EXCEPTIONAL. While there's something to be said for such a principle, I think that it would be overbroad to apply it generally to instructors teaching Chinese or Buddhist philosophy without graduate-equivalent preparation. Nonetheless, working through these arguments should remind us of the care that all of us, as philosophy instructors, need to take in the presentation of our material.

Costs and Benefits of Responsibly Diversifying the Curriculum

Absent some principle like EXCEPTIONAL, we may presumptively conclude that a lack of graduate-equivalent preparation does not obstruct someone's ability to responsibly teach Chinese or Buddhist philosophy. Accordingly, *if* such considerations about responsible teaching are the decisive obstacle to someone's diversifying their own teaching, then they should go ahead. Yet other considerations may be relevant as well. I have not given an accounting of the *costs* of responsibly diversifying the curriculum, especially as they accrue for those who do the bulk of undergraduate philosophy instruction.

A responsible attempt to diversify the curriculum will require purchasing literature and communicating with established experts on the subject. These activities have straightforward monetary costs for the necessary material goods, for instance, travel expenses to meet with experts and the price of books. While we may hope that institutions will help defray such costs, a moment's attention to adjunct policies will reveal that hope as Panglossian for many. But the matter gets further complicated once we countenance those indirect opportunity costs. It is no small thing to ask an instructor on the job market or the tenure-track to set aside their efforts toward publication. And the threat of negative course evaluations resulting from forays into new material can reasonably chill the blood of adjuncts and visiting faculty.

I cannot give a full accounting of the costs of learning to diversify the curriculum for individual philosophy instructors. The contexts and constitutions of philosophy instructors vary too widely to admit of any easy generalities. Each philosophy instructor will have to reflect and decide for themself whether the costs of diversifying the curriculum outweigh the value of realizing it in their own teaching.

Nonetheless, I can provide some fodder for such reflection. My own experience learning to teach Chinese and Buddhist philosophy is some evidence of these costs, especially for those similarly situated (e.g., with similar privileges). Specifically, I will focus on my experience as it relates to the common currency of professional success: peer and student course evaluations, publications, and employment opportunities. If my experience is any indication, then there is some reason to think that the costs of diversifying one's own teaching, on this metric, are low. Moreover, the costs of diversifying one's teaching to one's professional success can be substantially offset by the benefits. In brief, diversifying my teaching has expanded my network of professional contacts, both within and outside of the field of philosophy, improved my course evaluations, and improved my prospects on the job market, at the cost of, roughly, a couple of publications. However, I note, my experience involves preparing to teach a full course rather than just a course module or smattering of material on non-Anglo-European philosophy.

Here's the setup: I began preparations to teach Chinese and Buddhist philosophy as a two-year sabbatical replacement at a small liberal arts college. Due to hiring constraints, the department could not afford to hire any further faculty but desired to offer a Chinese philosophy class which had gone untaught since the retirement of a sinologist in the history department a few years earlier. To that point, my total exposure to Chinese philosophy had been a single undergraduate course taken in my first year of college—ironically, from that retired sinologist. Nonetheless, in the spring semester of my first year, I agreed to teach a Chinese philosophy course the following spring.

To prepare, I applied to the annual summer *Institute on Infusing Chinese Studies into the Undergraduate Curriculum* offered by the Asian Studies Development Program (ASDP) jointly hosted by the East-West Center and the University of Hawai'i at Mānoa. At the ten-day intensive institute, I studied under two philosophers working on Chinese philosophy and began to compile a list of texts and translations suitable for my undergraduates as well as more advanced secondary sources for myself. After returning from the institute, I reached out to the Chinese literature professor and sinologists working at my school to discuss both pitfalls and how my course might fit together with theirs. Throughout the rest of the summer, and during the breaks of the fall semester, I read translations of primary texts, sometimes multiple translations, secondary literature, and developed a syllabus with a straightforward historical structure (e.g., Confucius to Zhu Xi). Three summers later, I would return to the ASDP for a four-week National Endowment for the Humanities Summer Institute on *Buddhist East Asia*, where I developed a syllabus on Buddhist Philosophy.

An immediate and continuing result of this preparation was a dramatic increase to my network of contacts both within and outside of the field of philosophy. In addition to the philosophers, sinologists, and literature professor mentioned above, I became involved in a transdisciplinary reading group on Buddhism—when I moved to another visiting position—where I met translators, scholars in Religious Studies, and more philosophers. I have also made contacts among my fellow participants at these summer institutes. In addition to benefiting my teaching, these contacts have served as professional references and given me opportunities to publish and present at conferences.

As for the courses themselves, they have been well received by peers and students alike. Indeed, that first Chinese philosophy course now marks a high point in my career evaluations. Part of my own efforts to "quality control" was to invite these colleagues to sit in on my classes and give feedback. When they've generously done so, their remarks have been both positive and constructive.

My preparation has also been a benefit on the job market. Critics such as Van Norden and Jay Garfield correctly worry that, in general, philosophy departments in the United States neglect non-Anglo-European philosophy. But a small yet significant number of departments desire faculty with the ability to teach non-Anglo-European philosophy (though this desire is often coupled with a desire for faculty who specialize in other areas such as applied ethics). For such departments, the ability to teach Chinese and/or Buddhist philosophy enhances the desirability of a faculty member, whether as a candidate in a job search or as current faculty seeking promotion. And, indeed, I was explicitly told that my preparation and experience teaching Chinese philosophy was a decisive factor in my being hired for my second visiting position (after the sabbatical replacement position mentioned above).

Of course, there have been costs. My time spent at summer institutes, reading secondary literature over two summers and a fall, winter, and spring break, and preparation of new material while teaching the course prevented me from working on articles for publication. Given my sense of how long it takes me to publish an article, from conception to completion, I estimate that diversifying my teaching has cost me around two publications.

By my own estimation, this has been well worth the cost. Professional success aside, I've found the process intellectually stimulating. I have also learned a great deal of history and more about religious practices, poetry, and art than ever before in my education. My hope in sharing my own experience goes beyond its evidentiary role in my argument. I also hope that my experiences can serve as a rough guide for those who recognize the worth of diversifying the curriculum and wish to realize that value in their own teaching.[20]

Notes

1. Bryan W. Van Norden, *Taking Back Philosophy* (New York: Columbia University Press, 2017).

2. Trevor Griffey, "Decline of Tenure for Higher Education Faculty," LAWCHA. org, accessed June 2, 2019, https://www.lawcha.org/2016/09/02/decline-tenure-higher-education-faculty-introduction/.

3. This assumption is not without support. As a survey of positions posted at Philjobs.org will attest, these schools, taken individually, do not post nearly as many job advertisements as R1 schools. Second, those who receive graduate training in non-Anglo-European philosophy comprise a much smaller proportion of those seeking philosophy positions.

4. Van Norden, *Taking Back Philosophy*, 38.

5. There is a danger here. Anne Cheng (2005) critiques those who engage with Chinese philosophy but "limit their scope to ancient thought," which is "tantamount to confining Chinese thought to the museum." While my own experience focuses on historical Chinese philosophy, I emphasize that the scope of my argument is not limited to it.

6. Henry Rosemont Jr., "Translating and Interpreting Chinese Philosophy," in *The Stanford Encyclopedia of Philosophy*, ed. Edward N. Zalta (Fall 2019 Edition), https://plato.stanford.edu/archives/fall2019/entries/chinese-translate-interpret.

7. Leah Kalmanson, "The Ritual Methods of Comparative Philosophy," *Philosophy East and West* 67, no. 2 (April 2017): 400.

8. Leah Kalmanson, "The Ritual Methods of Comparative Philosophy," 401–402.

9. Leah Kalmanson, "The Ritual Methods of Comparative Philosophy," 409.

10. Van Norden, *Taking Back Philosophy*, 61.

11. Van Norden, *Taking Back Philosophy*, 66–68.

12. Pierre Hadot, *Philosophy as a Way of Life: Spiritual Exercises from Socrates to Foucault*, trans. Arnold Davidson (Malden, MA: Blackwell, 1995).

13. For an illustrative example, consider: Natalie Helberg, Cressida J. Heyes, Jaclyn Rohel, "Thinking through the Body: Yoga, Philosophy, and Physical Education," *Teaching Philosophy* 32, no. 3 (Sept. 2009): 263–84.

14. Sally Haslanger, "Social Meaning and Philosophical Method," *American Philosophical Association 110th Eastern Division Annual Meeting*, December 2013, 15.

15. Sally Haslanger, "What Is a (Social) Structural Explanation?" *Philosophical Studies* 173, no. 1 (Jan. 2016): 126.

16. Yoko Arisaka (2000) considers how philosophy is sometimes conceived of as uniquely Western. But this conception is then subtly conflated with a conception of philosophy as concerning important questions (e.g., of ethics, reality, knowledge) in a Eurocentric manner. The conspicuous absence of non-Western philosophies may contribute to this insidious conflation.

17. As Ming-huei Lee (2018) notes, this historical failure partially consists of the delegitimization of Chinese philosophy. That is, even if we recognize that there is such a thing as Chinese philosophy, some doubt whether it provides anything of philosophical value.

18. I thank an anonymous reviewer for pushing me to explicitly address this point.

19. Does realizing these other sorts of values require graduate level training in alternative methodologies (e.g., Buddhist literary analysis or Chinese sociology)? Given the limits of my own experience and training, I can only speculate. In some cases, perhaps. But, not in all cases.

20. I am grateful to Whitney Kelting, Leah Kalmanson, Sarah Mattice, Jacob Sparks, the editors of this anthology, and the audiences at the 2019 Eastern and Central Meetings of the American Philosophical Association for their helpful comments on this chapter.

Bibliography

Arisaka, Yoko. "Asian Women: Invisibility, Locations, and Claims to Philosophy." In *Women of Color in Philosophy*, edited by Naomi Zack, 209–34. New York: Blackwell, 2000.

Cheng, Anne. "The Problem with 'Chinese Philosophy.'" *Revue Internationale de Philosophie* 232, no. 2 (2005): 175–80.

Griffey, Trevor. "Decline of Tenure for Higher Education Faculty." LAWCHA.org, accessed June 2, 2019, https://www.lawcha.org/2016/09/02/decline-tenure-higher-education-faculty-introduction/.

Hadot, Pierre. *Philosophy as a Way of Life: Spiritual Exercises from Socrates to Foucault.* Translated by Arnold Davidson. Malden, MA: Blackwell, 1995.

Haslanger, Sally. "Social Meaning and Philosophical Method." *American Philosophical Association 110th Eastern Division Annual Meeting*, December 2013.

———. "What Is a (Social) Structural Explanation?" *Philosophical Studies* 173, no. 1 (January 2016): 113–30.

Helberg, Natalie, Cressida J. Heyes, Jaclyn Rohel. "Thinking through the Body: Yoga, Philosophy, and Physical Education." *Teaching Philosophy* 32, no. 3 (September 2009): 263–84.

Kalmanson, Leah. "The Ritual Methods of Comparative Philosophy." *Philosophy East and West* 67, no. 2 (April 2017): 399–418.

Lee, Ming-huei. "Reviewing the Crisis of the Study of Chinese Philosophy—Starting from the 'Legitimacy of Chinese Philosophy' Debates." In *Concepts of Philosophy in Asia and the Islamic World*, edited by Raji C. Steineck, Robert Gassmann, and Elena Lange, 128–40. Leiden: Brill, 2018.

Rosemont Jr., Henry. "Translating and Interpreting Chinese Philosophy." In *The Stanford Encyclopedia of Philosophy*, edited by Edward N. Zalta (Fall 2019 Edition), https://plato.stanford.edu/archives/fall2019/entries/chinese-translate-interpret.

Van Norden, Bryan W. *Taking Back Philosophy*. New York: Columbia University Press, 2017.

Chapter 4

Brains, Blades, and Buddhists

Pedagogical Skirmishes at the Intersection of Philosophy of Mind, the Way of the Sword, and Buddhism

Jesús Ilundáin-Agurruza

Through the sword, how is non-aggressive peace to be established?

—Hashimoto Sensei, from Robert Carter,
The Japanese Arts and Self-Cultivation

What makes swordsmanship come closer to Zen than any other art that has developed in Japan is that it involves the problem of death in the most immediately threatening manner.

—Daisetz Suzuki, *Zen and Japanese Culture*

Challenges and Remedies Come in Threes: Introduction

The philosophy of mind is one of the most challenging areas in the philosophical curriculum today.[1] Highly technical and interdisciplinary, it sprouts ever-growing connections with the "sciences of the mind": cognitive science, psychology, neuroscience, linguistics, to name a few. Consequently, its thematic concerns are varied and complex. The nature of the mind, the body and mind relation, consciousness and the subjective character of experience, whether we think by processing information or in some other way, and what the self is, come to mind.

101

We will be hard-pressed, however, to find *genuine* engagement of non-Western philosophies in the curriculum. In the English-speaking world, an analytic perspective carries the day. Some offerings include phenomenology and bring novelty via animal and artificial minds, while others incorporate forays into "embodied cognition." Invariably, they all remain a heady *intellectual* affair disengaged from comparative elements and praxis.

A philosophy of mind course that includes East Asian views and favors a holistic stance that emphasizes conceptual continuities rather than divisions faces three pedagogical challenges: One, how to make the discipline's technical material manageable to a variety of undergraduate students. Two, the possibility of incorporating rigorous, legitimate, and revealing *practice* into a theoretical endeavor. And three, how best to integrate East Asian philosophy.

Congruently, the three challenges and three main structural pedagogical elements of the course match. These elements work synchronously and bring together conceptual and practical aspects throughout the course. They concern: (1) theoretical views on the mind/body—standard philosophy of mind offerings and this course's holistic alternative; (2) embodied practice, incorporated via swordsmanship; and (3) Buddhism—specifically Japanese Rinzai, Shingon, and Sōtō schools. Beyond metaphysical disputes, the course is designed to act as a catalyst that enables intellectual growth and vital transformation.

To stay within the Buddhist boundaries of this volume, the second section, Minds, Brains and Living Bodies, provides a highly condensed overview of traditional philosophical approaches to the mind/brain and their challengers, presenting the minimal background needed to appreciate the merits of Buddhism's holistic alternative. The Sword of No-Sword, the third section, details the novel pedagogy of weekly swordsmanship practice based on Japanese *dō* (道 artistic pursuits for personal flourishing). The fourth section, Finding Peace in the Maelstrom, probes into key Buddhist tenets as they relate to (no)self, virtuosic performance, and compassion. Finally, an appendix lists supplementary materials accessible via a weblink.

Briefly put, this chapter presents a potential game-changer in philosophical pedagogy in which the *seemingly* disparate elements of brains, blades, and Buddhism valuably come together.

Minds, Brains, and Living Bodies: Controversies in the Philosophy of Mind

Given the many themes discussed in this portion of the course, the first subsection below pithily discusses just two representative and foundational basic issues: the metaphysics of mind and the "mechanics" of thinking. The second subection considers phenomenology and embodied cognition—expressly enactivism—which present challenges to themes discussed in the first subsection and lay the foundation for Buddhism.

MAINSTREAM METAPHYSICS AND MENTAL MECHANICS

Conventional philosophy of mind takes a 4-I stance: it is Intellectualist, Internalist, Individualist, and Information processing–based. To sequentially explain, it favors mind and reason over body and emotion, keeps thoughts inside the skull, limits cognition to the individual thinker, and thinking is viewed as involving rules that process symbolic representations of worldly inputs. It also emphasizes metaphysics, for instance, the nature of mind and body and their interaction.[2] Conceptual analysis and reductive methodology prevail: the whole amounts to the sum of its parts. Highly influential, scientism—the view that science is *the* way to knowledge—leads to a mechanistic position whereby we are complex machines whose workings are explainable in terms of causal interactions that mathematical models best capture.

Seventeenth-century French polymath René Descartes was at the forefront of such efforts. His dualistic legacy—he split us into mind and body—has left an enduring metaphysical headache and division in the West.[3] Even the name of the discipline, philosophy of *mind*, ratifies such foundational and fundamental rift. In his wake, a long parade of views touts various solutions among which physicalism (materialism) is most influential.[4] Basically, physicalism equates mind/ideas with body/matter such that a thought *is* just a physical process.[5] Ironically, for a view intended to undercut dualism, it begets a brain/body dualism[6] and other dichotomies such as the separation between organism and environment. The main objection to physicalism, ominously called the Hard Problem of Consciousness, argues that no matter how detailed our physical descriptions there remains an ever-elusive quality about what phenomena *feel like*, for example, the sensation of the katana's heft.[7]

Phenomenology addresses this, but beforehand let's concisely consider the mechanics of the mind, how we think. Starting in the 1950s, cognitive science became the "go-to" source for models of thought as it embraced computational cognitivism as the model of the mind: our thinking works like a computational system according to which algorithmic rules process abstract symbols that encode information about the world—the fourth "I."[8] The consensus is that we process or compute representations—cognitive content.[9] On the whole, this 4-I program makes nary a connection to our *lived* experience, much less do we find actual hands-on learning.

Phenomenological and Embodied Alternatives

Phenomenology and embodied cognition offer viable alternatives. The first pays attention to our experience while the second promisingly relates to East Asian views by arguing for intelligent bodies *constitutively* intertwined with their environment (which valuably aligns with Buddhist notions of causal interdependence, see section four, Interdependence and *muga*). Together, they expediently sow the ground for pertinent Buddhist tenets, proving vital for a holistic account that finds its highest expression in virtuosic performance (section four, Compassion and *Upāya*).

While complex, phenomenology has a clear and basic concern: lived experience and how it is structured such that both our unique and shared aspects of experience can be *qualitatively* described—thereby correcting scientistic bias toward quantification. Crucially, it is not about the mere subjective report of personal feelings; it seeks intersubjective corroboration by and objective agreement with others' experiences. Basically, phenomenology tries to reveal the invariant structure of our experience while suspending judgment on whether a phenomenon exists. It sets aside scientific knowledge to simply *pay* attention. This reveals *how* we experience phenomena. Take how it discloses the workings of human vision: when appraising a katana's blade, we perceive it as whole even if at any given moment we only see "slices" of it, for example, just the top or left side; we do not think the bottom or right side are missing. Phenomenology also analyzes our contributions.[10] If, through it all, the katana remains the same, what changes is the manner of our engagement (e.g., when tired, we find the katana cumbersome to wield).

Intentionality, crucial methodologically, is concerned with the "about-ness" of experience and includes how personal and environmental circumstances affect us. We look at an opponent's blade and may see it as polished, deem it nonthreatening, and, further, we can imagine, remember, or fear it. Merleau-Ponty[11] developed the notion of "motor intentionality," which endows our actions with purpose, intentionality, and intelligence, even at the level of habits. We have a "knowledge in the hands" that understands "skilled action as a form of embodied knowledge,"[12] which, alongside intelligent habit, enables fluid, seamless, and attuned action. For samurai in the thick of the action, this integrates the sword as an extension of themselves (section three, The Way of the Sword).

Complementarily, embodied cognition offers a holistic alternative. In contrast to the dichotomous 4-I's, we encounter the radical continuities of the 4-E's: Embodied, Enacted, Extended, and Embedded. Respectively, these argue that our cognition is: affected by nonneural elements (muscles, joints); partially constituted by action; located in the external environment to varying degrees; and coupled with the environment. Enactivism, the most suitable E presently, makes embodied action pivotal for our cognitive engagements with the world.[13] Unlike computational accounts, enactivism rejects mental representations as essential.[14] Instead of a representation-mediated relation with the world, it posits that intelligent and skilled engagements are a matter of responding and relating, taking shape through organisms' active explorations of their environment. This unmediated engagement fits well the model of relationality that Buddhism seeks with others and our environment (at least under Chan/Zen auspices).

Enactivism posits a two-layered view of intelligence: a representation-based level that involves semantic content (meaning) that typifies sociocultural practices, and a basic-cognition level without representations or mental content that *still* engages intentionality to target the environment. To explain this via *kenjutsu* (劍術), Japanese sword techniques: the skills and underlying philosophy codified in manuals—such as Yagyū Munenori's (1571–1646) *Heihō Kadensho* (兵法家伝書), *Book of Family Traditions*—require linguistic competence; then there is *actual* practice which, operating *without* performance-encumbering mental representations,[15] is executed in dynamic attunement with adversaries. The epitome is expert improvisational action (section four, Compassion and *Upāya*), as when Munenori instantly jumped to defend his daimyō (大名 feudal lord) and killed seven enemy samurai while the rest of his retinue froze.

The theoretical and practical shift is to recast "philosophy of mind," whose currency of thought is mentality, as a philosophy of embodied minds or minded bodies, whose fundamental unit is the brain/body/environment; alternatively, the organism-environment coupling. How this play outs practically follows next.

The Sword of No-Sword: Pedagogy and Swordsmanship

It is time to see how books and *bokken* (木劍 wooden training swords), go together. One way is to appeal to the notion of *bunbu ryodō* (文武両道), the two ways of the sword and the brush. Eventually, samurai had to endeavor to become cultivated warriors whose hands were equally skilled with katana and brush. Another way is to evoke enactivism's cognitive model whereby basic intelligence and its nonrepresentational situated engagements with the world support representational modes of intelligence. Yet another way is to note that East Asian traditions inherently join theory and praxis holistically: intellectual learning is insufficient for mastery in life, hands-on practice steers the way. Ideally, both work together like the two wheels of a cart. The section "Pedagogical Skirmishes" looks at how theory/practice integration works pedagogically, while "The Way of the Sword" delves into Japanese swordsmanship manuals as preparatory "kata" for Buddhism.

PEDAGOGICAL SKIRMISHES

The introduction listed three pedagogical challenges to amalgamating brains/minds, swords, and Buddhism: subject matter complexity, genuine integration of practice, and incorporation of Buddhist perspectives. The ensuing is concurrently descriptive chronicle, rationale, and illustrative explanation.

The course meets these challenges by making practice the keystone to theoretical understanding, skillful development, and existential awakening within an East-West comparative framework. The philosophical component progresses from traditional topics and methodologies toward a holistic pedagogy premised on embodiment. As for the practical facet, it will be ineffective and fail to be transformative unless substantially engaged. Students rightly correlate task importance with allotted class time and evaluated deliverables. Besides regular instructional time, there is a semester-long weekly hour-and-a-half laboratory. Just as there are readings, presentations, papers, and exams, there is ample *bokken* time with graded benchmarks.

The hands-on practice on the way of the sword combines Japanese *kenjutsu* and historical European swordsmanship techniques. Crucially, this is *practice,* not training: the former focuses on process subordinate to course philosophical themes; the latter centers on progress circumscribed to martial expertise within a *dōjō's* (道場 training hall) milieu. In short, the goal is not martial prowess, and exercises do not follow a specific martial arts school curriculum. The aim is the development of skill as object of study, a means for theoretical inquiry and deep insight. Moreover, Buddhist texts and concepts are not engaged praxically as means of indoctrination but philosophically. Consequently, there are no *zazen* (座禅), seated meditation, or *sanzen* (参禅), koan study, sessions—which would necessitate a *rōshi's* (老師) guidance.[16]

Wielding their *bokken,* students connect technical theoretical aspects with *felt* movement: they cut and parry their way through recent and cutting-edge philosophical analyses or traditional perspectives, whether these be functionalism or Buddhist notions of causality and karma. This opens the possibility for students to appreciate the Buddhist "philosophy of the bodymind" for both its philosophical perspective and its transformative potential (nothing fosters empathy like being hit sometimes!) toward creative and responsive relational dynamics and compassion (section four, Compassion and *Upāya*).

Some might frown and others turn their noses up, judging this to be gimmicky perhaps. Consider, however, that Plato argued that we learn best when we play: "We should live out our lives playing at certain pastimes— sacrificing, singing and dancing—so as to be able to win Heaven's favour and to repel our foes and vanquish them in fight."[17] (Rather appositely, incidentally.) Drills, kata, even sparring incorporate legitimate disciplined play—something Rinzai priest Ōmori Sōgen (1904-1994) fully endorses (section 3, The Way of the Sword; section four, Ignorance and *Mushin*, and Compassion and *Upāya*).[18]

How does this *actually* work? Two examples illustrate this: embodied practice itself,[19] and an exercise called "press-flow."

The laboratory provides an advantageous setting to investigate embodiment dynamically. The abstract distinction between *körper*, the anatomical body as thing-like object, and *leib*, the lived, subjective, organic body, comes literally alive as students learn to phenomenologically *pay attention*: from the feeling of being (im)balanced to exploring the rich proprioceptive and kinesthetic dynamics of movement through *their* moving bodies—and which Sheets-Johnstone[20] best helps elucidate. Arguably, our dynamic psychosomatic unity is better rendered in terms of "bodymind," as well as the adjectival "bodyminded" and verbal "bodyminding."[21] These come closer to East Asian notions of the heartmind.

Ancient Chinese conceived of what Westerners call "mind" as the heartmind, *xin* (心, Jpn. *shin*). The character, representing a blood-pumping heart, integrates emotions, reason, and vitality. Japanese language is particularly expedient. With equivalents to the phenomenologist's *leib* (*shintai* 身体), and *körper* (*karada* 体), it offers revealing distinctions: the homophonous kanji *shinshin* (心身) refer to "heartmind" and "body" respectively, and being reversible help emphasize different dynamics—mindful body (心身) or corporeal mind (身心).[22] Most interesting presently, *shinshin ichinyo* (心身一如), oneness of bodymind, designates the highest level of integration and virtuosic performance. If nonpareil swordsman Miyamoto Musashi (1584–1645) seems the obvious exemplar, in virtue of her loftier spiritual development Buddhist nun Ōtagaki Rengetsu (1791–1875) is a far better choice. She was a consummate poet, potter, painter, calligrapher, *and* licensed master martial artist of several disciplines who gently yet *firmly* put in their place "overeager" courters to her and her female friends.[23]

This practical approach, furthermore, includes a transformative aspect that connects to normative dimensions of embodiment found in China and Japan. As to the Middle Kingdom, Wang argues how moral self-cultivation in the Confucian tradition involves *xiushen* (修身), bodily cultivation.[24] In the Land of the Rising Sun, Saito explains, artistic training and bodily aesthetic factors nurture virtues through disciplined training and activity.[25] The laboratory concretely blends and contextualizes these facets.

The "press-flow" exercise connects with units on neuroanatomy, cognitive psychology, and phenomenology, specifically attention, visual perception, and neural signaling.[26] In the drill, partners keep their *bokken* in constant contact while trying to outmaneuver each other to tap below the shoulders.

Seven iterations target different theoretical and scientific aspects, which are discussed after each bout. The first relates to the physiology of vision, optic pathways, and the primary visual cortex's neural columnar organization. The second iteration considers neural signaling via action potentials and ion channels. The third is connected to processing speed at the nervous system, and neural signaling levels; the fourth bout, blindfolded, dwells on intentionality and the phenomenology of kinesthetic and proprioceptive dynamics. The fifth analyzes attentional focus in relation to performance with the sword. The sixth examines explanatory misattributions in martial arts and sports that fly in the face of neurocognitive evidence, for example, keeping the eye on the ball (or blade).[27] The last one delves into the "Quiet Eye" hypothesis[28] and is contrasted with Musashi's advice on where to direct one's gaze in his *Go Rin No Sho* (五輪書), or *Book of Five Rings*.[29] Practically, the exercise teaches students *not* to look at the blade and to trust their kinematics and "sense" of blade location to better anticipate opponents' actions; theoretically, it shows how the different explanatory levels and methodologies coalesce into a fuller understanding congruent with martial and Buddhist precepts (section four, Compassion and *Upāya*).

Swordsmanship exercises give hands-on practice tied to course theoretical outcomes such that they: (1) explain neurophysiological processes vis-à-vis specific techniques; (2) incorporate East/West embodied phenomenological stances as related to intentionality, kinesthesia, etc.; (3) engage Japanese scholarship and medieval *kenjutsu* treatises (see The Way of the Sword below); and (4) develop an appreciation for the imperturbably focused mind on which these manuals discourse (that enactivism best explicates, see section two, Phenomenological and Embodied Alternatives and section four, Ignorance and *Mushin*). This pedagogical framework is inspired in the artistic practices of self-cultivation from Japan, to which we now turn.

THE WAY OF THE SWORD

Japanese *dō* (Chin. *Dao*, 道, Way) encompass a diverse number of practices such as *chadō* (茶道), the way of tea, *kyūdō* (弓道), the way of the bow, or *kendō* (剣道), the way of the sword. Performed with artistic sensibility and committed action—imparting ethical and aesthetic values—they seek to perfect performance and performer.[30] They are soteriological methods to enlightenment through personal improvement. Put differently, *dō* are transformative paths toward excellence. Critically, this transformation evolves from the initial functionally dualistic psychosomatic disconnection typical of beginners to the harmonious bodyminded integration of consummate experts. Put in philosophical and pedagogical terms, this pragmatic and phenomenological *modus operandi* places practical achievement, and not mere intellectual comprehension, at the heart of the process. As Carter avows, "There is nothing like this understanding in the West, which does not employ its arts and crafts, or its sports to achieve spiritual self-transformation."[31]

Another important aspect not found in the West is the sustained life-long dedication inherent to *dō* known as *shugyō* (修行). It derives originally from the Buddhist practice of *sennichi shugyō* (千日修行), one thousand days of practice, wherein acolytes would strive to perfect themselves through arduous exercises. The gist of it is that these paths are no mere cakewalk, but earnest endeavors undertaken for spiritual awakening.

Shugyō, usually rendered as self-cultivation, presents significant translation challenges as Yuasa explains: in contrast to the agricultural associations that cultivation has of tilling the earth or cultural refinement, "the connotations embraced by the Japanese word "*gyō*" [carry] the sense of strengthening the mind (spirit) and enhancing the personality, as a human being, *by training the body*."[32] He clarifies that East Asian (holistic bodyminded) unity is missing in Western monastic ascetic practices (closest to the Japanese) since these are premised on dualistic bodily neglect and repression thereof in pursuit of spiritual salvation. For our purposes, *shugyō* can be reformulated as enduring transformative flourishing, or alternatively as steadfast skillful striving.[33] A pivotal facet to highlight is the normative value that skills and techniques accrue within the context of *dō* and *shugyō*. It is praxis and actual movement—bodyminded practice—that impart deep insight and true understanding. The following three cases illustrate *shugyō*.

Sport philosopher Abe Shinobu's remark regarding his own *kendō* training embodies the lifelong commitment and ethos *Shugyō* necessitates: "I see practice as a never-ending struggle with myself to correct my faults."[34] More dramatic because of its resolve, given that it involves the practice of *zazen* and not swordsmanship, *Sōtō* Zen (曹洞宗) founder Dōgen Zenji (1200–1253) writes in *Shōbōgenzō* (正法眼蔵), *Treasury of the True Dharma Eye* (or Repository of the Eye for the Truth):[35] "Just concentrate on your intention and make your utmost effort to pursue the Way. In your pursuit of the Way, *train as if you were facing a life-and-death situation*."[36] In Ōmori, we find an exceptional confluence of paths toward thriving via *Shugyō*. It sprung from three fountains: Zen, *kendō*, and calligraphy, ways to which he devoted himself following Dōgen's guidance, willing that he was to stake his life.[37] He once undertook a grueling challenge to perform the *hōjō no kata* (法定之形), a complex four-part sword form, one hundred times a day for a week—an ordeal he felt at one point would kill him before pushing through his limits to a higher state.[38]

The bond between Zen and swordsmanship is both surprising yet plausible. Unexpected because of the nonviolence (*ahimsa*) that Buddhism espouses[39] and the lethality inherent to the sword; understandable because, as Suzuki's opening epigram explains, swordsmanship and Zen are closer than any other Japanese *dō* because of the immediate threat of death. Further, Ōmori, who viewed martial arts as integrated ideal in terms of *bunbu ryodō*, advanced that even if our existence is mired in strife the martial way *can* transform the art of killing into creative and nonlethal play.[40] Leaving the deadly aspect for the last section, we can further explore the way of the sword, blade-in-hand, alongside samurai Issai Chozanshi's (1659–1741) treatise *Tengu Geijutsuron* (天狗芸術論), *Demon's Sermon on the Martial Arts*,[41] and Munenori.[42]

Unlike Musashi's famed manual, Chozanshi's syncretic treatise, which combines Confucian, Daoist, and Buddhist ideas, does not describe a single technique.[43] Rather, a *tengu* (天狗)—a mountain demon resembling a human-sized bird of prey that is highly skilled with the sword—imparts lessons to fellow *tengu*, nuanced and sophisticated analyses of consciousness and psychophysical phenomena aimed at expert performance. As we read, "Swordsmanship is a matter of victory or defeat. Nevertheless, extended to its ultimate law, it is nothing other than the mysterious function of the very nature of the essence of the mind."[44]

The text's neo-Confucian leanings exhibit antagonism toward Buddhism at worst or begrudging forbearance at best, yet the latter invariably infuses the deepest lessons. Native syncretist tendencies meant that Confucianism, Daoism, Shinto, and Buddhism intermingled in various ways throughout Japanese history.[45] For instance, the following instruction partakes of both Confucian reference to a cultivated warrior and Buddhist equanimity in the face of death, "When you meet an opponent, you simply execute the action appropriate to you, and happily look death in the face. What then could distress you? It is considered essential not to break the sole resolve of a proper cultured warrior."[46] A bit of hermeneutic *jūjutsu* (柔術, jiu-jitsu) cordially blends these traditions, facilitating examination of pertinent insights.

First, endorsing *bunbu ryodō,* Chozanshi makes clear the need for both techniques developed through arduous work and insight into the nature of the heartmind. On the one hand, even when researching technique and its underlying principle beforehand, "if it has not penetrated your [heartmind], if the technique has not matured, and if you have not piled up great effort upon effort into training, you will not be able to grasp its mystery."[47] Relying overly on technique preempts bodyminded integration and fluidity of vital energy, *ki* (氣; Chi., *qi*). On the other hand, knowing only "in terms of principle," without grasping "with your body" means that one cannot perform.[48] In other words, in accordance with Buddha's Middle Way, whatever our hands are busy with, either extreme is ill-advised. The two wheels must synchronize. After all, as Chozanshi sentences, "Principle is explained from the top down, while training is sought after from the bottom up, and this is just the way things are."[49] Understanding is a theoretical enterprise but performing expertly is a practical one that relies on an enactive intelligence premised on flexible habits and responsive attunement. Munenori helps explain, "When you have exclusively learned the various practices and techniques and made great efforts in disciplined training, there will be actions in your arms, legs, and body but none in your [heartmind]. You will be unaware of where your [heartmind] is. . . . Training is done for the purpose of reaching this state. With successful training, training falls away. This is the secret principle toward which all Ways progress."[50] This is an enactive model of performance. In the thick of it, representations (as propositional truth, veridicality conditions, or similarly construed mental content) fall by the wayside.[51] Yet, intelligent attunement remains; what matters is dynamic adjustment to opponents. This is explored just below, sword-in-hand, then looking at the adversary with samurai eyes (section four, Compassion and *Upāya*).

Phenomenologically, performing with flawless form and fluidity means integrating tools into one's body schema, "You must not be contrary to the character of the bow, and you and the bow must become one."[52] The reason being that, "The highest principles are contained within techniques and follow the self-nature of the utensil."[53] In other words, the utensil, whether katana or bow, sets the kinematics and biomechanics: how to hold and move tools such that they become extensions of oneself much as Merleau-Ponty wrote about the blind person and her cane.[54] Ultimately, integration and performance are distilled into principles. But these principles, while helping with deliberative analysis and basic to improved performance, are not how action unfolds during intense training or combat. In swordsmanship, fluidity, efficacy, and swiftness are paramount: "Following the perceptions of the mind, the *speed* of practical application is like opening a door and the moonlight immediately shining in."[55]

The moon reflecting on water is a common Buddhist trope. Munenori uses it variously in several chapters, for instance, to explain timing and distance, or to advise seeing the heartmind as the moon and the sword as the water in order to better ponder spontaneous action.[56] Chozanshi cites Emperor Sutoku's poem, "Though there is a reflection, The moon reflects itself Without thought. Without thought, too, the water: Hirozawa Pond."[57] Chozanshi explains the poem is about an enlightened state of heartmind regarding action according to which one reacts spontaneously, in a state of *mushin* (無心, explained below in section four, Ignorance and *Mushin*). The state to be in when confronting a skilled enemy: without distraction and completely committed.

Moreover, this concords with enactivist rejection of mental content. As Chozanshi notes in the context of fast reaction when fighting, "If you don't have conceptualization, form will not have aspect. Aspect is the shadow of concept, and is what manifests form. If there is no aspect to form, the opponent you are supposed to face will not exist."[58] For Ōmori, the gift of fearlessness is the removal of fear or anxiety from the heartmind.[59] Thus, the way not to fear your opponent is not to think of her as an opponent *at all* even as you see her sword trained on your head (section four, Interdependence and *Muga,* and Ignorance and *Mushin*). With the basis for the way of the sword laid down, it is advisable to leave the lair of the *tengu* and enter the realm of the *Buddhas*.

Finding Peace and Compassion in the Maelstrom: Buddhism

Hashimoto Sensei's epigraph throws down the gauntlet: How do we institute peace through the sword? The challenge is to transform, within an enactively consistent framework, the killing sword into a life-giving sword in accordance with Mahayanistic values. As other chapters discuss Buddhist notions such as the four noble truths, the focus falls on three pairs of concepts best related to the ongoing narrative: interdependence and *muga* (無我, no-self); ignorance and *mushin* (better left untranslated; see Ignorance and *Mushin* below); and compassion and *upāya* (improvisational virtuosity).

INTERDEPENDENCE AND *MUGA*

The teaching of *Pratītyasamutpāda* is one of the most fundamental in Buddhism. Harvey explains, "The understanding of conditioned co-arising is so central to Buddhist practice and development that the Buddha's chief disciple, Sāriputta, said, 'Whoever sees Conditioned Co-arising sees Dhamma, whoever sees Dhamma sees Conditioned Co-arising.' "[60] Translated also as dependent origination, dependent co-arising, and conditioned arising among others, presently "interdependence" will be used for reasons of parsimony and relevance.

Essentially, all beings and phenomena are causally connected such that they do not exist independently of other beings or phenomena. Fittingly, it closely connects theoretically to concepts such as *anitya*, impermanence, and *anātman*, no-self. The exception to universal interconnectedness is *nirvāṇa*, as it cuts bondage to *dukkha*, suffering or dissatisfaction, attainment of which requires realizing bone-to-bone the truth of interdependence. Otherwise, existence and its quality remain conditioned, arising in connection with other phenomena that karmically bind us. The causal nexus among mutable phenomena means impermanence is the one constant we can count on.

The self, or rather lack thereof, is rather suitable to elucidate how interdependence manifests and works. The Buddhist doctrine of *anātman*, or no-self (Jpn. *muga*), rejects a permanent and unique self or soul. Five *skandhas*, or aggregates, form the "self." These are psychophysical factors that causally effect clinging: form, sensation, perception, mental formations, and consciousness. There is no "what" or "who" over and above this heap of five conditions/aggregates. This also accounts for how *samudāya*, clinging, arises. Addtionally, this aggregation gives rise to "our" karma in virtue of which good or bad deeds accrue merit. In other words, there is no self or soul, but "we" are not off the hook: there is a forensic sense of "person" to which moral responsibility attaches. Noteworthy is the relevance for Buddhist merit—within a karmic context—of constraint. Precisely because we are highly constrained in abilities and possibilities, that is, because we have to strive and accumulate merit, there is karmic "hope" of eventual release from karma's cosmic workings.

How does this insight into *muga* manifest itself? What practical outcome/s may we expect? Its manifestation, supposedly, should lead to a phenomenologically distinct experience. Japanese novelist and avid runner Haruki Murakami's musings on what he thinks while he runs are revealing. A sixty-two mile race he ran resulted in some profound changes. Unsurprisingly, perhaps, he lost the motivation to run for a long time. But, this was preceded or caused by the gradual erasure of his ego or self. He writes, "My mind went into a blank state you might even call philosophical or religious. Something urged me to become more introspective, and this newfound introspection transformed my attitude toward the act of running."[61] This introspective act, paradoxically, produced no substantive self or experiential locus but rather a blank-state "emptiness" after which Murakami strives: "Really as I run, I don't think much of anything worth mentioning. I just run. I run in a void. Or maybe I should put it the other way: I run in order to acquire a void."[62]

Swordspersons of old knew how to strive after this void or emptiness at the heart of who "we" fancy to be. Hayashizaki Temple's records on swordsmen performing *iaidō* (居合道), the way of drawing the sword, for seven continuous days detail that the top three performed more than ninety thousand draws—the equivalent of skillfully drawing and sheathing the sword about thirteen thousand times daily.[63] This relentless practice whittles the (sense of) self, cut by cut, such that in the end only the drawing of the sword remains.

Some may despondently resist the "loss" of self, but there are advantages to accepting, even embracing *muga*: without a self, there is no reason to worry about what happens to it. Rinzai monk Takuan Sōhō's (1573–1645) *Fudōchi Shinmyōroku* (不動智神妙録), *The Mysterious Record of Immovable Wisdom*[64]—a letter he wrote to Munenori explaining Zen's innermost insights in relation to the intricacies of skilled swordsmanship—puts this to good use. In kenjutsu, upon realizing *muga*, you come to see that, "For the striking sword, there is no [heartmind]. For myself, who is about to attack, there is no [heartmind]. The attacker is Emptiness. His Sword is Emptiness. I, who am about to be struck, am Emptiness."[65] Truly liberating.

Suitably paradoxical, the psychological shedding of an emotional concern for "self" leads to worry-free action. Munenori and Chozanshi approvingly echo Takuan's words. On board also is enactivism. It rejects minimal self-awareness: there is no sense of self *as* self originally. It argues that this is a late-developing phenomenon tied to narrative practices.[66] This process and insight may lead to a state associated with superior performance called *mushin* in Japan.[67] A preliminary step, however, is to confront ignorance.

IGNORANCE AND *MUSHIN*

Avidyā, ignorance, to which Dōgen refers as "the darkness of spiritual ignorance," comes first in his "Twelve Links in the Chain of Dependent Origination," which lead to *dukkha*.[68] As part of the wheel of karmic desert and "comeuppance," these are unranked, but it is telling that Takuan begins his letter to Munenori discussing ignorance, which also involves delusion. In essence, it concerns delusion about impermanence and no-self (and consequently interdependence), and how these lead to *dukkha* and karmic "reinvestment." Zen masters are also renowned for fighting such ignorance through playful shenanigans. It is no coincidence that the laboratory involves the sword: what begins in ignorance (how often do people wield swords nowadays?) and playfulness (who does not enjoy doing so?) soon becomes a path for committed practice. Amenably, Ōmori viewed martially developed playfulness as a privileged way for ego transcendence.[69] Ignorance is overcome with *kufū* (工夫), purposeful and skillful striving after awakening. Far from being a one-time permanent revelation, such enlightenment must be rehearsed continually in the spirit of *shugyō*.

To confront our ignorant ways, let's turn to Takuan again. Ignorance leads to entrapment, a stopping or dwelling that prevents fast, free, and fluid *right* action. In terms of swordsmanship, he elaborates for Munenori, "When your opponent advances to strike you, your eyes immediately catch the movement of the sword. If you are 'stopped' by this movement of the sword towards you your [heartmind] loses its freedom and you are sure to be killed. This is because your mind 'freezes,'"[70] an indication of karmic fettering by any other (s)word. His solution: learn about *fudōshin*, the immovable wisdom of the Buddhas, from Fudō Myō-ō—Shingon Buddhism's embodiment of sagely immovability that leads us toward awakening by severing the shackles of ignorance/craving (the three poisons of desires, hatred, and delusion) with his sword Karikara.

Less esoteric and more practical, drawing from Kasulis' work, McRae[71] examines Takuan's *fudōshin* epistemically in terms of how we think we know reality: there are three stages to get from ignorance to *fudōshin*. First, *shiryō* (思量), thinking: our intentionality focuses on objects and tries to rationally figure them out; useful in many contexts but not dueling or seeking enlightenment. This abides in ignorance for Takuan. Second, *fushiryō* (不思量), not-thinking: it lacks intentionality and negates thinking, rendering our heartmind like a stone; not helpful in duels or soteriological endeavors either. And third, *hishiryō* (非思量), non-thinking: bypassing subject-object dichotomies—astride between thinking and not-thinking—it rides freely everywhere and nowhere. Takuan emphasizes that such non-thinking must be lightning fast, like a spark from a struck flint, leaving not even a hairbreadth of room between perception and action.[72] It is immediate. That is, this immovability is not about a passive, "frozen" bodymind but rather an imperturbable state that responds creatively and freely. McRae elaborates, "*Fudōshin* is a desirable state for the martial artist because it promotes a state of hyperpraxia in which there is no thought between thought and action."[73] Some call this state *mushin*.

Mushin is traditionally rendered as no-mind or without-mind—aptly concise but inaptly inaccurate as both lack any kind of nuance to instead suggest a zombie-like mindlessness. Hence, *mushin* will be left untranslated in lieu of counsel to think of it as committed, awakened, virtuosic, and engaged *presence*. Murakami gifts us with yet another insight that helps qualitatively appreciate *mushin*: "Your quality of experience is based not on standards such as time or ranking, but on finally *awakening to an awareness of the fluidity within action itself.*"[74]

Performers in this state act peerlessly in mindfully fluid awareness that, as Takuan[75] elucidates, because it does not abide anywhere is free to be everywhere. The swordsperson's or performer's heartmind and attention are like the eye of a hurricane: immovable, in Takuan's sense, while chaos unleashes all around. This bespeaks practiced, poised readiness to engage the situation at hand in whichever fashion it arrives, even the problem of death in the most immediately threatening manner, such that, "If the man makes one false movement he is doomed forever, and he has no time for conceptualization or calculated acts."[76] This evidently concurs with enactivism: *mushin*'s non-thinking is effectively explained in terms of nonconceptual and nonrepresentational cognition synched with its environment.[77]

Notwithstanding this congruence, we must be leery of relinquishing too much control at the hands of automaticity. Scholars struggle to make room for attentional control and flexibly intelligent habit, instead appealing to effortless automatization,[78] unconscious operation,[79] the implicit system,[80] or other offline processes. *Mushin* lies far from the sort of mindless coping that some phenomenologists attribute to skilled habitual action,[81] and which are popularly transferred to *mushin* (and flow) states. An enactive stance maintains automatized subroutines precisely and to the extent that they liberate attentional resources to mind what matters.[82] Indeed, *mushin,* for all its apparent esotericism, Munenori expounds, "is not a state of having no mind at all. It is simply your ordinary mind."[83] Hershock helps clarify, in relation to Chan master Mazu, "Of course, it is ordinary mind with a difference: the absence of any boundary or horizon on the other side of which lies something 'more' or 'better' or 'mystically complete.' "[84] Whereas *dharma* transmission, or awakening, is done from heartmind to heartmind, *ishin denshin* (以心伝心), without relying on language or sacred texts,[85] this does not mean that words are entirely useless, as Dōgen *writes.*[86] Fostering *mushin,* as method, is not just advisable but peremptory for karmic liberation and superior performance. Hearteningly, for all its unique ordinariness, *mushin* can be improved through committed practice by endeavoring not to be taken in by phenomena, that is, training our ability for engaged presence—at which Buddhism, with its many techniques, excels.

Chozanshi wrote a delightful tale, *Neko no Myōjutsu* (猫の妙術), Wondrous (or Mysterious) Technique of the Cat.[87] A long-in-the-tooth sagely cat, after nonchalantly taking care of a ferocious rat that has bested the efforts of a samurai and the town's best cats, expounds that when facing off with an opponent, *the* technique to overcome gripping anxiety is *mushin* expressed as spontaneous, natural action. Yet, the cat recounts of another even more aged cat in its neighborhood that slept all day and had no vitality but wherever it was no rats were found. Unresponsive to any questioning, the sagely cat concluded, "That cat had even forgotten that it had forgotten itself, and had returned to a state of 'Nothingness.' The very spirit of the martial, it killed nothing."[88] Indeed, endowed with the power to kill or let live, ready-at-hand, facing dire scenarios, agents (cat, swordsperson, monk, or layperson) better act with compassionate creativity in order to face come what may in a way that improves their karmic prospects.

COMPASSION AND *UPĀYA*

There is a short and a long answer to Hashimoto sensei's question. The short and somewhat inaccurate one,[89] simply alludes to Japan's martial history:

what began as *bujutsu* (武術), deadly warrior techniques, and which prevailed for much of its medieval history, during the pacified Tokugawa era (1600–1868 CE) gradually evolved into *budō* (武道), way of the warrior or martial way. Thus, *kenjutsu* transformed into *kendō,* which emphasized ethical development. The long answer is, expectedly, more interesting if complex.

To simplify crudely but clearly, the central difference between Theravada and Mahayanistic Buddhist schools is that the latter emphasize compassion for all living beings rather than personal salvation. Those who reach enlightenment become *Bodhisattvas,* awakened ones who choose to remain until all beings are liberated. How to transmit the message most efficiently and effectively is crucial, then. Siddhārtha Gautama, the historical Buddha, used many creative techniques to impart the most intricate lessons, such as the insight behind interdependence. These techniques fall under the rubric of *upāya.*

Usually translated as expedient or skillful means, Hershock's more fine-grained rendition views it as liberating, contributory, improvisational, attentional, and relational virtuosity.[90] Schroeder[91] explicates that, unlike orthodox Western philosophical understandings of Buddhism, *upāya* is not concerned with logical and grammatical solutions to metaphysical issues but rather with finding the most efficacious pedagogical and heuristic way to transmit *dharma.*

Arguably, one of the most creative ways to do so *must* be sword-in-hand. This ingenious and transformative response is typical of Chan Buddhism and exemplifies Hershock's responsive virtuosity. Improvisation thus understood, while looking forward—being anticipatory—is based on a rich repertoire acquired through *exploratory* relentless practice, deliberate training, reflection, and constant testing. Hershock, much as Takuan, admonishes against dwelling on any "thing" because it "means an end to improvising, a resistance of the impermanence of things, [whereas . . .] the possibility of successfully relinquishing all horizons for responsibility depends on the practice of emptiness (K'ung)."[92] An emptiness, Hershock clarifies, understood as expansiveness, as oceanic receptivity, which Chan formulates as "according with the situation and responding as needed."[93]

In fact, Munenori,[94] discussing deception in martial arts equates deceit with *upāya.* Unlike Takuan, his intent is to transmit fencing know-how not Buddhist insight. Yet, his text is decidedly steeped in Buddhist lore. He so often refers to, cites from, and evokes imagery from the Buddhist canon that it is sensible to attribute an underlying Buddhist ethos to the textual and strategic evolution from killing sword to life-giving sword to no-sword. By some lights, this can propound the ability to kill or let live when facing, even without a blade, a katana-wielding adversary.[95] The following passage is an apposite example: "When you intone the name of Lord Fudo you make your posture correct, press your palms together, and contemplate his unmoving form in your consciousness. At this time, the Three Conditions of Karma—body, mouth, and consciousness—are made one and equal, and concentration is undisturbed. This is called the Universalization of the Three Mysteries."[96] Body, mouth, and consciousness represent deeds, words, and thoughts, as Wilson explains.[97] To be noticed are the importance of praxis and full bodyminded engagement that begins with proper posture (in addition to whom the intonation is addressed!).

Prowess and improvisational acumen under a Buddhist aegis finds apt attainment in the creed of *bushi no me* (武士の目), eyes of a warrior. It bespeaks of peaceful and compassionate wielding of the sword. There are five levels that range from: *nikugen* (肉眼で)—the naked eye—a superficial view from one's perspective that does not see beyond what *literally* meets the eye to the most refined, *shingen/hōgen* (神眼), compassionate eye (literally view from the gods, *kami*), which understands interdependence, karmic law, and therefore engages in compassionate action.[98] Skill and Buddhist insight are pivotal to duly managing karmic relational dynamics. The saying *Saya no Naka no Kachi* (鞘の中の勝ち), victory while the sword is still in the scabbard, helps display this in full yet perfectly restrained force. Another way to think of this is that drawing the sword from the scabbard means one has already lost. There will be scant opportunity for compassion and plenty for bloodshed once the blades cross.

The following account exhibits this compassionate restraint: Musashi, walking through a castle town, crossed paths with a fearsome looking retainer. They eyed each other and instantly recognized each other as Musashi and Yagyū Hyōgonosuke (Hyogo, nephew to Munenori). Fast becoming friends, they never fought. Musashi explained why: " 'It is a mysterious work of the mind without reason, that I acknowledged Hyogo directly. Why didn't we cross swords? This was not necessary because we tacitly knew our skill." Their meeting was like that between Shakyamuni and Kasyapa on Mount Grdhrakuta: it was an even match.[99] This amounts to an *ai nuke* (合抜), a draw that signals that two fighters of peerless, equal skill leave the encounter unscathed. Ōmori celebrates *ai nuke* as the world of absolute peace that transcends winning and losing.[100]

Compassion—from "com" (together) and "pati" (to suffer)—necessarily involves others. At its best it is the empathetic committed concern for others that, beyond mere sympathy, acts. If compassion allows us to contribute to others, the community teaches, supports, and enables us to flourish. Sensibly, given the arduous path to enlightenment, the historical Buddha instituted the *sangha*—the monastic community of monks and nuns. This is not the occasion to delve further.[101] Suffice it to remark that such relational and poised responsive virtuosity can be fruitfully integrated within a holistic and enactive comparative framework where our bodyminded expressions and explorations shine brightest.

In summary, the preceding validates how an instrument conceived for killing can become a means for personal and communal compassion, flourishing, and peace.

Conclusion: The View from the Top

This chapter has described, explained, and argued for a comparative East-West perspective, specifically combining Buddhism and enactivism. It endorses holistic rather than reductive cognition: the 4-E's supplant the 4-I's, and highlight an enactivist action-constituted intelligence. This incorporates phenomenological analyses of the lived body that bridge bodyminded East-West views. Buddhism (Rinzai, Shingon, and Sōtō schools), as integrated in Japanese *dō*, is theoretically, pragmatically, and pedagogically central. It establishes a joint theory/praxis path to understanding bodyminded phenomena. A pedagogy that integrates a rigorous weekly hands-on practicum on the way of the sword fosters this. Besides intellectual clarification, this opens transformative opportunities where the sword becomes a path to peace(fulness)—personal and collective. The course's educative arc summits to an open vista of the perspectival possibility of appreciating how committed practice and theoretical study may lead to a liberating and engaged presence that encourages *kufū* as personal and steadfast skillful striving. To close with a citation from a course handout, *On the Cutting Edge*: "All the different elements blend into a holistic view of consciousness . . . enriched via contemplative techniques that lead to empathy and peacefulness. Selecting the originally violent way of the sword underscores the point: if swordsmanship can become a means of self-knowledge and peace, the potential is indeed limitless."

Appendix: Supplementary Materials

The link below leads to a repository of documents in the section "Course Materials—Philosophy of Mind." https://linfield.academia.edu/JesusIlundain Agurruza/. These include:

- *On the Cutting Edge.* A précis that theoretically frames the way of the sword in relation to consciousness, philosophical contemplation, and compassion

- *The Place of Mind.* A chart that visually summarizes basic philosophy of mind concepts

- *Philosophy of Mind—An Overview.* A preview, resource, and summary of thematic lines of inquiry

- Sample Practice Lesson Plans

- Chozanshi's *Tale of the Old Cat* (*Neko no Myōjutsu*)

- Syllabus

- Extended version of this chapter with detailed discussion of philosophy of mind and fictional narrative

Notes

1. This work was supported by the Australian Research Council Discovery Project, "Minds in Skilled Performance." DP170102987.

2. Initially, signaling a split, the chapter uses dualistic mind and body phrasings. Once the holistic framework is introduced, it uses words that designate psychosomatic union (bodymind).

3. Dualist and monist views are found in East and West philosophies well before the modern period in the West (mid-1600s onward). Over two millennia ago, we find *soma* and *psyché* in ancient Greece, *atman* and body in Indian Hinduism, and a monist physicalism in Indian Carvaca materialism. (See section three, The Way of the Sword, for East Asian views.)

4. These include a number of "isms" (behaviorism, emergentism, functionalism, etc.), which the course covers in detail. For a thorough review, see Garrett Thomson and Philip Turetzky, "A Simple Guide to Contemporary Philosophy of

Mind," in *The Experience of Philosophy*, ed. Daniel Kolak and Raymond Martin (Oxford: Oxford University Press, 1996), 444–58.

5. Exactly how this works is much disputed, with monist, reductive, and eliminativist variants.

6. This is termed the mereological fallacy as per Max Bennett and Peter Hacker, *Philosophical Foundations of Neuroscience* (Malden, MA: Blackwell, 2003).

7. David Chalmers, "Facing Up to the Problem of Consciousness," *Journal of Consciousness Studies* 2 (1995): 200–219. For those who might be unfamiliar with Japanese swords, a katana is the long sword that was typically carried by samurai alongside a shorter blade, the wakizashi.

8. There are two main approaches. Consider seeing an opponent's high guard. Cognitive scientists favor a top-down model where brain-encoded "sword" and "body" representations interpret incoming signals from the eyes. Neuroscientists opt for a bottom-up approach wherein eyes send signals via the optic nerve to the visual cortex, which are interpreted as "adversary with sword."

9. Philosophers understand mental representations as intensional, bearing semantic meaning or content with satisfaction conditions. Cognitive scientists and neuroscientists view these as neural codings. Nonetheless, all postulate a stand-in that mediates between cognition and world.

10. Phenomenology brings into focus subjective contributions by analyzing how different structures of subjectivity as experienced correlate and underlie the rich kinds of experiences we enjoy.

11. Maurice Merleau-Ponty, *Phenomenology of Perception* (London: Routledge, 1945/2012).

12. Merleau-Ponty, 41.

13. Shaun Gallagher, *Enactivist Interventions* (Oxford: Oxford University Press, 2017).

14. Dan Hutto and Erik Myin, *Radicalizing Enactivism* (Cambridge, MA, and London: MIT Press, 2013).

15. Jesús Ilundáin-Agurruza, Kevin Krein, and Karl Erickson, "High Performance, Risk Sports, and Japanese Thought and Culture," in *The MIT Press Handbook of Embodied Cognition and Sport Psychology*, ed. Maximilian Cappuccio (Cambridge, MA, and London: MIT Press, 2018), 446–483.

16. See "On the Cutting Edge" (Appendix) for more details. Upon completion, some students choose to join a cohort of former pupils. There is a shift to training now. Although I have practiced swordsmanship for two decades, I am not a certified sensei/instructor. Thus, my role becomes that of a collaborator: we *jointly* research and learn techniques. Blunt steel blades replace *bokken* for more realistic blade behavior that also puts "something" on the line.

17. Plato, *Laws. Vol. 2*, trans. R. G. Bury (New York: P. Putnam's Sons, 1926), 55.

18. Hosokawa Dogen, *Omori Sogen: The Art of the Zen Master* (New York: Routledge, 2011), 107ff.

19. See Section four, Compassion and *Upāya*, specifically the discussion on "eyes of a samurai." Its five levels are explained in the laboratory related to Mahayanistic Buddhist compassionate aspirations, each in a separate session.

20. Maxine Sheets-Johnstone, *The Primacy of Movement*, 2nd Ed. (Amsterdam: John Benjamins, 2011).

21. Critically, this is a phenomenological point and not a metaphysical distinction: it affords informative descriptions of psychophysical dynamics while avoiding claims about "ultimate" nature.

22. David E. Shaner, *The Bodymind Experience in Japanese Buddhism: A Phenomenological Study of Kūkai and Dōgen* (Albany: State University of New York Press, 1985); Jesús Ilundáin-Agurruza, *Holism and the Cultivation of Excellence in Sports and Performance: Skillful Striving* (London: Routledge, 2016); Jesús Ilundáin-Agurruza, "A Different Way to Play," in *Philosophy: Sport*, ed. Scott R. Kretchmar (Farmington Hills, MI: Macmillan, 2017), 319–43.

23. John Stevens, *Rengetsu: Life and Poetry of Lotus Moon* (Brattleboro, VT: Echo Point Books and Media, 2014).

24. Robin Wang, "The Virtuous Body at Work: The Ethical Life as *Qi* 氣 in Motion," *Dao: A Comparative Journal* 9 (2010): 339–51.

25. Yuriko Saito, "Bodily Aesthetics and the Cultivation of Moral Virtues," in *New Essays in Japanese Aesthetics*, ed. A. Minh Nguyen (Lanham, MD: Lexington Books, 2018), 61–73.

26. Michael O'Shea, *The Brain: A Very Short Introduction* (Oxford: Oxford University Press, 2005) is the main text for this unit (supplemented with other materials).

27. This misguided advice is based on misinterpreted "observations," as ball and sword-tip move too fast for human visual tracking abilities.

28. Joan N. Vickers, *Perception, Cognition, and Decision Training: The Quiet Eye in Action* (Champaign, IL: Human Kinetics, 2007).

29. Musashi, Miyamoto, *The Book of Five Rings*, trans. Thomas Cleary (Boston: Shambhala, 1993), 3–92.

30. This normative aesthetic/ethical aspect is also evident in *kendō*'s *zanshin* (残心), remaining heartmind. See Yoshiko Oda and Yoshitaka Kondo, "The Concept of Yuko-Datotsu in Kendo: Interpreted from the Aesthetics of Zanshin," *Sport, Ethics and Philosophy*, 8, no. 1 (2104): 3–15.

31. Carter, Japanese Arts, 4.

32. Yuasa Yasuo, *The Body, Self-cultivation, and Ki-energy* (Albany: State University of New York Press, 1993), 10 (emphasis added).

33. Ilundáin-Agurruza, *Skillful Striving* (esp. ch. 9).

34. Abe Shinobu, "Zen and Sport," *Journal of the Philosophy of Sport* 13, no. 1 (1986): 47.

35. Thomas Kasulis, *Engaging Japanese Philosophy: A Short History* (Honolulu: University of Hawai'i Press, 2018).

36. Dōgen. *Shōbōgenzō*, trans. Hubert Nearman (Mount Shasta, CA: Shasta Abbey Press, 2007), 380 (emphasis added).

37. Hosokawa Dogen, 38.

38. Hosokawa Dogen, 15.

39. Nonetheless, some Chan and Zen masters employed violent means to help others reach enlightenment. For more on violence and nonviolence in Buddhism, see chapter 1 of this volume.

40. Hosokawa Dogen, 110–11.

41. Issai Chozanshi, *The Demon's Sermon on the Martial Arts*, trans. William Scott Wilson (Tokyo: Kodansha International, 2006).

42. In translated citations, "heartmind" replaces translators' use of "mind" as a more accurate rendition of the original Japanese. While "mind" might be more relatable for Western readers, it lacks holistic and embodied connotations.

43. Their respective biographies help account for this. Musashi lived in one of the most turbulent times in Japan's history, had extensive warfare experience, and survived sixty duels by the time he was thirty; Chozanshi was a retainer in pacified Tokugawa (Edo Period) Japan.

44. Chozanshi, 53.

45. Martin Collcutt, "The Legacy of Confucianism in Japan," in *Confucian Heritage and Its Modern Adaptation,* ed. Gilbert Rozman (Princeton: Princeton University Press, 1991), 111–54.

46. Chozanshi, 126.

47. Chozanshi, 101.

48. Chozanshi, 138.

49. Chozanshi, 102.

50. Yagyu, The Life-Giving Sword, 75.

51. Ilundáin-Agurruza, Krein, and Erickson, *High Performance*, 454–60.

52. Chozanshi, *Demon's Sermon*, 100.

53. Chozanshi, *Demon's Sermon*, 96.

54. Merleau-Ponty, *Phenomenology.*

55. Chozanshi, 118; author's emphasis.

56. Yagyu, *The Life-Giving Sword.*

57. Chozanshi, 133.

58. Chozanshi, 118.

59. Dogen, H., *Omori Sogen*, 112.

60. Harvey, Peter, "The Conditioned Co-arising of Mental and Bodily Processes within Life and between Lives," in *A Companion to Buddhist Philosophy,* ed. Steven M. Emmanuel (Chichester: John Wiley and Sons, 2013), 46.

61. Murakami Haruki, *What I Talk about When I Talk About Running: A Memoir* (New York: Alfred K. Knopf, 2008), 116–17.

62. Murakami, 16.

63. Tokitsu Kenji, *Miyamoto Musashi: His Life and Writings* (Boston: Shambhala, 2004), 290.

64. Takuan Soho, *The Unfettered Mind: Writings of the Zen Master to the Sword Master*, trans. Williams S. Wilson (Tokyo: Kodansha, 1986).

65. Takuan, Unfettered Mind, 37.

66. Daniel Hutto and J. Ilundáin-Agurruza, "Selfless Activity and Experience: Radicalizing Minimal Self-Awareness," *Topoi: An International Journal of Philosophy* (2018): 1–11. https://doi.org/10.1007/s11245-018-9573.

67. Flow states are often equated with *mushin* states. Functionally equivalent, on account of cultural permeation, these should be considered phenomenologically sui generis. See Kevin Krein and Jesús Ilundáin-Agurruza, "An East-West Comparative Analysis of Mushin and Flow," in *Philosophy and the Martial Arts*, ed. Graham Priest and Damian Young (London and New York: Routledge, 2014), 139–64; and Ilundáin-Agurruza, Krein, and Ericksen, *High Performance*, 460–68.

68. Dōgen, *Shōbōgenzō*, 308.

69. Dogen Hosokawa, 112.

70. Nobuko Hirose, ed. and trans., *The Teachings of Takuan Soho: Immovable Wisdom* (N.P.: Floating World Editions, 2013), 22.

71. McRae, James, "Art of War, Art of Self: Aesthetic Cultivation in *Japanese Martial Arts*," in *New Essays in Japanese Aesthetics*, ed. A. Minh Nguyen (Lanham, MD: Lexington Books, 2018), 121–36.

72. Takuan, *Unfettered Mind*; Hirose, *Teachings of Takuan Soho*.

73. McRae, 127.

74. Murakami, 170; emphases added.

75. Takuan, *Unfettered Mind*; Hirose, *Teachings of Takuan Soho*.

76. Suzuki, 182.

77. Ilundáin-Agurruza (2016); Ilundáin-Agurruza, Krein, and Ericksen, *High Performance*.

78. Bruya, Brian, *Effortless Attention* (Cambridge, MA, and London: MIT Press, 2010).

79. Suzuki, *Zen and Japanese Culture*.

80. Carter, Robert, *Nothingness beyond God: An Introduction to the Philosophy of Nishida Kitaro* (Saint Paul: Paragon House, 1997).

81. Dreyfus, Hubert, "Intelligence without Representation—Merleau-Ponty's Critique of Mental Representation. The Relevance of Phenomenology to Scientific Explanation," *Phenomenology and the Cognitive Sciences* (2002): 367–83.

82. Ilundáin-Agurruza, *Holism*, 257ff.

83. Yagyu, 93.

84. Peter Hershock, *Chan Buddhism* (Honolulu: University of Hawai'i Press, 2005), 1.

85. Chozanshi, *Demon's Sermon*; Munenori, *Life-Giving Sword*.

86. Dōgen, *Shōbōgenzō*.

87. Chozanshi, *Demon's Sermon*; Chozan. Niwa, *The Subtle Art of a Cat* (n.p: n.d). https://www.themathesontrust.org/library/subtle-cat-art-neko-no-myojutsu; John Stevens, *Budo Secrets: Teachings of the Martial Arts Masters* (Boston and London: Shambhala, 2013).

88. Chozanshi, 185.

89. In fact, the historical record does not support this progressive evolution as Karl Friday and Seki Humitake point out in *Legacies of the Sword: the Kashima-Shinryū and Samurai Martial Culture* (Honolulu: University of Hawai'i Press, 1997), 8. This is a terminological matter to some extent, however, since the nature of martial culture did progress, in accord with the changing political landscape, from warfare toward peaceful self-cultivation.

90. Peter Hershock, *Liberating Intimacy* (Albany: State University of New York Press, 1996).

91. John Schroeder, *Skillful Means: The Heart of Buddhist Compassion* (Honolulu: University of Hawai'i Press, 2004).

92. Hershock, *Liberating Intimacy*, 133.

93. Hershock, *Liberating Intimacy*, 150.

94. Yagyu, 76.

95. As Karl Friday and Seki Humitake explain in *Legacies of the Sword*—in classical *Bugei* (武芸)—*Setsunin-tō* (殺人刀), the Killing Sword, and *Katsujin-ken* (活人剣), the Life-Giving Sword, terms derived from Buddhist allegory, refer not to the weapon itself but to how to wield it: either attacking or drawing out adversaries' reactions respectively. It is not opponents who are killed or given life, but their responses and fighting spirit. Nonetheless, we can argue that a compassionate and virtuosic swordsperson is able to engage antagonists without lethal force. To add another layer from a Buddhist perspective, the sword—cutting through delusion, attachment, and hesitation—becomes a teaching tool for how to live.

96. Yagyu, 96.

97. Yagyu, 180 fn. 69.

98. Shimabukuro, Masayuki and Leonard J. Pellman, *Flashing Steel: Mastering Eishin-Ryū Swordsmanship* (Berkeley: Blue Snake Books, 2008), 21–44.

99. Hirose, 20.

100. Dogen Hosokawa, *Omori Sogen*, 102.

101. Hershock, in *Liberating Intimacy*, has revealingly explored this in a Buddhist context.

Bibliography

Abe, Shinobu. "Zen and Sport." *Journal of the Philosophy of Sport* 13, no. 1 (1986): 47.

Bennett, Max, and Peter Hacker. *Philosophical Foundations of Neuroscience*. Malden, MA: Blackwell, 2003.

Bruya, Brian. *Effortless Attention*. Cambridge, MA, and London: MIT Press, 2010.

Carter, Robert. *The Japanese Arts and Self-Cultivation*. Albany: State University of New York Press, 2008.

———. *Nothingness beyond God: An Introduction to the Philosophy of Nishida Kitaro*. Saint Paul: Paragon House, 1997.

Chalmers, David. "Facing Up to the Problem of Consciousness." *Journal of Consciousness Studies* no. 2 (1995): 200–19.

Chozanshi, Issai. *The Demon's Sermon on the Martial Arts*. Translated by William S. Wilson. Tokyo: Kodansha International, 2006.

Collcutt, Martin. "The Legacy of Confucianism in Japan." In *Confucian Heritage and Its Modern Adaptation*, edited by Gilbert Rozman, 111–54. Princeton: Princeton University Press, 1991.

Dogen, Hosokawa. *Omori Sogen: The Art of the Zen Master*. London and New York: Routledge, 2011.

Dōgen. *Shōbōgenzō*. Translated by Hubert Nearman. Mount Shasta, CA: Shasta Abbey Press, 2007.

Dreyfus, Hubert L. "Intelligence without Representation—Merleau-Ponty's Critique of Mental Representation. The Relevance of Phenomenology to Scientific Explanation." *Phenomenology and the Cognitive Sciences* 1 (2002): 367–83.

Friday, Karl F., and Fumitake Seki. *Legacies of the Sword: the Kashima-Shinryū and Samurai Martial Culture*. Honolulu: University of Hawai'i Press, 1997.

Gallagher, Shaun. *Enactivist Interventions*. Oxford: Oxford University Press, 2017.

Harvey, Peter. "The Conditioned Co-arising of Mental and Bodily Processes within Life and Between Lives." In Steven M. Emmanuel, *A Companion to Buddhist Philosophy*, 46–68. Chichester: John Wiley and Sons, 2013.

Hershock, Peter. *Chan Buddhism*. Honolulu: University of Hawai'i Press, 2005.

———. *Liberating Intimacy*. Albany: State University of New York Press, 1996.

Hirose, Nobuko, ed. and trans. *The Teachings of Takuan Soho: Immovable Wisdom*. N.P.: Floating World Editions, 2013.

Hutto, Daniel, and Erik Myin. *Radicalizing Enactivism*. Cambridge, MA, and London: MIT Press, 2013.

Hutto, Daniel, and Jesús Ilundáin-Agurruza. "Selfless Activity and Experience: Radicalizing Minimal Self-Awareness." *Topoi an International Journal of Philosophy* (2018): 1–11. https://doi.org/10.1007/s11245-018-9573.

Ilundáin-Agurruza, Jesús. *Holism and the Cultivation of Excellence in Sports and Performance: Skillful Striving*. London: Routledge, 2016.

———. "A Different Way to Play." In *Sport. Philosophy*, edited by Scott R. Kretchmar, 319–43. Farmington Hills, MI: Macmillan, 2018.

———, Kevin Krein, and Karl Erickson. "High Performance, Risk Sports, and Japanese Thought and Culture." In *The MIT Press Handbook of Embodied Cognition and Sport Psychology*, edited by Maximilian Cappuccio, 446–83. Cambridge, MA, and London: MIT Press, 2018.

Kasulis, Thomas. *Engaging Japanese Philosophy: A Short History*. Honolulu: University of Hawai'i Press, 2018.

Leggett, Trevor. *Samurai Zen: The Warrior Koans*. London: Taylor and Francis, 2013.

McRae, James. "Art of War, Art of Self: Aesthetic Cultivation in the Japanese Martial Arts." In *New Essays in Japanese Aesthetics*, edited by A. Minh Nguyen, 121–36. Lanham, MD: Lexington Books, 2018.

Merleau-Ponty, Maurice. *Phenomenology of Perception*. London: Routledge, 1945/2012.

Murakami, Haruki. *What I Talk about When I Talk About Running: A Memoir*. New York: Alfred K. Knopf, 2008.

Musashi, Miyamoto. *The Book of Five Rings*. Translated by T. Cleary. Boston: Shambhala, 1993.

Oda, Yoshiko, and Yoshitaka Kondo. 2014. "The Concept of Yuko-Datotsu in Kendo: Interpreted from the Aesthetics of Zanshin." *Sport, Ethics and Philosophy* 8, no. 1: 3–15.

O'Shea, Michael. *The Brain: A very Short Introduction*. Oxford: Oxford University Press, 2005.

Plato. *Laws. Vol. 2*. Translated by R. G. Bury. New York: G. P. Putnam's Sons, 1926.

Saito, Yuriko. "Bodily Aesthetics and the Cultivation of Moral Virtues." In *New Essays in Japanese* Aesthetics, edited by A. Minh Nguyen, 61–73. Lanham, MD: Lexington Books, 2018.

Schroeder, John. *Skillful Means: The Heart of Buddhist Compassion*. Honolulu: University of Hawai'i Press, 2004.

Shaner, David E. *The Bodymind Experience in Japanese Buddhism: A Phenomenological Study of Kūkai and Dōgen*. Albany: State University of New York Press, 1985.

Sheets-Johnstone, Maxine. *The Primacy of Movement*. 2nd ed. Amsterdam: John Benjamins, 2011.

Shimabukuro, Masayuki, and Leonard J. Pellman. *Flashing Steel: Mastering Eishin-Ryū Swordsmanship*. Berkeley: Blue Snake Books, 2008.

Stevens, John, *Rengetsu: Life and Poetry of Lotus Moon*. Brattleboro, VT: Echo Point Books and Media, 2014.

Suzuki, Daisetz. *Zen and Japanese Culture*. Princeton: Princeton University Press, 1993.

Takuan, Soho. *The Unfettered Mind: Writings of the Zen Master to the Sword Master*. Translated by William S. Wilson. Tokyo: Kodansha, 1986.

Thomson, Garrett, and Philip Turetzky. "A Simple Guide to Contemporary Philosophy of Mind." In *The Experience of Philosophy*, edited by Daniel Kolak and Raymond Martin, 444–58. Oxford: Oxford University Press, 1996.

Tokitsu, Kenji. *Miyamoto Musashi: His Life and Writings*. Boston: Shambhala, 2004.

Vickers, Joan. N. *Perception, Cognition, and Decision Training: The Quiet Eye in Action*. Champaign, IL: Human Kinetics, 2007.

Wang, Robin. "The Virtuous Body at Work: The Ethical Life as Qi 氣 in Motion." *Dao: A Comparative Journal* 9 (2010): 339–51.

Yagyu, Munenori. *The Life-Giving Sword: Secret Teachings for the House of the Shogun.* Translated by William S. Wilson. Boston and Tokyo: Kodansha International, 2003.

Yuasa, Yasuo. *The Body, Self-cultivation, and Ki-energy.* Albany: State University of New York Press, 1993.

Chapter 5

Revitalizing the Familiar

A Practical Application of Dōgen's Transformative Zen

George Wrisley

A central aspect of Dōgen's Sōtō Zen that sets it apart from other forms of Zen—and Buddhism more generally—is his soteriological approach to language. That is, instead of seeing language as merely a means or, worse, the main obstacle to enlightenment, Dōgen views language as integral to the salvific process and the realization, the enactment, of enlightenment. In his *Shōbōgenzō, the Treasury of the True Dharma Eye*, the mainstay of Dōgen's literary approach is to take a kōan[1] or a passage from Buddhist texts, quite often from *Chan*[2] (禪; Jpn. Zen) sources, and comment on it extensively. This is a vital component in Dōgen's own Zen practice. That is, he not only teaches thereby but actualizes his own enlightenment by way of composing these texts. One of the things that makes Dōgen's approach so interesting and influential is that he, as Steven Heine emphasizes following Hee-Jin Kim, "exhibits a kind of alchemical capacity to alter literature significantly by twisting and even distorting conventional expressions in order to uncover the underlying theoretical significance embedded in speech acts."[3] Dōgen will take a passage and pull it apart, word by word, line by line, to use it to express his understanding of the true Dharma. In doing so, he often takes passages that would be familiar or well known and imbues them with new meaning, revitalizing them with new significance using his "literary alchemy."

In this chapter, I attempt to convey Dōgen's unique understanding of the Dharma by demonstrating Dōgen's approach on something with which an English language reader is likely to be quite familiar, namely, the nursery rhyme "Row, row, row your boat." Doing so has the following pedagogical advantages over a more conventional approach to conveying Dōgen's Zen. First, the nursery rhyme itself is *akin* to a kōan and has many of the elements that can be found in Zen texts and Dōgen's own writings, for example, boat imagery, streams and water, an activity (here, rowing), the question of emotion ("merrily"), and the idea of the dreamlike nature of life and reality, something Dōgen takes up explicitly in his *Shōbōgenzō* fascicle "Talking of a Dream within a Dream." Second, commenting on the nursery rhyme will take something familiar to the reader and memorably make it new, revitalizing it, and thereby making it a fruitful doorway into a better understanding of Dōgen's methodology and Sōtō Zen. Third, as Dōgen expresses, for example, in his fascicle "Buddha Sutras," "The sutras are the entire world of the ten directions. There is no moment or place that is not sutras."[4] That is, all things might function, if properly attended, as Buddhist sutras, that is, Buddhist texts. Hence, we should feel confident in appropriating the nursery rhyme as a kind of Buddhist text. Thus, though the nursery rhyme was not written by a Zen master or as a Buddhist text at all, its imagery and familiarity make it highly attractive for the pedagogical purposes for which it will be used.

After a brief look at Dōgen's biography, this chapter lays out the central aspects of Dōgen's Zen, situating it in relation to other forms of Buddhism and Zen; it lastly demonstrates Dōgen's method by way of a "Dōgen-esque" commentary on, "Row, row, row your boat," indicating that the student reader should use the earlier parts of the chapter, its exposition on Dōgen's Zen, to try to unpack the meaning of the commentary on the nursery rhyme. To help facilitate this, questions are given at the end of the chapter to help guide the student through the process.

Dōgen's Biography

In line with Buddhism's notion of dependent co-arising, when considering Dōgen's biography we should note the broader social-historical context in which he lived. First, his birth (1200 CE) coincided with the beginning of Japan's Kamakura period (1192–1333), following on the Heian period (710–1192 CE). This period shift is marked by the aristocracy's waning power, based in Kyoto, and the increasing power of the military class, based in Kamakura. The aristocracy in the Heian period was marked, as it had been for some time, by a deep aesthetic appreciation of life. As Hee-Jin

Kim notes, "Despite its outward pomposity, the aristocratic way of life was permeated by an awareness of beauty shadowed by a sense of sorrow due to beauty's inherently ephemeral character."[5] Further, while beauty and religion went hand in hand for the Heian aristocracy, this was not so for aesthetic and ethical considerations. The aristocracy understood themselves to be karmically privileged and thus did not seriously consider the lot of the underprivileged masses.[6] These two aspects coming into the Kamakura period were important for Dōgen. First, since he was born into the aristocracy, his education included literary and aesthetic material, whose influence would later become apparent in his masterful use of language, both Chinese and Japanese. Second, he, like several other Buddhist innovators of his time, would be concerned to put forward a religion accessible to the masses, though here, too, Dōgen's aristocratic background would show.

Another important aspect of the period of Dōgen's life was that it was widely held that the time of the Degenerate Law (*mappō*) had begun. *Mappō* was purportedly prophesied by the Buddha as a time when society and morality would decline; it would be a time of great difficulty, including difficulty in making progress along the Buddhist path. Social, political, and climatic turmoil in the late Heian and early Kamakura heavily reinforced the idea that *mappō* was truly at hand. While many bought into these ideas, Dōgen refused to give in to the idea that enlightenment was any harder to achieve than it had been before.

With these basics of Dōgen's historical context in place, we can begin Dōgen's biography by noting that he was born in 1200 CE into an aristocratic family in Kyoto. He quickly came to know the truth of impermanence, as he lost his father at the age of two and his mother at the age of seven. On her deathbed, his mother is supposed to have expressed to Dōgen her desire that he become a Buddhist monk seeking the truth and the way to help all people.[7] Dōgen is said to have been deeply moved by the expression of impermanence made by the rising smoke from the incense sticks at his mother's funeral.

In 1213, at the age of thirteen, Dōgen became a monastic and began his formal study and practice of Buddhism at Mt. Hiei, northeast of Kyoto. At this time, Buddhism was flourishing in Japan, with Tendai being the most dominant of the schools and with a number of "new" schools coming into existence. It has been said that in 1191 Myōan Eisai transmitted *Rinzai Zen* (Chinese: Linji School of Chan) from China to Japan; however, Steven Heine emphasizes that "[Eisai] always thought of himself as a Tendai monk who featured meditation mixed with various traditional ritual elements."[8]

Nevertheless, Eisai did found Kenninji temple in Kyoto in 1202, where he remained until he died in 1215. Kenninji was "at the time not only the center of Zen, but was also the center of studies for Tendai, Shingon, and other schools of Buddhism,"[9] while being a rival of Mt. Hiei. Having traveled to China in 1223, Dōgen would return in 1227 to establish what he saw as the authentic Dharma, what became Sōtō Zen, staying at Kenninji for the first several years upon his return. However, before we get there, we should take care to note what seems to have been the impetus for Dōgen's journey to China.

At the age of fourteen, Dōgen is said to have begun to have his crisis of "great doubt" in his Buddhist practice. The crisis concerned the "time-honored Mahāyāna"[10] doctrine of original enlightenment (hongaku); this doctrine holds that all things, not just humans, are intrinsically enlightened. Dōgen's great doubt was: Why practice with great effort if everything is already the awakened state of Buddhahood? As Kim notes in this context, faith without real practice, "which required no strenuous religious or moral exertion, became readily associated with the antinomian cynicism inspired by the Age of Degenerate Law [mappō]."[11] Even at such a young age, Dōgen was disturbed by the antinomian temptations of (possible interpretations of) the doctrine of original enlightenment.

Dōgen traveled around to different teachers, looking for an answer to his question regarding the necessity of intense, difficult Buddhist practice in the face of the hongaku doctrine. He apparently could not find a satisfactory answer to this question wherever he went in Japan, whomever he asked. After wandering for some time, Dōgen returned to Kenninji in 1217 where he studied with Eisai's disciple Myōzen until 1223, at which point Dōgen, Myōzen, and a small group of others, left for China. As much as Dōgen appreciated Myōzen's understanding of the Dharma, his "great doubt" had not been assuaged by him.

In China, during his first two years there, Dōgen would continue to wander from temple to temple in the Five Mountains Temples area, looking for a true teacher of the authentic Dharma. It was not until 1225 that Dōgen found his true teacher, namely, Tiantong Rujing. During the three-month practice period of intense zazen that year (1225), it is said that Dōgen was practicing zazen next to a monk who had fallen asleep. Rujing, upon seeing the sleeping monk admonished him severely, saying, "In zazen it is imperative to cast off the body and mind. How could you indulge in sleeping?"[12] Dōgen is said to have had at this moment a deep realization concerning his great doubt and the need for practice.

Rujing conferred Dharma transmission to Dōgen, certifying his awakening. Dōgen became the first Japanese monk to receive transmission from the Caodong School of Chan Buddhism, and the Zhenxie Qingliao line. In 1227, Dōgen returned to Japan, purportedly "empty-handed," that is, without the various things traveling monks would usually return with, for example, sūtras and other documents and iconography.

Back in Japan, Dōgen slowly began to orient himself and his mission of establishing the true Dharma. Moreover, he was interested in a religion open to all, regardless of social rank, intelligence, or ability. Further still, like other new Buddhist schools in Japan, Dōgen had a purportedly singular method for achieving enlightenment, namely, zazen-only. That is, it was through seated meditation that enlightenment is enacted. We'll see more later what this means. Here, let us note that while others in Japan, such as Shinran and Nichiren, had singular methods, as well, theirs were more aimed at ease of use by the common folk living, as they believed, in the Age of Degenerate Law (*mappō*).

Despite his desire to establish a widely accessible form of practice, Dōgen's zazen-only approach to enlightenment was more rigorous and less easily enacted than, for example, putting one's faith in the recitation of a Buddha's name, as was practiced in the Pure Land school of Shinran. Moreover, as is clear from his writings, Dōgen did not write for the non-erudite. Moreover, he early on had a kind of ambivalence regarding whether lay practitioners can attain enlightenment. This ambivalence seems to have faded into apparent pessimism, as Dōgen, in his later years, focused ever more on the monastic community.[13] However, one aspect we should note in this context is that Dōgen wrote primarily in vernacular Japanese, especially in the informal talks collected as the *Shōbōgenzō*, where he utilized his knowledge of Japanese literary techniques to great advantage in expressing his understanding of the Dharma. He was the first to write in vernacular Japanese; as Kazuaki Tanahashi notes, "Until then Buddhist teachings had been studied and written almost exclusively in the Japanese form of Chinese."[14] Thus began Sōtō Zen by way of Dōgen's earnest pursuit of the authentic Dharma in answer to his great doubt.

From Duality to Nonduality

A helpful way to begin grappling with Dōgen's Zen is by examining his treatment of a number of seeming dualities—for example, *saṃsāra*/enlightenment, self/other, practice/enlightenment, and so forth. Through a thorough application of emptiness (San. *śūnyatā*), Dōgen deconstructs and then reconstructs them as nondualities. As Dōgen's expositions show, a purported duality is nondual when the existence of two *seemingly separate* "things" is not truly separate, since their existence is entangled; yet they are not one and the same thing either.

Once we understand a duality as nondual, we can "jump off both sides"[15] and not fall into the trap of being attached or averse to either "side," or extreme, for instance, *form* or *emptiness*. It is all too easy to mistake the Zen path as one of movement from understanding/behavior that takes the world to divide into fixed, unchanging *forms,* to behavior and understanding that takes the world to consist of radically unfixed and continually changing *emptiness.* In Zen practice properly understood, we don't linger on either focal point/duality, nor does either exist without the other; there is both form and emptiness, but they are nondually one. Hence, Dōgen's statement of nonduality, "Though not identical, they are not different; though not different, they are not one; though not one, they are not many,"[16] which can be applied to every duality, every "thing" that appears separate/different. It is because of both the transitory and interdependent "nature" of things in emptiness that Buddhism, and Zen in particular, has this understanding of nonduality. And it must be applied to everything (including emptiness itself), including the large set of apparent dualisms found in Zen Buddhism, for example, *saṃsāra*/enlightenment, substance/emptiness, practice/enlightenment, self/other, self/self (over time), language/silence, among others.

A tempting way to see these dualities is that the lefthand side is problematic or incomplete (in the case of practice) and the righthand one is desirable/complete, such that one needs to transition (via some method such as zazen) from the one to the other. But these dualisms are not to be affirmed such that the correct soteriological practice is to move from the left to the right, but rather, the idea is that these dualities are to be nondually taken up and navigated, explored and creatively engaged so as to *actualize* their soteriological potentials for *enacting* enlightenment. And, thus, there is, for Dōgen, never any *absolute* affirmation of the one "side" over the other.

Enlightenment is awakening to the true nature of *saṃsāra,* to all of its complexities and "entangled vines" of language and concepts and myriad relationships. This is why Hee-Jin Kim, for example, sees Dōgen's Zen as thoroughly philosophical: it is a form of religio-philosophical practice where all difference is critically engaged nondually. This is the practice of grappling with what Kim calls both the deconstructive and reconstructive aspects of emptiness.[17] *Deconstruction* is in service of removing substantialist views and attachments; *reconstruction* is the *negotiating* of reality in light of a rehabilitated understanding of a world of "things."[18] In this light, we can understand Dōgen's writing: "The endeavor to negotiate the Way (*bendō*), as I now teach, consists in discerning all things in view of enlightenment, and putting such unitive awareness (*ichinyo*) into practice in the midst of the revaluated world (*shutsuro*)."[19] Let's explore some of the above dualities in more depth and what it means to engage them nondually through the reconstructive lens of emptiness.

Saṃsāra and Enlightenment

In Buddhism, *saṃsāra* is "the world" of *dukkha*, of suffering, of dissatisfaction rooted in delusion; it is "the world" of birth, death, and rebirth, such that *enlightenment/Nirvana* (*Bodhi*) is "the world" of freedom from *dukkha*, from delusion, and the rest. The *duality* of this distinction is found explicitly in such imagery as the Buddha's teachings being a raft to get to the other shore (enlightenment). This imagery goes well with a common assumption that the Buddha's teachings outline a method, a means (the raft), for getting from one shore to the other. Such a means-end conception of practice is problematic in Zen generally, but in particular for Dōgen, as we will examine in detail below. For Dōgen, *saṃsāra* and enlightenment are not different places or times; the world of *saṃsāra* is the *same* world as that of enlightenment/*nirvana*—moreover, Dōgen's teachings do not outline a method or means to *achieve* enlightenment but rather explicate how enlightenment is to be *enacted* in this very *sahā* world (mundane world) in which practice and enlightenment are (nondually) one; this nonduality will be discussed in detail below along with Dōgen's view of a means-ends conception of practice. *Enlightened activity is the skillful negotiation of the nonduality of delusion and enlightenment.* Hence, for Dōgen, Buddhas greatly enlighten delusion and "those greatly deluded amid enlightenment are sentient beings."[20] And, further: "Just understand that birth-and-death itself is nirvana, and you will neither hate one as being birth-and-death, nor cherish the other as being nirvana. Only then can you be free of birth-and-death."[21]

Sentient beings are greatly deluded amid enlightenment because of how they comport themselves in a world that is empty. Ignorant of, or flaunting, emptiness, "sentient beings" take the dream nature of the world as solid, projecting their fixed concepts, expectations, and desires onto it, attempting to bend it to their will; rejecting the empty, dreamlike nature of the world, labeling it as "bad" when it does not conform to their wills, their desires and expectations; labeling it as "good" when it does. As we will see, for Dōgen, it is not so much a matter of *ridding* ourselves of delusion once and for all—for there is no "once and for all" in life—but rather of skillfully and continuously navigating the reality of delusion.

The world in all of its aspects is enlightenment itself, but, as Dōgen indicates with the story of Zen Master Pao-ch'e,[22] though the wind (enlightenment) may be everywhere that does not mean that we do not have to fan ourselves, that is, that does not mean that we do not have to continuously practice, negotiating the nondual reality of delusion and enlightenment.[23] Liberation (enlightenment) occurs only through overcoming delusion continuously. This is particularly the case given the recognition of continuous change. That is, there is never a fixed point where reality does not present unique situations that prompt the overcoming of delusion.

Substance and Emptiness

A fundamental way we are deluded is by our taking the world to be composed of substances, of things, each of which exists as the same, identical "thing" over time, and whose nature is what it is independently of everything else. The tree that grows in the yard today was planted thirty years ago when I was a child; it is the *same* tree now as the one planted all those years ago. And it exists, is what it is, because of its intrinsic "tree" nature. Dug up and transplanted across the country or the world, it's still the *same* tree. However, this way of viewing the tree constitutes delusion, since, in Zen Buddhism, everything is *empty* of substantial natures of that kind. Emptiness (*śūnyatā*) characterizes everything. That is, nothing persists as the same, identical "thing" over time—the tree today isn't *straightforwardly* the *numerically same* tree that was there thirty years ago—and everything that is, is what it is in complete dependence on all the things ordinarily taken not to be it—the tree's existence is completely dependent upon non-tree elements such as the rain, the sun, the soil and its nutrients, carbon dioxide, the producers of carbon dioxide, etc. Take any of those elements away and you take away the tree.[24]

Here we see an important point that Dōgen likes to emphasize regarding the dreamlike (empty) nature of existence. On the one hand, we might think that enlightenment is waking up from the dream of ignorance, delusion, and suffering. Yet, from a different angle, we can see a kind of paradox, but one whose grasping is central to enlightenment. For we also speak of dreams as nonsubstantial, not real, and not (fully) in our control. Yet in our deluded, "unenlightened" dreamlike position, we take things in the world to be substantial, "real," and (largely) in our control, which is to say, *not like dreams at all.* Thus, "waking up" in Zen means *awakening* to the *dreamlike nature of everything in emptiness.*

A perhaps surprising point here is that it is only *in the dream* that some "thing" can exist—there is not a more substantial reality possible. Without time, without interdependence, nothing could exist, nothing could be an experience or a happening—this is one reason that Dōgen insists upon seeing existence as time/time as existence. Hence, too, Dōgen's point that it is only a painted (i.e., empty) rice cake that can satisfy hunger. Dōgen transforms—*makes new*—the ideas some in Zen had that the dreamlike, empty nature of everything means that no desire can be satisfied, since trying to satisfy a desire in the context of emptiness is like trying to satisfy hunger with a painted rice cake. Dōgen recognizes that there is no such thing as a rice cake (i.e., anything) that is not "painted." It is exactly with "painted rice cakes" that one becomes satisfied, if one is going to find satisfaction at all (through authentic practice).[25]

Practice and Enlightenment

Building on what we have seen so far, we can well grasp now a pivotal duality that Dōgen deconstructs and reconstructs according to his view of authentic practice of the Way, namely, the duality of practice and enlightenment. Again, it is all too easy to think of practice as a necessary means to achieving *the* special *state of mind* that is enlightenment (consider the Buddha under the Bodhi tree)—practice is how we move from the deluded world of conventional truth to that of ultimate truth. On this view, you must diligently work at perfecting the skills needed to awaken the mind to the true nature of reality so that you no longer suffer. This may take years, a lifetime, or many lifetimes of rebirth to achieve. For example, if zazen or seated meditation is taken to be a primary mode of practice, then one must engage in zazen until one has achieved awakening. Further, the fundamental truth of Buddhism is that there is nothing that can be grasped, as everything is continuously changing according to the interdependent web of being/process of which it is a part and has its being. Hence, we suffer when we negotiate the world with a grasping mind that attaches to ideas, expectations, desires, etc. The sooner we come to see into the nature of this situation, the sooner we'll be able to let go of our attachments. Studying the sutras and sitting zazen are means, then, to insight and wisdom that will facilitate letting go. Similarly, the Eightfold Path outlined by the Buddha gives a method and means for achieving enlightenment, or so we might think.

We find, however, Dōgen thoroughly repudiating this complex picture, going so far as to call it "non-Buddhist": "The view that practice and enlightenment are not one is a non-Buddhist view. In the Buddha-dharma they are one. . . . for practice itself is original enlightenment."[26] What does it mean to say that practice and enlightenment are "one." In the fascicle "*Busshō*," Dōgen puts forth one of his most well-known linguistic transformations. That is, he purposefully "misreads" the line, "All sentient beings without exception have the Buddha-nature" as "*entire being* is the Buddha-nature."[27] The original line from the *Nirvana Sutra* is usually understood to mean that inherent to sentient beings' nature is the *potential* to become Buddhas. But it is a potential that requires practice to develop and actualize. Dōgen's purposeful "misreading" says instead that all that exists, "entire being," is the Buddha-nature. As we saw earlier, one way of focusing on Buddha-nature is as the transitory aspect of all existence. We can further identify Buddha-nature as *emptiness* such that to speak of Buddha-nature is to speak of the emptiness of things. Insofar as we might think of enlightenment as the deep realization of the emptiness of all things, we can think of enlightenment itself, original enlightenment, as the emptiness of things itself, that is, Buddha-nature. Thus, we ourselves *are already enlightenment itself insofar as we are Buddha-nature*—yet while we are enlightenment itself, we are continually having to practice not falling into delusion, that is, the denial of Buddha-nature in the context of lived life. Practice, then, is the enacting of emptiness; this is not simply a state of mind, but a particular kind of activity, namely, letting go, moment to moment. What does this mean?

The twentieth-century Japanese Zen master Kodo Sawaki had a wonderful saying: "Zazen is good for nothing."[28] What he means is that we often think of things in terms of their instrumental value, what they can get us. The job is *good for* earning money, the bike is *good for* getting around, zazen is *good for* practicing concentration and gaining insight. By saying that zazen is good for nothing, Sawaki is trying to jar us out of the all too easy temptation of thinking of zazen as an instrument, *a means*, for attaining enlightenment. For such means-ends thinking makes them two;

we end up with (1) the means (zazen), and (2) the end (enlightenment), that is, a duality. Sawaki wants us to let go of that way of thinking and to understand the way in which practice and enlightenment are not two, while not numerically identical either.

Whenever we conceptualize (explicitly or not) something as a means to an end, we split our minds, so to speak. If we hang the clothes up *so that* they may dry, then when we do the hanging, our minds are (often unconsciously) in two places. We are doing the hanging, but we are also thinking of (we are implicating) the future point when they will be dry. The only way to be fully in the moment with whatever *is*, is to treat each moment as an end in itself. While we, of course, know that hanging up the clothes is to dry them, it is possible to be fully present to the hanging of the clothes whereby one views the hanging as an end in itself. One lets go of all that is future, all the possible results of hanging the clothes, and simply hangs them (after all, they may fail to dry). This would, in a sense, be to treat the hanging of the clothes *as good for nothing*.

If we think of sitting in zazen *as good for* something, then we are treating the sitting as a means to achieve something outside of, or separate from, the sitting. In many books on Zen, this is how practice is discussed. For example, in the important and influential *Three Pillars of Zen* by Philip Kapleau, Zen is a matter of achieving, through zazen, "concentration and absorption by which the mind is first tranquilized and brought to one-point-edness, and then awakened."[29] Here, "awakening" is *satori*, a Japanese term, which Kapleau defines as "enlightenment, that is, Self-realization, opening the Mind's eye, awakening to one's True-nature and hence of the nature of all existence. See also 'kenshō.' "[30] The term he references at the end, *kenshō*, he explains thus, "kenshō (literally, 'seeing into one's own nature'): Semantically, kenshō and satori have virtually the same meaning and are often used interchangeably. In describing the enlightenment of the Buddha and the patriarchs, however, it is customary to use the word *satori* rather than kenshō, the term satori implying a deeper experience."[31] However, practicing zazen as a means to achieve the end of *kenshō/satori* means that when one sits, one's mind is divided between the moment of sitting now and the future moment of hoped for attainment of *satori*.

For Dōgen, by contrast, as we saw above, you *are already enlightenment itself*, since you are the Buddha-nature; but, again, this does not negate the need for practice. Remember, the issue of "original enlightenment" was at the heart of Dōgen's great doubt, the central question that drove him to China in search of the authentic Dharma. While we are through and through enlightenment, that is, Buddha-nature, what must be done is to *practice this enlightenment* by *just sitting*, what Dōgen calls in the Japanese, *shikantaza*. This is "the practice-realization of totally culminated enlightenment."[32] "If you concentrate your effort single-mindedly, you are thereby negotiating the Way with your practice realization undefiled."[33] For Dōgen, we defile practice (zazen) by using it as a means. What he wants us to do is to treat practice as an end in itself. You sit just to sit and this *just sitting* (*shikantaza*) is actualizing Buddha-nature by letting things simply be what they are, unfolding in time, as time, in their interdependent web of process/being. For Dōgen, *satori* is not best thought of as a particular mental state that is the experiential/phenomenological apprehension of Buddha-nature, but rather the continuous practice of enacting Buddha-nature by letting go, moment by moment, again and again. Similarly, with the Eightfold Path, it can be viewed not merely as a means to enlightenment but *enlightenment itself*—the "endless" path is the goal itself.

While there may be a sense of *satori* that is a particular experience of deep insight into the nature of reality in all of its nonduality, such experiences are just something else to become attached to.[34] The danger is that we will come to *prefer* enlightened (*satori*) experiences over nonenlightened (*deluded*) experiences. But as Dōgen writes, "If the least like or dislike arises, the mind is lost in confusion."[35] Typically, to "like something" is to want to hold onto it; to "dislike something" is to want to be rid of it. We have a "bad," busy-mind experience, and we dislike it; we have a "good," ecstatic *satori* experience, and we want to hold on to it. But this is not the reality of Buddha-nature. Nothing is fixed. Nothing persists unchanging. To enact that reality, to enact Buddha-nature, to enact enlightenment, there is nothing to do but let go, again and again, and allow the changing, interdependent reality to unfold. Hence, Uchiyama Roshi writes, "Whether fantasies arise one after another or whether you sit there with a perfectly clean slate, let go of either one. Seeing both, illusions or realizations, with the same eye is what is critical here."[36] As Okumura Roshi writes, though he's been sitting zazen for more than forty years, sometimes his mind is perfectly still and sometimes it is clouded with much thought, but whatever happens, the point is to let go.[37]

Regarding practice, we have focused here primarily on the idea of seated meditation. However, we should note that there are two important aspects of practice that we have had to leave aside but which should be mentioned. The first is that Dōgen makes clear that his Zen of "zazen-only" of "just sitting" does not mean that the only kind of practice is literal sitting. For one thing, you can practice "zazen-only" off the cushion in the context of ordinary activities. This he makes clear, for example, in the fascicle "Instructions for the Head Cook" ("Tenzokyōkun"), as the cook does not have the same opportunities to sit as the rest of the sangha. The cook's "sitting" is the various tasks associated with the planning and preparing of meals. The second thing we should note is that Dōgen's Zen is that of Mahāyāna Buddhism and as such it is the Bodhisattva vehicle. This might have been another point of focus for us; if we had done so, then we would have emphasized the role of compassion in enacting enlightenment.[38]

Self and Other, and Self and Self, through Time

"Self" in Buddhism is a way of referring to (separate) identities. That is, there is a "self" when there is an *identifiable* "thing" that exists as distinguishable from other such things. For example, a chair is a *self* insofar as it has a purported identity/existence that is separate from the self of the table and the person sitting, eating at the table. A further aspect of "selves" is that in addition to being identifiable and separate, they persist through time. The chair that is separate from the table this morning is the same chair that was there last night at dinner. It is this sense of self as a separate *and* persisting "thing," that Buddhism, and Dōgen, challenge so vehemently through various deconstructive applications of emptiness. The two central foci of emptiness are unceasing transitoriness and interdependence: nothing persists and every "thing" exists interdependently with everything else.

In this way, the dualities of self/other and self/self-over-time are taken apart (deconstructive aspect of emptiness) and put back together (reconstruction aspect of emptiness) and, thus, rendered nondual. For example, Dōgen quotes approvingly the line "Old man Zhang drinks, and old man Li gets drunk"[39] as a way to express the interdependence of all things. Drinking alcohol is an interesting image here, since it implicates both body and mind. One drinks the alcohol with one's body-mind and very quickly one's body-mind is affected. The drunk person is drunk in both bodily and mental behavior together.

Yet, as Dōgen writes, "not one of the four great elements or the five skandhas can be understood as self or identified as self."[40] The five *skandhas* are a central way Buddhists have traditionally analyzed a person into parts; they are: form, feeling, perceptions, mental formations, and consciousness. I, my*self*, drink a beer, and you, your*self*, don't get drunk—we ordinarily think. And while there is an appropriate sense of *you* as separate from *me*, nevertheless, in emptiness, my *self* is nondual with your *self*: self and other interpenetrate. I drink and stumble around; in your mind-body there arises compassion and concern—the five *skandhas* referred to by your name change. Thus, your existence is interdependent with mine: the nature of your mind, its content, the you (self) that exists in this moment is what it is only because of my drinking, my stumbling body-mind (and, of course, the rest of the world, past and present, and future). And your body-mind then acts to help me along. Our very being, *our-self* is what it is only in relation to our "separate" selves and their interactions. Self and other as a duality are interwoven, *entwined like vines,* in nonduality. The apparent duality is deconstructed in emptiness and reconstructed as a nondual "unity." And it is in this way that our understanding does not fall into the mistake of taking each self to be "truly" a separate, independent self, nor does it fall into the mistake of thinking that there is no sense of self with which you may identify. You do not literally get drunk when I drink, yet in my drunkenness and your reaction/response, we are nondually one.

We can see that for Dōgen the nonduality of self and other is not "merely" that of *persons,* but rather all purportedly separate "selves." That is, every "thing" that exists is nondual with every other "thing." This has radical implications for how we are to come to understand "our" *selves.* Dōgen makes this clear with such passages as: "Everything that comes forth from the study of the way is the true human body. The entire world of the ten directions is nothing but the true human body. The coming and going of birth and death is the true human body."[41] In the nondual context of self and other, I might start with this body birthed by my mother, but when I appropriately apprehend interdependence, I come to understand that the entire earth, all that exists, as it unfolds moment to moment is my true body: all aspects of my "I" exist only because "that" exists, and thus *I* and *that* are nondually one. However, this does not erase the body-mind that goes by my name. If that were the case, then we would fall into the mistake of taking one half of the duality of self and other (entire earth/unity of reality) as the one true thing. Instead, we must come to see the way in which this body-mind (this lump of red flesh, as Dōgen likes to say) is interdependent with the rest of the world, each making the other what they are through the reciprocating interactions of causes and conditions. Thus, the following boat metaphor from Dōgen:

Quietly think over whether birth [life] and all things that arise

together with birth are inseparable or not. . . . Birth is just like
riding in a boat. You raise the sails and you steer. Although you
maneuver the sail and the pole, the boat gives you a ride, and
without the boat you couldn't ride. But you ride in the boat,
and your riding makes the boat what it is. . . . Thus, you make
birth what it is, you make birth your birth. When you ride in a
boat, your body, mind, and environs together are the undivided
activity of the boat. The entire earth and the entire sky are both
the undivided activity of the boat.[42]

Riding in the boat, you make the boat a boat but the boat makes you a
"boater"—hence, reciprocal conditioning and the dynamic inseparableness
of you and the boat at any given moment. At the time of sailing the
boat—i.e., at any given moment, as the boat is metaphor—there is, from
your perspective, nothing but the world of the boat, the world of this given
moment, with all of its interpenetrating particulars.

As we usually take "you" to be a different self from "me," we also
usually take ourselves to be the *same* selves over time, to persist through
time. Counter to this, Dōgen employs another boat analogy; this time, we
are to note that if we look at the world, it seems as if it, like the shore seen
from a boat, is what changes/moves, while we stay the same/unmoving. Yet,
if we look at ourselves, we'll see that we *are* changing/moving: "If he turns
back within himself, making all his daily deeds immediately and directly
his own, the reason all things have no selfhood becomes clear to him."[43]
It is all too easy to see the transitoriness of the world around us but fail
to see the transitoriness of ourselves. After all, we seem to feel a sense of
continuity over time. We remember doing and thinking and saying, and so
forth, a large variety of things, not only from yesterday but from last year
and many years before that. This is like being on the boat with the shore
passing us/the boat by. Yet, if we pay attention, cultivating and practicing
awareness, in zazen and daily life, we see that we are "moving."

Again, for Dōgen, just as with interdependence, impermanence does not
flatfootedly negate your existence over time. He expresses this forcefully in
his firewood analogy,[44] where he makes clear the nonduality of each moment
in time. Let's say you practice diligently and one day realize the truth of
Dōgen's Zen and you thereby actualize enlightenment in your realization.
In doing so, the fire of your desires burns itself out in the peace of your
realization. One way to think of this story is that there was a time when
you were not enlightened and a later time in which you became enlight-

ened. Here, we have a kind of duality of *unenlightened* self-at-one-time and *enlightened* self-at-a-later-time and these "two" selves are really one, really numerically identical. Dōgen finds this way of understanding things to be deeply deluded. The problem he has here is with the idea of subsequent, discrete moments simply following each other (in time), and, in particular, ones where the selfsame person persists across them.

Yet, it is not that he wants to say that there is *no* sameness over time. Again, we must understand each moment's nonduality. At the moment of firewood, there is nothing but firewood, which is firmly located in what Dōgen calls its *dharma-position* [*hōi* 法位][45] and cut off from everything else that is not it. Each moment, each particular, is all that exists—there is no before or after to speak of at any given moment. Nevertheless, there is a before and after rooted in the moment of the firewood. After all, the firewood is what it is only interdependently with the rest of the world: the sun, the soil, the air, the water, that gave rise to the tree that became the wood; there is the ash of "the future." Now, there is nothing but the firewood, it is cut off from all else; yet, because of emptiness, the firewood is nondual with the before (the tree, etc.) and after (the ash, etc.). Similarly, the *you* that is the unenlightened self-at-one-time and enlightened self-at-a-later-time is that particular *you* because at each given moment, that moment is both cutoff from all other moments while being interdependent with them "over time." Therefore, in emptiness, we have a kind of temporal unity of selves *over time*.

Given the above, one way, then, to express a fundamental implication for Dōgen is that in practice, one forgets, that is, one lets go of, one's separable, limited self-concern and in the realized context of emptiness, one's (small-) self-concern is now concern for the self that is the entire world, entire being. And in the reconstructed understanding of each moment and each particular, one realizes that the entire world is engaged by engaging *this* moment and *this* particular, whether *this* cup of coffee or *this* dog, or *this* political problem. Thus, to neglect this moment and its particulars is to neglect all being. It is in this way that we are *the nondual unity of all particulars*; and we avoid falling into either extreme in our understanding of particularity and unity.

We are now in a position to understand how it is, in Dōgen's thorough application of emptiness, that when we authentically practice and realize emptiness, it is not only a denial, a "no" (deconstruction), of individuality or self. Rather, it is simultaneously a complete affirmation, a "yes" (reconstruction), of each particular, each moment, such that each moment, each particular, "pops out" as the only particular, the only moment, there is, yet "containing" all else—this is Buddha-nature; this is time; this is existence; this is you; this is me. In this way, the ordinary becomes extra-ordinary, the familiar becomes new and unfamiliar in its radical temporality of denial and affirmation, moment to moment.[46]

Language and Enlightenment

To fully appreciate Dōgen's views on language,[47] it is important to understand the view(s) that one usually finds in Buddhism, particularly Mahāyāna Buddhism and other forms of Zen. For example, Mario D'Amato notes that "a dominant theme in Mahāyāna soteriological thought is that language and conceptualization are at the root of the problem with sentient existence."[48] Further, discussing what he takes to be the third of three ways one may describe something, Garma C. C. Chang writes that direct pointing, as with a finger, *without employing concepts*, is "the best and in fact the only genuine way to describe Emptiness. . . . It is this approach which is frequently applied in Zen Buddhism."[49] And not only are concepts supposedly unnecessary for describing/pointing to emptiness, but concepts and explanations are taken to actually occlude how things really are—most notably the reality of emptiness (*śūnyatā*). The latter is a point that Thomas Kasulis emphasizes numerous times in his *Zen Action, Zen Person*. For example, he writes, "Concepts are *saṃvṛti*; they literally 'cover' or 'obstruct' the way things are actually experienced."[50] Further: "The Zen Buddhist view is that intellectualizations, concepts, even language itself are inadequate for expressing our experience as it is experienced."[51] As Toru Funaki puts it, "In Zen Buddhism . . . the practitioner aims at reaching an absolute stage where language is of no import as that stage lies beyond linguistic understanding."[52]

Let's be clear about what is at issue in these claims. First, we have the idea that language lies at the root of suffering, presumably because its use creates a reification of emptiness, that is to say, it seems to make "solid" that which is in truth empty; put differently, since language creates the illusion of individual and persisting objects, it allows for the projection of "selves" onto the world, and, thus, is a precondition of craving. Second, language/concepts are not simply unnecessary for "pointing to," for example, emptiness, but the only genuine way to do so is without language/concepts. Third, language/concepts occlude reality as it really is. Fourth, language is inadequate to describe reality as we actually experience it. Fifth, there is a stage of understanding that is nonlinguistic/nonconceptual, and that is the "place" where you want to get to with your practice—*prajñā* (wisdom) is nonlinguistic.

It is certainly true that our use of language and concepts[53] can be problematic. Our use of noun words, for example, can give the impression that the world is populated by individual, persisting things—cats, cars, countries, donuts—when, in fact, anything we call a cat is a complex, dynamic process that we label "cat" as a helpful way to engage reality over time. Along these lines, we discriminate between things, preferencing one thing over another by using language to divide the world into kinds of things, some we like, some we don't. Further, we often get caught up in the future with our plans that we formulate in language; we get caught up in the past, using language to help form a picture of what (we take to have) happened. We use language to conceptualize one thing as a means to another, thereby defiling the nonduality of the moment. Indeed, we could go on and on in regard to all of the ways we are deluded through language.

However, we have already seen a number of things from Dōgen that challenge the above five points raised against language. Going in reverse order, first, for Dōgen, *prajñā*/wisdom, enlightenment, is not a matter of achieving some special mental state, but rather is the continuous practice of letting go with full presence. And as he makes clear in his "Instructions for the Tenzo,"[54] there is enlightened activity that employs concepts and makes discriminations.

Second, while the uninitiated may not be able to know what exactly it is like to drink coffee simply by my describing it, that does not mean that such a description cannot help prepare one for what to look for when first drinking coffee. The same applies to describing aspects of enlightened practice. Further, one of the things Dōgen is often doing in the writings he presents to monks and lay followers is not simply describing but rather acting like a kind of cheerleader. He admonishes, encourages, gives warnings, and presses question after question.

Third, while it is possible that language can function to occlude the nature of reality, namely, its emptiness, words do not have to do so. For one thing, as we have done here, we can use words to describe the true nature of reality (according to Zen) in all of its emptiness. Further, we can have at least two different attitudes toward a thing and the word we use to pick it out. That is, when I use "cat" to refer to one of the furry animals in our home, I can have either of the following two attitudes: (1) this "cat" is a separate, persisting thing or (2) this "cat" is a dynamic, interdependent, transitory process. Using "cat" does not force me to comport myself along the lines of (1). I can use "cat" to keep track of this collection of *skandhas* over time and to discriminate between it and the dog without that meaning I've deludedly hypostatized a separate, persisting thing.

Fourth, it is not clear what it would mean to point to emptiness outside a linguistic/philosophical/cultural context. The example that Chang appeals to is that of a Zen master "enlightening" a student by asking him to kneel down and then unexpectedly kicking him in the chest. Suddenly the student has a breakthrough (*kenshō*) type experience and is awakened to the true nature of reality (emptiness/Buddha-nature).[55] While these issues are complex and we cannot fully address them here, let's simply note that outside the broader context of Buddhism, its teachings, and so on, and the more specific context of a Zen master and disciple, all of which are through and through a complex linguistic/philosophical/cultural context (as Dōgen would say, with many entwined vines), we've no reason to think a kick to the chest would give rise to such an experience of awakening. A person with no knowledge of Buddhism and Zen could not be led to understand all that it is about simply by nonlinguistic means, much less be led to an experience of awakening by a kick to the chest.

Fifth, we have already seen how language can, indeed, be a contributing factor to delusion and suffering. However, we have also seen how it need not be. And, in fact, Dōgen is often taken to be *the one* to show how language can be most productively harnessed to encourage authentic practice. As with everything else for Dōgen, we must apply both the deconstructive and reconstructive aspects of emptiness to language and concepts. Further, it is, actually, quite possible that something Dōgen writes might be all you need to have a deep realization into a point central to practice.

Consider, as a kind of summary note on the above five points about the importance of language for enlightened practice, Kim: "Enlightenment, from Dōgen's perspective, consists of clarifying and penetrating one's muddled discriminative thought in and through our language to attain clarity, depth, and precision in the discriminative thought itself. This is enlightenment or vision."[56]

The other main aspect of Dōgen and language to consider is his treatment of kōans. Kōans are often taken to be short enigmatic, if not incomprehensible, sayings, questions, or dialogues, often between Zen masters or masters and students. One way, often in Rinzai Zen, they are utilized is as objects on which to focus the practitioner's attention; their enigmatic/ nonsensical content is like a giant rock that the practitioner's conceptual thought crashes against, breaking apart, allowing the practitioner to have a *kenshō*-type experience of seeing things as they truly are: empty.

Dōgen, however, does not treat them this way in his writings. Many of his writings, particularly in the *Shōbōgenzō*, consist of extended commentary on kōans, treating them as perfectly understandable (at least to those with the proper understanding of the Dharma).[57] It is in these contexts that Dōgen expresses his understanding of the authentic Dharma by way of his creative and masterly use of language. Waddell and Abe nicely summarize a key aspect of Dōgen's writing. In their introductory comments to Dōgen's "Bussho" fascicle, which, as we've seen, is where he transforms "All sentient beings without exception have the Buddha-nature" into "entire being is the Buddha-nature," they write: "Perhaps the most striking feature of his treatment of the theme [of Buddha-nature] is the clear priority he gives to religious meaning over grammatical syntax, often reading the passages he quotes from various texts in ways that are, in strict grammatical terms, dubious at best. He does this to focus attention on what he feels are inadequacies in the traditional ways the texts are read and to rectify those inadequacies based on his own understanding."[58] What I want to emphasize is that one of the central things Dōgen is doing by appropriating and modifying the language in the kōans and sutra passages he treats is to make them, in a sense, new. That is, not only does he seek to do what Waddell and Abe suggest above, but he also seeks to make that which is familiar, *unfamiliar*, thereby *revitalizing* it, and in the process bring the listener/reader into a deeper realization of the Dharma.

Along these lines, I want to do something similar. However, for most Western students, particularly beginners, many of the kōans/passages Dōgen might use and comment on are not already familiar such that they can be *made new* and *revitalized* for the reader. Nonetheless, we can try to demonstrate Dōgen's method of commentary by using a short "kōan" that the reader is likely to be familiar with, namely, the nursery rhyme, "row, row, row your boat." While the nursery rhyme is obviously not an actual kōan, it has the character of kōans in many ways, and it has the further advantage of being familiar to contemporary English readers. I take it that it is familiar to the point of being unremarkable to the reader, thus making it ripe for reinterpretation and revitalization in the way Dōgen does with kōans that would have been familiar to his audience, as well.

What I would like the reader to do is to first study carefully all that we've discussed so far about Dōgen's Zen and then go on to read my attempt to recreate a Dōgen-like kōan commentary on the nursery rhyme, thereby demonstrating some typical moves Dōgen makes while also giving the reader a chance to make connections with what has been straightforwardly described above. Teachers may use the set of questions that follow the commentary to guide students in drawing connections with what they have learned about Dōgen's interpretive method and the practice of Sōtō Zen.

Dream Rowing / The Rowing of a Dream

A monk once asked a Master, "How should I understand the unity of practice and enlightenment and the reality of time?" The Master turned, walked away, and broke into a short song, "*Row, row, row your boat, gently down the stream, merrily, merrily, merrily, merrily, life is but a dream.*" The monk's mouth dropped open and then with tear-filled eyes he began to sing the same song.

You should enter the Buddha's eye, ceaselessly studying these words "row row row your boat." Consider, what is rowing? Consider, where is your boat? Does *merrily* exclude *non-merrily*? Who is the dream that rows the boat? Ask these questions and enumerable more until you have thoroughly mastered the truth of *row, row, row your boat.*

Is there ever a time that is not *row, row, row*? Is *row, row, row* not just Zen Master Pao-ch'e fanning himself? Does rowing not exhaust the activities of Buddhas and Patriarchs? If you say that you do not need to row because the current is swift and permanent, then you understand neither swiftness nor permanence—neither time nor impermanence. Where is your continuous practice if all is not *row, row, row*? *Row* such that you go *beyond rowing.*

Penetrate unceasingly *gently down the stream*. Do not mistakenly think this stream is a stream. Time does not simply flow. Each moment is all time, all being, *all being is time.* This we must practice diligently. Yet, what does it mean to practice being as time? It means to move *gently down the stream* with your rowing. But this *movement* is what we fail to understand. *Time does not rush* if you paddle faster; *time does not drag* if you hold the paddle against the water. Does *this* moment move anywhere?

How do we go *merrily, merrily, merrily, merrily*? Is *merrily* a boat full of laughter? At the time of neither liking nor disliking, is *merrily, merrily, merrily, merrily* not the same as crying, crying, crying, crying? Only fools who are ignorant of the authentic Buddha eye believe that *merrily* is nothing but merrily. What is the full range of merrily? Is it not simply *what comes thus*? Sitting facing the wall, letting the sky be the sky, whether cloudless or full of low, dark billows? The sun peeking through or the sun not seen for days? Is the full range of the sky's colors not *merrily, merrily, merrily, merrily*?

Seeing into the truth of *life is but a dream* requires plucking out the Buddha's eyeball and replacing your own with your own, as you replace your body with the true human body. It is *just this*. Penetrate unceasingly: In a dream are you not awake? Ordinary people view a dream as unreal and waking up as reality. Do not be so foolish! When you fall down in a dream, having tripped over the ground, do you not pick yourself up using the same ground? Is that ground not solid? Is it not a dream? Just remember: If *life* were not *but a dream* then there would be no awakening. Time is dreaming; dreaming is time. Thus, *life* cannot be *but a dream*.

Questions to Answer Regarding "Dōgen's": *Dream Rowing / The Rowing of a Dream*

1. What is the connection being made between "rowing" and the fanning of Zen Master Pao-ch'e who demonstrated the need for continuous practice by fanning himself even though the wind is everywhere?

2. In what ways are the boat "metaphors" and their meanings, as discussed in the section "Self and other and self and self-over-time," found in the commentary here on the "Row, row, row . . ."?

3. In what way is time not like a river? How does this relate to the question of self/selves?

4. How is the meaning of "gently down the stream" transformed in the commentary?

5. We might think that being enlightened makes everything joyful or "merry." However, how does the commentary transform this understanding of "merrily, merrily, merrily, merrily"?

6. In what, perhaps, negative sense is life called "but a dream" in the original nursery rhyme? How is this transformed in the context of this "Dōgen-esque" commentary?

7. What does it mean to say that when one falls because of the ground it is the ground that one must use to pick oneself up? What is the point of talking about dream ground?

8. In what ways do we see the nonduality of dream and non-dream (solidity) in the commentary?

9. What other connections can you make between the "Row, row, row . . ." piece and other aspects of Dōgen's Zen?

Notes

1. Generally speaking, kōans are enigmatic sayings formulated by master practitioners of Chan/Zen. Their nature and use will be discussed further below.

2. "Chan" refers to the Chinese school that is the source of Japanese Zen.

3. Steven Heine, "Dōgen on the Language of Creative Textual Hermeneutics," in *The Oxford Handbook of Japanese Philosophy*, ed. B. W. Davis (New York: Oxford University Press, 2020), 215.

4. Dōgen, *Treasury of the True Dharma Eye: Zen Master Dōgen's Shobo Genzo*. Ed. K. Tanahashi (Boston: Shambhala, 2012), 538.

5. Hee-Jin Kim, *Eihei Dōgen: Mystical Realist* (Boston: Wisdom, 2004), 14.

6. Kim, *Eihei Dōgen*, 14.

7. Kim, *Eihei Dōgen*, 19.

8. Steven Heine, *From Chinese Chan to Japanese Zen: A Remarkable Century of Transmission and Transformation* (New York: Oxford University Press, 2018), 82.

9. Kim, *Eihei Dōgen*, 24.

10. Kim, *Eihei Dōgen*, 22.

11. Kim, *Eihei Dōgen*, 23.

12. Quoted in Kim, *Eihei Dōgen*, 36.

13. These issues are well dealt with in Steven Heine, *Did Dōgen Go to China?: What He Wrote and When He Wrote It* (New York: Oxford University Press, 2006)—a highly recommended text.

14. Dōgen, *Treasury of the True Dharma Eye*, lii–liii.

15. Nishiari Bokusan, "Commentary on Dogen's Genjo Koan," in *Dōgen's Genjo Koan: Three Commentaries*, trans. S. M. Weitsman and K. Tanahashi (Berkeley: Counterpoint Press, 2011), 33.

16. Quoted in Hee-Jin Kim, *Dōgen on Meditation and Thinking: A Reflection on His View of Zen* (Albany: State University of New York Press, 2007), 67.

17. See Kim, *Dōgen on Meditation and Thinking*, 44ff.

18. See Kim, *Dōgen on Meditation and Thinking*, 92.

19. From "Bendōwa"; Quoted in Kim, *Dōgen on Meditation and Thinking*, 21.

20. See "Genjokoan" in Dōgen, *The Heart of Dōgen's Shōbōgenzō*, trans. N. Waddell and M. Abe (Albany: State University of New York Press, 2002), 40.

21. Dōgen, *The Heart of Dōgen's Shōbōgenzō*, 46.

22. See "Genjokoan" in Dōgen, *The Heart of Dōgen's Shōbōgenzō*, 44. "Pao-ch'e" in the Wade Giles system; "Baoche" in Pinyin.

23. See "Genjokoan" in Dōgen, *The Heart of Dōgen's Shōbōgenzō*. See also Kim, *Dōgen on Meditation and Thinking*, ch. 2, for example.

24. Thich Nhat Hanh has a lovely discussion of this in *The Heart of Understanding: Commentaries on the Prajnaparamita Heart Sutra* (Berkeley: Parallax Press, 1988), 3.

25. See "Painting of a Rice Cake," in Dōgen, *Treasury of the True Dharma Eye*.

26. "Bendowa" quoted in Kim, *Dōgen on Meditation and Thinking*, 23.

27. Dōgen, *The Heart of Dōgen's Shōbōgenzō*, 60 and 61.

28. Kosho Uchiyama and Shohaku Okumura, *The Zen Teaching of Homeless Kodo* (Boston: Wisdom, 2014), 138.

29. Philip Kapleau, *The Three Pillars of Zen: 25th Anniversary Edition* (New York: Anchor Books Doubleday, 1989), 385.

30. Kapleau, *The Three Pillars of Zen*, 377.

31. Kapleau, *The Three Pillars of Zen*, 369.

32. Dōgen, *The Heart of Dōgen's Shōbōgenzō*, 4.

33. Dōgen, *The Heart of Dōgen's Shōbōgenzō*, 5.

34. See Uchiyama Roshi's lovely discussion of these issues in Kosho Uchiyama and Shohaku Okumura, *Deepest Practice, Deepest Wisdom: Three Fascicles from Shōbōgenzō with Commentaries*, trans. D. T. Wright and S. Okumura (Somerville: Wisdom, 2018), 103–104.

35. Dōgen, *The Heart of Dōgen's Shōbōgenzō*, 3.

36. Uchiyama and Okumura, *Deepest Practice, Deepest Wisdom*, 123–24.

37. Shohaku Okumura, *The Mountains and Waters Sūtra: A Practitioner's Guide to Dōgen's "Sansuikyo"* (Somerville: Wisdom, 2018), 139.

38. See George Wrisley, "The Role of Compassion in Actualizing Dōgen's Zen," *Japan Studies Review* XXIV (2020): 111–36. This work takes up the role of compassion in actualizing Dōgen's Zen, and in doing so draws the connections between "just sitting" and compassion.

39. Dōgen, *Dōgen's Extensive Record: A Translation of the Eihei Kōroku*, trans. T. D. Leighton and S. Okumura, ed. T. D. Leighton (Boston: Wisdom, 2010), Vol. 1, no. 32, 101.

40. Dōgen, *Treasury of the True Dharma Eye*, "Only a Buddha and a Buddha."

41. Dōgen, *Treasury of the True Dharma Eye*, "Body and Mind Study the Way."

42. Dōgen, *Treasury of the True Dharma Eye*, "Zenki."

43. Dōgen, *The Heart of Dōgen's Shōbōgenzō*, "Genjokoan," 42.

44. See Dōgen, *The Heart of Dōgen's Shōbōgenzō*, "Genjokoan."

45. Hee-Jin Kim, "Existence/Time as the Way of Ascesis: An Analysis of the Basic Structure of Dōgen's Thought," *The Eastern Buddhist*, New Series 11, no. 2 (1978): 43–73.

46. For further interesting and helpful discussions of issues concerning (Zen) Buddhism and the self, see Joan Stambaugh, *The Formless Self* (Albany: State University of New York Press, 1999); Leah Kalmanson, "Buddhism and bell hooks: Liberatory Aesthetics and the Radical Subjectivity of No-Self," *Hypatia* 27, no. 4 (2012), 810–27; Erin McCarthy, "The Embodied Ethical Self: A Japanese and Feminist Account of Nondual Subjectivity," in *Asian and Feminist Philosophies in Dialogue*, ed., J. McWeeny and A. Butnor (New York: Columbia University Press, 2014), 203–22; and Hsiao-Lan Hu, "*Kamma*, No-Self, and Social Construction: The Middle Way Between Determinism and Free Will," in *Asian and Feminist Philosophies in Dialogue*,ed., J. McWeeny and A. Butnor (New York: Columbia University Press, 2014), 37–56.

47. The following discussion is merely supplemental to the far greater discussion of Dōgen and language by others. See, for example, Kim, *Dōgen on Meditation and Thinking*, ch. 4, and Heine, "Dōgen on the Language of Creative Textual Hermeneutics."

48. Mario D'Amato, "Why the Buddha Never Uttered a Word," in *Pointing at the Moon: Buddhism, Logic, Analytic Philosophy*, ed. M. D'Amato, J. L. Garfield, and T. J. Tillemans (Oxford: Oxford University Press, 2009), 41–42.

49. G. C. C. Chang, *The Buddhist Teaching of Totality: The Philosophy of Hwa Yen Buddhism* (University Park: The Pennsylvania State University Press, 1971), 63.

50. T. P. Kasulis, *Zen Action, Zen Person* (Honolulu: The University Press of Hawai'i, 1981), 23.

51. Kasulis, 55.

52. Toru Funaki, "The Notion of the 'Words that Speak the Truth' in Merleau-Ponty and Shinran," in *Merleau-Ponty and Buddhism*, ed. J. Y. Park and G. Kopf, 113–32 (Lanham, MD: Rowman and Littlefield, 2009).

53. And from now on I will write simply of language and take that to include concepts; while there might be concepts that we use that do not have words associated with them, I am going to simply fold that possibility into my discussion of language.

54. In Dōgen, *Dōgen's Pure Standards for the Zen Community: A Translation of Eihei Shingi*, trans. Taigen Daniel Leighton and Shohaku Okumura (Albany: State University of New York Press, 1996).

55. G. C. C. Chang, *The Buddhist Teaching of Totality: The Philosophy of Hwa Yen Buddhism* (University Park: The Pennsylvania State University Press, 1971), 63.

56. Kim, *Dōgen on Meditation and Thinking*, 63.

57. See Dōgen's "The Mountains and Waters Sutra" (for example, in Okumura, *The Mountains and Waters Sūtra*) for an explicit repudiation of the view that kōans have nonsensical "content."

58. Dōgen, *The Heart of Dōgen's Shōbōgenzō*, 59.

Bibliography

Bokusan, Nishiari. "Commentary on Dogen's Genjo Koan." In *Dōgen's Genjo Koan: Three Commentaries*. Translated by S. M. Weitsman and K. Tanahashi. Berkeley: Counterpoint Press, 2011.

Chang, G. C. C. *The Buddhist Teaching of Totality: The Philosophy of Hwa Yen Buddhism*. University Park: The Pennsylvania State University Press, 1971.

D'Amato, Mario. "Why the Buddha Never Uttered a Word." In *Pointing at the Moon: Buddhism, Logic, Analytic Philosophy*, edited by M. D'Amato, J. L. Garfield, and T. J. Tillemans, 41–56. Oxford: Oxford University Press, 2009.

Dōgen. *Dōgen's Pure Standards for the Zen Community: A Translation of Eihei Shingi*. Translated by Taigen Daniel Leighton and Shohaku Okumura. Albany: State University of New York Press, 1996.

———. *The Heart of Dōgen's Shōbōgenzō*. Translated by N. Waddell and M. Abe. Albany: State University of New York Press, 2002.

———. *Dōgen's Extensive Record: A Translation of the Eihei Kōroku*. Translated by T. D. Leighton and S. Okumura. Edited by T. D. Leighton. Boston: Wisdom, 2010.

———. *Treasury of the True Dharma Eye: Zen Master Dōgen's Shobo Genzo*. Edited by K. Tanahashi. Boston: Shambhala, 2012.

Funaki, Toru. "The Notion of the 'Words that Speak the Truth' in Merleau-Ponty and Shinran." In *Merleau-Ponty and Buddhism*, edited by J. Y. Park and G. Kopf, 113–32. Lanham, MD: Rowman and Littlefield, 2009.

Heine, Steven. *Did Dōgen Go to China?: What He Wrote and When He Wrote It*. New York: Oxford University Press, 2006.

———. *From Chinese Chan to Japanese Zen: A Remarkable Century of Transmission and Transformation*. New York: Oxford University Press, 2018.

———. "Dōgen on the Language of Creative Textual Hermeneutics." In *The Oxford Handbook of Japanese Philosophy*, edited by B. W. Davis, 215–29. New York: Oxford University Press, 2020.

Hu, Hsiao-Lan. "*Kamma*, No-Self, and Social Construction: The Middle Way Between Determinism and Free Will." In *Asian and Feminist Philosophies in Dialogue*, edited by J. McWeeny and A. Butnor, 37–56. New York: Columbia University Press, 2014.

Kalmanson, Leah. "Buddhism and bell hooks: Liberatory Aesthetics and the Radical Subjectivity of No-Self." *Hypatia* 27, no. 4 (2012). 810–27.

Kapleau, Philip. *The Three Pillars of Zen: 25th Anniversary Edition*. New York: Anchor Books Doubleday, 1989.

Kasulis, T. P. *Zen Action, Zen Person*. Honolulu: The University Press of Hawai'i, 1981.

Kim, Hee-Jin. "Existence/Time as the Way of Ascesis: An Analysis of the Basic Structure of Dōgen's Thought." *The Eastern Buddhist*. New Series 11, no. 2 (1978): 43–73.

———. *Eihei Dōgen: Mystical Realist*. Boston: Wisdom, 2004.

———. *Dōgen on Meditation and Thinking: A Reflection on His View of Zen.* Albany: State University of New York Press, 2007.

Leighton, Taigen Dan. *Faces of Compassion: Classic Bodhisattva Archetypes and Their Modern Expression: An Introduction to Mahayana Buddhism.* Somerville, MA: Wisdom, 2012.

McCarthy, Erin. "The Embodied Ethical Self: A Japanese and Feminist Account of Nondual Subjectivity." In *Asian and Feminist Philosophies in Dialogue*, edited by J. McWeeny and A. Butnor, 203–22. New York: Columbia University Press, 2014.

Nhat Hanh, Thich. *The Heart of Understanding: Commentaries on the Prajnaparamita Heart Sutra.* Berkeley: Parallax Press, 1988.

Okumura, Shohaku. *Realizing Genjōkōan: The Key to Dōgens Shōbōgenzō.* Boston: Wisdom, 2010.

———. *The Mountains and Waters Sūtra: A Practitioner's Guide to Dōgen's "Sansuikyo."* Somerville, MA: Wisdom, 2018.

Stambaugh, Joan. *The Formless Self.* Albany: State University of New York Press, 1999.

Uchiyama, Kosho, and Shohaku Okumura. *The Zen Teaching of Homeless Kodo.* Boston: Wisdom, 2014.

———. *Deepest Practice, Deepest Wisdom: Three Fascicles from Shōbōgenzō with Commentaries.* Translated by D. T. Wright and S. Okumura. Somerville: Wisdom, 2018.

Wrisley, George. "The Nietzschean Bodhisattva—Passionately Navigating Indeterminacy." In *The Significance of Indeterminacy: Perspectives from Asian and Continental Philosophy*, edited by Robert H. Scott and Gregory Moss, 309–29. New York: Routledge, 2019.

———. "The Role of Compassion in Actualizing Dōgen's Zen." *Japan Studies Review* XXIV (2020): 111–36.

Part 2

East Asian Buddhisms and the Humanities

Ethics, Art, and Politics

Chapter 6

The Finger that Points to the Earth

East Asian Buddhism as a Conceptual Resource for Environmental Philosophy

James McRae

Introduction: Life in the Unsatisfactory Anthropocene

The First Noble Truth of Buddhism tells us that all life is profoundly unsatisfactory (Pli. *dukkha*). This is particularly true in the Anthropocene, which is the proposed name for the current geologic epoch that spans the period in which human beings have reshaped the planet.[1] This change has not always been for the best. We are currently in the midst of an unprecedented environmental crisis that threatens to make the planet unlivable for human beings, which would bring the Anthropocene to a screeching halt. The environmental degradation characteristic of this era comes as the result of our worldview, the philosophical presuppositions that guide our lives. If we want to survive the Anthropocene, we need to reconceptualize our worldview.

The purpose of this paper is to give an overview of how Buddhist environmental ethics can reshape our worldview. The first section examines our current environmental crisis and the effects that environmental degradation can have on economic and political stability. The next section uses Buddhist philosophy to criticize the consumerist worldview that has caused this environmental degradation, and offers an alternative worldview grounded in the concept of symbiosis (*kyōsei/tomoiki*). The third section argues that Buddhism is not an anthropocentric ("human-centered") ethic, but rather an ecocentric ethic that recognizes the intrinsic value of human beings, nonhuman organisms, and even the inorganic components of the natural world. The final section explains how East Asian Buddhism can be understood as a type of environmental virtue ethics. Ultimately, East Asian Buddhism is a valuable conceptual resource for environmental ethics because it forces us to critique many of the foundational assumptions that we have taken for granted, such as consumerism and anthropocentrism, and it encourages us to cultivate intellectual and moral virtues that promote a flourishing existence.

Our Current Environmental Crisis

The Earth is facing the worst environmental crisis in human history due to climate change. Since the Industrial Revolution, human beings have utilized fossil fuels such as coal and oil as their main energy sources. Burning these fuels releases greenhouse gases such as carbon dioxide into the atmosphere, where they inhibit the radiation of infrared energy (heat) into space. Over time, this has led to the gradual increase of the average temperature of the planet: since the late nineteenth century, the Earth's average surface temperature has risen by one degree Celsius, and it is expected to rise by another 0.5 degrees by as early as 2030.[2] (Note that this refers to the *average* temperature of *Earth's* climate, so just because we have cold weather in some places does not mean that the planet as a whole is not heating up.) The majority of this temperature change has happened over the last thirty-five years, with the six warmest years on record (as of 2022) taking place from 2014–19.[3] There is a near-universal consensus among scholars publishing in peer-reviewed scientific journals, where 97 percent of the articles argue that climate change is anthropogenic (caused by human beings).[4] This temperature increase, known as global warming, will cause significant long-term changes to climate systems, including sea-level rise due to melting polar ice, temperature extremes in inhabited regions, significant precipitation changes (droughts or flooding, depending on the region), species extinction, food and water shortages, and economic growth. Human beings are responsible for climate change, but we also have the ability to minimize its effects. The IPCC recommends that limiting global warming to a total increase of 1.5 degrees Celsius will significantly minimize climate change compared to an increase of 2 degrees or more.[5]

Climate change poses a particularly salient threat in terms of environmental security, which refers to the ways that national security issues are affected by ecosystem sustainability and the demands placed upon the natural world by human populations. Our environmental impact can lead to negative socioeconomic effects, which in turn can promote violent conflict. The environmental impact of human beings can be described by the equation I = PAT: environmental impact (I) is a function of population (P), affluence (A), and technology (T).[6] Our impact upon the environment is affected by our population (how many people are using resources), affluence (how many resources a person expects to use to meet a certain standard of living), and technology (which can be clean, like wind turbines and solar power, or polluting, like coal or oil). When large populations of consumerism-driven human beings use polluting technology, it creates negative environmental impacts such as global warming, ozone depletion, acid rain, deforestation, land degradation, water shortages, and overfishing. These impacts produce significant socioeconomic consequences, including decreased agricultural production, economic decline, population displacement (environmental refugees), and the disruption of social relations (due to group identity conflicts). At this point, societies can either adapt to these changes by limiting environmentally irresponsible activities (changing individual habits, cultural norms, laws, and policies), or they can fail to adapt by maintaining the status quo. Successful adaptation promotes sociopolitical stability, while unsuccessful adaptation typically leads to violent conflict.[7] Thus, what is at stake with climate change is not just the disruption of our natural environment, but also the social and political systems that we depend upon for peace and order.

Buddhism offers a solution to this problem on three different levels. First, it rejects consumerism, which is the main force that drives our negative environmental impact. Second, it rejects anthropocentrism—the idea that only human beings have moral worth—in favor of an ethic that values nonhuman animals and the natural environment. Finally, Buddhism endorses an environmental virtue ethic that encourages the good habits (virtues) that promote environmental sustainability and discourages the bad habits (vices) that interfere with it. The following sections investigate these themes in detail to demonstrate how Buddhist philosophy can help to minimize our environmental impact and help us to reconceptualize the way that we treat the natural world.

Against Consumerism

As the previous section demonstrated, our environmental impact is heavily influenced by our affluence, the standard of living that we expect. If

I commute to work by myself in a gas-guzzling sports car, I will have a greater environmental impact than if I carpool in a fuel-efficient vehicle, utilize public transportation, or walk. Exotic foods imported from all over the globe consume more fossil fuels than locally grown food. Heating my overly large home to seventy-two degrees Fahrenheit in the middle of winter will consume more electricity from the coal-fired power plant than if I lived in a more modest home heated to sixty-six degrees and wore a sweater (not to mention the benefits of replacing that coal-fired plant with wind turbines or solar energy). Contemporary American culture emphasizes *consumerism*, which is the obsession with the acquisition of consumer goods. This phenomenon is not just confined to the United States, but is common in many industrialized nations (at least in part due to the influence of American culture).

John de Graaf, David Wann, and Thomas H. Naylor have dubbed this malaise "affluenza," which they define as "a painful, contagious, socially transmitted condition of overload, debt, anxiety, and waste resulting from the dogged pursuit of more."[8] Americans are "addicted to stuff" and our obsession with acquisition is ruining both our lives and our environment. Since the late '90s, more Americans have declared bankruptcy than have graduated from college. Americans feel compelled to work constantly to pay for consumer goods, but the acquisition of material objects does little to bring actual happiness. On the contrary, consumerism leads to stress, exhaustion, and debt while disrupting interpersonal relationships. We work jobs we don't enjoy so that we can spend money we don't have on stuff we don't need to impress people we don't really like. For many Americans, affluenza produces a profound sense of ennui, existential boredom due to the meaninglessness of one's existence.[9]

Our obsession with consumerism has serious consequences for the environment. The level of affluence to which most Americans have become accustomed has to be supported by an enormous quantity of natural resources such as petroleum, coal, metals, water, trees, fish, and farmland. Most of our easily extracted resources have been used up, and getting at the remaining coal, oil, and precious metals is expensive, dangerous, and polluting (e.g., consider the Deepwater Horizon oil rig or the Kennecott Copper Mine disasters). Many of our waterways are polluted with chemicals, agricultural runoff, sewage, and plastic waste. Fish populations have been severely depleted. Our demand for arable farmland and timber has led to deforestation and widespread species extinction. The average world citizen uses 30 percent more resources than the earth can sustainably provide. If the entire world were to use resources at the same rate as the United States, we would need five more planets to sustain us.[10]

Buddhist philosophy is a helpful treatment for affluenza because it rejects consumerism. The foundation of Buddhist thought is the Four Noble Truths, which the historical Buddha Siddhartha Gautama revealed in his first sermon in Deer Park.[11] The First Noble Truth states that life is characterized by *duḥkha* (San.; Pli. *dukkha*), which can be translated as "suffering," "sorrow," "unsatisfactoriness," or "stress." As discussed above, consumerism leads to suffering because it creates both personal problems (exhaustion, debt, psychological distress, etc.) and environmental problems (pollution, climate change, species extinction, overpopulation, etc.). The Second Noble Truth argues that *duḥkha* arises due to craving. We passionately desire the things that we should not or cannot have because we are ignorantly attached to false ideals. We assume that personal wealth is the only measure of happiness, that the Earth has an unlimited amount of resources to sustain this wealth, and that our actions have no consequences for the planet. In contrast, Buddhism argues that there is no self (San. *anātman*; Pli. *anattā*), so egoistic acquisition of material goods is meaningless, that all things are impermanent (San. *anitya*; Pli. *anicca*), so natural resources can be used up, and that all things are interdependent (San. *pratitya-samutpāda,* Pli. *paṭicca-samuppāda*), so everything that we do affects the environment, which affects us in turn. The Third Noble Truth offers a solution to this problem: if we can eliminate the ignorant attachment to false ideals that causes us to crave, we can eliminate suffering. The Fourth Noble Truth describes how this may be accomplished by following the Eightfold Path, which involves the cultivation of wisdom (San. *prajñā*; Pli. *paññā*), right conduct (San./Pli. *śīla*), and discipline (San./Pli. *samādhi*). Only through self-discipline can one cultivate the intellectual and moral virtues needed to overcome ignorance, craving, and suffering.[12]

The rejection of consumerism does not entail a rejection of capitalism, but we do need to rethink the way in which we practice capitalism. One of the most important conceptual resources for contemporary environmental ethics and business ethics is the concept of *kyōsei,* or "symbiosis." The word *kyōsei* is composed of two Japanese characters: 共 (*tomo* or *kyō,* "together") and 生 (*ikiru* or *sei,* "life") and literally means "living together." In ethics, *kyōsei* refers to the idea of living and working together in a mutually beneficial manner that promotes a harmonious coexistence.[13] This idea has roots in multiple different Japanese traditions, one of the most important of which is Buddhism. The Japanese characters for *kyōsei* 共生 can also be read as "*tomoiki*,"[14] and it is the latter pronunciation that appears in twentieth-century Buddhist thought. What follows is a brief intellectual history of the development of *kyōsei* as a concept in science, Buddhist philosophy, and applied ethics.

The term *kyōsei* was first used in reference to the concept of symbiosis in biological science. In 1879, Anton de Bary coined the term *symbiosis* to refer to the ways that different species live together in nature.[15] There are six different types of symbiosis:

- *Competition*: Organisms from different species fight over limited resources, which causes harm to these creatures. For example, the green anole, a lizard indigenous to Florida, competes with the invasive Cuban brown anole for food and habitat.

- *Amensalism*: One organism harms the other without being harmed itself. A black walnut tree exudes a toxin from its roots that prevents plant growth around the base of the tree.

- *Agonism* (sometimes called *antagonism*): One organism is benefited by the relationship while the other is harmed. Fleas use dogs as a food source, which causes the latter animal to suffer.

- *Neutralism*: Organisms from two species live in the same environment, but neither harm nor benefit one another (e.g., trout and rabbit might spend their lives only a few dozen yards away from one another, but never interact).

- *Commensalism*: One organism benefits from the relationship while the other is unaffected. Cows stir up insects as they graze, which are eaten by the cattle egret, a bird that harmlessly follows the herd.

- *Mutualism*: Both organisms benefit from the relationship. Clown fish live among the tentacles of sea anemones. The fish, which are immune to the anemones' sting, get a home with a built-in security system in exchange for serving as custodians that keep the anemone clean.[16]

The term *kyōsei* first appeared in Japan in an 1888 article by Miyoshi Manabu in *The Journal of Japanese Botany*, where it was used to translate "symbiosis" in reference to lichen (an organism arising from the mutualistic relationship between algae and fungi).[17] It was not until the twentieth century that *kyōsei* took on a second, ethical meaning.

In 1922, the Pure Land Buddhist priest Benkyō Shiio used the term *tomoiki* to refer to the idea of "living together." Shiio did not draw this concept directly from biology. Rather, he was inspired by phrases in the fifth-century Indian Buddhist monk Vasubandhu, the seventh-century Chinese Pure Land monk Shan-tao, and the tenth/eleventh-century Japanese Tendai monk Genshin that referred to "passing into the Pure Land together with all living beings." Shiio viewed rebirth in the Pure Land as an extension of living harmoniously in this world.[18] He argued that *tomoiki* is an extension of the Buddhist concept of interdependence (Jpn. *engi* 縁起; Pli. *pratītyasamutpāda*). Because human beings are fundamentally interconnected with all things, they affect (and are affected by) their environments with every action. However, Toshio Horiuchi argues that interdependence does not necessarily entail ethical obligations, since one can be causally related to something and still treat it inappropriately. He suggests that *tomoiki* is best grounded in the *Dīgha Nikāya's* four immeasurables of loving kindness, compassion, empathetic joy, and—most importantly for Horiuchi—equanimity. One who cultivates these traits will not cause unnecessary injury to living beings (or the resources upon which they depend) and will not fall victim to grasping or aversion.[19] These virtues are discussed in detail in the last section of this chapter.

Shiio's concept of *tomoiki* eventually made its way into the business world using the alternative pronunciation, *kyōsei*, taken from biology. In addition to his role as the chief abbot of Zōjōji Temple, Shiio was an educator: he founded Tōkai Middle School in Nagoya and taught at Waseda University and Taisho University (eventually becoming president of the latter). One of Shiio's students at Tōkai Middle School was Kisho Kurakawa, who went on in 1987 to write *The Concept of Symbiosis* (*Kyōsei no Shisō* 共生の 思想).[20] Kurakawa's book dealt primarily with architectural principles, but he nonetheless used *kyōsei* as a moral paradigm. The concept quickly bled over into business ethics. That same year, Canon Inc. chair Ryūzaburō Kaku applied *kyōsei* to corporate social responsibility, arguing that the concept encourages a business philosophy of "living and working together for the common good."[21] Though Kaku's understanding of symbiosis is drawn from multiple sources, including Japanese Confucian thought, he was also influenced by the Buddhist concept of *tomoiki*.[22] Kaku was one of the founders of the Caux Round Table (CRT) for Moral Capitalism, an international association of business and political leaders who work to promote ethical business practices. The CRT includes *kyōsei* as one of their Seven Point Principles for Business Conduct.[23] According to Kaku, symbiosis represents the idea that there should be a "harmony between profit and social justice" and corporations should cultivate synergistic relationships that maximize the good of all stakeholders.[24] In business ethics, this view is known as "stakeholder theory" and it stands in contrast to the more traditional approach known as "shareholder theory." Shareholder theory argues that managers have one—and only one—moral obligation: to maximize profits for those with a financial stake in the company (the shareholders). Stakeholder theory expands upon this narrow view of management to address the moral significance of all those affected by a corporation's actions: financiers, employees, suppliers, customers, and the communities in which the firm is located.[25] *Kyōsei* demands that we strive to maintain mutualistic relationships with these groups rather than parasitic (agonistic) relationships. In other words, in business, we should try to be more like clown fish and less like fleas.

Kyōsei and *tomoiki* were embraced by other branches of Buddhism outside of the Pure Land tradition. In the mid-1990s, Sōtō Zen began to emphasize a "harmonious coexistence with nature" (*shizen to no tomoiki* 自然との共生) and developed a Green Plan that involved minimizing desire and wasteful living. The Tendai tradition has embraced the idea of living in harmony (*kyōsei/tomoiki*) with all things, which is grounded in the idea that all things manifest buddha-nature. The Tendai "Light up One Corner" (一隅を照らす *ichigu wo terasu*) movement, which began in 1969, has embraced a "three practices" slogan that includes "life" (*inochi* 命), "service" (*hōshi* 奉仕), and "living in harmony" (*kyōsei* 共生). In 2011, in response to the Fukushima Daiichi nuclear reactor disaster, Rinzai Zen issued an antinuclear declaration with the goal of creating a harmonious society (*kyōsei shakai* 共生社会).[26] These are just a few examples of how *kyōsei* has influenced contemporary engaged Buddhism.

Kyōsei (*tomoiki*) has become a predominant moral paradigm for engaging applied ethics issues, both in and outside of the Buddhist world. If affluenza is caused by craving, then *kyōsei/tomoiki* might be the cure. Consumerism operates in a parasitic manner, using the natural environment, nonhuman animals, and human beings as nothing more than raw material for one's own personal satisfaction. Affluenza makes us indifferent to the suffering of others, so that our relationships are often agonistic, amensal, or competitive (i.e., at least one party gets hurt). *Kyōsei* encourages us to pursue relationships that are neutral, commensal, or mutualistic (where at least no harm is done and, ideally, all parties benefit). The success of symbiosis as a paradigm for international business ethics shows us that "going green" can have two meanings: we can simultaneously promote ecological and economic stability. Many people reject environmental concerns because going green is allegedly bad for the economy. *Kyōsei* proves otherwise.

Anthropocentrism, Biocentrism, and Ecocentrism

One of the key questions for environmental ethics is, "What has value?" Do only human beings matter ethically, or should we consider nonhuman animals, plants, and even nonliving things when making ethical decisions? This section investigates the extent to which Buddhism can be understood as an ecocentric ethical system: one that places value on the whole of nature.

Anthropocentric, or "human-centered," ethical systems argue that only humans have moral value.[27] According to this view, humans have unique abilities that give us, and us alone, rights: rationality, interests, self-awareness, language, goal-directed activity, etc.[28] Nonhuman animals may be used purely as means to the end of human satisfaction, though they should be treated humanely when possible. The more human-like an animal is, the more rights it might be granted, so cetaceans (like dolphins) and higher primates (like western lowland gorillas) might be treated better than mice or fish. Human beings might have responsibilities to one another concerning the natural world, but we have no direct responsibilities to nature. For example, we might limit deforestation to guarantee that we have resources for future generations of humans, but not because the forest or its inhabitants (such as the spotted owl) have any intrinsic value.[29] *Non*-anthropocentric environmental ethics fall into two categories: biocentric and ecocentric.

Biocentric, or "life-centered," ethical systems support the idea that nonhuman animals have comparable value to human beings. One of the most prominent biocentric theorists is the utilitarian Peter Singer, who argues that *sentience* (the ability to experience pleasure or pain) is the primary criterion for moral considerability. It is wrong to harm a human because of the suffering it causes. Compared to human beings, animals are equally capable of suffering and pleasure, and all suffering is equally bad, so we must acknowledge that animal suffering is morally problematic. The arbitrary exclusion of nonhuman animals from the sphere of moral consideration is *speciesism*, a type of human-chauvinism whereby we treat nonhuman animals badly simply because they are different (which, Singer argues, is wrong for the same reasons that sexism and racism are wrong). Eating meat (particularly from factory farming), hunting, wearing fur/leather, zoos, and conducting animal experimentation are morally wrong because they cause unnecessary suffering to nonhuman animals, who are just as sentient as human beings[30] The deontologist Tom Regan reaches similar conclusions for different reasons. He argues that it is wrong to harm human beings because we are each a "subject-of-a-life": we each have beliefs, desires, perception, memory, and a sense of the future, all of which give a human life value. Animals might not be able to articulate their values, but they nonetheless value their lives (as evidenced by their fight or flight reactions when threatened). While human beings are *moral agents* (free and rational beings capable of doing ethics), nonhuman animals are *moral patients* (like human babies, who cannot comprehend ethics, but are nonetheless valuable).[31] While Singer and Regan offer different perspectives on biocentric ethics, they agree that most nonhuman animals have value in much the same way that human beings have value.

Ecocentric ethical systems value not just human beings or nonhuman animals, but the entire ecosystem, including things such as plants, soils, mountains, and rivers. One of the best examples of ecocentric ethics is the land ethic, which was first articulated by environmental scientist and conservationist Aldo Leopold, and then later developed into a robust ethical system by philosopher J. Baird Callicott. Traditionally, human beings have acted as though they are conquerors of nature, treating all living and nonliving things that are not human as natural resources to be harvested. However, from a scientific perspective, there is nothing morally special about human beings; we simply have certain evolutionary adaptations that have enhanced our ability to survive and thrive. Leopold argues that we should not view ourselves as conquerors of the land, but rather as "plain members and citizens of the biotic community."[32] Organic bodies such as a human body have discernable parts that operate together to form a second-order whole. The ecosystem can be understood as a "third-order organic whole" that is "a unified system of integrally related parts."[33] The duties toward self-preservation (the maintenance of organic integrity) and noninterference that we endorse on the individual level can be extended to the biotic community. Leopold's summary maxim for the land ethic is, "A thing is right when it tends to preserve the integrity, stability, and beauty of the biotic community. It is wrong when it tends otherwise."[34] Leopold argues that over the history of human civilization, the boundaries of moral considerability have expanded: we have moved from valuing just ourselves (egoism) to include family, then community, then country, and then to all humankind. Leopold calls this the "ethical sequence": the progressive extension of value to all the groups to which one is interdependent. The sequence can be further extended to the biotic community because of the realization that the land itself is part of our community (which is a fact of ecology). Eventually, this will become part of the collective cultural consciousness once we have achieved "universal ecological literacy."[35]

Another ecocentric approach to environmental ethics can be found in deep ecology, which was founded by Arne Næss in 1973 and expanded by thinkers such as Bill Devall and George Sessions. Deep ecology argues that human beings must realize that they exist as part of an organic whole, which is grounded on an objective, biological consciousness rather than a subjective, anthropocentric consciousness. Anthropocentrism has produced technocrat/industrial societies that view human beings as separate from nature, which they are justified in dominating to serve their needs. By contrast, deep ecology endorses two ultimate norms: Self-realization and biocentric equality. The Western notion of the self—as an insulated ego striving for hedonistic gratification or individual salvation—is wrong. True self-cultivation occurs when we see beyond ego and identify with other people, other species, and the environment as a whole. A human being is a "self-in-Self": a particular individual (lowercase s self) contextually grounded in a greater organic whole (capital S Self). Biocentric equality refers to the idea that all things in the biosphere have an equal right to life and self-realization within a larger Self-realization. Granted, species will prey on one another, but this is the way nature functions. However, humans must consider themselves "plain citizens" of the biotic community rather than masters over all. Humans have vital needs that go beyond nourishment and shelter to include relationships and self-cultivation. Technocratic societies encourage false needs through consumerism. These two ultimate norms entail certain basic moral principles such as respecting the intrinsic value of all life, promoting the richness and diversity of life, pursuing only vital needs (rather than consumer desires), controlling population growth, limiting human interference, improving laws and policies, and emphasizing quality of life over affluence. Ultimately, we all have an obligation to act to protect the natural world.[36]

So, where does Buddhism fit into all these theories? At first glance, it might seem that Buddhism is inherently anthropocentric because it emphasizes the overcoming of *human* suffering. The Buddha's primary concern is not for whole ecosystems, but rather for the awakening of human beings. Because of this pragmatic emphasis upon soteriology, the Buddha does not develop a complex theory of nature. However, there are a number of core

Buddhist principles that conflict with anthropocentrism and resonate with an ecocentric perspective.[37]

First, Buddhism rejects the idea that human beings are in possession of a fundamental self that is separate from and superior to the rest of nature. As Buddhism moved from India into East Asia, it affirmed to a greater extent the value of the natural world.[38] One of the core principles of Buddhism is the doctrine of interdependent arising, which asserts that all things are causally interconnected. People affect their environment and are affected by it in turn. One does not have an essential "self"; one is instead part of an "extended web of interconnection."[39] David Hall and Roger Ames describe the traditional Chinese view of the person as the "focus-field self." Human beings are not individuals who are separate from their environment, but rather "radically situated as persons-in-context" who are defined by their relationships with other people and the natural world.[40] Environmental degradation is typically caused by the belief that human beings (as individuals or as a group) are separate from and superior to nature. The Buddhist doctrine of no-self rejects egoism (the idea that an individual is inherently better than others) and anthropocentrism (the idea that humans are intrinsically better than other species). Callicott argues that "desire plus self-consciousness equals egocentrism equals *dukkha*."[41] Our attachment to the notion of a self reinforces our desires and leads to suffering. Buddhism asserts that the term *self* is really just a useful linguistic handle to describe the temporary aggregate of matter and energy that is a human body. There is no fundamental "soul" that defines an individual. There is a self in the nominal sense, "but when we unravel it we are left with *mu*—no-thing; that is, nothing."[42] In Buddhism, all things are impermanent, including human beings and the planet. The concept of impermanence is important because environmental degradation is often the result of the mistaken notion that human beings cannot have negative effects on the environment; we think we cannot possibly influence the "natural cycle" of climate or wipe out entire species. Impermanence tells us that all things are ephemeral and can be destroyed, so we must care for them if we want them to survive. While change is inevitable, we can choose to be positive agents of change and shape the world productively rather than passively accepting our fates or acting in ways that promote suffering. Each of us must realize that we are not separate from or superior to other humans or nonhumans. Our actions affect—and are affected by—others, and we *can* actually destroy the environment . . . or preserve it.

The second reason that East-Asian Buddhism is ecocentric comes from the idea of "Buddha-nature." The original Indian Mahāyāna doctrine of Buddha-nature stated that all human beings have the potential for enlightenment: it is in our nature to be Buddhas, though we need training to awaken to this reality. This view was progressively expanded by Chinese Buddhist traditions, including Sānlùn, Fǎxiàng, and Tiāntāi, and the idea carried over as Buddhism moved into Korea and Japan. Buddha-nature was first extended to all sentient beings, including nonhuman animals, and later to plants as well. Japanese Shingon master Kūkai argued that even inanimate objects have Buddha-nature.[43] Zen master Dōgen went a step farther to argue that all things *are* Buddha-nature. For Dōgen, Buddha-nature is not a property of things; rather, it is the true nature of reality as an impermanent, interdependent process in which all things participate. The world is the body of the Buddha and nature manifests the dharma. Dualisms such as self/other or human/nonhuman are meaningless.[44] This directly parallels ecocentric environmental ethics, which views nature as an interdependent process with intrinsic value.

Third, the ethics of the Mahāyāna tradition emphasize *ahiṃsā* (Chi. *bù hài*, Jpn. 不害 *fugai*) or non-injury. Enlightenment involves an epistemological shift in which one realizes the profound interdependence of all things, which leads to a sense of compassion and a desire for the well-being of all things. *Ahiṃsā* entails that one will not harm other beings unless it is absolutely necessary.[45] According to the traditional Buddhist concept of *saṃsāra,* human beings can be reborn as nonhuman animals, which is why the first of the ten precepts (Jpn. 十戒 *jikkai*) prohibits the killing of all creatures, not just human beings. Though humans are the only species that can realize enlightenment, all species are part of the struggle for liberation. Though not all Buddhist traditions or practitioners are vegetarian, many Buddhist schools do discourage or prohibit the eating of meat.[46] However, East Asian Buddhism is not a strictly biocentric perspective that is concerned with only the suffering of sentient beings. As indicated above, Buddha-nature is ascribed to inanimate objects. Dōgen argues that it is not just sentient beings (*shujō* 衆生) that are Buddha-nature, but rather the whole-being (*shitsū* 悉有). All things in nature have value, which is consistent with a holistic, ecocentric perspective.[47]

Though Buddhism is nonanthropocentric and resonates with ecocentric perspectives on environmental ethics, we must be careful not to try to draw a one-to-one parallel with any particular Western tradition. While Buddhism has many parallels with the land ethic and deep ecology, it offers a unique perspective on environmental ethics that should be appreciated on its own terms. The next section offers an overview of how Buddhism can be understood as a distinct type of environmental virtue ethic.

Buddhism as an Environmental Virtue Ethic

Buddhism endorses a perspective on environmental philosophy that can be best categorized as a type of environmental virtue ethic. The virtue ethics tradition is the oldest approach to ethics in the history of philosophy, dating back to the time of Socrates in ancient Greece and the Vedic period in ancient India. Unlike modern, principle-based ethical systems such as deontology and utilitarianism that ask, "What is the right thing to do?" virtue ethics asks instead, "What kind of person should I be?"[48] Virtue ethics differs from deontology and utilitarianism because it places emphasis on the character, rather than just the actions, of the individual. Jonathan Glover argues that each person has a moral identity, which is a "a conception of what we are like, and of the kind of person we want to be, which may limit what we are prepared to do to others."[49] A virtuous person is dedicated to being a particular type of person with certain traits of character. There is an ideal sort of life that we can lead that will produce the greatest sense of satisfaction, and this is accomplished by cultivating ourselves to become ideal people who fully actualize their potential as human beings. The way that we become exemplary humans is by developing virtues, character traits that allow us to pursue the good life, and avoiding vices, those habits that interfere with the good life.[50] One's character—and the motivations for cultivating it—are of central importance for virtue ethics.[51] Because justice, prudence, and compassion are all included as virtues, virtue ethics is able to address many of the concerns raised by deontology (e.g., justice as fairness), utilitarianism (e.g., maximizing happiness and minimizing suffering), and care ethics (e.g., moral sentiment).

One of the most important virtue ethicists is Aristotle, who argued that every human activity, including morality, is directed toward some ultimate goal (*telos*). He states that the highest goal, to which all other goals are subordinate, must possess three attributes: (1) it must be desired for its own sake, (2) all other things must be desired for the sake of the goal, and (3) the goal must never be chosen for the sake of anything else.[52] Based on these criteria, Aristotle argues that the goal toward which all human life aims is best understood as *eudaimonia*.[53] While this term is often translated as "happiness," Aristotle does not mean that we should dedicate our lives to hedonism. He condemns the life of pleasure-seeking in favor of a life devoted to health, knowledge, wisdom, and virtue. The ultimate human aim of *eudaimonia* is best understood as "well-being."[54] When a virtue ethicist like Aristotle talks of "flourishing," he refers to a life of *eudaimonia* in which one continually cultivates oneself to the highest possible degree. The virtues are those aspects of a person's character that help one to "achieve well-being or to live the good life."[55] *Eudaimonia* is the deep sense of satisfaction experienced by a person who can look at themself with a sense of pride that comes from having lived well as a good person.[56]

For Buddhism, the goal (*telos*) toward which human life should be directed is nirvana. It is the ultimate goal of Buddhist cultivation because it represents the state of awakening in which one has realized the truth of interdependent arising and transcended the karmic cycle that binds one to an existence of suffering.[57] A flourishing life is one that is characterized by enlightenment. Not only will it bring a deep sense of satisfaction on the individual level, but if everyone were to pursue enlightenment as goal, the world as a whole would flourish.[58] Enlightenment is realized by following the Eightfold Path, which is made up of three major branches: wisdom (knowing the truth about reality through right views and right intention), conduct (acting with compassion through right speech, right action, and right livelihood), and discipline (the method by which one cultivates oneself according to right effort, right mindfulness, and right concentration).

In the Mahāyāna traditions of East Asian Buddhism, self-cultivation is based on the simultaneous cultivation of wisdom (San. *prajñā*; Jpn. 知恵 *chie*) and compassion (San. *karuṇā*; Jpn. 慈悲 *jihi*). Enlightenment is more than just understanding the true nature of reality; it also involves an ethical transformation. When a person realizes that all things are co-dependently interconnected (San. *pratītyasamutpāda*; Jpn. *engi* 縁起), they see that their actions have consequences for them and everyone around them. When they realize that they have no essential self, they see that egoism is meaningless. Enlightened beings view themselves as part of an "extended web of interconnection," which produces a profound sense of compassion for other beings.[59] Wisdom and compassion need to be cultivated simultaneously. An enlightened person cannot have one without the other.[60]

East Asian Buddhism represents an environmental virtue ethic because it emphasizes the cultivation of specific character traits—virtues—that promote the universal goal of nirvana, which is the elimination of suffering through awakening. David E. Cooper and Simon P. James identify three broad categories of Buddhist environmental virtues. They call the first category "foundational virtues," which refers to those habits necessary for the cultivation of all other virtues. These foundational virtues include things such as mindfulness, personal responsibility, and moral shame. They do not tell one how to act, but rather are prerequisites for having any serious concern about how one ought to act or what kind of person one ought to be. The second and third categories refer to self-regarding and other-regarding virtues, which provide specific guidance about how one ought to act with respect to oneself and others. It is these virtues to which Cooper and James devote most of their study.[61]

Cooper and James identify three self-regarding Buddhist environmental virtues: humility, self-mastery, and equanimity. The virtue of humility is opposed to the vice of egoism, which is a major driver of consumerism. When a person realizes that there is no fundamental self that is separate from and superior to the world around them, a sense of humility arises that diffuses prior desires to pursue selfish motives. An individual's needs are not more important than the needs of others, and they are not entitled to a greater share of resources because of their alleged "superiority." This humility extends beyond individuals to humanity as a whole: human beings must reject the idea that they hold a special place in nature that allows them to exploit it for their own personal gain. Self-mastery—which is developed through the Buddhist practices of right effort, right mindfulness, and right concentration—is a virtue associated with people who seek to transform their lives through self-cultivation. It entails a constant dedication to developing the faculties that allow one to flourish. A person dedicated to self-mastery is constantly on the lookout for false ideals and goals that might lead them astray, and thus self-mastery involves a frugal existence that emphasizes the cultivation of character over the acquisition of unnecessary resources. One must "guard one's sense-doors" so that one is not led astray by misguided views that promote a life of hedonism and acquisitiveness. Finally, equanimity, one of the four immeasurable states in Mahāyāna Buddhism, is the virtue that allows one to maintain calm composure, especially when faced with difficult situations. It is based on the realization that all things are impermanent and interdependent: fundamentally, there is nothing that is really "mine" to own. Equanimity is opposed not only to the cravings that promote acquisitiveness, but also the vice of willful ignorance, which many people embrace to avoid the fear associated with change.[62] For example, when confronted with the truth about climate change, some people choose to claim that it's a "liberal hoax" or "part of a natural cycle" or that "further study is needed" so that they do not have to face the reality that they need to change their lifestyles to avoid environmental catastrophe. (Jesse Butler's chapter in this volume will have a lot more to say about this issue.) By contrast, the equanimous person accepts this reality and calmly adjusts their life to avoid disaster.

The three Buddhist other-regarding virtues enumerated by Cooper and James are solicitude, nonviolence, and responsibleness. Solicitude is an umbrella term that refers to loving-kindness, compassion, and empathetic joy (the other three immeasurable states of Buddhism besides equanimity). Loving-kindness (San. *maitrī*, Jpn. 慈 *ji*) is the desire for all beings to be happy, compassion (San. *karuṇā*, Jpn. 慈悲 *jihi*) is a sensitivity to the distress of others and a commitment to help relieve their suffering, and empathetic joy (San. *muditā*, Jpn. 喜 *ki*) is happiness at the flourishing of others. Solicitude helps foster wisdom because it dispels the delusions that separate us from other beings and encourages sympathy for others, including nonhuman animals. It stands in opposition to the vice of cruelty, which represents an indifference to the suffering of others (or in extreme cases, enjoyment of their suffering).[63] The second other-regarding virtue is nonviolence (San. *ahiṃsā*, Jpn. 不害 *fugai*), which is one of the five general moral precepts of Buddhism. A nonviolent person will not only avoid doing unnecessary harm to sentient beings, but will also refrain from causing gratuitous injury to the nonsentient natural world, which manifests Buddha-nature. John Daido Loori argues that nonviolence applies not only to individual beings, but to entire species, since anthropogenic species extinction represents "the worst kind of killing."[64] Nonviolence also refers to a spirit of intellectual humility and nonattachment to particular views: a virtuous person does not cling dogmatically to ignorant points of view and then attack the views of others, but rather is critically reflective and willing to learn.[65] This is particularly important in our current political climate, where some individuals are unwilling to revise their views about climate change despite overwhelming contrary evidence. Nonviolence is opposed to the vice of violence, which is the disposition to intentionally cause unnecessary harm.[66] The final other-regarding virtue is responsibleness, which refers to a willingness to accept one's moral responsibilities (and is tied to the concepts of karma and skillful means). A virtuous person cannot shirk their moral duties and sit idly by while others suffer harm. In this sense, responsibleness is opposed to the vice of passivity, a tendency to neglect one's duties, to hide one's head in the sand and ignore the obligations that one has to other beings.[67] Many people allow their fear of climate change to paralyze them into inaction. They feel as if they can do nothing to change the world, so they pretend that the crisis does not exist. By contrast, a virtuous person takes responsibility for the deleterious effects that human beings have had upon the environment and acts to improve the situation. Though one person might only have a limited effect on the environment, when many people act together, they can radically transform it. That is how we got into this mess in the first place, and it is the only way that we are going to get out of it.

A final point should be made about Buddhist environmental virtue ethics: the natural world can be a valuable resource for moral cultivation. Psychologist Mihaly Csikszentmihalyi pioneered research into "flow states," which is the name given to optimal experiences in which an individual is completely engaged with the task at hand. Flow states are a type of "negentropy" in which the distractions of one's chaotic, everyday mind fall away and one's performance is optimized as one lives fully in the present moment. Athletes often refer to this as "being in the zone," where they feel that they are moving in perfect harmony with both the field and the other players. Human beings are happiest while in flow states, and the most enjoyable lives are those in which one spends the most time in flow states. Csikszentmihalyi explicitly identifies flow states with Buddhist meditation, though they can be produced by any activity in which one is fully absorbed by one's experience.[68] I have argued elsewhere[69] that these flow states parallel Zen master Takuan Sōhō's concept of *fudōshin,* the state of "unfettered mind" in which one is fully unified with one's experience. Buddhist texts contain numerous references to the meditative value of experiences of the natural world. Cooper and James argue that while nature can be a testament to suffering, a "more prominent theme in the scriptures, however, is that of experience of nature as conducive to tranquility, equanimity, self-restraint and control, selfless pleasure, humility—to, indeed, most of the virtues clustered under our three headings."[70] An experience of nature, like the experience of art, "enables the acquisition of self-transforming virtues by inducing, and indeed instantiating, a sense of ourselves as beings capable of self-transformation, of liberation from a conditioned state towards an enlightened one."[71] Experiences of nature are conducive to producing flow states, which are characteristic of enlightenment because they allow one to effortlessly participate in the interdependent process that is the natural world. The more time one spends in nature, the more likely one is to experience these states on a regular basis. Thus, nature can be a medium for self-cultivation.

Conclusion

There is an old Buddhist metaphor, used by everyone from Thich Nhat Hanh to Bruce Lee, that says the teachings of Buddhism are like a finger pointing at the moon: if we focus on the finger, we will miss the beauty of the heavenly body it is trying to indicate. Here, the teachings of Buddhism are the finger while the moon represents enlightenment. Buddhist teachings are nothing more than a vehicle to move one toward awakening, and students of the Way should be careful not to mistake the vehicle for the Way itself.[72] I have argued in this chapter that Buddhism points not only to the moon, but also to the Earth. It offers an environmental ethic that critiques the consumerist worldview that encourages us to adopt vicious attitudes that result in meaningless lives, negative environmental impact, and the destabilization of economic and political systems. But does this environmental ethic only apply to Buddhists, who comprise about a half-billion people in a world that contains more than seven billion human beings?

Buddhism is a philosophy in the sense that it is a way of thinking critically about the world so that we can understand it better and thereby live better.[73] Though it is typically practiced as a religious tradition, many of its ideas can be readily adopted by secular organizations. *Kyōsei* is a prime example: though it originated from the Buddhist concept of *tomoiki*, it went on to become one of the key moral paradigms for international business ethics. Perhaps a secularized version of the general argument of this paper can be made that can apply to non-Buddhist worldviews.[74] Let's call it the "Four Noble Truths of Environmental Ethics":

1. The earth's environment is suffering, and we are suffering with it. We are facing the worst environmental crisis in history due to climate change, which threatens to destabilize our economies and political systems, and possibly make the planet uninhabitable for human beings.

2. Consumerism-driven human activity ("affluenza") is the cause of these environmental problems. Our booming population, obsession with wealth, and use of polluting technology all increase our negative environmental impact. Because many of us are afraid to change our lifestyles, we ignore the overwhelming evidence and remain ignorantly attached to false ideals.

3. If we reject consumerism, we can eliminate our negative environmental impact. We caused this mess, but we have the power to clean it up.

4. We can change the environment by cultivating ourselves to be better human beings with better goals and habits. We

can practice capitalism responsibly by following a stakeholder model that embraces mutualistic symbiosis as its goal. We can realize that human beings do not have a privileged status as a species, but are rather, as Aldo Leopold puts it, plain citizens of the biotic community. As a result, we must learn to value the environment and nonhuman species. By changing our outlook and our way of life, we can not only heal the planet, but also lead happier, more satisfying lives through our experience of nature.

Buddhism teaches us that we are the authors of our own suffering, but we can rewrite the narrative to give it a much happier ending. If we want to survive the Anthropocene, we had better get to work.

Notes

1. Will Steffen et al., "The Anthropocene: Conceptual and Historical Perspectives" *Philosophical Transactions of the Royal Society A* 369, no. 1938 (2011): 842–67.

2. "IPCC, 2018: Summary for Policymakers," in Global Warming of 1.5°C: an IPCC Special Report on the impacts of global warming of 1.5°C above pre-industrial levels and related global greenhouse gas emission pathways, in the context of strengthening the global response to the threat of climate change, sustainable development, and efforts to eradicate poverty, ed. Valérie Masson-Delmotte et al., accessed June 22, 2020, https://www.ipcc.ch/site/assets/uploads/sites/2/2019/05/SR15_SPM_version_report_LR.pdf. The complete report can be found at https://www.ipcc.ch/sr15/. The Intergovernmental Panel on Climate Change (IPCC) is a body of the United Nations tasked with providing scientific information about climate change and the risks it poses to nature, politics, and economics. For a clear and concise summary of the environmental problems associated with climate change, see the first chapter of Graham Parkes's How to Think about the Climate Crisis: A Philosophical Guide to Saner Ways of Living (New York: Bloomsbury, 2021), 22–39.

3. These figures are based on the latest data from NASA, which are regularly updated on their "Global Climate Change: Vital Signs of the Planet" website: https://climate.nasa.gov, accessed June 22, 2020.

4. John Cook et al., "Consensus on Consensus: A Synthesis of Consensus Estimates on Human-Caused Global Warming," *Environmental Research Letters* 11, no. 4 (2016), accessed June 22, 2020: https://iopscience.iop.org/article/10.1088/1748–9326/11/4/048002. This paper is a meta-study written by the authors of seven previously published climate consensus studies, including Naomi

Oreskes, Peter T. Doran, William R. L. Anderegg, Bart Verheggen, Edward Maibach, J. Stuart Carlton, and John Cook.

5. "IPCC, 2018: Summary for Policymakers."

6. Paul R. Ehrlich and John P. Holdren, "Impact of Population Growth," *Science* 171, no. 3977 (1971): 1212–17.

7. James McRae, "Triple-Negation: Watsuji Tetsurō on the Sustainability of Ecosystems, Economies, and International Peace," in *Environmental Philosophy in Asian Traditions of Thought*, ed. J. Baird Callicott and James McRae (Albany: State University of New York Press, 2014). See also Thomas F. Homer-Dixon's articles, "On The Threshold: Environmental Changes as Causes of Acute Conflict," *International Security* 16, no. 2 (Fall 1991): 76–116 and "Environmental Scarcities and Violent Conflict: Evidence from Cases," *International Security* 19, No. I (Summer 1994): 5–40. See also Richard A. Matthew, Ted Gaulin, and Bryan McDonald, "The Elusive Quest: Linking Environmental Change and Conflict," *Canadian Journal of Political Science* 36, no. 4 (Sept. 2003): 857–78.

8. John de Graaf, David Wann, and Thomas H. Naylor, *Affluenza: How Overconsumption Is Killing Us—And How to Fight Back* (San Francisco: Berrett-Koehler, 2014), Apple Books edition, 24. Italics removed. See also de Graff, Wann, and Naylor's *Affluenza: The All-Consuming Epidemic* (San Francisco: Berrett-Koehler, 2005).

9. De Graff, Wann, and Naylor, *Affluenza: How Overconsumption Is Killing Us*. See also De Graff, Wann, and Naylor, *Affluenza: The All-Consuming Epidemic*.

10. De Graff, Wann, and Naylor, *Affluenza: How Overconsumption Is Killing Us*, 195–98. See also Joseph DesJardins, *Environmental Ethics: An Introduction to Environmental Philosophy*, 4th Ed. (Belmont, CA: Thomson-Wadsworth, 2006), 70–72.

11. "Four Noble Truths" is the most common translation of *ārya-satya* (Sanskrit) or *ariya-sacca* (Pāli). "Noble" or "Ennobled One" (*ārya/ariya*) refers to one who is spiritually awakened to the true nature of reality (*satya/sacca*). One becomes "noble" through self-cultivation and spiritual discipline. John Koller prefers "Noble Fourfold Truth," while Peter Harvey uses "The Four True Realities for the Spiritually Ennobled." See John M. Koller, *Asian Philosophies* (New York: Routledge, 2018) and Peter Harvey, *An Introduction to Buddhism: Teachings, History, and Practices* (New York: Cambridge University Press, 2013).

12. Koller, 53–62 and Harvey, 50–86. For a detailed discussion of how craving promotes environmental degradation, see J. Baird Callicott, *Earth's Insights: A Survey of Ecological Ethics from the Mediterranean Basin to the Australian Outback* (Berkeley: University of California Press, 1997), 59–62.

13. Toshio Horiuchi, "Upekśa as a Potential Basis for Kyosei in Buddhism," *Journal of International Philosophy* (国際哲学研究) 1 (2012): 281.

14. Japanese characters—known as kanji—can be read in different ways. Each character has both an *on-yomi* and a *kun-yomi* reading, the former of which is derived from the Chinese pronunciation of the character and the latter of which reflects the Japanese pronunciation. As a result, the characters 共生 can be read either

kyōsei (on-yomi) or *tomoiki (kun-yomi)*. Though the pronunciations are different, the meaning of the word is the same.

15. Horiuchi, 282.

16. James McRae, "From *Kyōsei* to *Kyōei*: Symbiotic Flourishing in Japanese Environmental Ethics," in *Japanese Environmental Philosophy*, ed. J. Baird Callicott and James McRae (New York: Oxford University Press, 2017), 47–61. See also James McRae, "Symbiosis and Sustainability: *Kyōsei* as a Moral Paradigm for Water Resource Management," *Water Resources IMPACT* 19, no. 3 (2017): 22–24. See also McRae, "Triple-Negation" 368–69. For a thorough exposition of the science of symbiosis, see Surindar Paracer and Vernon Ahmadjian, *Symbiosis: An Introduction to Biological Associations*, 2nd ed. (New York: Oxford University Press, 2000), 6–8, and Jan Sapp, *Evolution by Association* (Oxford: Oxford University Press, 1994).

17. Horiuchi, 282.

18. Horiuchi, 283. Shiio's *tomoiki* was a significant influence on the development of *kyōsei* as a business ethics principle. See Henri-Claude de Bettignies, Kenneth E. Goodpaster, and Matsuoka Toshio, "The Caux Roundtable Principles for Business: Presentation and Discussion," in *International Business Ethics: Challenges and Approaches*, ed. Georges Enderle (Notre Dame, IN: University of Notre Dame Press, 1999), 133.

19. Horiuchi, 285–88.

20. Horiuchi, 283.

21. McRae, "From *Kyōsei* to *Kyōei*," 49–50. See also McRae, "Triple-Negation," 368–69 and Richard E. Wokutch and Jon M. Shepard, "The Maturing of the Japanese Economy: Corporate Social Responsibility Implications," *Business Ethics Quarterly* 9, no. 3 (1999): 536–37.

22. Bettignies, Goodpaster, and Matsuoka, "Caux Roundtable Principles," 131–42.

23. For more information about the Caux Round Table, see https://www.cauxroundtable.org.

24. McRae, "From *Kyōsei* to *Kyōei*," 50. See also Bettignies, Goodpaster, and Matsuoka, "Caux Roundtable Principles," 133–34.

25. McRae, "Triple-Negation," 369. See also Kenneth E. Goodpaster, "Bridging East and West in Management Ethics: Kyosei and the Moral Point of View," in *International Business Ethics: Challenges and Approaches*, ed. Georges Enderle (Notre Dame, IN: University of Notre Dame Press, 1999), 150–51, and Thomas M. Jones, Andrew C. Wicks, and R. Edward Freeman, "Stakeholder Theory: The State of the Art," in *The Blackwell Guide to Business Ethics*, ed. Norman E. Bowie (Malden, MA: Blackwell, 2002), 19–20.

26. Ugo Dessì, " 'Greening Dharma': Contemporary Japanese Buddhism and Ecology," *Journal for the Study of Religion, Nature and Culture* 7 no. 3 (2013): 334–55.

27. DesJardins, 12.

28. The characteristics listed here are Mary Anne Warren's criteria for personhood. See Mary Anne Warren, "Difficulties with the Strong Animal Rights Position," in *Contemporary Moral Problems*, 8th ed., ed. James E. White (Belmont, CA: Thomson Wadsworth, 2006), 396–403 and Mary Anne Warren, "On the Moral and Legal Status of Abortion," in *Contemporary Moral Problems*, 8th ed., ed. James E. White (Belmont, CA: Thomson Wadsworth, 2006), 114–25. See also McRae, "Cutting the Cat in One," 133.

29. DesJardins 12–13. See also J. Baird Callicott, *In Defense of the Land Ethic: Essays in Environmental Philosophy* (Albany: State University of New York Press, 1989), 18.

30. Peter Singer, *Animal Liberation* (New York: Ecco, 2002) and Peter Singer, ed., *In Defense of Animals* (New York: Basil Blackwell, 1985). See also Callicott, *In Defense of the Land Ethic*, 18–20.

31. Tom Regan, *The Case for Animal Rights* (Oakland: University of California Press, 1983).

32. Callicott, *In Defense of the Land Ethic*. Callicott bases this argument largely upon Leopold's essay, "The Land Ethic," in *A Sand County Almanac* (New York: Random House, 1990). See also, Steve Odin, "The Japanese Concept of Nature in Relation to the Environmental Ethics and Conservation Aesthetics of Aldo Leopold," in *Environmental Philosophy in Asian Traditions of Thought*, ed. J. Baird Callicott and James McRae (Albany: State University of New York Press, 2014), 247–65.

33. Callicott, *In Defense of the Land Ethic*, 22–23.

34. Callicott, *In Defense of the Land Ethic*, 21.

35. Callicott, *In Defense of the Land Ethic*, 81–82.

36. Bill Devall and George Sessions, *Deep Ecology: Living as if Nature Mattered* (Salt Lake City: G. M. Smith, 1985). See also Deane Curtin, "Dōgen, Deep Ecology, and the Ecological Self," in *Environmental Philosophy in Asian Traditions of Thought*, ed. J. Baird Callicott and James McRae (Albany: State University of New York Press, 2014).

37. David E. Cooper and Simon P. James, *Buddhism, Virtue, and Environment* (New York: Routledge, 2017), Kindle Edition. See chapter 5 in particular.

38. David Barnhill, "Buddhism—East Asian," in *Encyclopedia of Religion and Nature*, ed. Bron Taylor (London: Thoemmes Continuum, 2005), 237.

39. Robert Carter, *Encounter with Enlightenment: A Study of Japanese Ethics* (Albany: State University of New York Press, 2001), 80, 86–87. See also McRae, "Cutting the Cat in One," 130.

40. David L. Hall and Roger T. Ames, *Thinking From the Han: Self, Truth, and Transcendence in Chinese and Western Culture* (Albany: State University of New York Press, 1998), 264. See also McRae, "Cutting the Cat in One," 130.

41. Callicott, *Earth's Insights*, 64.

42. J. Baird Callicott, "Afterword: A Plea for Environmental Philosophy as an Extension of Natural Philosophy," in *Japanese Environmental Philosophy*, ed. J. Baird Callicott and James McRae (New York: Oxford University Press, 2017), 290.

43. Barnhill, 237–38.

44. Dōgen, *Moon in a Dewdrop: Writings of Zen Master Dōgen*, ed. and trans. Kasuaki Tanahashi (San Francisco: San Francisco Zen Center, 1985), 41, 65, 79, and 146. See also Barnhill, 237–38. I offer a detailed exposition of Dōgen's ecocentric philosophy, particularly as it applies to nonhuman animals, in McRae, "Cutting the Cat in One."

45. McRae, "Cutting the Cat in One," 133–34.

46. Damien Keown, *Buddhist Ethics: A Very Short Introduction* (New York: Oxford University Press, 2005), 39–42, 49. Also see Dōgen, *Moon in a Dewdrop*, 339 and McRae, "Cutting the Cat in One," 133–34.

47. Abe Masao, *A Study of Dōgen: His Philosophy and Religion*, trans. and ed. Steven Heine (Albany: State University of New York Press, 1992), 54–55. See also Deane Curtin, "Dōgen, Deep Ecology, and the Ecological Self."

48. Simon P. James, *Zen Buddhism and Environmental Ethics* (New York: Routledge, 2016), Kindle Edition, Singer, Peter. *Animal Liberation* (New York: Ecco, 2002), ch. 2. Since e-books do not typically have universal page numbers, I am providing the chapter in which this information can be found (and I do the same in these notes for all digital editions that do not provide page numbers).

49. Jonothan Glover, *Humanity: A Moral History of the Twentieth Century* (New Haven: Yale Nota Bene, 2001), 22.

50. James, ch. 2.

51. Cooper and James, ch. 1.

52. Aristotle, *Nichomachean Ethics*, trans. Terence Irwin (Indianapolis: Hackett, 1999), 1094a18–25. Also see Damien Keown, *The Nature of Buddhist Ethics* (New York: Palgrave, 2001), 197.

53. Aristotle 1095a12–21.

54. Douglas Birsch, *Ethical Insights: A Brief Introduction* (Boston: McGraw-Hill, 1999), 137. Also see Aristotle, 1097a14–1098a20. This notion of "well-being" closely parallels James Griffin's understanding of the good of utilitarianism.

55. Birsch, 136; italics removed.

56. James, ch. 2. See also Cooper and James, ch. 1.

57. Damien Keown offers a detailed exposition of Buddhist virtue ethics in *The Nature of Buddhist Ethics*.

58. James, ch. 2. Cooper and James, ch. 4.

59. Carter, 80. See also McRae, "Cutting the Cat in One," 130.

60. Carter, 88. See also McRae, "Cutting the Cat in One," 130–31 and Dōgen, *The Heart of Dōgen's Shōbōgenzō*, trans. Norman Waddell and Masao Abe (Albany: State University of New York Press, 2002), 40–41.

61. Cooper and James, ch. 4.

62. Cooper and James, ch. 4–5.
63. Cooper and James, ch. 4–5.
64. James, ch. 3.
65. Cooper and James, ch. 4.
66. Cooper and James, ch. 5.
67. Cooper and James, ch. 4–5.
68. Mihaly Csikszentmihalyi, "Happiness Revisited," ch. 1 in *Flow: The Psychology of Optimal Experience* (New York: HarperCollins, 2008), Kindle edition. See also Mihaly Csikszentmihalyi and Rick E. Robinson, *The Art of Seeing: An Interpretation of the Aesthetic Encounter* (Los Angeles: Getty Publications, 1990).
69. James McRae, "Art of War, Art of Self: Aesthetic Cultivation in Japanese Martial Arts," in *New Essays in Japanese Aesthetics*, ed. Minh Nguyen (New York: Lexington Books, 2018).
70. Cooper and James, ch. 5.
71. Cooper and James, ch. 5.
72. Thích Nhất Hạnh, *Old Path, White Clouds* Vol. 2 (Berkeley: Parallax Press, 1991), 106–107. Bruce Lee famously uses this metaphor in *Enter the Dragon* (Warner Bros., 1973). See also Alejandro Jodorowsky, *The Finger and the Moon: Zen Teachings and Koans* (Rochester, VT: Inner Traditions, 2016).
73. To say that Buddhism is a philosophy is not to say that it cannot also be a religion. See Sarah Mattice's chapter in this volume for a detailed exposition of the dangers of labeling Buddhism as just a philosophical system or just a religious tradition.
74. It should be noted that the author of this chapter is a Buddhologist (one who studies Buddhism academically), but not a Buddhist (a practitioner of the religion). Although I am a non-Buddhist, Buddhist philosophy nonetheless informs my worldview and I utilize Buddhist meditation methods for my own self-cultivation (including seated meditation, breathing exercises, and moving meditation in the martial arts). Many of the ideas and practices of Buddhism can be utilized by practitioners of other faith traditions (like the Trappist monk Thomas Merton), or by those who ascribe to no faith tradition ("religious nones").

Bibliography

Abe, Masao. *A Study of Dōgen: His Philosophy and Religion*. Edited and translated by Steven Heine. Albany: State University of New York Press, 1992.
Aristotle. *Nichomachean Ethics*. Translated by Terence Irwin. Indianapolis: Hackett, 1999.
Barnhill, David. "Buddhism—East Asian." In *Encyclopedia of Religion and Nature*, edited by Bron Taylor, 236–39. London: Thoemmes Continuum, 2005.
Birsch, Douglas. *Ethical Insights: A Brief Introduction*. Boston: McGraw-Hill, 1999.

Callicott, J. Baird. *In Defense of the Land Ethic: Essays in Environmental Philosophy.* Albany: State University of New York Press, 1989.

———. *Earth's Insights: A Survey of Ecological Ethics from the Mediterranean Basin to the Australian Outback.* Berkeley: University of California Press, 1997.

———. "Afterword: A Plea for Environmental Philosophy as an Extension of Natural Philosophy." In *Japanese Environmental Philosophy*, edited by J. Baird Callicott and James McRae, 287–302. New York: Oxford University Press, 2017.

Carter, Robert. *Encounter with Enlightenment: A Study of Japanese Ethics.* Albany: State University of New York Press, 2001.

Cook, John, Naomi Oreskes, Peter T. Doran, William R.L. Anderegg, Bart Verheggen, Ed W. Maibach, J. Stuart Carlton, Stephan Lewandowsky, Andrew G. Skuce, Sarah A. Green, Dana Nuccitelli, Peter Jacobs, Mark Richardson, Bärbel Winkler, Rob Painting, and Ken Rice. "Consensus on Consensus: A Synthesis of Consensus Estimates on Human-Caused Global Warming." *Environmental Research Letters* 11, no. 4 (2016), accessed June 22, 2020: https://iopscience. iop.org/article/10.1088/1748–9326/11/4/048002.

Cooper, David E. and Simon P. James. *Buddhism, Virtue, and Environment.* New York: Routledge, 2017. Kindle Edition.

Csikszentmihalyi, Mihaly. *Flow: The Psychology of Optimal Experience.* New York: HarperCollins, 2008, Kindle edition.

———, and Rick E. Robinson. *The Art of Seeing: An Interpretation of the Aesthetic Encounter.* Los Angeles: Getty Publications, 1990.

Curtin, Deane. "Dōgen, Deep Ecology, and the Ecological Self." In *Environmental Philosophy in Asian Traditions of Thought*, edited by J. Baird Callicott and James McRae, 267–89. Albany: State University of New York Press, 2014.

De Bettignies, Henri-Claude, Kenneth E. Goodpaster, and Matsuoka Toshio. "The Caux Roundtable Principles for Business: Presentation and Discussion." In *International Business Ethics: Challenges and Approaches*, edited by Georges Enderle, 131–42. Notre Dame, IN: University of Notre Dame Press, 1999.

De Graaf, John, David Wann, and Thomas H. Naylor. *Affluenza: The All-Consuming Epidemic* (San Francisco: Berrett-Koehler, 2005).

———. *Affluenza: How Overconsumption Is Killing Us—And How to Fight Back.* San Francisco: Berrett-Koehler, 2014. Apple Books edition.

DesJardins, Joseph. *Environmental Ethics: An Introduction to Environmental Philosophy*, 4th Edition. Belmont, CA: Thomson Wadsworth, 2006.

Dessì, Ugo. "'Greening Dharma': Contemporary Japanese Buddhism and Ecology." *Journal for the Study of Religion, Nature and Culture* 7, no. 3 (2013): 334–55.

Devall, Bill, and George Sessions. *Deep Ecology: Living as if Nature Mattered.* Salt Lake City: G. M. Smith, 1985.

Dōgen. *Moon in a Dewdrop: Writings of Zen Master Dōgen.* Edited and translated by Kasuaki Tanahashi. San Francisco: San Francisco Zen Center, 1985.

————. *The Heart of Dōgen's Shōbōgenzō*. Translated by Norman Waddell and Masao Abe. Albany: State University of New York Press, 2002.

Ehrlich, Paul R., and John P. Holdren. "Impact of Population Growth." *Science* 171, no. 3977 (1971): 1212–17.

Glover, Jonathan. *Humanity: A Moral History of the Twentieth Century*. New Haven: Yale Nota Bene, 2001.

Goodpaster, Kenneth E. "Bridging East and West in Management Ethics: Kyosei and the Moral Point of View." In *International Business Ethics: Challenges and Approaches*, edited by Georges Enderle, 150–59. Notre Dame, IN: University of Notre Dame Press, 1999.

Hall, David L., and Roger T. Ames. *Thinking from the Han: Self, Truth, and Transcendence in Chinese and Western Culture*. Albany: State University of New York Press, 1998.

Harvey, Peter. *An Introduction to Buddhism: Teachings, History, and Practices*. New York: Cambridge University Press, 2013.

Homer-Dixon, Thomas F. "On the Threshold: Environmental Changes as Causes of Acute Conflict." *International Security* 16, no. 2 (Fall 1991): 76–116.

————. "Environmental Scarcities and Violent Conflict: Evidence from Cases." *International Security* 19, no. I (Summer 1994): 5–40.

Horiuchi, Toshio. "Upekśa as a Potential Basis for Kyosei in Buddhism." *Journal of International Philosophy* (国際哲学研究) 1 (2012): 281–88.

James, Simon P. *Zen Buddhism and Environmental Ethics*. New York: Routledge, 2016. Kindle Edition.

Jodorowsky, Alejandro. *The Finger and the Moon: Zen Teachings and Koans*. Rochester, VT: Inner Traditions, 2016.

Jones, Thomas M., Andrew C. Wicks, and R. Edward Freeman. "Stakeholder Theory: The State of the Art." In *The Blackwell Guide to Business Ethics*, edited by Norman E. Bowie, 19–37. Malden, MA: Blackwell, 2002.

Keown, Damien. *The Nature of Buddhist Ethics*. New York: Palgrave, 2001.

————. *Buddhist Ethics: A Very Short Introduction*. New York: Oxford University Press, 2005.

Koller, John M. *Asian Philosophies*. New York: Routledge, 2018.

Leopold, Aldo. *A Sand County Almanac*. New York: Random House, 1990.

Masson-Delmotte, Valérie et al. *Global Warming of 1.5°C: an IPCC Special Report on the Impacts of Global Warming of 1.5°C above Pre-industrial levels and Related Global Greenhouse Gas Emission Pathways, in the Context of Strengthening the Global Response to the Threat of Climate Change, Sustainable Development, and Efforts to Eradicate Poverty*, accessed June 22, 2020, https://www.ipcc.ch/site/assets/uploads/sites/2/2019/05/SR15_SPM_version_report_LR.pdf.

Matthew, Richard A., Ted Gaulin, and Bryan McDonald. "The Elusive Quest: Linking Environmental Change and Conflict." *Canadian Journal of Political Science* 36, no. 4 (September 2003): 857–78.

McRae, James. "Triple-Negation: Watsuji Tetsurō on the Sustainability of Ecosystems, Economies, and International Peace." In *Environmental Philosophy in Asian Traditions of Thought*, edited by J. Baird Callicott and James McRae, 359–75. Albany: State University of New York Press, 2014.

———. "From Kyōsei to Kyōei: Symbiotic Flourishing in Japanese Environmental Ethics." In *Japanese Environmental Philosophy*, edited by J. Baird Callicott and James McRae, 47–61. New York: Oxford University Press, 2017.

———. "Symbiosis and Sustainability: *Kyōsei* as a Moral Paradigm for Water Resource Management." *Water Resources IMPACT* 19, no. 3 (2017): 22–24.

———. "Art of War, Art of Self: Aesthetic Cultivation in Japanese Martial Arts." In *New Essays in Japanese Aesthetics*, edited by Minh Nguyen, 121–36. New York: Lexington Books, 2018.

NASA. "Global Climate Change: Vital Signs of the Planet," accessed July 17, 2020, https://climate.nasa.gov.

Nhất Hạnh, Thích. *Old Path, White Clouds*, Vol. 2. Berkeley: Parallax Press, 1991.

Odin, Steve. "The Japanese Concept of Nature in Relation to the Environmental Ethics and Conservation Aesthetics of Aldo Leopold." In *Environmental Philosophy in Asian Traditions of Thought*, edited by J. Baird Callicott and James McRae, 247–65. Albany: State University of New York Press, 2014.

Paracer, Surindar, and Vernon Ahmadjian. *Symbiosis: An Introduction to Biological Associations*, 2nd ed. New York: Oxford University Press, 2000.

Parkes, Graham. *How to Think about the Climate Crisis: A Philosophical Guide to Saner Ways of Living*. New York: Bloomsbury, 2021.

Regan, Tom. *The Case for Animal Rights*. Oakland: University of California Press, 1983.

Sapp, Jan. *Evolution by Association*. Oxford: Oxford University Press, 1994.

Singer, Peter. *Animal Liberation*. New York: Ecco, 2002.

———, ed. *In Defense of Animals*. New York: Basil Blackwell, 1985.

Steffen, Will, and Jacques Grinevald, Paul Crutzen, and John McNeill, "The Anthropocene: Conceptual and Historical Perspectives," *Philosophical Transactions of the Royal Society A* 369, no. 1938 (2011): 842–67.

Warren, Mary Anne. "Difficulties with the Strong Animal Rights Position." In *Contemporary Moral Problems*, 8th ed., edited by James E. White, 396–403. Belmont, CA: Thomson Wadsworth, 2006.

———. "On the Moral and Legal Status of Abortion." In *Contemporary Moral Problems*, 8th ed., edited by James E. White, 114–25. Belmont, CA: Thomson Wadsworth, 2006.

Wokutch, Richard E., and Jon M. Shepard. "The Maturing of the Japanese Economy: Corporate Social Responsibility Implications." *Business Ethics Quarterly* 9, no. 3 (1999): 527–40.

Chapter 7

Ecological Self-understanding in Chinese Buddhism

Investigating an Epistemic Virtue

JESSE BUTLER

Awareness of our environmental impact is not necessarily new, but in recent times it has become clear that we humans are active participants in a global ecological crisis. Of course, the details are incredibly complicated and there are many ways in which our dynamic world has always been changing irrespective of what we ourselves may or may not have been doing. However, there is widespread evidence and expert consensus that we humans, collectively speaking, bear a great deal of responsibility for climate change and other environmental problems that are increasingly wreaking havoc throughout the biosphere on an unprecedented scale, to the point that the future of humanity itself is at stake, not to mention myriad other species and life systems with which we share the world.[1]

In the face of global ecological crisis brought about by the human species, it is imperative that we reevaluate ourselves and our place on the planet, not only in regard to our concrete behaviors, practices, and policies as consumers and citizens, but also in terms of our more general understanding of ourselves through the philosophical and religious aspects of human culture that frame how we view our place in reality. All worldviews should take into account the ecological context of our lives and the circumstances that we face together as a species on planet Earth, but our focus here will be on Buddhism, which of course is a major philosophical and religious tradition that has framed human understanding across borders throughout history and continues to shape the lives of hundreds of millions of people around the world today.[2] Juxtaposing this longstanding worldview with our current ecological circumstances brings us to the driving questions that we will explore in this chapter: How does Buddhism fare with regard to understanding and responding to our current ecological circumstances? Are there forms of Buddhism that acknowledge the ecological context of our existence and offer a viable framework for understanding ourselves in terms of our relationships with the natural world? Or, alternatively, are there any problems or barriers within Buddhism that stand in the way of viable ecological understanding?

Of course, Buddhists themselves have spoken on the matter, with many notable contemporary Buddhists voicing significant concern regarding environmental issues. As one of the most globally visible examples, the current Dalai Lama recently requested that his ongoing series of interactive dialogues with scientists through the Mind and Life Institute meet on the theme of "Ecology, Ethics, and Interdependence," turning from their usual focus on collaborative research between cognitive scientists and contemplative practitioners (a burgeoning new field known as "contemplative neuroscience") to express unequivocal concern for our current ecological crisis and what we should do about it.[3] There are numerous other examples, and at a more general level one could argue that Buddhism has been intertwined with environmental studies for decades now, not only through the work of Buddhists themselves but also through environmentalists who have turned to Buddhism for wisdom and insight.[4]

These observations are suggestive of a positive answer to our inquiry. However, despite the emergence of "Green Buddhism" in recent times, there are some reasons to question the extent to which Buddhism itself may offer genuine insight regarding environmental problems. Our current awareness of the global scale of our environmental circumstances is largely due to modern science, which of course has affected Buddhism in various ways, but which is also fairly clearly distinct from Buddhist philosophy and religion per se. Moreover, the cultural context of the formative stages of Buddhism, both in ancient India as well as in the time of its reception in China, Korea, and Japan in the first to seventh centuries, lacked anything akin to the contemporary environmental movement, or even a discernable conception of the natural world as a direct object of inquiry or moral concern.[5] Taking this historical context into consideration, environmentally oriented Buddhism might only be a recent development that retrospectively projects contemporary concepts and issues back onto a far older domain that simply does not share our current environmental concerns. That is not to say Buddhism cannot engage in beneficial dialogue with environmental scientists and others in addressing our ecological crisis—indeed, Buddhism is an actively evolving worldview continuously reshaping itself in myriad ways, in conjunction with the changing relational dynamics of human history as it unfolds—but it does bring into question to what extent Buddhism itself can be regarded as an ecologically minded worldview, with regard to its own longstanding repertoire of beliefs and practices. This chapter is an attempt to investigate this issue, by introducing a cross-cultural conception of ecological self-understanding as an epistemic virtue for human worldviews in general and analyzing to what extent Buddhism exhibits this virtue, through representative details drawn from some prominent traditions in China in particular.

Before we begin, some clarifications about the nature and scope of the project of this chapter are in order. By far most of the attention given to Buddhism on these matters has been in terms of environmental ethics, regarding issues such as whether or not nature has intrinsic value, apart from our instrumental use of it for our own purposes, or what kind of moral character is exhibited by our actions and their consequences for the environment. However, this investigation will emphasize a somewhat different orientation. The focus here will be more epistemological than ethical, aimed toward normative concerns regarding human belief and understanding.[6] For those who might be unfamiliar with the field, epistemology is the area of philosophy concerned with knowledge and other related concepts, such as truth, wisdom, and understanding. Generally speaking, epistemology pertains to our cognitive relationship to reality: Do we have true beliefs about ourselves and the world, such that we can know what is really going on in reality? Do our belief systems cultivate wisdom and understanding in our representations of ourselves and the world around us? Or, alternatively, do our beliefs fail to properly grasp reality in some form or other, leading to falsity or delusion rather than truth and understanding? What features should we look for in our beliefs and belief-forming processes, to equip our minds with virtuous qualities that can reliably lead us to truth and understanding? These kinds of questions form the conceptual background of this chapter, and we will take a virtue epistemology approach to responding to them, introducing the concept of ecological self-understanding as an epistemic virtue to analyze how different worldviews frame human understanding of self-environment relationships.[7]

Also, while our focus here is on Buddhism as a specific wordview, it is important to recognize that Buddhism is a vast collection of diverse beliefs and practices that exhibit considerable variety across ideological differences and cultural transformations. In this respect, perhaps it is more accurate to speak of Buddhisms rather than Buddhism, as another recent anthology in this series recommends.[8] This does not mean that there are no commonalities across diverse forms of Buddhism, however. The different Buddhisms of the world, however diverse they may be, are all still forms of Buddhism after all. In this project, I will discuss some general concepts that are shared throughout the Buddhisms of the world (though still variably interpreted, as we will see), but I will also constrain our focus to some more specific forms of Buddhism prominent in East Asia, particularly China.[9] Focusing on Chinese Buddhism will make our task more manageable and help us avoid overgeneralizations across all forms of Buddhism, while also leaving analogous investigations into other Buddhist traditions for further inquiry.

Moreover, there are some reasons to think that Chinese Buddhism might be a particularly revealing place to look for ecological understanding, given its confluence with other aspects of Chinese culture. As Buddhism spread from India, the Mahāyāna branch grew into a range of traditions, combining with varied indigenous cultural roots throughout South and East Asia. With regard to China, such transformations are generally regarded to have made Buddhism somewhat more "this-worldly" than was earlier imbued by the more mystical and transcendentally oriented Indian cultural traditions within which it arose, through infusion with the practically oriented character of Confucianism and the naturalistically oriented Daoism of Chinese culture.[10] As Nicholas Brasovan has argued, ecological self-understanding can be identified in these Chinese worldviews and their contextual understandings of what it is to be a person in the world.[11] Consequently, if we want to identify forms of Buddhism that properly recognize the ecological context of our lives, Chinese Buddhism is a reasonable place to look. We will consider some general Buddhist concepts that are not limited to Chinese Buddhism as well, but for these reasons I will focus on prominent Chinese Buddhist traditions as we proceed, looking at details from Tiantai, Huayan, Chan, and Pure Land Buddhism in particular.[12]

Ecological Self-understanding as an Epistemic Virtue

Before analyzing Chinese Buddhism through the concept of ecological self-understanding, we first need to develop the concept itself to establish a general foundation for our inquiry. Accordingly, this section will develop the concept of ecological self-understanding as a general epistemic virtue that can function as a normative ideal for any worldview. Epistemic virtues (or "intellectual virtues," as they are also called) are desirable traits for the cultivation of knowledge and understanding. As defined in the *Stanford Encyclopedia of Philosophy*, they are "characteristics that promote intellectual flourishing, or which make for an excellent cognizer."[13] They are *Virtues of the Mind*, as the epistemologist Linda Zagzebski's influential book by the same name puts it.[14] Just as ethical (or moral) virtues such as courage, patience, and compassion are desirable character traits for human conduct, epistemic (or intellectual) virtues like open-mindedness, humility, and conscientiousness are desirable traits for the pursuit of truth, knowledge, and understanding.

Following this general understanding of epistemic virtue, I propose that ecological self-understanding is a particularly salient epistemic virtue for our time, in terms of being a desirable cognitive disposition for framing human understanding in ways that cultivate veridical recognition of the ecological context of our existence. This proposal is based upon my recent work on ecological self-understanding as a cross-cultural epistemic virtue, in which I define and illustrate this particular virtue through examples from contemporary indigenous philosophy.[15] Here is a definition adapted from this work: Ecological self-understanding is *veridical recognition of human beings as embodied agents in the world, including both a general grasp of the fact that we humans exist as part of a broader earthly ecology and a first-personal acknowledgment of oneself and one's actions as situated within interdependent relations with one's actual environment.* The goal of this definition is to identify a generalizable cross-cultural epistemic virtue regarding how we humans ought to understand ourselves and our place in reality. In this respect, my overarching project here (including both this chapter and my prior work on the topic) can be seen as a kind of applied virtue epistemology, proposing a normative conception of human understanding to analyze and compare worldviews in regard to what extent they appropriately recognize self-environment relations in their cultivation of knowledge, wisdom, and understanding. At the same time, I intend for this virtue to apply at the individual level as well, which can be seen with the inclusion of the first-person perspective in the definition above.[16] Worldviews that exhibit the virtue of ecological self-understanding should not only take into account the ecological context of our existence in general but also cultivate a first-personal grasp of an individual's ecological interdependence from within their own perspective on themselves and the world, thereby framing how individuals understand and actualize their agency as human beings in the world.

Let's begin with an example at the individual level for illustration. Suppose three co-workers who commute together are stuck in traffic on their way to work. Bill, the driver, angrily complains, "Why won't these fools get out of my way?! They're going to make me late!" Dan, the front seat passenger, replies, "We're all going to be late but there's nothing we can do about it, so there's no point in getting angry. Relax and we'll get there when we get there." Finally, Emma, another passenger in the back, leans forward and says, "Look, we are just as much a part of this as anyone else. This traffic is a problem, but we're traffic too. What can we do about it? Maybe we can get management to let us telecommute part-time."

Out of our three commuters, only Emma exhibits ecological self-understanding. She is the only one who acknowledges their role as active components in the traffic they face, and also thereby takes responsibility to actualize her agency in her understanding of the situation. It is not just that they are stuck in traffic. They themselves are part of the traffic, and only Emma demonstrates the cognitive disposition to recognize this fact. Bill and Dan both fail to acknowledge their involvement in the traffic, although from somewhat different perspectives and different failures of understanding.

Further analyzing the examples of Bill and Dan, we can identify a couple of general vices that stand in contrast to the virtue of ecological self-understanding. Bill exhibits what we can call *the vice of egocentric-self-focused bias,* in that he views things from a privileged individualistic perspective that separates himself and his interests from the traffic in his environment, thereby feeling more entitled to travel on the road than the other people who are also equally stuck in traffic. Bill conceives of himself as an agent, but in a self-focused manner that blinds him from appropriately understanding his agency as a component of the situation. On the other hand, Dan exhibits *the vice of self-denial,* failing to acknowledge his agency altogether. Unlike Bill, Dan does not assume a privileged or transcendent standpoint on the situation. Instead, he is in denial of their active participation in creating the traffic, conceiving of himself and his co-workers as mere fated cogs in the machine, as it were, helplessly determined to be stuck in traffic as an unavoidable byproduct of circumstance. Only Emma approaches the situation in accord with *the virtue of ecological self-understanding,* acknowledging both their interrelatedness with the traffic and their own agency as active components situated within the broader environmental factors constituting their circumstances.

Building upon these examples, we can extend these concepts to general worldviews and their various ways of understanding the human condition.

Like Emma, worldviews that exhibit the virtue of ecological self-understanding recognize the ecological context of our lives and the fact that we exist as active responsible agents within the environmental relations that constitute our existence as beings in the world. Worldviews that exhibit the vice of egocentric-self-focused bias, on the other hand, regard humans as privileged beings that transcend their worldly relations and enable individuals to regard themselves and their own self-focused concerns uniquely apart from the environmental context of their existence. Worldviews with the vice of self-denial fail to properly acknowledge our selfhood by negating the agency we have as embodied beings in the world. Such worldviews might deny our selfhood altogether, or perhaps only deny our freedom or responsible agency in some form or other, but either way denying the facts of the embodied causality of our actions as self-conscious beings in the world.

We can now reframe our general inquiry with these concepts: Where does Buddhism fall in terms of this spectrum of virtue and vice for worldviews and their understanding of the human condition? Do different forms of Buddhism vary in this regard? Given that other aspects of Chinese culture exhibit notable elements of ecological self-understanding, do we find this virtue in Chinese Buddhism as well? To answer these questions, we will survey Buddhist views of self, dependent origination, and karma, with specific details drawn from Tiantai, Huayan, Chan, and Pure Land traditions in China, assessing to what extent they correspond to or diverge from the virtue of ecological self-understanding in the ways they frame human understanding of our place in the world.

Before turning to these details, however, one basic commonality between Buddhism and the way I have portrayed virtue here in general is worth some comment as well. As readers who are familiar with philosophical theories of virtue will have likely noticed, my characterization of ecological self-understanding as a virtue between the vices of self-denial and self-focused bias follows a common cross-cultural understanding of virtue as an ideal "golden mean," or middle state, between vices of deficiency and excess.[17] While not necessarily universal, this general understanding of virtue as an ideal mean can be found in classical philosophical traditions around the world, most famously with Aristotle's theory of ethics, the Confucian *Doctrine of the Mean*, and indeed the "Middle Way" of the Buddha.[18] The comparative details of these different virtue traditions are complex and variable, however, so we shouldn't assume too much in regard to this general commonality. With that in mind, we can safely assume that Buddhism is a tradition that is generally amenable to a virtue-based analysis of this kind, while taking it as an open question for investigation as to whether Buddhism exhibits the specific epistemic virtue of ecological self-understanding.

Anātman and Tiantai Buddhism

An obvious starting point for our investigation is the Buddhist view of the self itself. A core teaching in Buddhism is the concept of *anātman* (San.), which is standardly translated as "no self" in English (Chi. 無我 *wúwǒ*). Taken in a simple and direct manner, this central Buddhist tenet appears to be the assertion that there is no self. Now, if Buddhism advocates a strict denial of selfhood altogether, then this alone would seem to settle things pretty quickly out of the gate in our investigation: Buddhism would seem to fall under the vice of self-denial. Ecological self-understanding requires recognition of ourselves as acting agents in the world, so if Buddhism denies that there is such a thing as a "self" then Buddhism fails in the same way as Self-Denial Dan, by denying the actuality of oneself as a self, an acting agent in the world.

Like many hasty inferences, however, drawing such a conclusion would be fundamentally misguided. There is significant discussion and debate across different schools of thought in Buddhism as to what exactly *anātman* means and entails, one of which we will turn to shortly, but it is relatively clear and uncontroversial that the concept of *anātman* is not a denial of selfhood altogether, such that we simply do not exist at all in any form. Instead, it can be more plausibly understood as a denial of a certain conception of selfhood, a point that is entirely compatible with, if not also conducive to, ecological self-understanding.

To understand the Buddhist concept of *anātman,* we must first understand the concept of *ātman,* of which it is a negation. In the Indian philosophy that shaped the cultural context from which Buddhism originated, the Sanskrit term *ātman* refers to an enduring eternal self. In Vedic tradition, *Ātman* is not the temporary changeable experience of a human being but rather a more fundamental and unchanging self that defines one's underlying essential nature. The essential self of this *Ātman* is not just an individual identity but also the basis of all being, a pervasive eternal consciousness constituting all of existence, identified in the Upanishadic worldview with the one true ultimate reality of Brahman or God. The Sanskrit prefix *an* is a negation, so in negating this kind of concept of *ātman,* the Buddhist *anātman* doctrine is a denial of an eternal, unchanging self. In other words,

Buddhism departs from belief in an essential core entity as the underlying substrate of our identity. Importantly, however, this does not mean that there are no selves at all. There is no particular thing comprising an essential unchanging identity over time, and in that respect the idea of a substantive self is an illusion, but our ordinary everyday references to ourselves as beings in the world does not require or entail any such substantive self as a metaphysical entity. In this sense, the point of the Buddhist concept of *anātman* is not to deny selfhood altogether. It is to clarify how the self is not an unchanging eternal entity, as Vedic tradition held, but rather an unfolding impermanent process within a broader interdependent reality.

With this clarification in mind, we can now see how the central Buddhist concept of *anātman* meshes with the concept of ecological self-understanding. Notice that the concept of *anātman* does not tell us anything positive about what we are. It simply tells us what we are not: an unchanging thing that persists across time and which defines our essential identity. There is no such thing, and if we attach ourselves to such an illusion, we are falling for a false sense of our place in reality. In this respect, the negation of *anātman* acts as a kind of insurance against egocentric self-focused bias, countering our tendency to attach a falsely inflated sense of privileged selfhood to our actual existence and what we are as beings in the world.

Consider again our driver, Biased Bill. He is angry at the traffic that is keeping him from his work, focused on himself, to the exclusion of the world around him. Bill conceives of himself as a privileged entity with his own special interests, distinctly apart from the world he perceives as a problem for achieving his own ends. The irony of course is that Bill himself is part of the traffic that he despises, a fact that is hidden by his illusory removal of himself and his agency from the world. With this vice of self-focused bias in mind, we can regard the Buddhist denial of a substantial self as a reality check against our tendency to conceive of ourselves in this kind of way, with illusory regard for ourselves apart from our interrelatedness with the world.

One interesting and notable expression of *anātman* emerges within the indigenous Chinese tradition of Tiantai Buddhism, which emphasizes enlightenment through the realization that all of reality is Buddha-nature.[19] From the perspective of Tiantai, realization of Buddhahood entails that we, as individuals, have no stable unconditional nature unto ourselves (the only unconditional reality is the truth of Buddhahood itself) and are thereby conditionally intertwined with all other aspects of reality. As Brook Ziporyn describes it:

This also means that, the more fully one realizes that one is any particular being, the more one realizes that he or she is also all other, contrasted, things as well. This is how traditional Buddhist "non-self" doctrine comes to play out in Tiantai. I think I am already this self, Brook, but in reality, Buddhism tells me, I am not yet really any such self—for to be a self is to be unconditional, and that is impossible for "me," a conditional determinate being. Also, I am not yet enlightened—for enlightenment is unconditionality, the only freedom from suffering. To become unconditioned, as I'd thought I was when I thought I was a self, is to become enlightened. This non-self is the only thing that really fulfills my previous lust to be a self, to actually be me. I cannot become this by being me as a determinate being to the exclusion of all other beings, nor other beings to the exclusion of me. Rather, by the Three Truths, I can only become more and more me by becoming more and more everything else, and that is what it means to become more and more enlightened.[20]

The "Three Truths" referenced here consist of the mutually complementary observations that all phenomena appear and pass away (the provisional truth of impermanence), that each appearance is empty of self-same identity (the ultimate truth of emptiness), and that all things exist between this impermanence and emptiness (the middle truth of the center or mean).[21] Applying this line of thought to oneself and the concept of *anātman* undermines our illusory sense of discrete individual selfhood, as a being apart from other beings, and instead resituates our understanding of self in terms of our conditioned relationality with the rest of reality, with Buddhahood itself being the enlightened awareness of the interdependency of all things (a topic we turn to next as well), from enlightened Buddhas to lowly dung beetles and all else in between.[22]

This Tiantai understanding of selfhood resonates with ecological self-understanding by rejecting independent selfhood and resituating one's existence within the matrix of relations that comprise reality, which is a notable confirming observation for our inquiry. We must be careful not to conflate the Tiantai understanding of reality with contemporary ecology and its naturalistic focus on physical processes, however. For Tiantai (and many other forms of Buddhism), reality itself is fundamentally mental in nature, comprised of awareness and identical to the luminosity of enlightened Buddhahood. So, while the Tiantai understanding of *anātman* includes the observation that we humans are conditionally interrelated with the other beings of the world, there is no recognition that this matrix of being comprises a naturalistic ecology of the physical world. In this respect, longstanding historical Buddhist traditions such as Tiantai might be regarded as in accord with an ecological point of view, but perhaps not directly ecological in nature on their own, without also incorporating the detailed empirical observations we have of the actual world through science.

Dependent Origination and Huayan Buddhism

The connection between *anātman* and interrelatedness that we see in Tiantai naturally leads us to our next central Buddhist concept: dependent origination. Itself originating in the foundational teachings of the Buddha, dependent origination refers to the fact that all phenomena are fundamentally interconnected through relations that jointly constitute their existence. The Sanskrit term *pratītyasamutpāda* (Chi.: 緣起 *yuánqǐ*) has been variously translated as "interdependence," "dependent origination," and "dependent arising," with the key idea being that all phenomena are relationally interdependent with each other. Just as *anātman* denies that there is a substantive independent self apart from the changing processes and events that constitute our lives, so too does the concept of dependent origination deny independently existing things that stand apart from the web of relations constituting the changing flux of reality. In this respect, one could say that dependent origination is *anātman* writ large, applying the negation of essential unchanging selfhood and prioritizing relational dynamics in relation to all things.

One popular portrayal of this concept is the example of Indra's Net from the Chinese tradition of Huayan Buddhism.[23] Here is how Dushun (557–640; Chi.: 杜順 *Tushun*), the first patriarch of the Huayan tradition, described the idea:

> This imperial net is made all of jewels: because the jewels are clear, they reflect each other's images, appearing in each other's reflections, ad infinitum, all appearing at once in one jewel, and in each one it is so. . . . If you sit in one jewel, then you are sitting in all the jewels in every direction, multiplied over and over. Why? Because in one jewel there are all the jewels. If there is one jewel in all the jewels, then you are sitting in all the jewels too. And the reverse applies to the totality if you

follow the same reasoning. Since in one jewel you go into all the jewels without leaving this one jewel, so in all jewels you enter one jewel without leaving this one jewel.[24]

The analogy of an interconnected net of jewels provides a vivid illustration of how we can understand things in terms of their dependent relations with each other, and by further imagining oneself within the network of jewels as Dushun describes here, we get a very nice portrayal of how this recognition of interdependence leads to a kind of first-person self-understanding as well. Moreover, it is worth noting that Dushun also connected the lessons of Indra's Net with epistemological issues, using the idea to characterize knowledge itself as a matter of dependent conditions between things. As he put it: "Knowledge accords with things, being in one and the same realm, made by conditions, tacitly conjoining, without rejecting anything, suddenly appearing, yet not without before and after."[25] The ways these ideas overlap with the concept of ecological self-understanding are striking. Just as the science of ecology itself emphasizes the relationality of organisms to each other and their environment, and situates the acquisition of knowledge in terms of this relationality, so too does the Huayan Buddhist understanding of dependent origination emphasize the relationality of all things to each other, such that all things are deeply interconnected through relationships that mutually constitute their existence, and likewise situates the acquisition of knowledge within that relational context. However, again, we must be cautious in the conclusions we draw. Just as we saw in the case of Tiantai Buddhism above, the portrayal of dependent origination in Huayan Buddhism does not frame the deep relationality it emphasizes in the same empirical and naturalistic terms as ecology itself, and thus cannot be interpreted as an explicitly ecological viewpoint on the basis of these parallels. Nevertheless, if we consider the fact that Buddhists and ecologists alike are referencing the same experienced reality that they share as beings in the world together, the shared relationality of their systems of understanding puts them significantly in accord with each other. In this respect, Buddhism, and these forms of Chinese Buddhism in particular, can be seen as at least compatible with, if not also conducive to, ecological thinking about our place in the world.

Agency and Karma in Chinese Buddhist Belief and Practice

Through the foundational Buddhist concepts of *anātman* and dependent origination, we have seen how Buddhism emphasizes our fundamental relationality to the world. Acknowledging this relationality is a necessary condition for ecological self-understanding, with nonrelational views of self leading us to ignore or deny the ecological context of our lives through illusory identification with a separate self. However, recognition of this relationality is not alone sufficient. As we have seen, the explicit application of relationality to environmental matters requires empirical knowledge of the natural world as well. But even that is not enough to embody full-fledged ecological self-understanding: Recall that ecological self-understanding also emphasizes our agency, in addition to our relationality, regarding the fact that we are active components of the ecological relations through which we exist, responsible for the choices and actions we instantiate as agents in the world. So, a remaining crucial aspect of our inquiry is to investigate to what extent Buddhism, and Chinese Buddhism in particular, cultivates a responsible understanding of agency through its repertoire of beliefs and practices.[26]

The concept of agency can be complicated and difficult to nail down, but in the context of ecological self-understanding it can be understood as our capacity to be self-consciously aware of our own actions as intentional beings in the world, such that we contemplate decisions about what to do and make choices in response to the circumstances we face in relation to the environment through which we act. Like Emma in our earlier example, agents with ecological self-understanding recognize the environmental circumstances of their lives and properly take them into consideration in their understanding of themselves and their decisions about what to do in life. They are not overly focused on themselves, like Biased Bill, nor are they in denial of the environmental circumstances or choices they face, like Self-Denial Dan.

So, what does Buddhism, and Chinese Buddhism in particular, say about agency? Here too things can be complicated and difficult to nail down. A recent anthology with a variety of views on the topic is subtitled with the question *Agentless Agency?* for example, as one indication of the (at least seemingly) paradoxical nature of the concept.[27] Moreover, we cannot expect Buddhist conceptions of agency to correspond with how it is framed in Western philosophy and religion, which often assumes the same kind of persistent individual essence that the Buddhist concept of *anātman* denies. To understand agency in Buddhism, we need to consider not only the relevance of the prior concepts we have already discussed, but also other facets of Buddhism as well, particularly the central importance of karma (Chi.: 業 *yè*), different conceptions of which will illustrate a spectrum of traits in relation to our inquiry.

I have selected two prominent forms of Chinese Buddhism for comparative analysis on the topic of karma and its relationship to human agency: Chan Buddhism and Pure Land Buddhism.[28] With Chan Buddhism, we will see an understanding of karma that emphasizes our relational agency in a manner that resonates quite well with ecological self-understanding, while in the case of Pure Land Buddhism we will see a tradition that appears to minimize our agency in favor of devotion to transcendent salvation. We will also analyze the common Chinese Buddhist practice of releasing captive animals to generate positive karma, which further problematizes Buddhist agency and its environmental consequences.

While we will look at them individually, in relation to what each reveals about the presence or absence of ecological self-understanding within Buddhism, these traditions and practices are not necessarily always separate from each other, especially in the context of Chinese Buddhism, which (unlike Japanese Zen and Pure Land Buddhism) does not fragment into distinct branches of Buddhist orthodoxy and presents syncretic blends of both Chan and Pure Land together throughout its history.[29] Nevertheless, comparative analysis of them will demonstrate how they have some rather different qualities with regard to our focus on ecological self-understanding.

Karma is a long-standing concept that predates Buddhism, a part of the Indian cultural heritage from which Siddhartha Gautama originally articulated the Dharma. The central meaning of "karma" is "action," in reference to cause-and-effect patterns related to moral aspects of agency, but this concept is deeply intertwined with numerous philosophical and religious traditions that exhibit diverse conceptions of reincarnation and fate. Now, if karma is regarded in a fatalistic sense, as a kind of deterministic cause and effect system that fixes a course of events in some way or other, then this could lead toward the vice of self-denial, in terms of failing to acknowledge our efficacy as self-aware agents in the world. Just as Self-Denial Dan relinquished his agency as an active component of the traffic that he was resigned to accept, a fatalistic conception of karma could lead to a similar denial of the agency that is essential to ecological self-understanding.

However, this does not appear to fit with how we should understand karma in the context of Chinese Buddhism. As JeeLoo Liu describes in her account of Chinese Buddhism:

> The karmic law is not deterministic, since in every step of the causal chain the agent's volitional act or choice would have

the potential to produce various consequences. . . . Since they [Chinese Buddhists] believe that life conditions are affected by past deeds (in one's life or in one's past lives), their attitude is quite "fatalistic" with respect to their present state. But they are not fatalistic with respect to their future states. On the basis of perfuming causation and karmic laws, they believe that a better future can be created as long as they perform the right deeds, have the right thought *now*.[30]

In this sense, the cause-and-effect patterns of karma recognize the impact of past events but still provide a space for agency in response to our circumstances as they unfold in the present. Importantly, this responsiveness entails responsibility as well, as highlighted by Peter Hershock in the following description of karma from the perspective of the "responsive virtuosity" of Chan Buddhism, emphasizing our relational capacity for intentional transformation of our present experiential circumstances:

The Buddhist teaching of karma enjoins us to verify personally that, with sufficiently close and sustained attention, a meticulous consonance becomes evident between the complexion of our values, intentions and actions and the patterns of outcomes and opportunities we experience. The eventualities to which we find ourselves responding are neither fated nor foisted on us at the whim of some transcendent deity. Neither are they the result of pure chance. They are a function of patterns in the meaning-generating ways we have been present, from an incomprehensibly deep past up to and including this very moment. Seeing this is to see that every experienced reality implies responsibility and that all responsibilities imply opportunities for new angles of response.[31]

This understanding is very much in accord with the kind of agency that is acknowledged and cultivated through ecological self-understanding, emphasizing an attentive recognition of our ongoing responsibilities through our capacity to transform the patterns of relations between our intentions, actions, and outcomes as they unfold in experience.

Moreover, it is important to note that the Chan Buddhist tradition which Hershock is working from in the passage above is known for its emphasis on embodied practice and experience, situating our relational agency within the context of our experience of the actual world in which we find ourselves. Enlightened Buddhahood is not achieved through otherworldly devotion or transcendence to another domain after this life, but rather here and now, in this world. As Hui-neng, the sixth Patriarch of the Chan tradition, put it in the *Platform Sutra*, "Buddhism is in the world. It is not realized apart from the world. Seeking enlightenment apart from the world, is like looking for horns on a hare."[32]

These features, in conjunction with the generally more practical orientation of the Chinese culture within which it developed, further distinguish this Chan conception of karma from more fatalistic worldviews and connect it to the real-world relational agency required by ecological self-understanding, in terms of both our embodied relationality to the world and the situational agency we experience as we knowingly shape the world through our actions and intentions.

A rather different picture emerges when we add Pure Land Buddhism to the mix, however, which also grew to prominence in China to become one of the most popular forms of Buddhism in the world today. To be clear, Chan and Pure Land traditions are not always clearly distinguishable within Chinese Buddhism, with many figures and practitioners having participated in both in various ways (including Taixu, for example, as discussed below). Nevertheless, they exhibit qualities that are rather strikingly different for the purposes of our inquiry. With Pure Land Buddhism, emphasis is placed not on the transformative potential of our current situational embodiment but rather on the supernatural potential to be reborn in Amitābha's "Pure Land" through devotional practice.[33] Amitābha is a supernatural Buddha with infinite merit to supplement one's own acquired karma, and rebirth in Amitābha's Pure Land offers the potential for enlightenment through unperturbed beauty and happiness in a heavenly domain that is free from the *dukkha*-laden karma we face here on this troubled earth.[34] With this transcendent otherworldly orientation, coupled with a reliance upon supernatural agency rather than one's own embodied agency in the present world of experience, the worldview that emerges here seems to diverge in significant ways from the virtue of ecological self-understanding. Insofar as Pure Land Buddhism emphasizes alternative realities over actual embodied relationality, along with diminishing one's own agency in favor of supernatural assistance, I am afraid we find here a lack of ecological self-understanding. If, however, Pure Land beliefs and practices can be oriented toward transformation of the conditions of the world in which we actually live, perhaps there is potential for Pure Land Buddhism to cultivate viable ecological self-understanding and responsible environmental agency.

With regard to the latter possibility, we can consider the modern Chinese Buddhist Taixu (1890–1947; Chi.: 太虛 *Tàixū*), who was an influential precursor in the development of what is now known as "humanitarian" or "socially engaged" Buddhism, due to an emphasis on addressing real-world sociopolitical issues. Although steeped in traditional Pure Land (and Chan) practice, Taixu sought to reorient Buddhism in the modern world by integrating it with science and aiming for the development of a "Pure Land in the Human Realm." This sounds like an ideal way to bring Pure Land Buddhism in accord with ecological self-understanding, in terms of conjoining Buddhist insights into our relationality and transformative agency with the knowledge provided by science to address real-world issues, but recent work on Taixu adds some further interesting details that might complicate this ideal. As Charles B. Jones observes in his reading of Taixu:

> He notes that social reform only benefits people in this present life, and that the need for personal salvation and immortality may only be answered by recourse to traditional Pure Land practices, such as those leading to rebirth either in the Pure Land of Amitābha or the Tusita Heaven of Maitreya. While he did coin the term "Pure Land in the Human Realm," he defines the "Human Realm" very broadly as any place in the Buddhist cosmos where humans dwell, including not only the present world with all its problems, but also Uttarakuru, the Western Pure Land [The supernatural domain of Amitābha Buddha discussed earlier], and the domain of a cakravartin king.[35]

To be clear, this does not necessarily entail that Taixu saw rebirth as an escape from our conditioned agency and responsibility. Pursuing reform in our present life and pursuing salvation in an immortal afterlife are not mutually exclusive options. One can aim for both, perhaps even at the same time if they serve conjoining ends, so we shouldn't necessarily exclude Taixu from the scope of ecological self-understanding here, but the fact that he emphasized otherworldly supernatural concerns for salvation and immortality within his tradition of practice highlights how his engagement with social reform is not necessarily what, say, a contemporary climate scientist or environmental activist would have in mind in addressing issues of the human realm. To what extent these ideas are reconcilable is an exercise I leave to the reader.[36]

Another aspect of karma to consider is the Buddhist practice of releasing fish, birds, frogs, and other animals from captivity, known as *fangsheng* (Chi.: 放生 *fàngshēng*) in China. *Fangsheng* is performed with the merit-making intention of cultivating positive karma through the liberation of sentient beings, perhaps through a kind of anthropomorphic psychological catharsis projected onto the act of (supposedly) rescuing animals from suffering and death.[37] The doctrinal basis of this practice has roots in Chinese Pure Land (and Daoist) sources, and it is widely practiced by Buddhists in China and elsewhere today, but studies of the practice have revealed that it actually causes significant environmental harm, not only often resulting in the death of the released animals themselves but also contributing to the disruption of ecosystems by introducing invasive species and diseases, not to mention that many animals are caught and sold for the express purpose of using them in *fangsheng* ceremonies.[38] So, while the practice may serve an important role for Buddhist practice, and might even account for recent resurgences of Buddhism among contemporary urban populations in China,[39] it arguably shows a lack of ecological understanding in terms of its actual consequences in the world.

There is evidence that sharing ecological knowledge of these negative consequences with others can mitigate this problematic practice, so perhaps the problem with *fangsheng* is simply a matter of ignorance that can be rectified through sharing scientific knowledge on what actually happens to animals when they are released.[40] However, there might be some self-focused bias present here too, akin to the attitude of Bill in the traffic example we explored, in terms of merely using animals as a vehicle for one's own benefit. If it is the intention of *fangsheng* practitioners to acquire credit in their own personal karmic banking accounts, and they do so without regard for the broader relational consequences of their actions, then they not only simply lack information but also lack an ecological understanding of their own agency. On the other hand, if the intention of *fangsheng* is to cultivate generosity, liberation, and well-being through compassionate transformation of the ecological relations in which one exists, then the appropriate ecological knowledge might be instrumental to reforming problematic *fangsheng* practices, or perhaps even transforming them into a kind of ecological stewardship that actually facilitates the liberation of sentient beings through virtuous agency and understanding. Whether or not this is a realistic possibility is an open question I leave for readers and Buddhists alike to contemplate.

Conclusion

We have seen a spectrum of ecological virtue and vice across the sampling of Chinese Buddhist beliefs and practices we have surveyed. Bill, Dan, and Emma could all be Chinese Buddhists. Suppose they are. Could we make a reasonable inference as to what type of Buddhist each would be? No. Complex traditions do not readily reduce to simple categories of virtue and vice, so it would be a mistake to think that, say, Emma is most likely a socially engaged Chan Buddhist while Bill spends his weekends releasing invasive bullfrog species into the wild and Dan is just waiting to be reborn in Amitābha's Pure Land. As previously mentioned, these aspects of Buddhism are intertwined throughout the traditions and practices of Chinese Buddhism and cannot be parsed out in this simple way.

Nevertheless, there are some more general conclusions that stand out from our selective investigation. Buddhism offers valuable insights that can help demonstrate ecological self-understanding, whether one is a practicing Buddhist or not. The core concepts of *anātman* and dependent origination are powerful reminders of our relationality, and the conjunction of this relationality with an understanding of karma in terms of embodied experiential responsibility, impinging on both actions and intentions, illustrates how responsible agency can be cultivated through responsive attentiveness to one's relational circumstances. On the flip side, however, we have also seen some potentially problematic features of Buddhism, such as beliefs that may emphasize transcendent salvation over the concrete responsibilities of our present conditions, and practices that fail to recognize their harmful real-world consequences. With openness to the unfolding knowledge of empirical investigation, however, coupled with its own rich insights and transformative capacities, I am hopeful that Buddhism has the conceptual resources to embody ecological self-understanding within its own traditions and help illustrate this virtue to others as we humans navigate what we might call the collective karma of our relations with our earthly home.

Notes

1. This consensus is well documented and widely discussed across numerous authoritative sources, so I will not go into the details here. See the latest data and documentation of the Intergovernmental Panel on Climate Change established by the United Nations for more information: https://www.ipcc.ch/. See the first section of chapter 6 in this volume for more information about the scientific consensus on climate change.

2. For reasons to be explained in due course, I will focus our investigation on Chinese Buddhism in particular, with specific attention to Tiantai, Huayan, Chan, and Pure Land traditions, but I also discuss some more general aspects of Buddhism here and elsewhere to help frame the nature of this inquiry and address some pertinent features of Buddhism overall as well.

3. John D. Dunne and Daniel Goleman, eds., *Ecology, Ethics, and Interdependence: The Dalai Lama in Conversation with Leading Thinkers on Climate Change* (Somerville, MA: Wisdom, 2018).

4. See, for example, Stephanie Kaza and Kenneth Kraft, eds., *Dharma Rain: Sources of Buddhist Environmentalism* (Boston: Shambhala, 2000).

5. Peter Hershock, *Buddhism in the Public Sphere: Reorienting Global Interdependence* (New York: Routledge, 2006), 14.

6. To be clear, this is not to say that epistemology is separable from ethics (indeed, I do not think it is), but rather only to help specify our investigative focus. The relationship between epistemology and ethics is complicated and contentious, but we do not need to make any specific commitments in that regard for our purposes here. For one example of how these fields can overlap, see Andrew Chignell, "The Ethics of Belief," *The Stanford Encyclopedia of Philosophy*, Spring 2018 Edition, Edited by Edward N. Zalta, https://plato.stanford.edu/archives/spr2018/entries/ethics-belief/. For more on Buddhism and environmental ethics, see chapter 6 of this volume. Also, for some reflections on Buddhism and ecological aesthetics, see Fanren Zeng, "Buddhism's Wisdom Pertaining to Ecological Aesthetics," *Introduction to Ecological Aesthetics* (Singapore: Springer, 2019), 185–94.

7. Further details about how this inquiry draws upon virtue epistemology are given in the next section. For more on virtue epistemology in general, see John Turri, Mark Alfano, and John Greco, "Virtue Epistemology," *The Stanford Encyclopedia of Philosophy*, Fall 2019 Edition, Edited by Edward N. Zalta, https://plato.stanford.edu/archives/fall2019/entries/epistemology-virtue/.

8. Nicholas S. Brasovan and Micheline M. Soong, *Buddhisms in Asia: Traditions, Transmissions, and Transformations* (Albany: State University of New York Press, 2019).

9. For more on environmental perspectives in China more broadly, see Chia-ju Chang, ed., *Chinese Environmental Humanities: Practices of Environing at the Margins* (Cham, Switzerland: Palgrave Macmillan, 2019).

10. For an overview of the development of Chinese forms of Buddhism and their interrelations with other Chinese philosophies, see Whalen Lai, "Buddhism in China: A Historical Survey," in *Encyclopedia of Chinese Philosophy*, edited by Antonio Cua (New York: Routledge, 2003), 7–19. See also Wing-Tsit Chan, *A Sourcebook in Chinese Philosophy* (Princeton: Princeton University Press 1963) and JeeLoo Liu, *An Introduction to Chinese Philosophy: From Ancient Philosophy to Chinese Buddhism* (Malden, MA: Blackwell, 2006).

11. Nicholas S. Brasovan, "Ecological Self-Understanding in Early Chinese Philosophies," *International Communication of Chinese Culture* 3, no. 2 (2016): 293–303.

12. See Lai, "Buddhism in China: A Historical Survey" and the Introduction to this volume for history and background information on these traditions.

13. Turri, Alfano, and Greco, "Virtue Epistemology."

14. Linda T. Zagzebski, *Virtues of the Mind: An Inquiry into the Nature of Virtue and the Ethical Foundations of Knowledge* (Cambridge: Cambridge University Press, 1996).

15. Jesse Butler, "Ecological Self-Understanding: A Cross-Cultural Epistemic Virtue in Contemporary Native American and Confucian Philosophy," *Science, Religion and Culture* 6, no. 1 (2019): 42–49.

16. See Jesse Butler, *Rethinking Introspection: A Pluralist Approach to the First-Person Perspective* (New York: Palgrave Macmillan, 2013) for my epistemology of the first-person perspective.

17. In fact, the cross-cultural prominence of this way of understanding virtue is one of the factors in my original formulation of ecological self-understanding as a cross-cultural virtue. See Butler, "Ecological Self-Understanding."

18. See Shundo Tachibana, *The Ethics of Buddhism* (New York: Routledge, 1995) and the Introduction to this volume for background on the Buddha's "Middle Way" and the foundational role it has played in Buddhist teachings. For more on virtue in Aristotelian and Confucian philosophy, see Jiyuan Yu, *The Ethics of Confucius and Aristotle: Mirrors of Virtue* (New York: Routledge, 2007).

19. Tiantai emerged as a uniquely Chinese school of Buddhism in the sixth century, focusing on the Lotus Sutra as its primary text. It died out in the eleventh century in China, but remains active in Japan (Tendai) and Korea (Chon'tae). In China, however, its influence continues to show in Chan and Pure Land Buddhism today. See the Introduction to this volume for further background and general details on the tradition.

20. Brook Ziporyn, "Tiantai Buddhism," *The Stanford Encyclopedia of Philosophy*, Fall 2018 Edition, Edited by Edward N. Zalta, https://plato.stanford.edu/archives/fall2018/entries/buddhism-tiantai/.

21. Ziporyn, "Tiantai Buddhism."

22. Continuing with the quote from Brook Ziporyn above: "To 'become what I am,' to be a more fully realized version of myself, is to see myself, Brook specifically, as unconditional, which means as omnipresent and eternal, which means as expressing itself in and as all things, which also means, conversely, intersubsumed, i.e., as an expression of all other things, as something as which all other things are appearing. I cannot be myself until I am a Buddha, but I cannot be a Buddha until I can be more fully (i.e., more unconditionally, more all-pervasively) myself, and that means being more fully a devil, a fool, a table, a spaceship, or, in Siming Zhili's

example, a dung beetle. Buddhist practice is the progressively fuller manifestation of my latent Buddhahood—which means also the progressively fuller manifestation of my latent Dung-Beetlehood, and indeed, my allegedly long ago already actual but really hitherto merely latent Brookhood."

23. Huayan Buddhism emerged in sixth-century China, focusing on the Flower Garland Sutra after which it is named. After flourishing through a series of influential patriarchs, the school declined in the ninth century but remains active in Japan (Kegon) and Korea (Hwaeom). In China, its insights continue to have an impact on Chan and Pure Land Buddhism. See the Introduction to this volume for further background. For more detail on the philosophy of Huayan Buddhism, see Bryan Van Norden and Nicholaos Jones, "Huayan Buddhism," *The Stanford Encyclopedia of Philosophy*, Winter 2019 Edition, Edited by Edward N. Zalta, https://plato.stanford.edu/archives/win2019/entries/buddhism-huayan/.

24. Kaza and Kraft, *Dharma Rain*, 58–59.

25. Kaza and Kraft, *Dharma Rain*, 58.

26. For a more general account of how Asian philosophies such as Buddhism and Daoism may be conducive to moral agency regarding environmental issues, see Heesoon Bai, "Reclaiming Our Moral Agency through Healing: A Call to Moral, Social, Environmental Activists," *Journal of Moral Education* 41, no. 3 (2012): 311–27.

27. Rick Repetti, ed., *Buddhist Perspectives on Free Will: Agentless Agency?* (New York: Routledge, 2016).

28. See the Introduction in this volume for more on karma in East Asian Buddhism.

29. See the Introduction and chapter 1 in this volume for differences in kinds of Pure Land Buddhism.

30. JeeLoo Liu, *An Introduction to Chinese Philosophy: From Ancient Philosophy to Chinese Buddhism*, 216.

31. Peter Hershock, "Responsive Virtuosity: A Classical Chinese Buddhist Contribution to Contemporary Conversations of Freedom," in *Why Traditional Chinese Philosophy Still Matters: The Relevance of Ancient Wisdom for the Global Age*, edited by Ming Dong Gu (New York: Routledge, 2018), 85–101.

32. Quoted by JeeLoo Liu, *An Introduction to Chinese Philosophy: From Ancient Philosophy to Chinese Buddhism*, 317. See also Hui-neng, *The Platform Sutra of the Sixth Patriarch*, trans. with notes by Philip B. Yampolsky (New York: Columbia University Press, 1967).

33. Charles B. Jones, *Chinese Pure Land Buddhism: Understanding a Tradition of Practice* (Honolulu: University of Hawai'i Press, 2019).

34. Kenneth K. Tanaka, "Where is the Pure Land?: Controversy in Chinese Buddhism on the Nature of Pure Land." *The Pacific World* 3 (1987): 36–45. See the Introduction in this volume for an explanation of *dukkha* and the First Noble Truth of Buddhism.

35. Charles B. Jones, *Chinese Pure Land Buddhism: Understanding a Tradition of Practice*, 57.

36. For more on the location of Pure Land in relation to environmental issues, see William Yau-nang Ng, "Pure Land and the Environmental Movement in Humanistic Buddhism," in *Dao Companions to Chinese Philosophy* 9, ed. Y. Wang and S. Wawrytko (Dordrecht: Springer 2019), 419–40.

37. Der-Ruey Yang, "Animal Release: The Dharma Being Staged between Marketplace and Park," *Cultural Diversity in China* 1, no. 2 (2015): 141–63.

38. Henry Shui and Leah Stokes, "Buddhist Animal Release Practices: Historic, Environmental, Public Health and Economic Concerns," *Contemporary Buddhism* 9, no. 2 (2008): 181–96.

39. Yang, "Animal Release: The Dharma Being Staged between Marketplace and Park."

40. Xuan Liu et al., "Ecological Knowledge Reduces Religious Release of Invasive Species," *Ecosphere* 4, no. 2 (2013): 21.

Bibliography

Bai, Heesoon. "Reclaiming our Moral Agency through Healing: A Call to Moral, Social, Environmental Activists." *Journal of Moral Education* 41, no. 3 (2012): 311–27.

Brasovan, Nicholas S. "Ecological Self-Understanding in Early Chinese Philosophies." *International Communication of Chinese Culture* 3, no. 2 (2016): 293–303.

———, and Micheline M. Soong, eds. *Buddhisms in Asia: Traditions, Transmissions, and Transformations.* Albany: State University of New York Press, 2019.

Butler, Jesse. *Rethinking Introspection: A Pluralist Approach to the First-Person Perspective.* New York: Palgrave Macmillan, 2013.

———. "Ecological Self-Understanding: A Cross-Cultural Epistemic Virtue in Contemporary Native American and Confucian Philosophy." *Science, Religion and Culture* 6, no. 1 (2019): 42–49.

Chan, Wing-Tsit, trans. and comp. *A Sourcebook in Chinese Philosophy.* Princeton: Princeton University Press, 1963.

Chang, Chia-ju, ed. *Chinese Environmental Humanities: Practices of Environing at the Margins.* Cham, Switzerland: Palgrave Macmillan, 2019.

Chignell, Andrew. "The Ethics of Belief." *The Stanford Encyclopedia of Philosophy.* Spring 2018 edition. Edited by Edward N. Zalta. https://plato.stanford.edu/archives/spr2018/entries/ethics-belief/.

Dunne, John D., and Daniel Goleman, eds. *Ecology, Ethics, and Interdependence: The Dalai Lama in Conversation with Leading Thinkers on Climate Change.* Somerville, MA: Wisdom, 2018.

Hershock, Peter. *Buddhism in the Public Sphere: Reorienting Global Interdependence.* New York: Routledge, 2006.

———. "Responsive Virtuosity: A Classical Chinese Buddhist Contribution to Contemporary Conversations of Freedom." In *Why Traditional Chinese Philosophy*

Still Matters: The Relevance of Ancient Wisdom for the Global Age, edited by Ming Dong Gu, 85–101. New York: Routledge, 2018.

Hui-neng. *The Platform Sutra of the Sixth Patriarch*. Translated with notes by Philip B. Yampolsky. New York: Columbia University Press, 1967.

Jones, Charles B. *Chinese Pure Land Buddhism: Understanding a Tradition of Practice*. Honolulu: University of Hawai'i Press, 2019.

Kaza, Stephanie, and Kenneth Kraft, eds. *Dharma Rain: Sources of Buddhist Environmentalism*. Boston: Shambhala, 2000.

Lai, Whalen. "Buddhism in China: A Historical Survey." In *Encyclopedia of Chinese Philosophy*, edited by Antonio Cua, 7–19. New York: Routledge, 2003.

Liu, JeeLoo. *An Introduction to Chinese Philosophy: From Ancient Philosophy to Chinese Buddhism*. Malden, MA: Blackwell, 2006.

Liu, Xuan, et al. "Ecological Knowledge Reduces Religious Release of Invasive Species." *Ecosphere* 4, no. 2 (2013): 21.

Ng, William Yau-nang. "Pure Land and the Environmental Movement in Humanistic Buddhism." In *Dao Companions to Chinese Philosophy* 9, edited by Y. Wang and S. Wawrytko, 419–40. Dordrecht: Springer 2019.

Repetti, Rick, ed. *Buddhist Perspectives on Free Will: Agentless Agency?* New York: Routledge, 2016.

Shui, Henry, and Leah Stokes. "Buddhist Animal Release Practices: Historic, Environmental, Public Health and Economic Concerns." *Contemporary Buddhism* 9, no. 2 (2008): 181–96.

Tachibana, Shundo. *The Ethics of Buddhism*. New York: Routledge, 1995.

Tanaka, Kenneth K. "Where Is the Pure Land?: Controversy in Chinese Buddhism on the Nature of Pure Land." *The Pacific World* 3 (1987): 36–45.

Turri, John, Mark Alfano, and John Greco. "Virtue Epistemology." *The Stanford Encyclopedia of Philosophy*, Fall 2019 edition. Edited by Edward N. Zalta. https://plato.stanford.edu/archives/fall2019/entries/epistemology-virtue/.

Van Norden, Bryan, and Nicholaos Jones. "Huayan Buddhism." *The Stanford Encyclopedia of Philosophy*, Winter 2019 edition. Edited by Edward N. Zalta. https://plato.stanford.edu/archives/win2019/entries/buddhism-huayan/.

Yang, Der-Ruey. "Animal Release: The Dharma Being Staged between Marketplace and Park." *Cultural Diversity in China* 1, no. 2 (2015): 141–63.

Yu, Jiyuan. *The Ethics of Confucius and Aristotle: Mirrors of Virtue*. New York: Routledge, 2007.

Zagzebski, Linda T. *Virtues of the Mind: An Inquiry into the Nature of Virtue and the Ethical Foundations of Knowledge*. Cambridge: Cambridge University Press, 1996.

Zeng, Fanren. "Buddhism's Wisdom Pertaining to Ecological Aesthetics." In *Introduction to Ecological Aesthetics*, 185–94. Singapore: Springer, 2019.

Ziporyn, Brook. "Tiantai Buddhism." *The Stanford Encyclopedia of Philosophy*, Fall 2018 Edition. Edited by Edward N. Zalta. https://plato.stanford.edu/archives/fall2018/entries/buddhism-tiantai/.

Chapter 8

Wisdom and Compassion in Chinul, Korean Seon Buddhism, and Postmodern Ethics

ROBERT H. SCOTT

While there are many forms of Buddhism, including various forms of East Asian Buddhism, all forms of Buddhism share the core doctrine of the Four Noble Truths, which point to the Eightfold Path and the practices of wisdom (right views and intentions), morality (right speech, actions, and livelihood), and meditation (right effort, mindfulness, and concentration).[1] This chapter inquires into how the twelfth-century Korean Seon (Chi. Chan; Jpn. Zen) master Chinul (1158–1210 CE) played a pivotal role in shaping the ways Seon Buddhism cultivates the practices of wisdom, morality, and meditation. Further, the chapter brings into focus how the close ties Chinul weaves among meditation, wisdom, and compassion point to an ethic of responsive virtuosity that resonates with the ethical implications of recent work in postmodern phenomenological philosophy in providing an alternative to modern normative ethical theories, which center on the universalization of rules.

The aims of this chapter are threefold. First, I aim to show the key role Chinul played in shaping the distinct character of Korean Seon and in restoring harmony among Buddhist schools in Korea in a time of discord; second, the chapter will show how Chinul's life and work contributed to the development of a Seon ethic of responsive virtuosity and compassion, dynamically arising with the practices of meditation and wisdom; third, I show how the Seon ethic of responsive virtuosity resonates with work on ethics in contemporary phenomenology and postmodern philosophy. In particular, I highlight connections between the Seon ethic of Chinul and the ethical implications of work by the contemporary phenomenological philosopher John Russon.

Jin Y. Park, a contemporary, leading scholar of Seon/Zen Buddhism, suggests that certain figures and texts in Korean Seon, including Chinul, point the way forward to "a new direction in our understanding of ethical categorization itself."[2] Park goes on to show how Seon ethics resonates in many ways with several aspects of "postmodern ethical thinking," arguing that together Seon Buddhism and postmodern ethics harbor important resources for the development of a much-needed "alternative to normative ethics."[3] By "normative ethics," Park refers to the prevailing models of ethics in modern Western philosophy, particularly Kantian and utilitarian ethical theory, that privilege universalizability as the standard for ethical normativity. Pointing to a need for a new, multicultural ethical paradigm, Park draws on the work of Chinul, as well as several postmodern and East Asian philosophers, to introduce her proposal for an "ethics of tension" as an alternative to the ethics of universalization. Park links the ethics of tension to the central Buddhist virtue of compassion. She further notes that "how the logic of compassion functions in Buddhism has yet to be fully investigated."[4] This chapter builds on Park's work in developing an alternative to modern, normative ethics based on universalization and by inquiring further into how the logic of compassion functions in Buddhism and, more broadly, in contemporary phenomenological thinking about ethics.

I take as a starting assumption that there is a need for an alternative—or at least a supplement—to modern universalization-based theories of ethical normativity. Among the problems with universalization-based theories of ethical normativity are tendencies toward anthropocentrism, reduction of differences to accommodate rules, and a lack of adaptability to variations in cultural values. This chapter contributes to developing a multicultural ethical paradigm by drawing out links between the Buddhist ethic of compassion and responsive virtuosity and postmodern, phenomenological ethics. A key element of the new ethical paradigm, I argue, is the link between wisdom and compassion which can be traced in both Chinul's work and in the practice of phenomenology as developed by John Russon. I conclude that the link between wisdom and compassion in both Seon Buddhism and Russon's phenomenology support the viability of an ethic of compassion and responsive virtuosity as an alternative to modern normative ethics based on the universalization of rules.[5]

The life and work of Chinul—known in Korea by his posthumous title State Preceptor Puril Pojo, the Sun of Buddhahood That Shines Everywhere[6]—stands out, in part, for his role in restoring a spirit of ecumenism and harmony among Buddhist schools in late-twelfth-century Korea, which had been in a state of discord for more than a century when Chinul came of age. Throughout Chinul's writings, an ethic of compassion, ecumenism, and inclusion resonates. While he spent much of his life in small monastic communities, his role in restoring harmony among Buddhist schools in Korea and in cultivating a spirit of compassion and openness to other traditions, justifies considering him to be a kind of social activist of his day and a precursor to Engaged Buddhism movements of recent times.[7]

Sketching the Historical Context of Late-Twelfth-Century Korean Buddhism

Korean Buddhism today, Robert Buswell argues, has become "the most ecumenical (Buddhist) tradition in Asia," and Chinul played a major role in cultivating this spirit of openness and inclusion.[8] In order to understand the pivotal role Chinul played in the development of modern Korean Buddhism, an understanding of the historical context of late-twelfth-century Korea is necessary. Other factors contributed to the growth of an ecumenical spirit in Korean Buddhism, of course, including the role Korean monks embraced beginning prior to Chinul as "preservers and interpreters of the larger Buddhist tradition,"[9] exemplified, for instance, by their preservation of the *Tripitaka Koreana*. The *Tripitaka* is an immense repository of Buddhist scriptures (and other Buddhist writings), inclusive of writings from various Buddhist schools and originally preserved on hand-carved wooden blocks in the eleventh century, destroyed during a Mongol invasion in 1232 and, then, through a large-scale community effort, restored by 1248. Another important contributing factor to the spirit of ecumenism was the long-standing mutually beneficial relationship in Korea between rulers and Buddhist monks beginning in the seventh century with the unification of the peninsula under the Unified Silla Dynasty (668–937 CE) and continuing until the beginning of the Josŏn Dynasty (1392–1910), when the Korean state shifted sponsorship to neo-Confucian institutions and Buddhism declined in favor and influence. The state sponsorship of Buddhism in Korea from the seventh to the late fourteenth centuries provided institutional support and pragmatic motivation for the various Buddhist schools in Korea to cultivate a spirit of ecumenism and harmony. However, a break in harmony among Buddhist schools arose in the ninth century due to doctrinal disputes and was aggravated further by corruption among monks. The current of discord among Buddhist schools continued into the late twelfth century, when Chinul's efforts proved pivotal in restoring harmony.

During the Unified Silla period (668–937 CE), Korean Buddhist monasteries benefited from strong state support, and this led to "a golden age of Buddhist scholasticism" in Korea.[10] Several Buddhist schools flourished on the Korean Peninsula during this period, including Pure Land Buddhism, Cheontae, and Seon. The most widely embraced school of Buddhism, however, was Hwaeom, a scholastic school that holds the *Flower Garland Sutra* (San. *Avataṃsaka Sūtra*) as its focal scripture, and its widespread influence continued into the Goryeo dynasty (937–1392). While monks from the various Buddhist schools coexisted in harmony from the seventh until the ninth centuries, including sharing monasteries, tensions arose in the mid-ninth century between the scholastic schools (Hwaeom and Cheontae, primarily) and the Seon school. These disputes centered on differences over the value of the practice of meditation relative to the study of sutras and disagreements on soteriological doctrine. While the Seon school prioritized meditation over the study of sutras,[11] the scholastics prioritized the study of sutras. In regard to soteriology, the Seon soteriology (following the ninth-century Chan monk Linji) of sudden enlightenment through mind-to-mind transmission from master to student ("sudden enlightenment/sudden cultivation") came into conflict with the scholastic doctrine of gradual cultivation and the gradual attainment of enlightenment through the study of sutras and other forms of practice ("gradual enlightenment/gradual cultivation").[12] These disputes led to scholastic monks increasingly viewing adepts of Seon as unorthodox and practitioners of Seon viewing other forms of Buddhism as inferior. Tensions were further aggravated by corruption among some monks who, taking advantage of the close ties between the monasteries and the state, pursued the monastic life for economic gain or secular power more than out of a sincere commitment to a life of devotion. The combination of doctrinal disputes and corruption among monks led to a state of discord and moral decline in Korean Buddhism during the early Goryeo period, and this decline was considered by many to be a symptom of a long period of general decline for the dharma, known as *mòfǎ* (末法; Jpn. *mappō*; Kor. *malpop*).

In the throes of this current of discord, in the late eleventh century, the Cheontae monk Uich'ŏn (1055–1101 CE) attempted to bridge the divide between the scholastic and the Seon schools, but his efforts had little success. Uich'ŏn, who is recognized and honored as a founder of Cheontae Buddhism in Korea, advocated for "a comprehensive approach to doctrinal study"[13] that emphasized both meditation and the study of a wide range of sutras, in hopes of appealing to both scholastic and Seon schools.[14] While his efforts were sincere, Uich'ŏn's criticisms of Seon were too harsh for Seon adepts to accept, and his early death (at age forty-seven) cut short his work. In the late twelfth century, however, Chinul took up the project of mediating disputes, and we can trace a historical shift toward a restoration of harmony through his efforts. Why did a restorative shift toward harmony among Buddhist schools in Korea take place following the efforts of Chinul and not earlier? While many historical factors were involved in this shift, a look at Chinul's life and work can help us to understand how Chinul played a pivotal role in restoring harmony by applying an ethic of responsive virtuosity or skillful means (San. *upāya*).

Examples of Responsive Virtuosity in the Life of Chinul

Not much is known of Chinul's early life, but we do know that he was a sickly child, so much so that his father, Chong Kwang-u (d.u.), who was rector of the local state academy, made a vow to the Buddha that if his son could be cured of his illness, "he would have him ordained in the Buddhist order."[15] Shortly after Chong Kwang-u made this vow, the child recovered, and at the age of eight Chinul entered the monastery at Kulsansa, near Kaeseong (the capitol at the time) in the "Nine Mountains" school of Korean Seon. Chinul's master at Kulsansa was Chonghwi (d.u.), a Seon monk who received mind-to-mind transmission from the master Yan'guan Qi'an, the founder of Kulsansa monastery and the tenth-generation successor to Pomil (810–889 CE) of the Southern School of Chan (Hongzhou, China).[16] It is unknown how close the master/student relationship was between Chinul and Chonghwi, but it is apparent that Chinul never received mind-to-mind transmission from Chonghwi or any other master.[17] Nevertheless, tradition considers Chinul to be, through Chonghwi, part of the lineage of the Southern School of Chan. Whether or not his relationship with his master was close, Buswell notes that Chinul "made up for the dearth of personal instruction by drawing his inspiration from the Buddhist scriptures."[18] Given the emphasis placed on the practice of meditation by the Seon school at the time, Chinul's devotion to the study of sutras and commentaries is remarkable, and it evidently contributed to his ability to apply skillful means in mediating between the scholastics, who prioritized the study of sutras, and the Seon school of which he was a part.

As Peter Hershock puts it, "skillful means" (San. *upāya*) refers to "the creative devices employed by bodhisattvas in carrying out their vow to liberate all sentient beings."[19] The vow mentioned here refers to the vow of compassion, made by all bodhisattvas, which orients action toward the liberation of sentient beings from suffering. Skillful means, therefore, involves applying creativity in practicing compassion, a central Buddhist virtue. Hershock further notes that *upāya* can be translated as "responsive virtuosity,"[20] meaning the ability to respond in all situations in ways that steer relational dynamics toward the liberation of sentient beings.

While Chinul's path to enlightenment was atypical for a Seon master in its lack of mind-to-mind transmission and in its reliance on the study of sutras, he shows responsive virtuosity in telling the story of his path to enlightenment in ways that contributed to diffusing discord and restoring harmony among Buddhist schools. Chinul tells of his path to enlightenment through his accounts of three awakening experiences. Each of these accounts displays responsive virtuosity when considered in relation to the historical context of discord among Buddhist schools, in that the narratives affirm both the Seon emphases on meditation and sudden enlightenment as well as the scholastic emphases on the intense study of sutras and gradual cultivation leading to enlightenment. As will be discussed in more detail below, Chinul's accounts of his awakening experiences further demonstrate responsive virtuosity in cultivating an attitude of openness and inclusion toward other traditions and in showing members of his own school how the central doctrines of the scholastics can be drawn together with Seon into a more comprehensive form of Buddhist practice.

In identifying ways in which Chinul's accounts of his awakening experiences demonstrate responsive virtuosity we may first note that there were three and not just one awakening experience, which implicitly affirms the scholastic doctrine of gradual cultivation. Yet, in accordance with the Buddhist logic of nondualism, the accounts also affirm the Seon doctrine of sudden enlightenment. In one of his early works, Chinul illustrates his syncretic soteriology by way of a simile: "The two aspects of sudden awakening and gradual cultivation are like the two wheels of a cart: neither one can be missing."[21] While his first awakening experience marked a kind of sudden enlightenment, thereby affirming Seon soteriology, his subsequent two awakening experiences both support the idea of gradual cultivation in that, through each subsequent experience he attains new insights that remove residual attachments and karmic obstructions and further (that is to say, *gradually*) transform behavioral habits in liberating ways. In adopting the syncretic soteriology of sudden enlightenment/gradual cultivation, Chinul applies the Buddhist logic of nondualism and displays responsive virtuosity in ways that contribute to resolving doctrinal disputes and bridging the divide between the scholastic and Seon schools.

In addition to affirming sudden/gradual soteriology, Chinul's awakening experience accounts also demonstrate responsive virtuosity in relation to the situation of discord by foregrounding the intense study of Buddhist texts, including Seon sutras, thereby affirming the scholastic prioritization of the study of sutras without compromising Seon tradition and doctrine. Chinul's first awakening experience occurred in 1182 at the age of twenty-four, after leaving his home monastery of Kulsansa and having arrived at Chongwonsa in the southwestern part of the peninsula.[22] The experience occurred while reading the following passage from *The Platform Sutra* by Huineng (638–713 CE), the sixth patriarch of Chan: "The self-nature of suchness gives rise to thoughts. But even though the six sense-faculties see, hear, sense, and know, [the self-nature] is not tainted by the myriads of images. The true nature is constantly free and self-reliant."[23] The "self-nature" refers to the doctrine of Buddha-nature (San. *tathāgatagarbha*), which, according to Seon doctrine, is common to all sentient beings. Chinul reports that, prompted by this passage, he experienced a sudden awakening to the doctrine of Buddha-nature as the "true nature" which "is not tainted" and "is constantly free and self-reliant." This awakening experience marks, for Chinul, a kind of sudden enlightenment and fits with what he later describes as the initial "understanding-awakening," which, after further (gradual) cultivation, is followed by a more complete "realization-awakening."[24] The concepts of an initial understanding-awakening and a subsequent and more complete realization-awakening, discussed in more detail below (in the section on Chinul's third awakening experience), aid in clarifying how the nondual logic of sudden/gradual awakening works.

In 1185, Chinul left the monastery at Chongwonsa and spent the next three years at Pomunsa monastery in the southeastern part of the peninsula. His second awakening experience took place at Pomunsa in 1188, near the end of his time there, and his account of this experience further demonstrates responsive virtuosity in bringing into focus the primary Hwaeom scripture, "The Flower Garland Sutra" (San. *Avataṃsaka Sūtra*) thereby re-affirming the scholastic emphasis on the study of sutras, this time in reference to a central scholastic text. Chinul notes in this account that he was reading, along with the sutra, a commentary by the Huayan (Kor. Hwaeom) monk Li Tongxuan (635–730 CE), further affirming the value of scholastic teaching. The passage Chinul focuses on from "The Flower Garland Sutra" reads: "The wisdom of the *tathagātas* is just like this: it is complete in the bodies of all sentient beings. It is merely all these ordinary, foolish people who are not aware of it and do not recognize it."[25] Through his study of this passage and Li's commentary, Chinul awakens to an understanding that the message of Hwaeom and Seon are, in fact, the same. As he goes on to explain, he realizes the unity of the central Seon doctrine that all sentient beings possess the wisdom of the *tathagātas* (that is to say, the Buddhas) and the central Hwaeom doctrine that the study of the sutras leads to universal wisdom, which consists in the insight, as Li's commentary points out, that the true mind is "the Buddha of Immovable Wisdom."[26] Chinul further realizes that the central Seon doctrine that all sentient beings possess Buddha-nature converges with the central Hwaeom insight into the unimpeded interpenetration of all things (San. *pratītya-samutpāda*), illustrated in Hwaeom writings through the image of Indra's Jewel Net in which each knot is a jewel and each jewel that binds the net together reflects all the other jewels in the net. This second awakening experience had such a profound impact on Chinul that, upon reading the passage, he recounts that he put the sutra on his head with reverence and began to weep, and it marked a step forward for him in the process of gradual cultivation by removing residual attachments to ongoing doctrinal disputes between Seon and other schools.[27]

By adopting an ecumenical sudden/gradual soteriology, Chinul not only shows responsive virtuosity in diffusing tensions among Buddhist schools, he also guides Korean Seon in a distinct and more inclusive doctrinal direction, which had a lasting impact. In China, prior to the twelfth century, there were several doctrinal schools of Chan, among which the Linji school (founded by the ninth-century Chan monk Linji) eventually emerged as the principal school, also taking root in Japan where it is known as Renzai Zen. The Linji school of Chan/Zen affirms the soteriological doctrine of sudden enlightenment/sudden cultivation; hence, Chinul's adoption of sudden/gradual soteriology marks a departure from Linji Chan. It is important to note, however, that Chinul's adoption of sudden/gradual soteriology was not a complete departure from Chan tradition as it was grounded in a leading Chan soteriology from earlier in ninth-century China—that of the Heze school of southern China, which Chinul learned from the writings of the Huayan (Kor. Hwaeom) and Chan monk Zongmi (780–841 CE).

The topic of Chinul's last work was Zongmi's *Dharma Collection and Special Practice Record*.[28] In this text, Zongmi provides a detailed account of the debate over sudden versus gradual soteriology as it was carried out among Chan monks in the first half of the ninth century in southern China. In the initial debate, the sudden/gradual doctrine of the Heze school won the day. While the sudden/gradual doctrine eventually faded in influence in China in favor of the sudden/sudden doctrine of the Linji school, which appeared some years later, the former view was renewed in Korean Seon through Chinul. Integral to Chinul's creative application of skillful means was his recognition of the importance of Zongmi's text and the aptness of the sudden/gradual doctrine for contributing to resolving disputes in the volatile context of discord in twelfth-century Korean Buddhism.[29] Chinul's creative retrieval of sudden/gradual soteriology contributed both to restoring harmony among Buddhist schools in Korea and to setting in motion the development of a distinctly Korean form of Seon, which he would impact further, as we will see below, in his retrieval of the method of *huatou* meditation, drawn from the early–twelfth-century monk Dahui.

In addition to having three awakening experiences, Chinul is also well known for establishing the *Samādhi* and *Prajñā* Society, a devoted, open group that included practitioners of Daoism and Confucianism. Both his awakening experiences and his role in establishing this society bear significantly on answering the question of what made Chinul a transformative figure in Korean Buddhism, and both illustrate ways in which he displayed responsive virtuosity as a mediator in a time of discord.

The *Samādhi* and *Prajñā* Society and the Intertwinement of Meditation, Wisdom, and Compassion

Chinul's accounts of his first two awakening experiences convey a deep spirit of openness and inclusion toward the scholastic schools of Buddhism, along with a compassionate desire to restore harmony between the scholastic and Seon schools. Before turning to Chinul's third awakening experience, in this section I will show how Chinul further exemplifies the spirit of openness and inclusion through his role in establishing the *Samādhi* and *Prajñā* Society. At the end of this section, I will briefly outline how Chinul's effectiveness as a mediator can be linked with his clear conception of the interrelationships among the three core Buddhist disciplines of meditation, wisdom, and morality (e.g., compassion).

Chinul first proposed forming the *Samādhi* and *Prajñā* Society to a few of his fellow monks in 1180 (at age twenty-two), but the formation of the Society was delayed until 1188 due, in part, to delays in finding a location. In 1188, he accepted an invitation to help establish the Society at Kŏjosa temple in the southeastern part of the peninsula, and he remained there until 1197. In 1190, while at Kŏjosa, he published *Encouragement to Practice* in which he explained that two of the primary goals of the Society, which he saw as intertwined, included revitalizing Seon and cultivating an ethos of openness and inclusion. In the closing remarks of that work, he writes, "I humbly hope that men of high moral standards who have grown tired of worldly affairs—regardless of whether they are adherents of Seon, the scholastic sects, Confucianism, or Taoism—will abandon the dusty domain of this world, soar high above all things, and devote themselves earnestly to the path of inner cultivation which is commensurate with this aim."[30] In contrast to Ui'chŏn who, at times, directed overly harsh criticisms toward schools other than his own, we see in this passage how Chinul skillfully and directly expresses an attitude of welcome toward both various Buddhist schools and other traditions. Chinul's vision for the Society was to create an open and inclusive community, oriented by the vow of compassion, in which members could practice meditation aimed at attaining a state of calmness and alertness, which correlate with the ideals of *samādhi* (meditation) and *prajñā* (wisdom), respectively. The core practice of meditation, Chinul explains, enables the attainment of a state of calm alertness, which facilitates what he refers to as "tracing back the radiance of one's own mind" to the "true mind" or Buddha-nature. Having attained insight into the true mind as Buddha-nature, the practice continues by further attuning oneself to Buddha-nature and culminates in the attainment of a kind of wisdom (*prajñā*) which activates and amplifies compassion toward sentient beings. Chinul eloquently expresses the intertwinement of meditation, wisdom, and compassion in the following passage: "Since we have vowed to ferry across others, we must first cultivate *samādhi* and *prajñā*. Once we have gained the power of the path, our compassion will surge like billowing clouds; our ocean of practices will be like towering waves. Into the far distant future we will rescue all sentient beings, worship the three jewels, and continue the work of the family of buddhas. How can we be compared to adepts who are biased toward calmness?"[31] The vow mentioned in the first line of this passage refers to the "vow of compassion," which all bodhisattvas take, affirming their commitment to act with compassion in the service of liberating sentient beings. In the above passage, Chinul articulates the seamless connection between the three core disciplines of the Eightfold Path: meditation facilitates insight into the true mind (wisdom) and, through the attainment of meditative wisdom, compassion surges forward like "towering waves," aimed at liberating and rescuing sentient beings even into the "far distant future." This is not to say that meditation precedes wisdom; rather, meditation and wisdom are nondual, as calmness and alertness are aspects of the same practice.[32] The closing question in the passage alludes to a common criticism of the Seon school, namely, that it was a "do nothing" school lacking in emphasis on the core Buddhist value of compassion. In this passage, Chinul emphasizes that the Seon practices of meditation and wisdom, far from leading to inaction, activate compassion, and he demonstrates this point through the spirit of openness and inclusion actively embodied by the *Samādhi* and *Prajñā* Society.

Chinul provides further insight into the dynamic interrelationship between wisdom and compassion by drawing on the Seon doctrine of nonduality in his *Treatise on the Complete and Sudden Attainment of Buddhahood*. There, he describes the wisdom attained through sudden enlightenment in terms of an awakening to the true mind understood as "the buddha of Immovable Wisdom" or Buddha-nature.[33] With this wisdom, which recalls the insight attained in his second awakening experience, comes a recognition that the true mind and Buddha-nature are nondual. He further realizes that all the Buddhas interpenetrate each other and are therefore nondual. Drawing the link between wisdom and compassion, he notes that the awakening to the wisdom of Buddha-nature leads to various "fruitions" of buddhahood associated with various modes of wisdom and compassion. He writes,

Accordingly, the sublime wisdom that is devoid of mind, nature, and principle and that discerns the one vehicle, the three vehicles, and the causes and results of [rebirth among] humans and divinities—this is named Manjuśrī. To practice together in accordance with discriminating wisdom in order to benefit sentient beings while being aware of their respective spiritual faculties and without taking a moment of rest—this is named Samantabhadra. The vow to use one's great compassion in order to rescue all sentient beings—this is named Avalokiteśvara. To cultivate simultaneously these three [bodhisattvas'] states of mind—this is named Vairocana Buddha. When this becomes habitual, it is called self-reliance. When there is not one dharma that does not stand out clearly, it is called unimpeded.

In this passage, Chinul both recognizes distinctions among various bodhi-sattvas associated with differing modes of wisdom and compassionate action while, at same time, noting that they are nondual in that all manifest the same buddhahood. That is, while it is possible to draw distinctions between Manjuśrī (the Buddha of Immovable Wisdom), Samantabhadra (associated with discriminative wisdom in the service of others), Avalokiteśvara (the Buddha of compassion), and Vairocana (the Buddha of complete wisdom), all of these are also, under the logic of nonduality, the same buddhahood. In making this point, Chinul again demonstrates skillful means in bridging the divide with scholastics by drawing on scholastic sources, quoting the Huayan monk Li's *Exposition*: "Whether it is a causal buddha or a fruition buddha it is of one nature—buddhahood."[34] By illustrating, through the doctrine of nonduality, the difference and sameness among Buddhas associated with wisdom and those associated with compassionate action, Chinul provides further insight into the close interrelationship between wisdom and compassion.

In the final section below, I will show how a similar ethic to the Buddhist ethic of responsive virtuosity arising from the interrelationship of wisdom and compassion can be traced in the work of the contemporary phenomenological philosopher John Russon. But first, I will note the importance of Chinul's third awakening experience as it relates to the development of Korean Seon and Chinul's conception of an ethic of responsive virtuosity.

Chinul's Third Awakening, *Huatou* Meditation, and the Possibility of Unlimited Responsive Virtuosity

Chinul's third awakening experience occurred in 1198 CE in the southern part of the peninsula at Sangmuju on Mount Chiri while he and a few companions were taking a solitary retreat along their journey to Songgwangsa, which was to be the new site for the rapidly growing *Samādhi* and *Prajñā* Society. The experience occurred while Chinul read the following passage from Dahui (1089–1163 CE), a Chan monk of the Linji tradition: "Seon does not consist in quietude; it does not consist in bustle. It does not consist in the activities of daily life; it does not consist in ratiocination. Nevertheless, it is of first importance not to investigate [Seon] while rejecting quietude or bustle, the activities of daily life, or ratiocination. Unexpectedly, your eyes will open and you then will know that these are all things taking place inside your own home."[35] Working through this passage, we can infer that it must have provided for Chinul a rebuttal to the scholastic criticism that Seon is a "do nothing" school. The passage counters this common critique by indicating that Seon is not reducible to either solitary meditation or social action ("bustle"); nor is it reducible to interpretations of sutras (ratiocination). Nevertheless, practitioners of Seon should not reject or disparage the value of any of these activities (meditation, social action, and rational interpretation of sutras). The implication of the passage is that Seon involves all three, but is not attached to any of the three. In contrast to Chinul's accounts of his first two awakenings, however, his account of the third awakening experience does not elaborate on the meaning of the passage cited; instead, he writes, without explanation, "I understood this [passage] and naturally nothing blocked my chest again and I never again dwelt together with an enemy. From then on I was at peace."[36] In view of this response, we may infer that the full meaning of the experience lay beyond discriminative interpretation (ratiocination) but that the nonarticulable experience evidently enabled a further removal of remaining karmic blockages that had persisted in the form of attachments to passions or views. We may further infer that it marked for Chinul a "realization-awakening," the completion of the process of gradual cultivation that followed his previous two awakening experiences. At this stage, at the age of forty, Chinul expresses that he has attained a level of wisdom through which he is now "able to respond to things autonomously and without limitation,"[37] namely, with unlimited responsive virtuosity. That is, having attained the realization-awakening, he will be able to act, moving forward, unencumbered by attachments, with the highest degree of responsive virtuosity and compassion toward sentient beings. In the final twelve years of his life, this would involve primarily leading the growing *Samādhi* and *Prajñā* Society at Songgwangsa monastery and completing his writings for the benefit of future generations.

As Jin Park points out, interesting links can be drawn between Chinul's insights and recent work in postmodern ethics. Park highlights connections between what she describes as an "ethics of tension" in Chinul's writings and key concepts related to ethics in the work of Merleau-Ponty, Julia Kristeva, Jacques Derrida, and others.[38] In the discussion of Russon in the next section, I build further on the connections Park draws between Buddhist ethics and the work of postmodern philosophers on ethics, with special emphasis on the interrelationship between wisdom and compassion. Before turning to Russon's work, however, a bit more should be said about the influence of Dahui on Chinul's development of a new form of meditation practice called *huatou* (Chi.; Kor. *hwadu*) meditation, which would become a distinguishing feature of Korean Seon.

Through his reading of Dahui, Chinul learned and adopted *huatou* meditation, which became a standard form of meditation practice in what has since been known as *kanhua* ("observing the keyword") Seon. *Kanhua* Seon derives from *gong'an* (公; Chi.; Jpn. *kōan*) meditation,[39] which is widely practiced in the Linji Chan/Zen tradition in China and Japan. Traditional *gong'an* meditation involves guided meditation on a *gong'an* that typically consists of an enigmatic dialogue between a master and student. In traditional *gong'an* meditation, the student goes through all the possible interpretations of the meaning of the dialogue until all interpretations are exhausted, at which point the student might arrive at a breakthrough insight that cannot be put into words. Chinul adopts Dahui's innovation on this method, which focuses interpretation on a key word or phrase in the dialogue. Dahui's *huatou* method (like Zongmi's sudden/gradual soteriology) quickly faded in China in favor of traditional Linji *gong'an* practice, but Chinul retrieved and cultivated *huatou* meditation in the *Samādhi* and *Prajñā* Society and passed it on through his successor Hyesim who established it as a focal practice for *kanhua* Seon. *Hwadu* (Kor.) meditation remains the primary method of meditation practice in Korean Seon today. Before explaining this method further, it should be noted that with the introduction of *hwadu* meditation, we see another way in which Chinul had a transformative effect in shaping the distinct character of Korean Seon, in addition to his influences on Seon soteriology, its spirit of openness and inclusion, and his role as mediator in restoring harmony among schools.

As noted above, the *huatou* (Chi.; Kor. *hwadu*) method involves focusing on a "keyword" or phrase in the *gong'an*, rather than on the whole dialogue. *Huatou* means "head of speech," which refers to the source of language beyond words, as opposed to the "end of speech" (Chi. *huawei*), which refers to the possible interpretive meanings of the word(s). An example of a *huatou*, which Chinul discusses, is the "No!" *huatou* in which "No!" is the keyword in the *gong'an* that begins with the question: "Does a dog have Buddha nature?" In this form of meditation practice, the meditator focuses on the keyword "No!" (or, in phrase form, "dog has no Buddha nature").[40] From there, the meditation may take two approaches: (1) the adept can inquire into the "dead word," which takes a similar approach to traditional *gong'an* meditation by going through all the possible interpretations of the meaning of the keyword or phrase until all are exhausted, or (2) the adept can inquire into the "live word" which involves meditating on the keyword without interpretation. In the *huatou* method, the second approach, inquiry into the "live word," is considered to be the superior approach, for it enables adepts to bypass the pitfalls of attachments to particular interpretations[41] and gain access, relatively quickly, to a "point beyond which speech exhausts itself."[42] Chinul recognized that this form of meditation facilitates both "tracing back the radiance to the true mind" of Buddha-nature and removing remaining attachments to passions and views. Moreover, not having to go through countless (attachment-laden) interpretations makes this form of meditation "free of the ten maladies,"[43] and more concise in enabling practitioners to dissolve hindrances of passions, attachments, and interests that stand in the way of attaining complete wisdom. For this reason *huatou* is also referred to as "the shortcut method." Ultimately, *huatou* meditation, like other forms of meditation, facilitates the attainment of wisdom and the removal of karmic obstructions to acting with unlimited compassion or, as Chinul puts it, "to respond to things autonomously and without limitation."[44]

Chinul and Russon on Wisdom, Compassion, and Habit Transformation

The work of contemporary philosopher John Russon, while engaging primarily with Hegel, Merleau-Ponty, and others working in existentialism and phenomenology, is remarkably diverse and accessible in its treatment of themes relating to everyday life. Of particular interest here is that Russon's work engages with Buddhist themes, including the themes of suffering, vulnerability, and appropriate responses to suffering.[45] Before highlighting a few points of resonance between Chinul's writings and Russon's phenomenological descriptions of experience it is important to note some differences between the two. First, Russon's philosophy has no doctrinal ties, nor does Russon frame his discourse in religious terms such as that of tracing the mind back to its original nature (e.g., Buddha-nature), as does Chinul.[46] Second, while the Buddhist practice of meditation as embodied practice is one of the three core Buddhist practices, Russon does not discuss the practice of meditation and is more directly concerned with the embodied aspect of existence than Chinul.[47] Third, while Chinul and Russon both value openness, hospitality, and inclusion, Russon places greater emphasis on the value of multiculturalism than Chinul, though this difference may be attributed more to differences between modern globalized society and twelfth-century Korea than anything else. Despite these differences, we can find several compelling links between Chinul and Russon. In what follows, I show how Russon's phenomenological descriptions of experience, hospitality, multiculturalism, and the process of habit transformation resonate with Chinul's discussions of wisdom, inclusion, compassion, and the possibility of habit transformation.

As we have seen, for Chinul, the three core Buddhist disciplines of wisdom, morality, and meditation are closely tied together: meditation facilitates wisdom, and meditative wisdom activates compassion. Recalling Chinul's accounts of his awakening experiences, meditation, which can be assisted by the study of sutras, leads to a state of calm alertness, which culminates in the insight that the true mind is Buddha-nature. As Chinul's account of his second awakening experience reveals, insight into Buddha-nature is equivalent to the wisdom of the sutras: that all things are interpenetrated by and reflective of each other. Chinul goes on to affirm the dynamic interrelationship between wisdom and compassion in stating that through such wisdom, compassion "will surge like billowing clouds . . . like towering waves."[48]

Similarly, in his phenomenological descriptions of experience, Russon draws a connection between insight into the true nature of the self and the possibility of moral transformation. The method of phenomenology begins with the phenomenological reduction, which sets aside assumptions about the independent existence of things in order to focus philosophical description on the lived experience of what appears (the phenomena). Following this methodological approach, Russon arrives at insight into the non-fixed, open-ended nature of the self, which is a kind of wisdom, and this wisdom activates attitudes of openness and hospitality that can be associated with compassion. Russon writes, "Just as I experience things as making manifest a reality beyond their finite specificity, so does my experience of them make manifest a depth of subjectivity, a depth of 'I,' that defines me that offers me the promise of further possibilities, but that I can access in no way other than through the determinacies of my specific experiences. The 'I,' like nature, is a kind of infinite that shows itself in and through its finite presentation."[49] In this passage, Russon applies the method of phenomenology to describe how experiential engagement with things discloses the finite/infinite character of both things we encounter and the "I." Through engagement with things, the non-fixed "depth of subjectivity" is revealed, along with its "finite specificity," and things and other persons are also revealed as having a reality beyond "their finite specificity" such that everything in nature is shown to be "a kind of infinite." Analogous to the Seon Buddhist insight into the true mind as Buddha-nature, insight into the finite/infinite character of self, others, and things is a kind of wisdom which can activate an attitude of openness and a sense of compassion toward oneself and others. Russon develops the link between wisdom and compassion further, first, in terms of what he refers to as the call of conscience and the need to realize the infinite through our finite engagements with things and, more concretely, in terms of the need for a politics of pluralist multiculturalism. He writes, "In conscience, we experience both the inner need of the finite situation to be a realization of the infinite and the need of the infinite to be realized in actuality."[50] He then connects the call to realize the infinite in the finite with the need for an attitude of openness and inclusion in the establishment of a healthy sense of identity and home:

> Our nature is to be simultaneously communal and personal, simultaneously finite and infinite. To be, we must be determinate, which means we must be actual, finite. We exist, however, *as* not defined by our finitude, as possibility beyond determinacy. . . . This means we must be at home, but our home will only properly house us if it houses us as exceeding our home. A healthy home will allow us to live from a sense of identity in such a way as to support attitudes and practices of openness to what is outside and other.

A few pages later he goes on to say, "Because our nature is to be finite-infinite, because this nature is always realized in the establishing of a home, and because home is necessarily an edge, a kind of multiculturalism . . . will always be the last word in political life."[51] While Russon does not use the word *compassion* in these contexts, he uses terms closely associated with compassion—*openness, hospitality,* and *responsibility for . . . shared humanity*"[52]—to convey the moral implications of wisdom (e.g., insight into the finite/infinite character of the self, other, and things). Similar to how Chinul's accounts of his awakening experiences culminate in the attainment of the wisdom of Buddha-nature, which removes obstructions to the flow of responsive virtuosity and compassion, the wisdom of insight into the finite/infinite character of self, others, and things in Russon's phenomenology of experience untethers the I from attachments to harmful views and activates compassion, openness, and hospitality. In this way, for both Chinul and Russon, wisdom removes obstructions to the flow of responsive virtuosity and compassion. It is noteworthy that Chinul's role in restoring harmony among Buddhist schools in twelfth-century Korea, while stemming from compassion, was a form of political action akin to what Russon refers to as pluralist multiculturalism. We may further note that Chinul exemplifies the qualities of openness and hospitality, emphasized by Russon in his discussion of multiculturalism, in forming the *Samādhi* and *Prajñā* Society, as well as in his efforts to bridge the divide between the scholastic and Seon schools.

A further connection between Chinul and Russon concerns similarities in their discussions of the possibility of habit transformation. Both Russon and Chinul (and Buddhism in general) recognize that habitual attachments to wrong views about reality account for much suffering. Russon writes, "We typically have adopted inadequate concepts for thinking about reality, not just in our daily affairs but in our most advanced conceptual endeavors. These mistaken presumptions about human nature are at the foundation of much philosophy, much political theory, much social and legal policy, and much psychological practice."[53] For Russon, the possibility for overcoming habitually engrained wrong views about human nature arises through reflection on the contingency of habits of thinking which leads to the realization that habits can be changed. Such reflection, which Russon identifies as philosophical reflection, has the capacity to facilitate increased autonomy and set in motion the transformation of habits such that one becomes more capable of realizing the infinite in finite situations. Drawing on his experience as a jazz musician, Russon writes,

> Our identities were formed through the processes of habituation by which melodic sequences of action became transformed into harmonic backgrounds for action; self-transformation will require taking these harmonies and making them melodies again, that is, making those harmonic dimensions of our action the specific foci of our actions. . . . But inasmuch as these habitual patterns of harmony and rhythm are the very platform for our making sense of the world, the process of change is always working against itself, always drawing upon the very resources it is trying to change . . . this makes personal change a very difficult process.[54]

Personal transformation, he goes on to say, although challenging, is possible through philosophical reflection and by developing attentiveness to the infinite aspect of things. Similarly, for Chinul, gradual cultivation through the Buddhist practices of wisdom, morality, and meditation has the capacity to transform "habitual proclivities." In particular, through meditation on the emptiness (San. *śūnyata*) of habitual proclivities (or their nonsubstantial, contingent nature), habits lose their grip such that they "need neither be suppressed or removed." In this way, by meditating on the emptiness of habits, adepts "avail themselves of great compassion and wisdom and through the dharma are able to adapt to conditions."[55] Further connecting this process of gradual self-transformation with wisdom and compassion, Chinul continues, "Compassion and wisdom are gradually consummated, and in a sublime manner one conforms with the ring's center (*dharmadhātu,* that is to say, Buddha dimension). One then truly may be called a person who practices in accordance with reality."[56] In his discussion of habit transformation and gradual cultivation, Chinul draws together the three core Buddhist disciplines of wisdom, morality, and meditation. As the phrase "in accordance with reality" indicates, the wisdom of true views about the nature of the self is for Chinul, as for Russon, a key to changing bad habits, removing karmic blockages, and activating openness, compassion, and responsive virtuosity.

Conclusion

Through an overview of Chinul's life and work and, in particular, his three awakening experiences, we have seen how he displayed responsive virtuosity and played a transformative role both in resolving disputes among Buddhist schools and in shaping the distinctive character of Korean Seon through his ecumenism, his adoption of sudden/gradual soteriology, and his development of the practice of *hwadu* meditation. Chinul's efforts as a mediator in a time of discord both reaffirmed the ties among the core Buddhist disciplines of wisdom, morality, and meditation and steered the development of Korean Seon in a more ecumenical direction, which continues to inform its identity today. Further, we have seen how the ethical implications of Chinul's work resonate with recent work by John Russon in the development of an ethic of responsive virtuosity that centers on the close interrelationship between wisdom and compassion. While the ethic of responsive virtuosity affirms the normativity of acting with compassion in ways that contribute to the liberation of sentient beings, it also provides a promising alternative to modern normative ethical theories that center on the universalizability of rules.

Notes

1. For more on the core doctrines of Buddhism, see the introduction to this volume.

2. Jin Y. Park, "Wisdom, Compassion, and Zen Social Ethics: The Case of Chinul, Seongch'eol, and Minjung Buddhism in Korea," *Journal of Buddhist Ethics* Vol. 13 (2006): 28.

3. Jin Y. Park, "Wisdom, Compassion, and Zen Social Ethics."

4. Jin Y. Park, *Buddhism and Postmodernity: Zen, Huayan, and the Possibility of Buddhist Postmodern Ethics* (Lanham, MD: Lexington Books, 2008), 183.

5. Both Buddhism and phenomenology conceive of wisdom in ways that link theory and practice. Buddhism, through the doctrine of emptiness (*śūnyata*), and postmodern phenomenological philosophy, through various forms of critique of the history of metaphysics, reject the idea that wisdom involves knowledge of fixed, substantial essences and highlight an element of indeterminacy in our understanding of things. The insight that wisdom involves understanding the emptiness or indeterminacy of things opens theoretical wisdom to practical demands that link wisdom with compassion. For more on wisdom as involving an understanding of an element of indeterminacy associated with all objects of knowledge, see Robert H. Scott, "The Significance of Indeterminacy as Key to a Phenomenological Reinterpretation of Aristotle's Intellectual Virtues," in *The Significance of Indeterminacy: Perspectives from Asian and Continental Philosophy*, ed. Robert H. Scott and Gregory S. Moss (New York: Routledge, Taylor and Francis Group, 2019), 182–200.

6. Robert E. Buswell Jr., ed. and translator, *Numinous Awareness Is Never Dark: The Korean Buddhist Master Chinul's Excerpts on Zen Practice* (Honolulu: University of Hawai'i Press, 2016), 3.

7. For more on the engaged Buddhism movement in late-twentieth-century Korea, see J. Park, "Wisdom, Compassion, and Social Zen Ethics."

8. Robert E. Buswell Jr., *Tracing Back the Radiance: Chinul's Korean Way of Zen* (Honolulu: The Kuroda Institute for the Study of Buddhism and Human Values, 1991), 1.

9. Buswell, *Tracing Back the Radiance.*

10. Buswell, *Tracing Back the Radiance*, 6.

11. Buswell, *Tracing Back the Radiance*, 12. While Seon places a strong emphasis on meditation, it is important to note that the Chan/Seon reputation for deemphasizing the study of sutras was overstated by its opponents, as Chan/Seon has a great tradition of sutra study, including regular study of *The Platform Sutra of the 6th Patriarch* by Huineng (638–713) and many other sutras.

12. There were long-running debates within and among Buddhist schools over the question of whether enlightenment and cultivation are sudden or gradual. The Huayan/Hwaeom schools tended to embrace the view of gradual enlightenment/ gradual cultivation, and the Linji Chan school, which had decisive influence on the development of Chan/Zen in China and Japan, embraced the sudden enlight-

enment/sudden cultivation view. Chinul, by contrast, in a manner that would both contribute to restoring harmony among Buddhist schools in Korea and to distinguishing Korean Seon from the Linji Chan tradition, embraced Zongmi's view of sudden enlightenment/gradual cultivation. Zongmi (780–841) a patriarch of both the Chan and Huayan schools in China who had an important influence on Chinul's thinking, provides a detailed outline of these debates in his *Dharma Collection and Special Practice Record*, which Chinul discusses in depth in his final work, *Excerts from the "Dharma Collection and Special Practice Record" with Inserted Personal Notes*, published in 1209, one year before his death.

13. Buswell, *Tracing Back the Radiance*, 12.

14. Buswell, *Tracing Back the Radiance*, 19.

15. Robert E. Buswell Jr., "Introduction: Chinul's Life, Thought, and Writings," in *Chinul: Selected Works*, Volume 2 of *Collected Works of Korean Buddhism*, ed. and trans. Robert E. Buswell (Compilation Committee of Korean Buddhist Thought and the Jogye Order of Korean Buddhism, 2012), 12.

16. Richard D. McBride II and Insung Cho, "Shifting Contexts of Faith: The Cult of Maitreya in Middle and Late Silla," *The Eastern Buddhist* 47, no. 1 (2016): 9.

17. Buswell, *Tracing Back the Radiance*, 39. Some question Chinul's status as the primary founder of Korean Seon, citing his lack of a traditional "mind-to-mind transmission" enlightenment experience. In view of Chinul's atypical path to enlightenment (discussed in what follows), some point to T'aego Pon (1307–1382), a practitioner of Seon who received mind-to-mind transmission in China in the Linji Chan tradition, as the primary founder of Korean Seon.

18. Buswell, "Introduction," 12–13.

19. Peter Hershock, *Chan Buddhism* (Honolulu: University of Hawai'i Press, 2005), 63. *Upāya* or Skillful means is an important Buddhist virtue highlighted in the *Lotus Sutra*, the central text of the Cheontae school. It is also a central Chan/Seon/Zen virtue.

20. Peter Hershock, "Responsive Virtuosity: A Classical Chinese Buddhist Contribution to Contemporary Conversations of Freedom," in *Why Traditional Chinese Philosophy Still Matters: The Relevance of Ancient Wisdom for the Global Age*, ed. Ming Dong Gu (New York: Routledge, Taylor and Francis Group, 2018), 94. For more on skillful means and responsive virtuosity see chapters 4 and 7 in this volume.

21. Moguja's Secrets on Cultivating the Mind (Moguja Susim kyŏl 牧牛子修心訣) in Buswell, *Chinul: Selected Works*, 227.

22. The exact site of Ch'ŏngwŏnsa is unknown, as the temple no longer stands. It is likely that it stood near the coastal port of Mop'ko in the southwestern part of the peninsula, thereby providing a convenient location for interchange with mainland China, affording the possibility for monks to receive copies of Buddhist texts from China. See Buswell, *Tracing Back the Radiance*, 22, note 110.

23. Quoted from Buswell, "Introduction," 17.

24. For more on the distinction Chinul draws between "understanding-awakening" and "realization-awakening" see Chinul's *Treatise on Resolving Doubts*

about Observing the Keyword (Kanhwa kyŏrŭiron 看話決疑論) in Buswell, *Chinul: Selected Works*, 352–59.

25. Quoted from Buswell, *Tracing Back the Radiance*, 25.

26. Buswell, *Tracing Back the Radiance*, 25.

27. Buswell, *Tracing Back the Radiance*, 25.

28. Buswell argues that this was also Chinul's most important work. See Buswell, *Numinous Awareness Is Never Dark*, 3.

29. It is unknown how Chinul gained access to Zongmi's text. However, it was common practice for Korean monks to pay travelers to China, both traders and fellow monks, to bring back texts from the mainland, and this is likely how Chinul acquired it. See Buswell, *Tracing Back the Radiance*, 23.

30. Chinul, *Encouragement to Practice: The Compact of the Samādhi and Prajñā Society* (*Kwŏnsu Chŏnghye kyŏlsa mun* 勸修定慧結社文), in Buswell, *Chinul: Selected Works*, 192.

31. Chinul, *Encouragement to Practice*, 166–67.

32. For more on the relationship between meditation and wisdom in East Asian Buddhism, see chapters 2 and 5 of this volume.

33. Chinul, *Treatise on the Complete and Sudden Attainment of Buddhahood* (*Wŏndon sŏngbullon* 圓頓成佛論) in Buswell, *Chinul: Selected Works*, 258.

34. Chinul, *Treatise on the Complete and Sudden Attainment of Buddhahood*, 270. A "causal Buddha" refers to Mañjuśrī. Samantabhadra and Avalokiteshvara are "fruition Buddhas," in that they are associated with the activation of compassionate action toward sentient beings.

35. Quoted from Buswell, "Introduction," 25.

36. Quoted from Buswell, "Introduction," 25.

37. Chinul, *Treatise on Resolving Doubts about Observing the Keyword*, 363.

38. See Park, "Wisdom, Compassion, and Zen Social Ethics," 25–27, and Park, *Buddhism and Postmodernity*, 205–22.

39. See chapter 1 of this volume for a discussion of *kōan*s by Buddhist women and about the experience of Buddhist women. See chapter 5 of this volume for a discussion of *kōan* meditation as developed by Dōgen and the Japanese Sōtō Zen tradition.

40. Buswell, *Tracing Back the Radiance*, 68.

41. Chinul, *Resolving Doubts about Observing the Keyword*, 351.

42. Buswell, *Tracing Back the Radiance*, 68.

43. Chinul, *Resolving Doubts about Observing the Keyword*, 351.

44. Chinul, *Resolving Doubts about Observing the Keyword*, 364.

45. See John Russon, "Self and Suffering in Buddhism and Phenomenology: Existential Pain, Compassion, and the Problems of Institutional Healthcare," in *Cultural Ontology of the Self in Pain*, ed. S. K. George and P. J. Young (New Delhi: Springer India, 2016), 181–95, and John Russon, *Sites of Exposure: Art, Politics, and the Nature of Experience* (Bloomington: Indiana University Press, 2017), 65–66 and 83–84.

46. See chapter 1 of this volume by Sarah Mattice for an in-depth discussion of problems inherent to debates about the applicability of the terms *religion* and *philosophy* to Buddhism.

47. See chapter 2 of this volume for more on the relationships among meditation, embodiment, and wisdom in East Asian Buddhism. For an excellent in-depth discussion of the direct relevance of Buddhist meditation practices to liberation from embodied suffering and intergenerational trauma stemming from systemic racism, see Rima Vesely-Flad, *Black Buddhists and the Black Radical Tradition: The Practice of Stillness in the Movement for Liberation* (New York: New York University Press, 2022).

48. Chinul, *Encouragement to Practice*, 166.

49. Russon, *Sites of Exposure*, 24.

50. Russon, *Sites of Exposure*, 125.

51. Russon, *Sites of Exposure*, 112–13 and 118.

52. Russon, *Sites of Exposure*, 113 and 114.

53. John Russon, *Bearing Witness to Epiphany: Persons, Things, and the Nature of Erotic Life* (Albany: State University of New York Press, 2006), 62.

54. Russon, *Bearing Witness to Epiphany*, 119.

55. Chinul, *Encouragement to Practice*, 168.

56. Chinul, *Encouragement to Practice*, 164.

Bibliography

Buswell, Robert E. Jr. *Tracing Back the Radiance: Chinul's Korean Way of Zen.* Honolulu: University of Hawai'i Press, Kuroda Institute, 1991.

———, ed. and trans. *Chinul: Selected Works.* Volume 2 of *Collected Works of Korean Buddhism.* Compilation Committee of Korean Buddhist Thought and the Jogye Order of Korean Buddhism, 2012.

———, ed. and trans. *Numinous Awareness Is Never Dark: The Korean Buddhist Master Chinul's Excerpts on Zen Practice.* Honolulu: University of Hawai'i Press, Korean Classics Library, 2016.

Hershock, Peter. *Chan Buddhism.* Honolulu: University of Hawai'i Press, 2005.

———. "Responsive Virtuosity: A Classical Chinese Buddhist Contribution to Contemporary Conversations of Freedom." In *Why Traditional Chinese Philosophy Still Matters: The Relevance of Ancient Wisdom for the Global Age*, edited by Ming Dong Gu, 85–101, New York: Routledge, Taylor and Francis Group, 2018.

McBride, Richard D. II, and Insung Cho. "Shifting Contexts of Faith: The Cult of Maitreya in Middle and Late Silla." *The Eastern Buddhist* 47, no. 1 (2016): 1–28.

Park, Jin Y. "Wisdom, Compassion, and Zen Social Ethics: The Case of Chinul, Seongch'eol, and Minjung Buddhism in Korea." *Journal of Buddhist Ethics* 13 (2006): 1–28.

———. *Buddhism and Postmodernity: Zen, Huayan, and the Possibility of Buddhist Postmodern Ethics.* Lanham, MD: Lexington Books, 2008.

Russon, John. *Bearing Witness to Epiphany: Persons, Things, and Nature of Erotic Life.* Albany: State University of New York Press, 2006.

———. "Self and Suffering in Buddhism and Phenomenology: Existential Pain, Compassion and the Problems of Institutional Healthcare." In *Cultural Ontology of the Self in Pain*, edited by S. K. George and P. J. Young, 181–95. New Delhi: Springer India, 2016.

———. *Sites of Exposure: Art, Politics, and the Nature of Experience.* Bloomington: Indiana University Press, 2017.

Scott, Robert H. "Indeterminacy as Key to a Phenomenological Reinterpretation of Aristotle's Intellectual Virtues." In *The Significance of Indeterminacy: Perspectives from Asian and Continental Philosophy*, edited by Robert H. Scott and Gregory S. Moss, 182–200. New York: Routledge, Taylor and Francis Group, 2019.

Vesely-Flad, Rima. *Black Buddhists and the Black Radical Tradition: The Practice of Stillness in the Movement for Liberation.* New York: New York University Press, 2022.

Chapter 9

The Lovelorn Lady and the Stony Monk

Women, Sexuality, and Imagination in the *Kegon Engi Emaki*

Sujung Kim

Introduction

This chapter focuses on a seventh-century love story between a Korean Buddhist monk and a Chinese maiden as imagined by a thirteenth-century Japanese Buddhist monk. The legendary tale is found in the *Illustrated Narrative Picture Scrolls of the Kegon Sect Patriarchs* 華厳宗祖師絵伝 (also known as the *Kegon Engi Emaki* 華厳縁起絵巻, hereafter the *Kegon Engi*), arguably created by the Japanese Kegon 華厳 (Chi. Huayan, Kor. Hwaŏm) Buddhist monk Myōe 明恵 (1173–1232 CE).[1] The *Kegon Engi* belongs to a Buddhist literary genre called *emaki* 絵巻 or picture scrolls. *Emaki* emerged as early as the Nara period (710–794 CE) in Japan, but it was not until the eleventh century when they began to be popularly produced and to circulate in greater numbers. *Emaki* are scrolls containing both text and illustrations, and often contain the stories of eminent monks, famous temples, and historical events. *Emaki* illustrate these stories with a sequence of paintings, and individuals hold the scroll and roll or unroll it using both hands, which is meant to generate an intimate relationship between object and viewer.[2] In this sense, *emaki* function as a unique medium to allow "synthetic viewing," that is, "the process of synthesizing the multiple parts of a narrative image ensemble to form a coherent interpretation of the whole work."[3]

The *Kegon Engi* belongs to Kōzanji temple 高山寺 in northwest Kyoto. Kōzanji was initially built in 774 CE and was revived as a training center for the Kegon Buddhist school by Myōe.[4] Kegon Buddhism was transmitted to Japan from China and Korea sometime during the late seventh century. With the support of imperial patronage, it became one of the leading Buddhist schools during the Nara period. Tōdaiji temple 東大寺 in Nara, known for its colossal Vairocana Buddha statue, was the headquarters of the Kegon sect.[5] During the ninth century, however, the Kegon school declined when the capital was moved from Nara to Kyoto and the sects of Tendai and Shingon Buddhism rose to prominence.[6] In the Kamakura period (1185–1333 CE), several innovative Buddhist leaders emerged and started establishing new Buddhist schools such as Pure Land, Zen, and Nichiren, based on different Buddhist texts and beliefs. As a monk who lived through the late Heian (794–1185 CE) up to the mid-Kamakura period, Myōe took a unique intellectual position. Even though the Kegon sect declined in his time, he rediscovered the teachings of the *Avataṃsaka-sūtra* (Jpn. *Kegon-kyō* 華厳経) and dedicated himself to reviving Kegon Buddhism.[7]

The *Kegon Engi* illustrate the biographies of two eminent Silla monks: Ŭisang (義湘 625–702 CE, three scrolls, known as Gishō scroll) and Wŏnhyo (元曉 617–686 CE, three scrolls, known as Gangyō scroll) both of whom had a major influence on Korean Hwaŏm thought.[8] Although Wŏnhyo's biographical account is connected to that of Ŭisang, since the love story that concerns us is from the Ŭisang part, our discussion focuses on the Gishō scroll and Ŭisang.[9] Interestingly, although the title states it is a biography, the narrative primarily recounts Ŭisang's relationship with a Chinese maiden called Shanmiao 善妙 (Jpn. Zenmyō) and her miracle performance. Traditionally, Ŭisang's story has been understood as a didactic tale of the loftiness of the eminent monk. Modern scholarship uncritically joined this view, arguing that the scroll is primarily a story of female salvation by the monk's moral power. Under this logic, it was surmised that Myōe sponsored the *Kegon Engi* in order to "inspire" and "save" his female followers at Zenmyōji 善妙寺, a nunnery that he founded.[10]

Without either victimizing or romanticizing the image of women in Buddhism, this chapter reevaluates the androcentric interpretations of the scroll by shifting the focus more onto the female.[11] Taking the depiction of Zenmyō as a cue, the chapter examines how women and sexuality were represented in Myōe's thought, and how not Ŭisang but Zenmyō is in fact the source of Myōe's imagination and inspiration in both his dream and real life. Myōe's fascination with Zenmyō further grew and he became a supporter of a group of women who became nuns at Zenmyōji. While Myōe contributed to the establishment of Zenmyōji temple and provided his guidance to these nuns, it was they themselves who made their religious practices vibrant. In what follows, the chapter contextualizes Zenmyō's role in Myōe's life and illustrates how women, sexuality, and love became crucial forces that shaped and challenged Myōe's thought.

The Lovelorn Lady and the *Kegon Engi*

The narratives from the *Kegon Engi* are adaptations of stories about Ŭisang and Wŏnhyo based on a Chinese text, known as the *Song Gaoseng Zhuan* 宋高僧傳 (*The Song Version of the Biographies of Eminent Monks*, compiled in 988 CE by Zanning 贊寧, one of the leading monk officials at the Song court), a collection of biographies of eminent Buddhist monks. Making considerable changes to the original account by adding colorful illustrations to the text, as well as extensive commentary (only found at the end of the Gishō scroll), explanatory notes (Jpn. *kotobagaki* 詞書), and text within the image (Jpn. *ekotoba* 絵詞), the *Kegon Engi* presents the most dramatic parts of the life of Ŭisang in an exuberantly animated form. The literary devices known as *ekotoba* make the story come alive even more. In fact, the *Kegon Engi* is one of the earliest known works that include short captions within the image for the purpose of *etoki* performance. *Etoki* is a type of Buddhist storytelling in which monks and nuns explain tales for a wide range of functions, from proselytization to fundraising.[12] Another difference between the Chinese original text and the *Kegon Engi* is also worth noting here: whereas the *Song Gaosengzhuan* focuses on Ŭisang's whereabouts and his accomplishments as an eminent monk, the *Kegon Engi* highlights his romance with Zenmyō and her role in the foundation of the first Hwaŏm temple in Silla (contemporary South Korea).[13]

For the following discussion, I briefly describe the main plot of the Gishō scroll while highlighting the different narrative foci in the *Song Gaosengzhuan* and the *Kegon Engi*. The Gishō scroll opens with illustrating Ŭisang's preparations for his trip to Tang China (618–907). Ŭisang arrives in China and serendipitously meets Shanmiao (Jpn. Zenmyō) at a house of a Chinese layman who had offered lodging for the monk. Shanmiao immediately falls in love with Ŭisang. In the description of the meeting, the text states that when Shanmiao first sees Ŭisang, she "raises her seductive eyebrows and flatters him,"[14] a typical example of androcentric Buddhist rhetoric presenting the woman as a temptress, both a cause of sexual transgression and a signifier of worldly attachment.[15]

While the textual reference does not avoid the male-centric gaze on female sexuality, the visual representation of the episode speaks differently. With its vibrant images (the text from *Song Gaoseng zhuan* keeps silent about this part), the *Kegon Engi*'s illustration depicts Shanmiao's confession of love to Ŭisang, which makes for perhaps one of the most romantic scenes in Buddhist painting. Here, Ŭisang "listens, but even as he looks upon her finery his heart remains solid as a rock."[16] Upon her love confession, Ŭisang explains his determination as a Buddhist monk, and Shanmiao begins to see that he will not return her feelings in kind. According to the story, being inspired by his lofty mind, Shanmiao experiences a religious awakening and makes a vow to look up to him and to be his supporter.

After several scenes whose narrative and pictorial focus is solely on Shanmiao, Ŭisang, who, having just finished his ten years of study, comes back to the layperson's house to repay kindness before his return trip to Silla. When Shanmiao realizes that the monk is back in town and he is about to return to Silla, she prepares farewell gifts for him—a box filled with monk's robes and various receptacles. She runs to the port to give them to him only to find the ship has already disembarked.

For this very heightened moment in the story, the *emaki* leverages the advantage of pictorial components by providing highly expressive images of Shanmiao to dramatize the story even further. For instance, when the *Song Gaosengzhuan* describes the scene with a rather dry and perfunctory tone—"the girl cursed [the boat]"—the captions in the images of the *emaki* convey Zenmyō's vivid emotions: "When Zemmyō sees this she becomes even more distraught and throws herself on the shore; it was as if she were a fish cast up on dry land."[17] As the story goes on, the heartbroken Shanmiao throws herself from a cliff into the sea, but instead of dying, miraculously turns herself into a gigantic dragon and escorts the monk's ship all the way to Silla. Once a lovelorn maiden, now in her animal form she becomes a powerful "protector" of the eminent monk.

Although the scene after this part has been lost in the original scroll, we know from the *Song Gaosengzhuan* that Shanmiao's devotion to the monk continues. Upon his arrival, when he tries to establish a temple to propagate the Hwaŏm teachings that he had brought from China, he encounters adversaries. But now the dragon-lady magically transforms once again into a floating boulder and expels them, allowing Ŭisang to build the temple and spread his teachings. The temple, celebrating Shanmiao's miracle, is known as Pusŏksa 浮石寺 (lit. temple of the floating rock) in Korean.[18] This marks the end of the story from the Gishō scroll, but according to the local transmission of the tale in Korea, it is believed that Shanmiao in her stone-dragon form still resides underneath Pusŏksa.

Is the Lovelorn Lady a Victim or Savior?

The above story has enjoyed wide popularity in the East Asian Buddhist tradition. It is also one of the most compelling stories that deeply engage with questions such as women, sexuality, and love within Buddhism. According to Buddhist religious tenets, women and sexuality are generally denied in principle. Women are the source of desire and attachments, which prevent monks from achieving enlightenment. But at the same time, in other contexts such as medieval Japanese Buddhism, it is totally acceptable for monks to have sex—whether it is with a real or supernatural woman or man—under the logic of *upāya,* or skillful means. A story about Shinran 親鸞 (1173–1263 CE), the founder of True Pure Land (Jōdo Shinshū) Buddhism, is a good example of such. He claimed that he made love to the Bodhisattva Kannon, a savior figure in Buddhism who often appears in feminine form. According to him, one day the bodhisattva manifested in front of him and told him that "you are destined to know women so I shall transform myself into the woman you will make love to. I shall be by your side all your life to purify this act. When you leave this world, I shall lead you to the Pure Land."[19] As one of the first Japanese Buddhist priests who openly married, Shinran rationalized that the violation of celibacy did not prevent him from being reborn in the Pure Land, but in fact, it helped him achieve his religious goal. As seen in this story, eminent Buddhist monks' involvement with women suggests that women play a key role in granting legitimacy to monks' redemption and awakening, as well as to their sexuality.

In the rather convenient androcentric rhetoric, however, the role of women is also often downplayed, and the view is confirmed in the *Kegon Engi.* In the story, even if Zenmyō is powerful and capable enough to transform her body from that of a human to a dragon and boulder at will, she is not granted full agency: her body is still condemned to an animal form whose unfortunate existence needs to be saved, and she takes a secondary, assisting role to the eminent monk's great deeds.[20] Even though Zenmyō performs miracles twice, which eventually "saves" the eminent monk, the commentator of the *Kegon Engi* is not willing to acknowledge the miracles as her own power. Instead, Zenmyō's miracles were made possible by the virtue of the monk. Below is one of the explanatory notes (Jpn. *kotobagaki* 詞書) inserted in the *Kegon Engi*: "Had Zenmyō fallen for someone other than Ŭisang, such a miracle would not have been manifest, no matter how deep her love and respect . . . this was due to the teacher's virtue. . . . Zenmyō encountered knowledge in a previous life and heard the True Dharma. Yet still, she remained tainted with the dust of the world and could not escape the retribution of being born a woman."[21] As seen above, Buddhist misogyny runs long and deep. Already back in early Indian Buddhism, there existed a list of women's five obstructions, or the view that a woman cannot be reborn as a Brahmā, a Śakra (Indra), a Māra (an evil king), a *cakravartin* (an ideal king), or a Buddha, which became the doctrinal basis for a gendered soteriology. According to this view, women cannot attain Buddhahood simply because a negative karmic retribution resulted in their inferior body. Thus, every woman's goal has to be to experience rebirth as a male, the only legitimate and perfect body able to attain the highest echelon in Buddhism. It was in the medieval period that this idea, together with other notions (such as the inherent pollution of the female body), came to be fully institutionalized and internalized in East Asian Buddhism as a social and religious reality.[22]

While the interpretation of the lovelorn lady Zenmyō in the *Kegon Engi* certainly does not escape the masculine point of view and feeds into the general common theme of women as victims, the commentator of the *Kegon Engi* nevertheless does not hesitate to praise Zenmyō's virtue and elevate her love almost to the level of a bodhisattva's compassion. In particular, toward the end of the Gishō scroll, we find extensive comments on Zenmyō's deeds and the nature of her love for Ŭisang. In the three sets of soliloquizing question-and-answer, the commentator presents a learned explanation for how to understand the story of Zenmyō within the framework of Buddhist doctrine.[23] The last question concerns whether or not Zenmyō's transformation and her accompanying Ŭisang can be condemned as an attachment. By comparing Zenmyō's love to another love story,[24] the commentator expounds that beyond her physical transformation, she also transformed and transcended her devotion: from loving a human to loving the Dharma, that is, the Buddhist teaching:

If we said that her dragon transformation resulted from the sin of attachment, then could we honestly say that she became a rock without having knowledge? This we must realize: she achieved supernatural powers in her present body because of her great vow. Just like the thirty-three bodies of Kannon, her transformations were limitless. . . . Now in considering the nature and expression of the teachings of the Dharma, love is either for intimacy or for the Dharma. Love for the Dharma is completely pure, while love of intimacy is close to pollution. . . . Now, even though Zenmyō first showed a poor, tainted mind, later she evinced a pure and loving mind.[25]

In the above passage, we find a highly favorable interpretation of Zenmyō's deeds. What is also interesting is that it is not shy about discussing "love," a rather unusual topic in the Buddhist context. By analyzing Zenmyō's love in Buddhist terms—citing Zongmi 宗密 (780–841 CE), the fifth patriarch of Huayan Buddhism, and a major Buddhist sutra such as *Verses on the Treasury of Abhidharma* (Jpn. *Kusharon* 倶舎論, San. *Abhidharmakośa-bhāṣya*)—the commentator highlights Zenmyō's virtue and her ability to transcend her affection and achieve a religious awakening.

Given the writing style as well as erudition of doctrinal knowledge in these comments, it is highly likely that the commentator was Myōe. How, then, can we reconcile the conflicting voices of women, sexuality, and female salvation in Myōe's thought? And could we say that the *Kegon Engi* at once presents misogynic and yet favorable interpretations of the female? Before answering these questions, it might be helpful to historicize Myōe's life further in order to gain a more nuanced assessment while withholding our modern gaze and gender critiques for the moment.

Between the Real and the Imagined

Just as Shanmiao did to Ŭisang, Zenmyō played significant roles in Myōe's life, both real and imagined.[26] Myōe, similar to other prominent monks of his time, considered dreams as a vehicle to channel the Buddha's teachings. Myōe kept dream journals, known as the *Yume no Ki* 夢記 or "Dream Diary," as a way to track his spiritual progress toward the goal of enlightenment.[27] During sleep or meditation, he had various sorts of dreams and visions, which he recorded over a period of thirty-five years. One of his journal entries, dating sometime between 1220 and 1222 CE, provides us a clue for understanding how Ŭisang's love story significantly shaped Myōe's identity as a Kegon monk.[28] In his dream, Myōe found a Chinese doll made of stoneware. The young woman-shaped doll expressed to him her sorrow at having left her homeland. Myōe showed sympathy and told her that he was a highly respected monk in his country, at which point the doll flushed with joy and turned into a living woman. The thrilled Myōe took her under his care, but when they attended a Buddhist service together, another monk accused the girl of having mated with snakes. After waking up, in his interpretation of the dream Myōe was convinced that the girl was Zenmyō. A Buddhist monk's dream of a young female who was accused of having sex with a serpent is certainly imbued with sexual overtones, which might have been related to his own personal struggles to maintain celibacy and to attain enlightenment. We do not know how exactly the dream influenced his sponsorship of the *Kegon Engi*, but it significantly tells us that Zenmyō had a pivotal role in Myōe's spiritual life, and that he was captivated by her.

This dream of Zenmyō is also crucial because it establishes a direct link between Zenmyō and Myōe, skipping Ŭisang. Nevertheless, Ŭisang's Hwaŏm teaching was undoubtedly important to Myōe. According to the repository list of Kōzanji (Jpn. *Kōzanji Shōgyō Mokuroku* 高山寺聖教目録), Ŭisang's Chart of the *Dharma-World of the One Vehicle of the Huayan* (Kor. *Hwaŏm Ilsŭng Pŏpkye to* 華嚴一乘法界圖), a short verse that epitomizes the essence of the *Avataṃsaka-Sūtra*, was transcribed sometime between 1222 and 1287 CE at Kōzanji, suggesting that Ŭisang's teachings were treasured by Myōe.[29] It may have been possible that Myōe even considered himself to be a reincarnation of the Korean monk. Yet, based on our analysis of the *Kegon Engi* and his dream of Zenmyō, we can confidently say that what Myōe hoped to tap into—by bridging a six hundred–year temporal gap—was not necessarily the eminence of the monk, but rather the protecting power of Zenmyō to help him keep his monastic commitments, including adhering to precepts. Myōe's devotion to the *Avataṃsaka-Sūtra* also helps to discern his logic in ignoring the temporal difference, as the Kegon philosophy expressed in the sutra emphasizes the interdependence and interpenetration of space and time.[30]

Indeed, Myōe was very interested in bringing Zenmyō back to real life. In 1223 CE, near his temple, Kōzanji, Myōe founded Zenmyōji (obviously named after Zenmyō), dedicated to widows from the Jōkyū Disturbance 承久の乱 of 1221 CE and other women who wished to renounce their lives.[31] It was not uncommon for widows to become Buddhist nuns after losing their husbands in wars or social disturbances. Yet in medieval Japan, being a Buddhist nun was a double-edged sword: while some enjoyed a certain degree of economic independence (often from their parents-in-law) and social autonomy, for others, being a nun in thirteenth-century Japan was not an option but a forced social expectation—if a husband died, the widow was expected to perform Buddhist memorials in order to ensure him an ideal rebirth in the next life.[32] Myōe was very much invested in creating a space for these women.[33] The *Kegon Engi* was completed most likely between 1220 and 1222 CE. This strongly suggests that Myōe's interest in Zenmyō contributed to the foundation of Zenmyōji, or at the very least to his motivation to honor Zenmyō in his real life.[34] Right after the foundation of the temple, Zenmyō's statue was installed in 1224 CE. A record states that Myōe performed a ceremony to dedicate the statue.[35] All of this indicates that Zenmyō was the religious inspiration for Myōe.

Zenmyō further became an independent object of worship for the followers of Zenmyōji as well as Kōzanji. She was worshipped as a "native" deity (Jpn. *kami* 神), whereby she came to be called "Zenmyō Myōjin" (善妙明神, lit. "the bright deity of Zenmyō"). Having a "*myōjin*" title means that worshippers believed that despite her Buddhist origin she manifested her divine power for the Japanese local audience following the Japanese medieval Buddhist-Shinto syncretistic principle (Jpn. *honji suijaku* 本地垂迹).[36] Deified Zenmyō also inspired artistic imagination. In the *Kōzanji Engi* 高山寺縁起 (1253), or the origin story of the Kōzanji, we find a description of a statue of Zenmyō installed at Zenmyōji. What is intriguing about the description of the statue is the attribution of Zenmyō's ethnic identity. The text states: "Zenmyō myōjin is a goddess of Silla. She is worshipped here because she pledged to protect Kegon teachings."[37] Although her Chinese origin is obscured here for an unknown reason, it evidently explains that the foreign lady Zenmyō—whether she was perceived as a virtuous woman in China or a dragon-lady who later turned into a floating rock—was highly regarded by the audiences at Zenmyōji and Kōzanji as a protector of the Kegon teaching.

Zenmyō also made a significant impact on some of the Zenmyōji nuns. Just as Zenmyō refused to be separated from Ŭisang and jumped into the sea, when Myōe passed away in 1232, some of the Zenmyōji nuns killed themselves by jumping into the Kiyotaki (清滝) River, near the temple.[38] It might have been the case that they were emulating Shanmiao's example[39] or it could have been just an unrelated event. We simply do not know their motives, but what we do know is that Myōe gained great respect from the nuns of Zenmyōji.

Myōe maintained a close relationship with the female practitioners and donors,[40] but more broadly, Myōe's interest in reviving a nunnery and his involvement with female followers can be understood in the context of his devotion to Śākyamuni Buddha who emphasized the inclusion of women in the Buddhist community. Since the early twelfth century there was a renewed interest in the devotional practices centered on Śākyamuni in Japan. Myōe's devotion to Śākyamuni joined that of other reformist Buddhist leaders of this time, such as Jōkei 貞慶 (1155–1213) and Eison 叡尊 (1201–1290).[41] Throughout Myōe's life, Śākyamuni was central to his faith. It is well known that he twice attempted to go to India, the holy space of Śākyamuni, although the trip was aborted each time. Myōe saw Śākyamuni not simply as a past figure of India, but as a salvific figure who ensured the opportunity to be reborn in Tuṣita Heaven, one of the Buddhist heavens that include the female.[42] As much as Śākyamuni emphasized the egalitarian monastic community within the fourfold structure of Buddhism (male/female monks and male/female laypeople), Myōe's support of Zenmyōji nuns can be better understood through his adherence to Śākyamuni's radical social inclusion.[43]

One of Myōe's lecture notes tells us more about how he saw his role in relation to the Zenmyōji nuns. In his criticism of Chengguan 澄觀 (738–839), the fourth Chinese Huayan patriarch, who claimed the presence of women in Buddhism was a source of distraction, Myōe advocated instead for the view of Fazang 法藏 (643–712), the third Huayan patriarch, who fully accepted female practitioners in the Buddhist community.[44] Myōe thought that incorporating women into the Buddhist tradition could be done with strict adherence to Buddhist monastic rules (San. *vinaya*). Indeed, Myōe was convinced that, by correctly following the rules that Śākyamuni had instituted, the Buddhist nuns could be equally respected by their followers. In his dying wishes, Myōe exhorted the Zenmyōji nuns to keep monastic rules strictly, indicating that he thought this would be the most secure way to make the nunnery thrive.[45]

With the support of Myōe, Zenmyōji nuns became actively engaged in their religious activities and devoted themselves to Buddhist teachings. The Zenmyōji nun Myōgyō 明行 (fl. early thirteenth century) is a prime example. She joined Zenmyōji after she became a widow from the Jōkyū Incident. As a highly educated lady who could write Chinese characters, she was deeply engaged with the practice of sutra-copying. It is said that Myōgyō copied the complete *Five Hundred Vows of Śākyamuni* (Jpn. *Shaka no Gohyakudaigan* 釈迦の五百大願) with the utmost level of devotion (using her own blood to copy the text), and also copied the entire six hundred volumes of the *Great Sutra of Perfect Wisdom* (Jpn. *Daihannya-kyō* 大般若

經, San. *Mahāprajñāpāramitā Sūtra*), all of which suggests her persistence and devotion to her practice.[46] Myōgyō's example also demonstrates that Zenmyōji was not just a nunnery for widows, but a space that allowed serious religious practices.

Conclusion

What did Myōe intend to tell about himself through the *Kegon Engi*? We may not be able to definitively answer this question without additional textual or historical references.[47] However, what we know is that women evidently played a pivotal role in Myōe's life and shaped his identity as a Kegon Buddhist monk. As this chapter has explained, we see strong parallels between the life of Myōe and that of Ŭisang: (1) Ŭisang's accomplishment of studying in China prefigures Myōe's long, (although unfulfilled) wish to go to India to access the authentic teachings of the Buddha; (2) Shanmiao's miracle to transform herself into a dragon in Ŭisang's story echoes the Chinese doll in Myōe's dream who transformed into a living woman; and (3) Ŭisang's loyal female Buddhist follower mirrors Myōe's close relationship with Zenmyōji nuns and his female patrons. In these different threads, what ultimately connects the two monks who lived in vastly different times and spaces was Zenmyō. For both, Zenmyō was an obstacle yet a source of inspiration. At the same time, it should be recognized that for each monk Zenmyō's place and significance is different. In the story of Ŭisang, Zenmyō carries a more passive image of the female (a temptress and, at best, a protector in her animal form). For Myōe, however, combined with his admiration of Ŭisang, his imagined and idealized image of Zenmyō played a more independent role, which allowed him to establish a nunnery and to advocate for the full acceptance of women as members of the Kegon religious community. Through Zenmyō, Myōe found a way to engage with Zenmyōji nuns, and therefore she was not just a figure from a distant past but a source of imagination and inspiration who beckoned to be revived and reenacted.

Notes

1. Japanese scholars have suggested that Myōe is possibly the author or editor of the scroll. Karen Brock, however, argues that it may have been the case

for the Gishō scroll, but Myōe was not directly involved at least in the Gangyō scroll. Karen L. Brock, "Tales of Gisho and Gangyo: Editor, Artist, and Audience in Japanese Picture Scrolls" (PhD diss., Princeton University, 1984), 400.

2. Miyeko Murase, *Emaki: Narrative Scrolls from Japan* (New York: Asian Society, 1983).

3. Greg M. Thomas, "Concluding Remarks: Narrative Visualization and Embodied Meaning," in *Rethinking Visual Narratives from Asia*, ed. Alexandra Green (Hong Kong: Hong Kong University Press, 2013), 250.

4. Modern English scholarship has illuminated numerous aspects of Myōe: For Myōe's life and thought in English, see Hayao Kawai, *The Buddhist Priest Myōe: A Life of Dreams*, trans. Mark Uno (Venice: Lapis Press, 1992); Robert Morell, "Kamakura Accounts of Myōe Shōnin as Popular Religious Hero," *Japanese Journal of Religious Studies* 9 nos. 2–3 (1982): 171–98; Mark Uno, *Shingon Refractions: Myōe and the Mantra of Light* (Somerville: Wisdom Publications, 1997); George J. Tanabe, *Myōe the Dreamkeeper: Fantasy and Knowledge in Early Kamakura Buddhism* (Cambridge: Council on East Asian Studies, Harvard University, 1992). For Myōe's *Kegon emaki* and its mythological connection to the dragon, see Bernard Faure, "Kegon and Dragon: A Mythological Approach to Huayan Doctrine," in *Reflecting Mirrors: Perspectives on Huayan Buddhism*, ed. Imre Hamer (Wiesbaden: Harrassowitz, 2007), 297–307. In Buddhism, the *nāga*-palace is often considered a space where important Buddhist teachings are preserved before they are revealed to humans. For religious and social meanings of Myōe's cutting off his own ear, see Ryuichi Abé, "Swords, Words, and Deformity: On Myōe's eccentricity," in *Discourse and Ideology in Medieval Japanese Buddhism*, ed. Richard K. Payne and Taigen Dan Leighton (London: Routledge, 2006), 148–59. For Myōe's salvation discourse in connection to *hinin* (an outcast group) see Ryuichi Abé, "Mantra, Hinin, and the Feminine: On the Salvational Strategies of Myōe and Eizon," *Cahiers d'Extrême-Asie* 13 (2002): 101–25. For doctrinal debates between Myōe and Hōnen, see Eiji Suhara, "Can Bodaishin Be a Cause of Rebirth? Reconsidering the Doctrinal Conflict between Hōnen and Myōe," *Philosophy East and West* 65 no. 2 (2015): 444–65.

5. Vairocana Buddha is one of the several Buddhas that Mahāyāna Buddhists worship. According to the *Avataṃsaka-sūtra*, after Śākyamuni Buddha achieves enlightenment, he attains the transcendental body of Vairocana, the Cosmic Buddha who transcends both time and space. However, the identity of the giant statue was never fixed. A recent study on the statue, suggests that the Japanese monk Chōgen (1121–1206) identified the Great Buddha as Mahāvairocana and Amitābha. See, Evan S. Ingram, "Chōgen's Vision of Tōdaiji's Great Buddha as Both Mahāvairocana and Amitābha," *Japanese Journal of Religious Studies*, 46 no. 2 (2019):173–92.

6. The Kegon (Chi. Huayan) school was transmitted from China and Korea to Japan during the late seventh century. It became one of the most influential doctrinal schools during the Nara period (710–784), along with the Kusha, Hossō, Jōjitsu, Sanron, and Ritsu schools, all of whose temples were based in Nara. With imperial patronage, these so-called Six Buddhist schools gained significant political

and religious power and even interfered with court politics. When the new capital was established in Kyoto, Tendai (established by Saichō on Mt. Hiei near Kyoto) and Shingon (established by Kūkai on Mt. Kōya near Osaka) emerged as new Buddhist centers during the Heian period (794–1185). Both Saichō and Kūkai studied new Buddhist ideas and practices in China and not only transmitted but also transformed them for their Japanese audiences. Tendai doctrine revolves around the *Lotus Sutra*, whereas the teachings of Shingon are based on the *Dainichi-kyō* among many other texts, emphasizing the actualization of Buddhahood through physical, verbal, and mental acts of practitioners. Both Tendai and Shingon came to be specialized in esoteric rituals that benefited the royal and aristocratic family.

7. As one of the most significant Mahāyāna Buddhist scriptures, the *Avataṃsaka-sūtra* is particularly influential in the establishment of the Huayan (Kegon/Hwaŏm) Buddhist school. The text expounds a multidimensional and encompassing vision of reality and provided a rich source of inspiration for Buddhist artists in East Asia.

8. The kingdom of Silla, one of the three kingdoms of ancient Korea, existed in the Korean peninsula from 57 BCE to 935 CE With the support of Tang China, Silla subjugated the other two kingdoms—Paekche and Koguryŏ—and eventually ousted China as well, completing unification in 668 CE. Hwaŏm became particularly important from the eighth century onward in Korean Buddhism. See, Sujung Kim, "Korea I: 372–935 C.E.," in Brill's *Encyclopedia of Buddhism*, vol. 4 (forthcoming).

9. Wŏnhyo is described as a Hwaŏm master in several Japanese sources. Although he was deeply influenced by Hwaŏm teachings, his thought had been perceived as a synthesizer of different schools of thought in the Korean Buddhist tradition. There are numerous studies on Ŭisang and Wŏnhyo's Hwaŏm teachings. For an overview of Huayan studies in Korean Buddhism, see Yeonshik Choe, "Huayan Studies in Korea," in *Reflecting Mirrors: Perspectives on Huayan Buddhism*, ed. Imre Hamer (Wiesbaden: Harrassowitz, 2007), 69–85.

10. Murase, for instance, sees Zenmyō's transformation as "'carnal love' into spiritual devotion." See Murase, *Emaki*, 136. Brock also sees the scroll as a source of female inspiration and salvation. See Karen Brock, "Chinese Maiden, Sillla Monk: Zenmyō and her thirteenth-century Japanese audience," in *Flowering in the Shadows: Women in the History of Chinese and Japanese Painting*, ed. Marsha Weidner (Honolulu: University of Hawai'i Press, 1990), 185–211. Chan also shares the same view. See Yuk-yue Chan, "Dream, Pilgrimage and Dragons in the *Kegon Engi Emaki* (Illustrated legends of the Kegon patriarchs): Reading Ideology in Kamakura Buddhist Narrative scrolls" (Master's thesis, University of Hong Kong, 2006), 99–100. Slightly differently, Okuda sees Myōe's female followers as women who needed male mediation to be saved, and that Myōe provided that role with the production of the *Kegon Engi*. Isao Okuda, "Myoe to josei: Kegon engi, Zenmyo, Zenmyoji," *Seishin joshi daigaku ronso* 89 (1997): 31–51.

11. Noriko Kawahashi and Naoko Kobayashi, "Editor's Introduction: Gendering Religious Practices in Japan Multiple Voices, Multiple Strategies," *Japanese Journal of Religious Studies* 44, no. 1 (2017): 1.

12. For discussion of *etoki* in English scholarship, see Ikumi Kaminishi, *Explaining Pictures: Buddhist Propaganda and Etoki Storytelling in Japan* (Honolulu: University of Hawai'i, 2006); Naoko Gunji, "The Ritual Narration of Mortuary Art: The Illustrated Story of Emperor Antoku and Its Etoki at Amidaji," *Japanese Journal of Religious Studies* 40, no. 2 (2013): 203–45.

13. Tanabe, *Myōe the Dreamkeeper*, 134; Brock, "Chinese Maiden," 189.

14. I follow Brock's translation. Brock, "Tales of Gisho," 433.

15. For a fuller discussion of the history of women in Buddhism and women's diverse relations with Buddhist males, see Bernard Faure, *The Power of Denial: Buddhism, Purity, and Gender* (Princeton: Princeton University Press, 2003).

16. Faure, *The Power of Denial*, 433.

17. Brock, "Tales of Gisho," 425 and 435.

18. There are in fact two Pusŏksa temples with the same origin story: one in Yŏngju and the other in Sŏsan in South Korea.

19. Kenneth Doo Young, Lee, *The Prince and the Monk: Shotoku Worship in Shinran's Buddhism* (Albany: State University of New York Press, 2012), 19.

20. Dragon ladies have been widely favored in the Mahayana Buddhist literature. The *locus classicus* of the dragon lady (as well as a major Buddhist view on the female body and salvation) comes from the *Lotus Sutra*. In the Devadatta chapter of the *Lotus Sutra*, the eight-year-old Dragon King's daughter instantly transforms into a perfect male body and then attains complete enlightenment in response to the doubts of the Buddha's disciple Śāriputra. While here the *nāga* girl challenges normative assumptions of the male body—not only morally superior, but also a prerequisite for enlightenment—the "animal" girl still has to show her ability *instantly* (not through rebirth) to transform her female body into a male body.

21. Brock, "Tales of Gisho," 437–38.

22. For more on this, see Barbara Ambros, *Women in Japanese Religions* (New York: New York University Press, 2015), 76–96.

23. These questions are: "(1) If this were the doing of a truly ordinary person, then how, relying on the power of her great vow, could she have brought about such a miracle now, in her present body? (2) If, whether or not you did good deeds in the past, you meet with the Buddhist Dharma, should there not be some benefit from this? (3) If this were the doing of a truly ordinary person, then, even in loving the virtues of the master, to become a great dragon that follows someone is still quite extraordinary. Is this not the sin of attachment?" For the entire translation, see Brock, "Tales of Gisho," 437–43.

24. The story that the commentator refers to is a popular narrative, the *Dōjōji engi emaki* in which a woman who bore rancor turns into a snake and ends up killing a Buddhist monk who rejected her love. For an overview of the text, see Virginia Skord Waters, "Sex, Lies, and the Illustrated Scroll: The *Dōjōji Engi Emaki*," *Monumenta Nipponica* 52 no. 1 (1997): 59–84. *Dōjōji* is also one of the most popular Noh repertoires in Japan. For more about how the serpent-woman is

presented in the Japanese Noh theater, see Susan Klein, "Woman as Serpent: The Demonic Feminine in the Noh Play," in *Religious Reflections on the Human Body*, ed. Jane Marie Law (Bloomington: Indiana University Press, 1995), 100–36.

25. Brock, "Tales of Gisho," 440–42.

26. Tae Hirano, "Myōe to nisō tachi," in *Nihon bungaku josei e no manazashi*, ed. Okuda Isao (Tokyo: Kazama Shobō, 2004), 76–98.

27. Tanabe, *Myōe the Dreamkeeper*, 159–98.

28. Tanabe, *Myōe the Dreamkeeper*, 178–79.

29. Se-in Cho, "Kozanji e yujŏn toen Han'guk Pulgyo munhŏn." Paper presented at the conference, Tong'ashia e yujon toen Hanguk Pulgyo munhŏn gwa sasang (Seoul, May 2019), 31.

30. Pamela Winfield, *Icons and Iconoclasm in Japanese Buddhism: Kūkai and Dōgen on the Art of Enlightenment* (Oxford: Oxford University, 2013).

31. This refers to a revolt led by the Retired Emperor Go Toba (r. 1183–1198) against the military government in Kamakura, which resulted in the exile of the emperor.

32. Ambros, *Women*, 80–81. For various cases of Buddhist nuns or Buddhist women in Japan, see Barbara Ruch ed., *Engendering Faith: Women and Buddhism in Premodern Japan* (Ann Arbor: Center for Japanese Studies, University of Michigan), 2002.

33. His involvement in establishing Zenmyōji may have to do with his interest in helping socially marginalized groups. For instance, Myōe was known for opening his temple door to groups such as lepers and beggars. Abé, "Swords," 156.

34. There is no consensus on the exact dates of the text in modern scholarship. On the date of the *Kegon Engi* each scholar proposes different dates depending on how they interpret the motivations of the production. Chan, "Dream," 4–10.

35. Tanabe, *Myōe the Dreamkeeper*, 153–54.

36. The term *honji suijaku* (lit. "the original ground and its traces") refers to distinctive and yet pervasive Japanese interpretations of the relationship between Buddhist and Shinto divinities. Medieval Japanese religionists believed that while the buddhas and bodhisattvas in Buddhism are the true essence of gods, when they manifest themselves in Japan, they take the form of mundane local gods, known as kami.

37. Kōzanji Tenseki Monjo Sōgō Chōsadan, ed., *Myōe shōnin shiryō* vol. 1 (Tokyo: Tokyo Daigaku Shuppankai, 1971), 656–57. The particular statue that the famous Buddhist sculptor Tankei (1173–1256) made is not the same as the statue stored at Kōzanji.

38. For more about Zenmyōji nuns, see Brock, "Chinese Maiden," 205–10; Okuda, "Myōe to josei," 31–51.

39. Tanabe, *Myōe*, 131–35.

40. For instance, Lady Sami was Myōe's long-term elite female patron. Brock suggests that she may have been one of the sponsors of the *Kegon Engi*. Brock, "Chinese Maiden," 205–10.

41. For a fuller discussion on this, see Luke N. Thompson, "Returning to the Founder: Śākyamuni Devotion in Early Medieval Japan and Japanese Buddhist Conceptions of History" (PhD diss., Columbia University, 2017).

42. Fumihiko Sueki, "Myōe no Shaka shinkō," in *Iwanami kōza Nihon bungaku to Bukkyō*, vol. 3: genes to raise, ed. Konno Tōru, Satake Akihiro, and Ueda Shizutera (Tokyo: Iwanami Shoten, 1994), 223–46. The Pure Land, a more popular Buddhist paradise, excludes the female in the realm.

43. Eison was another major Buddhist monk who devoted his life to rebuilding the oldest Buddhist nunnery, known as Hokkeji. For more about Hokkeji, see Lori Meeks, *The Hokkeji and the Emergence of Monastic Orders in Premodern Japan* (Honolulu: University of Hawai'i Press, 2010).

44. Hirano, "Myōe to nisō," 92–93.

45. Hirano, "Myōe to nisō," 92.

46. Isao Okuda, "Zenmyōji no nisō: Myōgyō-Fūjyumon wo meggute," *Seishin joshi daigaku ronsō* 92 (1999): 157–77.

47. It is uncertain how the scroll was used at Kōzanji either, since temple documents postdating the year of 1630 have not been published. But visitors to Kōzanji from the seventeenth to the nineteenth centuries occasionally had an opportunity to see the scrolls. Brock, "Tales of Gisho," 48.

Bibliography

Abé, Ryuichi. "Mantra, Hinin, and the Feminine: On the Salvational Strategies of Myōe and Eizon." *Cahiers d'Extrême-Asie* 13 (2002): 101–25.

———. "Swords, Words, and Deformity: On Myōe's eccentricity." In *Discourse and Ideology in Medieval Japanese Buddhism*, edited by Richard K. Payne and Taigen Dan Leighton, 148–59. London: Routledge, 2006.

Ambros, Barbara. *Women in Japanese Religions*. New York: New York University Press, 2015.

Brock, Karen L. "Tales of Gisho and Gangyo: Editor, Artist, and Audience in Japanese Picture Scrolls." PhD diss., Princeton University, 1984.

———. "Chinese Maiden, Sillla Monk: Zenmyō and Her Thirteenth-century Japanese Audience." In *Flowering in the Shadows: Women in the History of Chinese and Japanese Painting*, edited by Marsha Weidner, 185–211. Honolulu: University of Hawai'i Press, 1990.

Chan, Yuk-yue. "Dream, Pilgrimage, and Dragons in the *Kegon Engi* Emaki (Illustrated legends of the Kegon patriarchs): Reading Ideology in Kamakura Buddhist Narrative Scrolls." Master's thesis, University of Hong Kong, 2006.

Cho, Se-in. "Kozanji e yujŏn toen Han'guk Pulgyo munhŏn." Paper presented at the conference, *Tong'ashia e yujon toen Hanguk Pulgyo munhŏn gwa sasang*, 77–90, Seoul, May 2019.

Choe, Yeonshik. "Huayan Studies in Korea." In *Reflecting Mirrors: Perspectives on Huayan Buddhism*, edited by Imre Hamer, 69–85. Wiesbaden: Harrassowitz, 2007.

Faure, Bernard. "Kegon and Dragon: A Mythological Approach to Huayan Doctrine." In *Reflecting Mirrors: Perspectives on Huayan Buddhism*, edited by Imre Hamer, 297–307. Wiesbaden: Harrassowitz, 2007.

Faure, Bernard. *The Power of Denial: Buddhism, Purity, and Gender*. Princeton: Princeton University Press, 2003.

Gimello, Robert, Frédéric Girard, and Imre Hamar, eds. *Avataṃsaka Buddhism in East Asia: Huayan, Kegon, Flower Ornament Buddhism Origins and Adaptation of a Visual Culture*. Wiesbaden: Harrassowitz, 2012.

Gunji, Naoko "The Ritual Narration of Mortuary Art: The Illustrated Story of Emperor Antoku and Its *Etoki* at Amidaji." *Japanese Journal of Religious Studies* 40, no. 2 (2013): 203–45.

Hirano, Tae. "Myōe to nisō tachi." In *Nihon bungaku josei e no manazashi*, edited by Okuda Isao, 76–98. Tokyo: Kazama Shobō, 2004.

Ingram, Evan S. "Chōgen's Vision of Tōdaiji's Great Buddha as Both Mahāvairocana and Amitābha." *Japanese Journal of Religious Studies* 46, no. 2 (2019): 173–92.

Kawahashi, Noriko, and Kobayashi Naoko. "Editor's Introduction: Gendering Religious Practices in Japan Multiple Voices, Multiple Strategies." *Japanese Journal of Religious Studies* 44, no. 1 (2017): 1–13.

Kawai, Hayao. *The Buddhist Priest Myōe: A Life of Dreams*. Translated by Mark Uno, Venice: Lapis Press, 1992.

Kaminishi, Ikumi. *Explaining Pictures: Buddhist Propaganda and Etoki Storytelling in Japan*. Honolulu: University of Hawaiʻi, 2006.

Kim, Sujung. "Korea I: 372–935 C.E." In *Brill's Encyclopedia of Buddhism*, vol. 4 (forthcoming).

Klein, Susan. "Woman as Serpent: The Demonic Feminine in the Noh Play." In *Religious Reflections on the Human Body*, edited by Jane Marie Law, 100–36. Bloomington: Indiana University Press, 1995.

Kōzanji Tenseki Monjo Sōgō Chōsadan, ed. *Myōe shōnin shiryō*. vol. 1 Tokyo: Tokyo Daigaku Shuppankai, 1971.

Lee, Kenneth Doo Young. *The Prince and the Monk: Shotoku Worship in Shinran's Buddhism*. Albany: State University of New York Press, 2012.

Meeks, Lori. *The Hokkeji and the Emergence of Monastic Orders in Premodern Japan*. Honolulu: University of Hawaiʻi Press, 2010.

Morell, Robert. "Kamakura Accounts of Myōe Shōnin as Popular Religious Hero." *Japanese Journal of Religious Studies* 9, nos. 2–3 (1982): 171–98.

Murase, Miyeko. *Emaki: Narrative Scrolls from Japan*. New York: Asian Society, 1983.

Okuda, Isao. "Myoe to josei: Kegon engi, Zenmyo, Zenmyoji." *Seishin joshi daigaku ronso* 89 (1997): 31–51.

————. "Zenmyōji no nisō: Myōgyō-Fūjyumon wo meggute." *Seishin joshi daigaku ronsō* 92 (1999): 157–77.

Ruch, Barbara ed. *Engendering Faith: Women and Buddhism in Premodern Japan*. Ann Arbor: Center for Japanese Studies, University of Michigan, 2002.

Sueki, Fumihiko. "Myōe no Shaka shinkō." In *Iwanami kōza Nihon bungaku to Bukkyō*, vol. 3: Genes to Raise, edited by Konno Tōru, Satake Akihiro, and Ueda Shizutera, 223–46. Tokyo: Iwanami Shoten, 1994.

Suhara, Eiji. "Can Bodaishin Be a Cause of Rebirth? Reconsidering the Doctrinal Conflict between Hōnen and Myōe." *Philosophy East and West* 65, no. 2 (2015): 444–65.

Tanabe, George J. *Myōe the Dreamkeeper: Fantasy and Knowledge in Early Kamakura Buddhism*. Cambridge: Council on East Asian Studies, Harvard University, 1992.

Thomas, Greg M. "Concluding Remarks: Narrative Visualization and Embodied Meaning." In *Rethinking Visual Narratives from Asia*, edited by Alexandra Green, 245–52. Hong Kong: Hong Kong University Press, 2013.

Thompson, Luke N. "Returning to the Founder: Śākyamuni Devotion in Early Medieval Japan and Japanese Buddhist Conceptions of History." PhD diss., Columbia University, 2017.

Uno, Mark. *Shingon Refractions: Myōe and the Mantra of Light*, Somerville: Wisdom Publications, 1997.

Waters, Virginia Skord. "Sex, Lies, and the Illustrated Scroll: *The Dōjōji Engi Emaki*." *Monumenta Nipponica* 52 no. 1 (1997): 59–84.

Winfield, Pamela. *Icons and Iconoclasm in Japanese Buddhism: Kūkai and Dōgen on the Art of Enlightenment*. Oxford: Oxford University, 2013.

Chapter 10

The Spirit of Shaolin on Screen

Buddhism and Cultural Politics in Chinese Cinema

MELISSA CROTEAU AND XIN ZHANG

In October 2011, the movie *Shaolin* premiered in theaters throughout China, meeting with a notable contrast between strong box office earnings and poor reviews. By mid-January of 2012, its box office was nearly 500 million yuan (US $70 million), yet it received a low score of 5.5 out of 10 from moviegoers on douban.com, the popular semi-professional review website in China. However, *Shaolin* was received more positively by international audiences; Rotten Tomatoes has this film at 74 percent among critics (with a 71 percent audience score). It seems that people who have less knowledge of Chan Buddhism are not as exacting as douban.com's reviewers, who represent the more aesthetically cultivated class in China. The movie followed the typical operational mode of blockbuster filmdom: a big-budget production with a famous director (Hong Kong film director Benny Chan), a star-studded cast, flashy promotion of kung fu action and chase scenes, and a family tragedy plotline. The disparity between the box office take and the poor reviews showed, however, that while the blockbuster formula of popular cinema might capture people's attention, it might not touch the minds and souls of the audience. Even in officially secular China, audiences have a sense of what is spiritually authentic and what is not, and *Shaolin* did not pass inspection.

Shaolin Temple is the birthplace of the Chinese Chan School of Buddhism as well as Shaolin martial arts. Its lasting historical influence in China is incomparable to any other Buddhist school. There are different versions of the origin story of Shaolin kung fu. According to one popular legend, the first Chinese patriarch of Chan, Bodhidharma, taught Shaolin monks kung fu for balancing their mental and physical development and avoiding the unhealthiness of sitting for long periods of time in meditation. However, many historians believe that this is a fiction, for Bodhidharma only stayed a short time at Shaolin Temple. In 495 CE, Emperor Xiaowen of Northern Wei built Shaolin Temple for the Indian monk Buddhabhadra, who became its first abbot. It was said that, while preaching, Buddhabhadra also taught monks Indian exercises. In the ancient period, most big temples located in the mountains had martially trained monks to protect their property from bandits. *Biographies of Shaolin Martial Monks* (少林武僧志) indicates that a disciple of Buddhabhadra, Sengchou (僧稠, 480–560 CE), was the earliest Shaolin martial monk. When Sengchou became the abbot of Shaolin temple, he promoted martial arts as well as Chan.[1] Martial arts are regarded as a way of and path to Chan, for they require rigorous discipline—firm control of body and mind—which helps monks to develop and maintain a better understanding of the self and to experience the interaction between the emptiness (San., *śūnyatā*) and suchness (San., *tathātā*) of the ephemeral phenomenal world.

As Shaolin kung fu plays an extremely significant role in China's martial arts world, it is only natural that we see images of Shaolin Temple and its monks appearing in kung fu films. However, this 2011 version of *Shaolin* is the first one that attempts to depict the "Shaolin Spirit." Before the movie's debut, the director, Chen Musheng (Benny Chan), averred, "Previous Shaolin films only tell you that Shaolin kung fu is spectacular to watch, but never tell you why you should learn, why you should practice Shaolin kung fu."[2] Indeed, great efforts were made to infuse what the director called "Shaolin elements" into the movie: 20 million yuan (US $2.8 million) were spent in reconstructing the Shaolin Temple structures, which were actually one-third larger than the original. With the exception of the leading roles, Shaolin monks were played by real Shaolin monks. Shi Yongxin, the current Abbot of Shaolin Temple, even served as the chief producer of the movie. The "Shaolin spirit" and ethos is reverently proclaimed in a stirring speech given by the protagonist Hou Jie, played by Liu Dehua (Andy Lau), during the climactic scene at the end of the movie when he stands in front of the monks on the steps of Shaolin Temple's Grand Hall and speaks to the frightened refugees for whom the monks have been caring. However, Chinese audiences found this oratory to be incongruent with the character of Hou Jie and the narrative of the film. Why was the Chinese audience drawn to Shaolin kung fu but not impressed by the so-called Shaolin spirit message? As will be argued, this film misrepresents the Chan Buddhist "Shaolin image" and marshals its themes of redemption, forgiveness, and compassion for nationalist aims on behalf of the ruling Chinese Communist Party of the People's Republic of China rather than endeavoring to portray any sort of authentic "Shaolin spirit."

The Big Picture: The Shaolin Temple as Political Canvas

When history goes to the movies, politics comes along, hand in hand. This principle holds true even in Chinese martial arts action films. What might be more surprising, especially in officially secular contemporary China, is that religion also is in the room. We see this quite clearly in Benny Chan's 2011 film *Shaolin*, which reviewers have compared to director Hsin-yen (Cheh) Chang's popular film *The Shaolin Temple*, made in 1982. This earlier film catapulted Jet Li, then an unknown, seventeen-year-old martial arts champion, to fame. The comparison between these two films is easy to make, particularly because, of the many Shaolin Temple kung fu films, they are the only two that have been sanctioned by the temple and made in cooperation with the temple's representatives. In both films, actual Shaolin monks play the monks in the film, and the films were shot on location at the Shaolin Temple, located in Henan Province's Dengfeng City. However, as Clarence Tsui states in his compelling review of Chan's *Shaolin* in the *South China Morning Post*, "Benny Chan . . . has stressed that his film is neither a simple remake of either Chang Cheh's [Hsin-yen Chang's] Shaolin Temple films from the 1970s, nor an update of the 1982 film of the same name." Tsui argues that the evolving, historically based narratives in Shaolin Temple kung fu films made from the 1970s to the present "allow viewers a glimpse of the political climate in which each film was made, and how Hong Kong cinema—or Hong Kong in general—has moved on in its relationship with its northerly neighbours." Indeed, as this chapter will point out, the developments in the relationship between Hong Kong and the People's Republic of China over the past fifty years are reflected particularly vividly in the plots, ideological agendas, themes, and production exigencies of this period's Shaolin-style kung fu films. Perhaps unexpectedly, the question of religion's place in contemporary China circulates within and around these films as well. In remarkable ways, the Shaolin epic retold by Chan in the eponymous film reflects the current uncertainty about religion in today's China.

Hsin-yen (Cheh) Chang was one of the most prolific filmmakers of the famous Shaw Brothers Studio of Hong Kong. His earlier Shaolin films, *Five Masters of Shaolin* (1974) and *Shaolin Temple* (1976), were creations entirely of the Hong Kong film industry and espoused the anticommunist ideology common to many of the Shaw Brothers' martial arts dramas. The protagonists of these films "are patriots trying to defeat the evil Manchus—the Qing court [1644–1912] was considered to be an interloper regime—and restore the country to Han rule."[3] Tsui also notes that "Chang had a close working relationship with Chiang Kai-shek's son, Chiang Ching-kuo, before he became a filmmaker in the 1950s," which leads him to the apt conclusion that "this narrative could easily be seen as an allegory of the Kuomintang's struggle to regain its footing on the communist-ruled mainland. The way its heroes fled to the south of the country to regroup also mirrors the way the Kuomintang government relocated to Taiwan after the establishment of the People's Republic in 1949."[4] Of course, the Chinese Communist Party's antagonistic views on religion of all kinds, particularly during the years of the Cultural Revolution (1966–1976), renders the making of a film focused on a renowned mainland Buddhist temple an act of subversion in the eyes of the leaders of the People's Republic of China (PRC).

However, it must be noted that the Kuomintang (KMT), after taking control of China in 1927 under Chiang Kai-shek, also censured the exceedingly popular genre of *wuxia* films—films featuring knights errant, physical battles, and spiritual/mythological means of salvation—of which kung fu films are a subgenre. According to film scholar Stephen Teo, the "left-wing" critics in the Chinese Communist Party (CCP) "viewed the espousal of heroism in *wuxia* mythology as an unhealthy trend because it transformed revolutionary class struggle into 'private feuds,'" while "[c]onservative traditionalists [of the KMT], on the other hand, feared that the genre might instigate anarchy and violence."[5] Some critics complained that the *wuxia* films "contained too much *wu* (violence) and too little *xia* (chivalry)."[6] By 1934, the KMT government had placed an outright ban on *wuxia* films, and much of the film industry based in Shanghai moved to Hong Kong and Taiwan to continue their film production. When the CCP took over the Chinese government in 1949, the remaining film industry on mainland China was mandated to serve the state by producing propaganda films in the socialist realism style that furthered the Communists' cause.

By the time *wuxia* films in the form of kung fu cinema came roaring back into the Hong Kong film industry of the 1970s, the religious and mythological overtones of the genre, as well as the focus on the individual hero, had become a political statement against the ideology of the CCP. Clarence Tsui reminds us that the "Qing soldiers' burning down of the Shaolin temple in [Hsin-yen] Chang's films also bears a resemblance to the real-life destruction of the institution during the Cultural Revolution, just years before the films were made [in the 1970s]. Mao Zedong set young men and women to subverting cultural and religious traditions. Red Guards shackled placard-wearing monks and subjected them to physical and mental abuse as well as emptying the monastery of its relics."[7] This example of violence against Buddhists during the Cultural Revolution certainly was not the first time the Shaolin Temple or Buddhism in general was severely attacked by government forces. During the Tang dynasty (618–907), Buddhism—which traveling Indian monks had introduced in China around 50 CE—experienced a surge in popularity. However, during the latter years of the dynasty, high-powered Confucianists of the aristocracy and intelligentsia put pressure on the government to impose rigorous controls on all "foreign religions."[8] As a result, in 845 CE the Tang government denounced Buddhism as a foreign influence and defunded monasteries, which forced thousands of them to close their doors and "laicized" much of the Buddhist clergy.[9] Indeed, as Daniel H. Bays asserts, "In terms of the most fundamental level of assumptions of the state toward religion, there has hardly been a Chinese political regime from the Tang dynasty . . . to the present that has not required a form of registration or licensing of religious groups or has not assumed the right to monitor and intervene in religious affairs. For a thousand years there has been apparatus for this purpose."[10] Taking this legacy into consideration, Chang's 1970s Shaolin films, which feature the conflagration and ultimate destruction of the Shaolin Temple and the southward escape of the monks, does seem to make a statement regarding the conspicuous liberty enjoyed by the Chinese who fled the mainland to live (ironically) in colonized Hong Kong. The fact that Chang could make these *wuxia* films about a legendary Buddhist temple while the mainland was suffering one of the most violent crackdowns on arts and religion in China's long history attests to this freedom.

Then, surprisingly, just a few years after Chang's first kung fu films, he was able to make *The Shaolin Temple* (1982) under very different circumstances, largely resulting from the death of Mao in 1976 and the ascension of Deng Xiaoping to the head of the CCP. *The Shaolin Temple* "received full backing from Beijing, and was among the first Hong Kong productions to be shot on the mainland as the country reopened its doors under the reforms Deng Xiaoping initiated in 1978."[11] The ideology of the 1982 Shaolin film had to be shifted to reflect and honor the increasingly amicable but fragile relationship between the British Crown Colony of Hong Kong and the PRC. *The Shaolin Temple* is based on a Shaolin legend and features Jet Li as the son of a slave who worked for, and was killed by, the tyrannical warlord Wang Shichong during the Tang dynasty. In the film, Wang has usurped the power of the true Tang Emperor. Jet Li's character escapes Wang's clutches and flees to the Shaolin Temple, where he trains in martial arts and then seeks revenge on the evil warlord. The Shaolin monks, including Jet Li's novice character, are the heroes, as in preceding films. However, in contrast to the earlier Shaolin films, Tsui points out that "the temple survived Wang's attacks thanks to the well-timed arrival of [the true Emperor's] forces, and . . . the monastery eventually received the blessing of the new royal court. This twist represents the reconciliation or even assimilation of Shaolin monks into the corridors of power."[12]

In the 1982 film, the temple survives and the monks bow to the superior political and spiritual power of the nation, represented by the new Tang Emperor. In other words, the monks have been co-opted into the cult of the Emperor; they no longer prioritize their Buddhist *dharma* over Tang dogma. (No mention is made of the Tang dynasty's later devastating blow to the Buddhist community.) The portrayal in the film of the religious devotees prioritizing their reverence for the Chinese Emperor above all else was a model for the behavior the CCP leaders expected from the Chinese people. Bays explains that dynastic governments, as well as the current CCP-driven government in China, have been "so insistent on monitoring and intervening in religious matters" because "the state itself had, and has today, religious pretensions and claims. Now, as then, in its mode of public discourse, in its sanctification of the existing political order, and in many other ways the Chinese government behaves as a theocratic organization."[13] Though the atheistic CCP attempted to eradicate religion from China in the 1950s and 1960s, it altered its policy on religion in 1978 and provided "limited space for religious believers to practice their faith" but also called for "comprehensive control measures to prevent religion from emerging as an independent force."[14] The Chinese government began officially to recognize (only) five religions: Buddhism, Taoism, Catholicism, Islam, and Protestantism. A few years later, Chang made *The Shaolin Temple* in tandem with the Chinese film industry and Shaolin Temple leaders. This Hong Kong–China co-production proved that formerly subversive and forbidden religiously oriented material could instruct mainland comrades how to put religion in its "proper" place, subservient to the needs and dictates of the state.

Nearly thirty years later, in 2009, director Benny Chan was able to acquire approval and support from the Shaolin Temple officials and the Chinese government to make his kung fu film on the historic site of the temple in the Henan Province of central China. It is significant that this was only the second film embraced by Shaolin Temple religious authorities, though dozens of Shaolin kung fu films were produced by the Hong Kong film industry after 1982. Significantly, the literal translation of the original Chinese title of Chan's 2011 film is *The New Shaolin Temple*. It is this nomenclature that inspired many critics to assume that Chan's film is a remake of Chang's *The Shaolin Temple*. Chan's comments about the relationship between his film and Chang's film are also suggestive. Journalist Boon Chan, in Singapore's *The Straits Times*, asserts that "Chan's *version* takes a different tack," and quotes Benny Chan, who declares, "The *original* was such a classic that I put all thoughts of it away and thought about the *message* here instead. I put more work into the drama, which delves into forgiveness and the *spirit of Shaolin*" (emphasis mine).[15] Boon Chan calling *Shaolin* a "version" of *The Shaolin Temple* and Benny Chan referring to the latter film as "the original" do give the impression that Benny Chan approached *Shaolin* as a remake. However, he also insists that he purposely "put all thoughts [of the earlier film] away" and emphasized markedly different aspects of Shaolin life in his film.[16] The connections between the two films are undeniable. Nonetheless, there is one striking change that makes all the difference in regard to the political and even spiritual messaging of this Shaolin drama: the film is set in the late 1920s rather than during the Tang dynasty.

As Benny Chan asserts, his Shaolin kung fu film foregrounds the spiritual subjects of forgiveness, compassion, and grace. These qualities are displayed in relationships that range from familial to communal to national. For instance, the protagonist Hou is forgiven for his terrible arrogance and selfishness by his long-suffering wife; Hou forgives and shows compassion to his maniacal protégé Cao, to the extent that Hou sacrifices his life to save Cao's; and the Shaolin monks have grace and forgiveness for the warlords and their soldiers who have been terrorizing the temple monks and the refugees under their care. While these selfless actions and expressions of compassion are in keeping with Shaolin's Chan Buddhist doctrines of no-self, emptiness, and nonduality, the film also conveys xenophobic and nationalistic messaging. By the end of the film, in the wake of the massive, brutal destruction of sacred space and innumerable Chinese lives, the humbled

Chinese survivors have learned that the true enemy of Chinese harmony is the evil, white foreigner along with internal divisiveness stemming from the avarice and lust for power displayed by the warlords.

This lesson is directly communicated to the audience during the Shaolin Temple's initiation ceremony for Hou, formerly a vicious warlord. The temple's Abbot proclaims, "All negative deeds are done out of greed," and announces that Hou has been so purified that nothing else remains. The Abbot then confers upon Hou his "spiritual name": Jingjue, meaning "pure enlightenment." In traditional Buddhist philosophy, enlightenment is gained by relinquishing and renouncing desire of all kinds, a process that is expected to take many years or even lifetimes. However, due to the synthesis of Taoism and Buddhism in China, Chinese Buddhism, and particularly the Chan (Jpn., Zen) tradition, has adopted the concept of sudden, or epiphanic, enlightenment. Although it does not happen overnight, Hou's path to profound enlightenment is rapid in *Shaolin*. Not long after his initiation ceremony, Hou's strength is tested when he bids farewell to his wife and restrains himself from killing Cao in order to prove to Cao that he (Hou) is truly transformed and, thereby, facilitate Cao's enlightenment. Hou asks Cao, "Power and wealth really mean so much to you?" and later gently declares, "Wake up, Cao. You possess more than you need. Let it go. Don't kill anymore." The physical battles between the monks and their attackers mirror the inward battle for enlightenment that all people experience. To renounce desire, to cease coveting and resenting what others have, is to embrace unity and harmony. It is not difficult to see why the Communist Party leaders agreed to support this project. It is a nationalist film with ideology conveniently provided courtesy of Chan Buddhism.

The enhanced spiritual elements in *Shaolin* have been noted by several journalists, many of whom complain that the film does not have enough spectacular martial arts scenes, but a few writers have noted the connection between the evident spiritual bent of the film and its nationalist project. Mark Jenkins and Clarence Tsui make cogent arguments to this effect. Jenkins, a reviewer for the United States' National Public Radio, asserts that the film treats the Shaolin monks

> more seriously than most. . . . The filmmakers have crafted an action scenario that's fairly . . . Buddhist. *Shaolin* is a tale of monstrous evil, spiritual transformation and ultimate self-sacrifice, all rendered in a subdued, misty palette. If the movie is grimmer than most battling-monk flicks, that's partially because it's set in

the 1920s. Railroads, machine guns and electricity—all presented as ominous—have arrived in China; several scenes depicting mass graves foreshadow the horrors of the Sino-Japanese War and Maoism.[17]

Indeed, as Jenkins points out, the setting of this film in the 1920s draws much attention to the Sino-Japanese War, with its genocidal atrocities, and the years leading up to the bloody battles between the Kuomintang and communist forces within China. The depiction in *Shaolin* of vaguely European/American white military leaders and their attendant armies taking advantage of the divisions between the Chinese warlords during this period—and, crucially, dealing the catastrophic final blow to the temple—communicate that xenophobia is rational, favorable, and wise. Of course, the most serious threat to China in the 1920s proved to be Japan, not the European nations, but the message regarding the perfidy, danger, and amorality of Western foreigners supports nationalist interests, nevertheless. The global situation of 2011 was vastly different from that of the early twentieth century, and *Shaolin*'s warning about the "unkindness of strangers" undoubtedly applies to economics and politics largely, though not entirely, outside the realm of armed conflict. China's battles in the twenty-first century revolve primarily around its strong economy and role as global financier. In many ways, as a global, economic power, China has the upper hand.

It is interesting that Mark Jenkins also connects the grimness of the China portrayed in *Shaolin* to the unspeakable suffering of the Chinese people under Mao Zedong. According to recent scholarship on Chinese history, Mao's Great Leap Forward from 1958 to 1962 resulted in the deaths of several million more Chinese people than previously thought.[18] The destruction of human life is staggering. However, as Chan's film is a co-production of Hong Kong and mainland China, filmed at Shaolin, surely the filmmaker has not alluded purposely to the trauma of China under Mao. While foreigners are always a worthy target of vitriol and disdain in China, Chairman Mao and his party are still off-limits to dissenters. What is fascinating is that a foreigner, such as Jenkins, might well see a palpable relationship between the gloomy grey-brown, mud-mottled, mist-haunted, and violence-saturated *mise-en-scène* of *Shaolin* and the darkness of human affliction in Mao's China. Nevertheless, this is not the connection the director, writers, or funders of the film intended or foresaw. However, as increasingly more is known about what took place in China during the 1950s through the 1970s, it is difficult for non-Chinese viewers to see the slaughter of Chinese citizens due to warlords' drive for power as well as the destruction of the renowned Buddhist temple in *Shaolin* and *not* draw parallels with mid-twentieth-century Chinese history. The CCP's positions regarding religion and human rights are well known. It is perplexing that Chinese censors did not perceive that these connections might be made by non-Chinese viewers.

There is no denying that Chan's *Shaolin* is rooted in political history. Clarence Tsui notes Chan's assertion that "he was inspired to make the film when he learned of the story of how Shaolin was burnt down in 1927 by the forces of Shi Yousan—a general notorious for his repeated switching of allegiances during the 1920s and 30s."[19] The chaos of this postdynastic period of battling warlords serves as a foil for the unity and stability the CCP claims to have brought to China. In *Shaolin*, the doctrines of Chan Buddhism—a tradition that has absorbed Taoistic pragmatism and respect for nature—are presented as concomitant with the CCP's alleged goals of cultivating a harmonious and united China. The monks even are willing and ready to participate in violent and underhanded activities as long as these are in the service of "the common people." This is evidenced by the episode in the film in which several monks break into a government storehouse and steal rice for the refugees (à la Robin Hood) and the dramatic martial arts sequence at Cao's compound in which the monks infiltrate the heavily guarded fortress to set free the innocent men whom Cao has ordered to be killed. A bloody battle ensues in which the monks kill many soldiers. All of this is justified, even though the monks are the aggressors, because they are defending the peasants from an evil ruler who is pandering to unscrupulous foreigners. Although Chan monks are known to separate themselves from secular affairs, the peace-loving warriors in this film use their skills for good. From a Mahāyāna Buddhist perspective, these actions could be rationalized with the doctrine of skillful means (San. *upāya*), which Peter Hershock defines as "the improvisational expression of *relational virtuosity* oriented toward the resolution of conflict, trouble and suffering."[20] In other words, these monks act in uncharacteristic ways (*upāya*) in order to alleviate the suffering of the refugees and innocent men, which is central to their vocation as Chan Buddhist practitioners.

Moreover, the spectacular and deadly kung fu used throughout the film by the spiritual devotees is par for the course in the *wuxia* genre. Nonetheless, many journalists and Benny Chan himself claim that this film is more "Buddhist" than previous Shaolin-based films. In *The Hollywood Reporter*, Maggie Lee declares that *Shaolin* "significantly altered the philosophy and screen representation of martial arts. Instead of vengeance, the theme is repentance and forgiveness, as it charts the hubris and spiritual rebirth of a warlord."[21] This film departs from the *dharma* of other Shaolin films in its renunciation of vengeance and embracing of forgiveness and redemption through enlightenment. Perhaps these Buddhist principles might be useful in a nation that endured an extremely turbulent and violent twentieth century. Forgiveness is indeed called for and could enhance the peace and unity of the nation. In addition, forgiveness and enlightenment, along with the renunciation of desire, might make for a more compliant society, in line with nationalist aims. Perhaps the Chinese government now sees the persuasive potential of utilizing religion in nationalistic propaganda, particularly if the religious principles or ideologies can be effectively separated from the religion to which they belong. To this end, there is a "Disclaimer" at the very end of the credits of *Shaolin* that states, "Any Buddhist ceremony portrayed in the film is depicted under artistic license and should not be construed religiously for the understanding and appreciation of the Buddhist faith." The selfless moral code of the brave Buddhist monks is to be admired and emulated, but not their faith. Clarence Tsui asserts, "Just like the film's predecessors, *Shaolin* finds the right target at the right time, revealing how political undertones lurk beneath the pyrotechnics and gravity-defying stunts."[22] As has been argued, this is undoubtedly true, but, just like the enlightened warrior Hou Jie at the end of *Shaolin*, the political messages in this film are ensconced in the hands of the great Buddha.

A Closer Look: The *Shaolin* Identity Lost

THE RED CROSS VERSION OF SHAOLIN

As demonstrated above, Benny Chan's *Shaolin* attempts to present a different Shaolin image from previous films, which generally emphasize the incredible martial arts skills of the Shaolin monks. Some viewers, however—Chinese viewers especially—might find the film's depiction of Chan monks to be unrealistic. At the beginning of the 2011 film, we see the Shaolin monks collecting corpses, providing aid to the sick and wounded, and offering help to war victims. They are doing so while the soldiers of opposing warlords fight on the battlefield, as if the Shaolin Temple is functioning as a modern version of the Red Cross in China. When the monks build pyres to burn the corpses and chant sutras to the heavens, we witness a rare scene of transcendent love and care. This Red Cross version of the Shaolin image was obviously created because the director wanted to give prominence to elements other than Shaolin kung fu, and beneficence is something that appeals to viewers. However, as the story unfolds, Chinese audiences cannot help but feel that this Red Cross version of Shaolin is poorly conceived.

Though the title of the movie is *Shaolin*, the Shaolin monks merely serve as a backdrop to the story of the heroic Hou Jie, the warlord turned monk. The Shaolin monks represent a worldview that is the polar opposite to that of the warlords, and the monks have a significant symbolic meaning in representing the Chan School of Chinese Buddhism. However, the monks' monastic lifestyle and state of mind, characterized by detachment from the rest of the world, only appears for a brief moment at the beginning of the movie, and then the monks begin an active secular life. As the story develops, the Shaolin monks resort to violence when necessary, stepping far beyond their community service role in the Red Cross vein, which would provide humanitarian aid, not martial protection. This unhesitating and uniform "turning to arms" of the monks, as rendered in the movie, conflicts with the film's intended justification of the Shaolin spirit of "Attaining Enlightenment through Martial Arts"—grasping the meaning of Chan Buddhism through peaceful physical practice and study. Conversely, it is also the case that Chan Buddhism cannot become a Red Cross–style, nongovernmental organization, for it is in essence a religious institution with Chan doctrine as its basic core and foothold. As a religious institution, the goal of Shaolin Temple is to provide monastic training and a consecrated space for seeking enlightenment; the temple is not meant to intervene in secular life. In the movie, when the monks turn to using force to save others, the monks do not show any mental struggle, which means the world-forsaking concept of Chan does not have any hold on the monks. Previous films featuring Shaolin do not include the secular humanitarian engagement of the monks that takes place in the 2011 film, in which Shaolin is a part of the world of *wuxia* that advocates for individual justice and heroism. Even this version of "Shaolin," despite efforts to transcend the previous monotonous depictions of kung fu battles and to prioritize the spiritual, cannot manage to leave behind the formula of secular heroism. Like the Shaolin films preceding it, this film relies on its glorification of kung fu through spectacular action sequences.

Is there any historical evidence for this sort of Red Cross version of Shaolin? Regrettably, Shaolin Temple has never in its history embraced a mandate to provide care to those in need nor has it expressed humanitarian aid to be a priority. Shaolin Temple was able to become a world-famous

Buddhist temple partly because of the support from the royal court of the Tang dynasty (618–907), as illustrated by the so-called legend of the "Thirteen Staff-Wielding Monks Rescuing the Tang Emperor," which served as the inspiration for the 1982 Shaolin film. To reward their meritorious military service in the war, the Tang royal court gave special authorization to allow Shaolin to retain its own fighting monks and conferred the title of General-in-Chief to monk Tan Zong. Shaolin Temple also was involved in the chaotic fighting between the warlords during the period of the Republic of China when the Shaolin Abbot led the fighting monks to join the army of the warlord Wu Peifu, which brought about the disastrous burning down of the Shaolin Temple in 1928 by their opponent Feng Yuxiang in retaliation when he had an upper hand. Shaolin's engagement with partisan politics demonstrates that even those in pursuit of spiritual transcendence cannot avoid the influence of political powers. Although faith directs people to the "other shore" of the spiritual world, a concrete, faith-based institution must face various issues found in the real world. Being detached from the world yet existing in its reality is a problem not easily handled by any serious faith or faith-based institution. Concomitantly, director Benny Chan had to negotiate with the politics of the film industry and the Chinese government while trying to portray a more spiritual Shaolin. Nonetheless, even for moviegoers who are mostly unaware of the history of Shaolin Temple's secular involvement, the simplistic rendition of the temple as a "Red Cross–style" place of refuge that resorts abruptly to violence does not ring true. According to the ten Shaolin commandments, which regulate the aim, attitude, and conduct expected when practicing Shaolin kung fu, the monks are "obliged to practice Buddhist compassion" and use martial arts "only for legitimate self-defense"; and "in travelling, a boxer should refrain from showing his art to the common people even to the extent of refusing challenges."[23] Although audiences might be familiar with secularized heroic stereotypes of Shaolin kung fu monks, Chan Buddhism, in doctrine and practice, cherishes life and refuses the use of violence.[24] If monks actively employ violence, such as killing jailors to liberate refugees, they are not safeguarding the Chan spirit of Shaolin.

THE U-SHAPED STORY OF THE PROTAGONIST

As previously noted, Benny Chan's *Shaolin* is not just a simple remake of the popular 1982 film *The Shaolin Temple*, as *Shaolin* is much more complex in terms of its protagonist and plot design than the earlier film. Put simply,

Chan's film introduces the U-shaped plot frequently seen in movies. The U-shaped plot refers to the experience of the protagonist whose life falls from a high point to the lowest point and then rises back to a high point; such a plotline is usually combined with the personal growth of the protagonist. At the beginning of the film, the tyrannical protagonist Hou Jie wantonly slaughters people in Shaolin Temple, losing his wife and daughter as a result of his transgressions. At his nadir, he is reduced to a fugitive hiding out in Shaolin Temple, where he learns Chan and Shaolin kung fu. This leads to his attainment of enlightenment and his arrival at the spiritual summit of his life, which results, finally, in the enlightenment of his adversary, Cao Man, at the cost of his own life.

Similar U-shaped plots and protagonists had appeared at least four times in Chinese kung fu films in the years leading up to *Shaolin*. 2004's *New Police Story* (dir. Benny Chan), with Jackie Chan; 2006's *Fearless* (dir. Ronny Yu), with Jet Li; 2010's *True Legend* (dir. Woo-Ping Yuen), with Zhao Wenzhuo; and 2011's *Shaolin* are all kung fu movies featuring established kung fu superstars. This plot structure is clearly commercially appealing. Chinese kung fu movies are based on Chinese kung fu novels, a literary genre of the Ming and Qing dynasties. Strong traditional Chinese character traits are carried by men of chivalry, by the "rivers and lakes" (a martial world similar to the American Wild West) and by the moral code of loyalty, filial piety, chastity, and righteousness (found in such kung fu novels as the classic *Three Heroes and Five Gallants* 三侠五义), as well as by clearly defined characters who are either good or evil. This classic moral code still prevails because the ethical concepts dominating the martial world and those of temples and courts are similar. In *The Literary Thousand Year Dream of Chivalry*,[25] Pingyuan Chen argues that the rivers and lakes are the virtual world of men of letters, a place not reached by the power of state apparatus, wherein men of chivalry become heroes who uphold justice, punishing evildoers and rewarding the virtuous. This kind of antiauthoritarian individualist hero is the main type of protagonist found in modern-day films, thus the successful modernizing of the chivalric novels in the kung fu film genre. 1982's *The Shaolin Temple* demonstrates the beauty and power of an individual through the violent spectacle of kung fu, which was still rare in mainland China at that time, though it later achieved tremendous success. *Shaolin* (2011) continues to employ these elements and adopts a more dramatic plotline in sensational settings to conform to popular cinematic conventions. However, it is doubtful whether the U-shaped plot really is suitable to communicate the Shaolin spirit, despite Benny Chan dedicating great efforts toward creating this impression.

Hou Jie (the name means *hero*) speaks of "Shaolin spirit" twice in the movie without clearly defining what this means. He says, "Shaolin spirit made me strong and brave," and uses the ambiguous term "Shaolin spirit" to encourage refugees. In addition, there is also the key defining scene of the film, its conclusion, when the hero's body falls into the palm of the enormous Buddha statue, lit by a chiaroscuro beam of light shining from the head of the Buddha. These signs suggest that, in his death, Hou Jie has reached the highest state of Buddhism, nirvana, for they hint that he has been accepted by Buddha and fulfilled the process of spiritual enlightenment. However, these scenes, which try to propagandize the "Shaolin spirit" directly, are the parts that Chinese viewers felt were most unconvincing. *Juewu* (觉悟, enlightenment) is a deep spiritual experience, but Hou Jie's spiritual journey is clichéd, vague, and unconvincing, no matter how thrilling the ride.

The appeal of the U-shaped protagonist is its depiction of a roller coaster–style dramatic plot, exaggerating the turbulence of life and heroizing the protagonist. In a sense, these are not suitable for the Buddhist or Chan worldview because sensationalism and hyperbole distract viewers' attention from the Buddhist worldview of *śūnyatā* (emptiness; the complete absence of desire) and *anattā* (nonexistence of self). The goal of Chan practitioners is to perceive transcendent truths and accept that the world is an illusion. A famous line from the Buddhist classic *The Diamond Sutra* elucidates this doctrine:

> As a lamp, a cataract, a star in space
> an illusion, a dewdrop, a bubble
> a dream, a cloud, a flash of lightning
> view all created things like this.[26]

Nothing is absolute and everything is transient, as life itself is governed by karma and destiny, and, therefore, one should maintain a peaceful state of mind. Throughout history, Buddhism, in its many forms, has developed corresponding kinds of aesthetics characterized by emptiness and quietness, with meaning expressed through various types of negative space and the imagery of ephemerality.[27] These Chan Buddhist aesthetic principles, more often associated with its Japanese counterpart, Zen, are not in harmony with the commercial movie logic of displaying graphic violence and dramatizing suffering.

From ancient times, there have been a variety of successful examples of the integration of Buddhism with literature and visual arts. However, the Chan Buddhist worldview of "nothingness and solitude" requires a corresponding aesthetic in its representation. As a U-shaped protagonist, Hou Jie is far too stubborn, even at the last moment when he enables the enlightenment of Cao Man (the name hints at usurpation and savagery) by giving his life. Hou Jie thinks that he is responsible for Cao's evil, so he sacrifices his life to enlighten Cao. Typically, in kung fu movies, the higher spiritual realm is arrived at only on the basis of defeating opponents by force. By contrast, *Shaolin* features a bizarre plot twist at the end, when, upon failing to persuade with words and after defeating Cao Man with kung fu, Hou Jie goes one salvific step further and sacrifices his life for Cao. At one moment, Hou Jie is an individualist hero, but at another, he is an eminent monk who redeems others with his own life. Sacrificing oneself for the sake of other people is regarded as a Buddhist trait, but the precondition for a monk's concern for others is nonattachment to the world. Without this precondition, the monk who cares for the world is not deemed pure and clean in his six roots of sensation,[28] which means he is not free from human desires and passions. Buddhism interprets the human world with laws of karma that are not controlled by humans. In the majority of Buddhist traditions, it takes many lifetimes to reach the highest state; however, it only takes Hou Jie several months in this movie. This could be chalked up to the Chan/Zen belief in "sudden enlightenment," but even this, generally, is thought to be accompanied by subsequent gradual cultivation. Typical Chinese moviegoers might not give much thought to these misrepresentations, but, being born in a historically Buddhist culture, they naturally feel the disconnection between Buddhism and the bravado they see on screen and, thus, are likely to reject the "Shaolin spirit" proposed by the film.

Authentic faith can be communicated effectively on screen, but achieving this requires a director who understands the meaning of, and has respect for, religious devotion, as well as viewers who are accustomed to this type of expression of faith. The director tried to add "Shaolin spirit" to spectacular violence in order to depict the conversion of an evil person, but the script displays little concern for modeling genuine Buddhist beliefs.

Conclusion: Specters of Shaolin Identity
Past, Present, and Future

What our approach to *Shaolin* (2011) reveals is that Chan Buddhism and cinematic genre conventions are utilized together in this film to relay nationalistic messaging. Though Chinese audiences may have perceived the film's portrayal of Chan Buddhism as superficial and inauthentic, despite the director's efforts to avoid this, *Shaolin* does vividly promote the narrative that Western foreigners and greedy Chinese warlords (symbols of the feudal, imperial system) betrayed the common folk of China. In a strange twist of cinematic fate, the Shaolin monks in this film perform Red Cross–style humanitarian work and even steal from the rich to give to the poor, behavior that lines up with communist aims (if not realities) of equal provision for all. Allegorically, then, "Shaolin spirit" in this film could be said to align with Communist Party doctrine, but herein lies the rub. The film's revisions of history and religion expose key problems with this comparison. *Shaolin's* depiction of the Western army's plunder during this period misrepresents the historical truth that it was the warlord Feng Yuxiang who burned down Shaolin Temple in 1928. The shift implies that the internal conflicts in this part of China partially originated from the covetousness of Western colonial powers. This historical emendation sidesteps Chinese responsibility and, thus, contradicts the Buddhist understanding of the origin of evil. In Buddhism, evil is believed to come from the "three unwholesome roots" in human beings—greed, hatred, and delusion—instead of external causes, and a Buddhist is to work on self-transformation to eliminate these. Attributing the worst type of avarice and destruction to foreigners and their influence seems an abdication of responsibility. Moreover, the appearance of white faces in the movie is abrupt and lacks specific motivation other than to shift blame. This dubious plotline, achieved by tampering with history, reflects late-twentieth-century and early-twenty-first-century CCP attitudes toward Western culture and is antithetical to the Chan Buddhist spiritual dimension the film attempts to capture.

Furthermore, Buddhism essentially does not endorse nationalism. In a debate over the relationship between Buddhism and the state during the Dong Jing Dynasty, Huiyuan (334–416 CE)[29] wrote an influential treatise *On Why Monks Do Not Bow Down Before Kings* (沙门不敬王者论, written in 404 CE). In the writing, he refutes the emperor's assumptions regarding "the supreme and all including authority and venerability of the Ruler, who as the mediator between Man and Heaven embodies the course of Nature . . . which all individuals have to obey."[30] Instead, Huiyuan indicates that monks are uniquely capable of illuminating the path (Way) to awakening and, thus, "open up the Way of Heaven and man." Hence, if a monk "fulfills his virtue, then the Way spreads to the six relations, and beneficence flows out to the whole world."[31] Therefore, Buddhist clergy have a spiritual, cosmic purpose and role that surpasses that of any emperor.

Huiyuan's treatise emphasizes the independent stance of Buddhism toward the state, and it succeeded in convincing his contemporary emperor of that principle. It is a shared sense of the Chinese people that Buddhists should remain relatively detached from the secular world as theirs is a transcendent goal, promoting nonattachment to all worldly desires; this has become an inextricable part of Buddhists' identity in China.

In addition, the film *Shaolin* deals specifically with Chan Buddhism, which, as noted above, is famous for the doctrine of "sudden enlightenment." Huineng (638–713), the Sixth Patriarch of Chan, taught this doctrine frequently in the *Platform Sutra*. For example, Huineng explains, "[W]hen I was with His Reverence Hongren, I became enlightened as soon as I heard him speak. I suddenly saw the fundamental nature of suchness. Therefore, I am disseminating this teaching so that you who study the Way may become suddenly enlightened and [achieve] bodhi," able to perceive the fundamentally illusory nature of all things.[32] However, even in Pure Land Buddhist traditions there are examples of sudden salvation. There is a proverb in China, "A butcher becomes a Buddha the moment he drops his cleaver,"[33] which originated from a story in the *Nirvana Sutra* that records a dramatic conversion of a butcher.[34] According to the legend, a monk master revealed the image of the Western Pure Land to the butcher Guang E (广额), for he saw the latter's "yuan (缘, which means fateful coincidence)" and guided him with the image. Consequently, Guang E voluntarily climbed a tree and fell from it to die in pursuit of the vision, thus, presumably, transmigrating immediately into the Buddha's celestial paradise. Perhaps with this proverb in mind, the director and writer of *Shaolin* attempted to combine Hou's version of "dropping the cleaver" with the U-shaped plot, that staple of cinematic narrative. However, as pointed out above, the dramatic plotline of extremes that defines the U-shaped journey of the protagonist does not reflect the narrative or aesthetic equivalent of Chan's core doctrines of emptiness and no-self, which are usually aligned with stillness, quiet, and greater attention to the natural world (a connection with Taoism): a move away from anthropocentrism rather than an emphasis on one individual's journey. Significantly, this U-shaped tale and the kung fu genre also undermine the communist ideal of cinematic socialist realism, as seen in many twentieth-century Soviet films and Chinese films during Mao's chairmanship, in which the protagonist is plural rather than singular and the group protagonist is represented as the "revolutionary" common people of the contemporary struggle. While there is a brave cadre of Shaolin monks in the film, the true hero of *Shaolin* is Hou.

In this film, Hou Jie ironically "becomes a Buddha" without "dropping his cleaver." He commits himself to the mission of enlightening his former righthand henchman Cao Man by oral persuasion, violence, and sacrificing his life, without considering Cao's karma and *yuan*. Hou's stubborn and fatal efforts demonstrate that he has not let go of worldly attachments, as he is determined to "save" Cao Man due to Hou's self-defined "responsibility" for Cao's evil behaviors. In addition, Hou's excessive sense of responsibility is a cliché of contemporary depictions of official Chinese heroes, which reflect neither Buddhism nor real life. In short, to extol the heroic and violent acts of any person violates fundamental principles of Mahāyāna Buddhism, which believes in the emptiness of all phenomena and refraining from harming all creatures. As a result, the magnificent image of the "martyr" Hou Jie lying in the hands of the grand Buddha statue, illuminated with a beam of light from heaven, provides a bankrupt metaphor that fails to move most Chinese viewers; although Western viewers, familiar with Westernized, more individualistic forms of Zen (Chan) Buddhism, might feel very differently. Though not all Chinese people are familiar with specific Buddhist teachings, they do live in a society with a strong Buddhist heritage and thus have inherent expectations of texts purporting to tell "Buddhist" stories that display the religion's values, such as *Shaolin*.

Though this film trades on a vague concept of the moral righteousness of "Shaolin identity," Shaolin today is more of a commercial brand than a spiritual path. There are hundreds of documentaries, both professional and amateur, about the place, its history, its kung fu styles, and its legends. Martial arts schools all over the world claim to teach "Shaolin kung fu," though the extreme rigor involved in this martial art practice and its inextricable connection to Chan make it highly doubtful that there is authenticity in these endeavors. Even the actual Shaolin Temple's religious significance is in question as it has become a pilgrimage site primarily for kung fu enthusiasts. Indeed, the temple's unique ability to exploit business opportunities for profit has caused its monks to be marginalized by the Buddhist community.[35] This is at least partly due to the Chinese Mainland's policies regarding religion, which, though greatly relaxed compared to before China's reform and opening up, still allow little space in public discourse for religion. Thus, while Shaolin monks can put on martial arts performances in public settings, this same group of people is not allowed to attempt to promote Buddhist doctrine in the same exact setting, though this is actually the monks' mandate. Faced with this difficult situation, Shaolin Temple's "commercialization" of its kung fu could be seen as an expedient measure (*upāya*) undertaken to spread the Buddhist faith. However, the reality is that the CCP is using Buddhist "products," in myriad forms, including this kung fu film, as its expedient means to inculcate forgiveness, compassion, and mercy, which conduce to a compliant populace—in other words, societal harmony. Harmony is a core, ancient East Asian ideal that is a noble goal, in itself, but governments the world over have used draconian and brutal measures against their people in the name of achieving harmony. Using Shaolin narratives, such as this film, for "harmony" propaganda is in keeping with its history: as dynasties replaced dynasties throughout Chinese history, Shaolin Temple was able to remain the Imperial Buddhist Monastery because of its willingness to cooperate with the Imperial Court. Currently, the People's Republic of China is promoting "traditional Chinese culture" both inside and outside its borders. However, the government's attitude toward "traditional culture" has always been instrumentalist, mainly to be used to promote or enforce immediate stability and unity in society: harmony. Whether or not this kind of "traditional culture" can be successfully integrated into the complexity of contemporary Chinese society or function in a spiritually redemptive fashion is not the focus of the government. The promotion of traditional culture by the government is pragmatic and, as shown, purposely steers away from traditions which are inextricable from religious beliefs.

Benny Chan's *Shaolin* is one of numerous kung fu movies that feature Buddhist monks and concepts, and it certainly is one of the most intriguing and beautifully made.[36] If it is not as entrancing as Hong Kong director King Hu's *wuxia* masterpiece, *A Touch of Zen* (1971), it does share with that film a true attempt to visualize Buddhist spiritual awakening in the midst of physical battles. Kung fu movies always have featured individualistic narratives, which conflicts with Buddhist principles, as has been demonstrated. The imaginary world of "rivers and lakes" featured in martial arts narratives implies a social system that remains outside of the official, government-centered milieu. Hence, it is unsurprising that kung fu movies first flourished in the more open atmosphere of Hong Kong, separated from the CCP's authority, as it was a British Crown Colony until 1997. Nevertheless, as Hong Kong is now united with the mainland and its special status is being challenged by increasingly controlling orders from Beijing,[37] cinematic storytelling in Hong Kong is in a period of transition; the narrational strategy of kung fu movies undoubtedly will shift. The confidence shown in the individual hero and his quest for justice may be destined to fade. Up to this point, Shaolin movies have been confined to the general framework of kung fu films, and the CCP has even been able to co-opt

Chan Buddhism for its own purposes in a few films, including *Shaolin*. However, those seeking to produce films in the kung fu genre and Shaolin subgenre, both in Hong Kong and on the mainland, such as Benny Chan, have to negotiate with and struggle for a new type of story and identity in the narrow space left for them. Shaolin Temple stands as an outstanding example of the assimilation and nationalization of Buddhism in Chinese culture. At the same time, while the ideology promoted by Buddhism is not necessarily in direct conflict with secular political powers, there is no way for it to be incorporated into the antireligious CCP worldview, which requires that its own preeminent precepts govern the lives and beliefs of Chinese citizens. Shaolin Temple's current extensive commercialization is its biggest opportunity but also its most serious crisis. Its future and destiny, as well as the restoration of its Buddhist "identity," will be closely bound with the continuing evolution of China's national policies on religion.

Notes

1. Deqian (德虔), *Biographies of Shaolin Martial Monks* 少林武僧志 (Beijing: Publishing House of Beijing Sport College, 1988).

2. "Interview with the Director of *Shaolin*, Chen Mucheng, the Film Uses the Past as a Metaphor for the Present," Sina, accessed June 15, 2020. http://dailynews.sina.com/bg/ent/film/sinacn/file/20110104/19492133950.html.

3. Clarence Tsui, "New Take." Rev. of *Shaolin* (2011), dir. Benny Chan, *South China Morning Post*, Jan. 23, 2011: 9, *Lexis-Nexis*, accessed Nov. 15, 2013. https://advance-lexis-com.libproxy.calbaptist.edu/api/document?collection=news&id=urn:contentItem:5213-8KJ1-JC8V-1183-00000-00&context=1516831. The Han Chinese were an ethnic group in ancient, central China who came to imperial power in 206 BCE and ruled until 220 CE. Han Dynasty rulers united and spread their culture throughout most of what is now known as the People's Republic of China. Approximately 92 percent of modern Chinese are ethnically Han. The Qing Dynasty (1644–1912) was established by Manchurian invaders from China's northeast region, and they were known to suppress the rights of Han Chinese during their reign, which was the final imperial regime in China.

4. Tsui, "New Take." Chiang Kai-shek (1888–1975) was the military leader and head of the Kuomintang (KMT), the Chinese Nationalist Party founded by Sun Yat-sen in 1911. The staunchly anticommunist Chiang led the KMT forces, representing the Republic of China, against those of the revolutionary Chinese Communist Party (CCP) in a civil war stretching intermittently from 1927 to 1949. Though the two armies took a break from their civil war to fight the invading Japanese (1931–1945), the Chinese civil war raged on from 1945 to 1949, when Chiang

and his forces were defeated by CCP Chairman Mao Zedong and his troops, and the KMT moved its leadership and adherents to Taiwan. The People's Republic of China has been governed by the Chinese Communist Party ever since.

5. Stephen Teo, *Chinese Martial Arts Cinema: The Wuxia Tradition* (Edinburgh: Edinburgh University Press, 2009), 40.

6. Stephen Teo, *Chinese Martial Arts Cinema*, 40.

7. Tsui, "New Take."

8. Daniel H. Bays, *A New History of Christianity in China* (Malden, MA: Wiley-Blackwell, 2012), 10.

9. Bays, *A New History of Christianity in China*, 10.

10. Daniel H. Bays, "A Tradition of State Dominance," in *God and Caesar in China: Policy Implications of Church-State Tensions*, ed. Jason Kindopp and Carol Lee Hamrin (Washington, DC: Brookings Institution Press, 2004), 26.

11. Tsui, "New Take."

12. Tsui, "New Take."

13. Bays, "A Tradition of State Dominance," 27.

14. Jason Kindopp, "Policy Dilemmas in China's Church-State Relations: An Introduction," in *God and Caesar in China: Policy Implications of Church-State Tensions*, ed. Jason Kindopp and Carol Lee Hamrin (Washington, DC: Brookings Institution Press, 2004), 2.

15. Boon Chan, "Andy the Director: Veteran Hong Kong Actor Andy Lau Is Not Shy When It Comes to Telling Movie Directors How to Film His Scenes," *The Straits Times* (Singapore) Jan. 22, 2011, *Lexis-Nexis*, accessed October 10, 2012, https://advance-lexis-com.libproxy.calbaptist.edu/api/document?collection=news&id=urn:contentItem:520P-5KS1-DYX3-Y4D8-00000-00&context=1516831.

16. Chan, "Andy the Director."

17. Mark Jenkins, "Finding Redemption (And New Moves) In 'Shaolin,'" NPR [National Public Radio], posted 8 Sept. 2011, accessed Sept. 4, 2012, http://www.npr.org/2011/09/08/140146859/finding-redemption-and-new-moves-in-shaolin.

18. See Bays, *New History*, 194, or Frank Dikötter, *Mao's Great Famine: The History of China's Most Devastating Catastrophe, 1958–1962* (New York: Walker, 2011).

19. Tsui, "New Take."

20. Peter Hershock, "Chan Buddhism," in *The Stanford Encyclopedia of Philosophy*, Spring 2019 Edition, ed. Edward N. Zalta (Stanford University Center for the Study of Language and Information, 2019), accessed June 26, 2020, https://plato.stanford.edu/archives/spr2019/entries/buddhism-chan/.

21. Maggie Lee, "The Bottom Line," Rev. of *Shaolin*, *The Hollywood Reporter*, July 13, 2011, accessed Nov. 15, 2013, https://www.hollywoodreporter.com/review/shaolin-film-review-210852.

22. Tsui, "New Take."

23. Owner of Zun Wo Building, *The Secret of Shaolin Boxing* (Beijing: Zhonghua Bookstore, 1983), 99.

24. While Buddhist doctrine rejects the use of violence, Buddhists have been involved in violence in various ways throughout history. For more on the complexities of violence and nonviolence in Buddhism, see Sarah Mattice's work in chapter 1 of this volume.

25. Refer Pingyuan Chen, *The Scholar's Thousand Year Dream of Chivalry* (Beijing: New World, 2002).

26. Red Pine, trans., *The Diamond Sutra and Perfect Wisdom* (Berkeley: Counterpoint, 2001), 27.

27. For example, see the poem by Wang Wei (699–761), a famous poet and painter in the Tang Dynasty and a lay Buddhist, "Birdsong Brook": "Idly I watch cassia flowers fall. / Still is the night, empty the hill in Spring. / Up comes the moon, startling the mountain birds. / Once in a while in the Spring brook they sing." Vikram Seth trans., *Three Chinese Poets: Translations of Poems by Wang Wei, Li Bai, and Du Fu* (New York: Harper Perennial, 1992), 4.

28. The six sense faculties are located in the eye, ear, nose, mouth, body, and mind.

29. Huiyuan: A master of Chan, who organized the Lotus Society and propagandized the Western Pure Land in China.

30. E. Zürcher, *Buddhist Conquest of China: The Spread and Adaptation of Buddhism in Early Medieval China*, trans. Stephen F. Teiser (Boston: Brill, 2007), 238. For the introduction of the debate, see 204–53.

31. Huiyuan, "A Monk Does not Bow Down before a King," in *Sources of Chinese Tradition*, vol. I, compiled by Theodor de Bary, Wing-tsit Chan, and Burton Watson (New York: Columbia University Press, 1960), 282. Three Vehicles means "postponing enlightenment in order to bring others closer to salvation, attaining enlightenment by personal exertions in an age which is not Buddha, and attaining enlightenment by hearing the Buddha's preaching," 282, n. 7.

32. Huineng, *The Platform Sutra of the Sixth Patriarch of Chan*, trans. John R. McRae (Moraga: BDK America, 2000), 32–33.

33. Pu Ji (普济), *Wu Deng Hui Yuan* (五灯会元) (Beijing: Zhong Hua, 1997), 1297.

34. Wuchen Tan (昙无谶) trans. *Nirvana Sutra* 涅槃经 (Beijing: Religious Culture, 2011), 311.

35. Currently in the Chinese Buddhist community, many people believe the touristy Shaolin Temple is no longer an appropriate place to practice Buddhism.

36. For an exhaustive look at the subgenre of Shaolin kung fu films up to the year 2000, see Leon Hunt, *Kung Fu Cult Masters: From Bruce Lee to Crouching Tiger* (London: Wallflower Press, 2003), especially chapter 2, "Burning Paradise: The Myth of the Shaolin Temple," 48–75.

37. The massive protests and violent clashes with the police in Hong Kong that have erupted over the past few years have become global news. Hong Kong itself is in a period of conflict and transformation.

Bibliography

Bays, Daniel H. *A New History of Christianity in China.* Malden, MA: Wiley-Blackwell, 2012.

———. "A Tradition of State Dominance." In *God and Caesar in China: Policy Implications of Church-State Tensions,* edited by Jason Kindopp and Carol Lee Hamrin, 25–39. Washington, DC: Brookings Institution Press, 2004.

Chan, Boon. "Andy the Director: Veteran Hong Kong Actor Andy Lau Is not Shy When It Comes to Telling Movie Directors How to Film His Scenes." *The Straits Times* (Singapore), 22 Jan. 2011. *Lexis-Nexis.* https://advance-lexis-com. libproxy.calbaptist.edu/api/document?collection=news&id=urn:contentItem:520 P-5KS1-DYX3-Y4D8-00000-00&context=1516831. Accessed Oct. 10, 2012.

Chen, Pingyuan. *The Scholar's Thousand Year Dream of Chivalry.* Beijing: New World, 2002.

Dikötter, Frank. *Mao's Great Famine: The History of China's Most Devastating Catastrophe, 1958–1962.* New York: Walker, 2011.

Hershock, Peter. "Chan Buddhism." *The Stanford Encyclopedia of Philosophy,* Spring 2019 Ed. Edited by Edward N. Zalta. Stanford University Center for the Study of Language and Information, 2019. https://plato.stanford.edu/archives/ spr2019/entries/buddhism-chan/. Accessed 26 June 2020.

Huineng, *The Platform Sutra of the Sixth Patriarch of Chan.* Translated by John R. McRae. Moraga: BDK America, 2000.

Huiyuan, "A Monk Does Not Bow Down before a King." In *Sources of Chinese Tradition,* Col. I, compiled by Theodore Bary, Wing-tsit Chan, and Burton Watson. New York: Columbia University Press, 1960.

Hunt, Leon. *Kung Fu Cult Masters: From Bruce Lee to Crouching Tiger.* London: Wallflower Press, 2003.

"Interview with the Director of *Shaolin,* Chen Mucheng, the Film Uses the Past as a Metaphor for the Present," *Sina,* http://dailynews.sina.com/bg/ent/film/ sinacn/file/20110104/19492133950.html. Accessed on 15 June 2020.

Jenkins, Mark. "Finding Redemption (And New Moves) In 'Shaolin'." *NPR* [National Public Radio], posted Sept. 8, 2011, accessed Sept. 12, 2012, http://www.npr. org/2011/09/08/140146859/finding-redemption-and-new-moves-in-shaolin.

Kindopp, Jason. "Policy Dilemmas in China's Church-State Relations: An Introduction." In *God and Caesar in China: Policy Implications of Church-State Tensions,* edited by Jason Kindopp and Carol Lee Hamrin, 1–22. Washington, DC: Brookings Institution Press, 2004.

Lee, Maggie. "The Bottom Line." Rev. of *Shaolin. The Hollywood Reporter,* posted July 13, 2011, accessed Nov., 15, 2013, https://www.hollywoodreporter.com/ review/shaolin-film-review-210852.

Owner of Zun Wo Building. *The Secret of Shaolin Boxing.* Beijing: Zhonghua Bookstore, 1983.

Pu Ji (普济), *Wu Deng Hui Yuan* (五灯会元). Beijing: ZhongHua, 1997.

Red Pine, trans. *The Diamond Sutra and Perfect Wisdom*. Berkeley: Counterpoint, 2001.

Seth, Vikram, trans. *Three Chinese Poets: Translations of Poems by Wang Wei, Li Bai, and Du Fu*. New York: Harper Perennial, 1992.

Teo, Stephen. *Chinese Martial Arts Cinema: The Wuxia Tradition*. Edinburgh: Edinburgh University Press, 2009.

Tsui, Clarence. "New Take." Review of *Shaolin* (2011), dir. Benny Chan. *South China Morning Post*, 23 Jan. 2011: 9. *Lexis-Nexis*, accessed Nov. 15, 2020, https://advance-lexis.com.libproxy.calbaptist.edu/api/document?collection=news&id=urn:contentItem:5213-8KJ1-JC8V-1183-00000-00&context=1516831.

Wuchen Tan (呈无谶), trans. *Nirvana Sutra* 涅槃经. Beijing: Religious Culture, 2011.

Zürcher, E. *Buddhist Conquest of China: The Spread and Adaptation of Buddhism in Early Medieval China*. Translated by Stephen F. Teiser. Boston: Brill, 2007.

Chapter 11

A Century of Critical Buddhism in Japan

JAMES MARK SHIELDS

The question of Buddhist involvement—or collaboration, to use a more loaded term—in modern Japanese nationalism and militarism was reopened in the late twentieth century by a number of books, including the compilation *Rude Awakenings: Zen, the Kyoto School, and the Question of Nationalism* (1994) and Brian Victoria's *Zen at War* (1997).[1] In *Zen at War*, Victoria argues that Buddhism—especially Zen—was at least partly responsible for prewar and wartime Japanese militarism. To the surprise of those who see Buddhism as avowedly pacifist in nature, the attempt to justify and support the Japanese war effort in Buddhist terms was in fact a disturbingly common occurrence, and not simply the work of a few zealots and hard-liners. A fair number of Zen masters, as well as most prominent intellectuals of the 1930s and 1940s were, at one time or another, quite ready to express their support of the so-called Great East Asia Co-Prosperity Sphere (Jpn. Dai Tōa Kyōei Ken 大東亜共栄圏) in terms that were often explicitly religious.[2] Yet for all the historical cases and incidents cited by Victoria, his work is limited, as he is quick to admit, by the fact that he is a historian, not an ethicist, philosopher, or religious critic. Thus, while the tone of the book expresses an undisguised evaluation of Buddhist betrayal, Victoria is reticent to pursue just *why* it happened in the first place. *Why* was Buddhism so easily manipulated—if that is the best way to phrase it—to suit militarism? And more generally, what is the relation, if any, between Buddhist doctrine, violence, warfare, and social ethics?

D. T. Suzuki (Suzuki Daisetsu, 1870–1966), whose writings from the 1930s through the 1960s were to have immense influence in shaping

Western attitudes toward Buddhism, seems to have answered this question decades ago, when he wrote that "Zen has sustained [the military classes] in two ways, morally and philosophically. Morally, because Zen is a religion which teaches us not to look backward once the course is decided upon; philosophically, because it treats life and death indifferently. . . . The military mind, being . . . comparatively simple and not at all addicted to philosophizing, finds a congenial spirit in Zen."[3] But is this a proper representation of Zen? Is this really the end-result of such a prominent strand of Buddhist tradition—that it is indifferent to pain, suffering, warfare, and genocide?

In the late 1980s, two Japanese Buddhist scholars—Hakamaya Noriaki and Matsumoto Shirō[4]—began to make their voices heard against this particular understanding of Buddhism and Buddhist ethics. Calling their movement Critical Buddhism (Jpn. *hihan bukkyō* 批判仏教), they proceeded to attack—in a forthright and highly polemical manner virtually unheard of in modern Japanese scholarship—prominent Japanese philosophical figures such as Suzuki, Nishida Kitarō (1870–1945), and Nishitani Keiji (1900–1990) of the Kyoto School, specific Buddhist doctrines such as "Buddha-nature" (Jpn. *busshō* 仏性) and "original enlightenment" (Jpn. *hongaku* 本覚), and even entire sects of Buddhism, including the one to which they themselves belonged—Sōtō Zen.[5]

In this chapter, after a brief examination of the central arguments of Matsumoto and Hakamaya, I provide a genealogy for Critical Buddhism by looking at two progressive Buddhist movements in early-twentieth-century Japan: the New Buddhist Fellowship (1899–1916) and the Youth League for Revitalizing Buddhism (1931–36). I argue that these three waves of Critical Buddhism focus on distinct aspects of the "failings" of Buddhism in the context of modernity. Though disparate in tone, emphasis, and effects, taken together these three movements can be instructive in thinking through the problems and possibilities of Buddhist ethics and politics in the contemporary global context.

The Case against Zen

As if in agreement with Suzuki, in an essay entitled "The Meaning of Zen," Matsumoto writes: "The essence of Zen thought is the denial of conceptual thinking, or, perhaps better, the cessation of conceptual thinking." He goes on to add, however: "It is clear that any 'Zen thought' that teaches the 'cessation of thinking' is anti-Buddhist."[6] Thus, while Matsumoto does not deny the accuracy of Suzuki's portrayal of Zen, he argues that Zen, as it has developed (or "degenerated") over eight centuries in Japan, has become profoundly "anti-Buddhist." As such, the so-called Imperial Way Zen (Jpn. *kōdō zen* 皇道禅) that flourished in the first half of the twentieth century and supported Japanese militarism was less an *aberration* than the inevitable *culmination* of Zen ethics—or, we might, say, lack of such.

Here, Hakamaya and Matsumoto, having been trained in the Zen tradition, may be faulted for assuming, like Suzuki, that Zen somehow "completes" Buddhism. Although they seek to undercut the Chan/Zen line at its roots, there remains in their work an assumption that, at its best— i.e., as expressed in the writings of thirteenth-century Sōtō master Dōgen (1200–1253)—"Zen is the integrating storehouse of Buddha-dharma."[7] And yet, while Zen clearly faces the brunt of Critical Buddhist attacks, it is not simply Zen that is being called into question, but Buddhism as it has been practiced (in India, South and West Asia, China, and Japan) for several thousand years. Perhaps the best way to understand this is to say that for Critical Buddhists, Zen represents an extreme of a tendency or set of characteristics that has existed in many forms of Buddhism from the classical Indian period up until today. In other words, they argue that Chan/Zen manifests both the best and worst possibilities of Buddhism—it is a storehouse, we might say, for Buddhist extremes.

According to Paul Swanson the Critical Buddhist analysis of Zen works on three distinct levels, as follows: (1) a *Buddhological* critique, which looks into the historical use—and abuse—of specific Buddhist doctrines such as Buddha-nature and *pratitya-samutpāda* or dependent origination; (2) a *sectarian* critique, which argues that modern and contemporary Sōtō Zen has misunderstood the teachings of the sect founder and philosopher Dōgen (1200–1253)—particularly with respect, once again, to the teaching of Buddha-nature; (3) a *social critique*, where an argument is made to the effect that both of the above have led to objectionable social structures and attitudes among Zen Buddhists—culminating in wartime apathy or collab- oration with Japanese nationalism and imperialism, as best exemplified in statements like Suzuki's.[8]

What is this "true" Buddhism against which modern Zen fails to measure up? What criteria for "truth" do the Critical Buddhists employ to make their normative claims? Hakamaya provides the most straightforward answer in his declaration that "Buddhism is criticism . . . [and] only that which is critical is Buddhism,"[9] which of course begs the question: What is *criticism*? For Hakamaya, criticism implies the ability to make distinctions, to be, in a literal sense, "discriminating," which in turn entails a reliance on reason, analysis, and clear language. He argues, in a fashion familiar to the rhetoric (if not always the reality) of the European Enlightenment and modern liberalism, that it is *only* critical thinking in this sense that can combat socioethical or political discrimination. Another way to put this is that the central problem with Zen (and other forms of Buddhism) is the tendency toward a metaphysics and soteriology that prizes "holism" and "harmony" and thereby neglects the pragmatic, ethical—and even political—spirit that, according to the Critical Buddhists, is the core of Buddhism.

In extrapolating this thesis, Hakamaya employs an opposition with a three-hundred-year legacy in Western thought, between what he calls the *criticalism* of Enlightenment thinker René Descartes (1596–1650) and the *topicalism* of Neapolitan jurist and philosopher Giambattista Vico (1668–1744). As odd as it may sound, especially to Western philosophers who have battled the ghost of Descartes for more than a century, this paradigm French rationalist serves as the standard bearer for the Critical Buddhist Reformation.[10] Vico, often called the father of historicism and a forefather of Romanticism, pointed out the ways in which Cartesian rationalism, and the critical method in particular, debilitated human thinking by obscuring the significance of the imagination and nonrational modes of experience.[11] Vico posited an alternative to the Cartesian method rooted in the Latin term *topica* (place, field, locus; from Greek *topos*), connoting a sense of intuition and holism. For Critical Buddhists, however, this approach to meaning and truth—whether in philosophical or religious guise—amounts to "an aesthetic mysticism unconcerned with critical differentiation between truth and falsity and not in need of rational demonstration."[12] Moreover, while they do not claim that Vico's work had any direct effect, the Italian jurist's turn away from Cartesian criticism gives expression to a mode that, Hakamaya and Matsumoto assert, has also come to infect the Mahāyāna Buddhist tradition as a whole and its Japanese offshoots (such as Zen) in particular.[13]

Elsewhere, Hakamaya suggests that in addition to a commitment to clear language and (discriminating, critical) reason, true Buddhism is rooted in an understanding and acceptance of the law of causation or dependent origination (San. *pratītya-samutpāda*), which, at least according to some Mahāyāna thinkers, entails an understanding of the "emptiness" (San. *śūnyāta*) of all phenomena.[14] Adherence to the doctrine of dependent origination counters the latterly derived—and, in their eyes, woefully misguided—doctrines of "Buddha nature" and "original enlightenment." According to the Critical Buddhists, a deep and unrelenting commitment to dependent origination pushes the practitioner away from the "selfish" enlightenment experience and toward the Other, as a manifestation of *mahākaruna* or Great Compassion lauded by classical Mahāyāna texts but lost in the topicalist turn taken by later derivatives such as Chan/Zen.

As such, the Critical Buddhists were not simply importing Western rationalism as the new way of understanding Buddhism or being Buddhist. Rather, they claim that their assault on topicalism is one that would have the support of the Buddha himself.[15] Indeed, they go so far as to suggest that Buddhism began as a revolt against topicalism in Indian thinking, and has ever since had to perform rearguard action against topical encroachments both within and outside the tradition, with varied success. Certainly, there has been a long tradition of criticism within Chinese and Japanese Buddhism. Whenever a new sect arose in China and Japan, the practice of *kyōsō-hanjaku* 競争半弱—"the judgement and interpretation of the various facets of Buddhist teachings"—was applied. According to Masao Abe, this practice was highly beneficial to Buddhist development, as it allowed for the application of new evaluative standards to various sutras and interpretations of texts and traditions.[16]

To summarize, the Critical Buddhist argument rests on a distinction between what they call "topicalism"—an understanding and experience of religion that stresses harmony, totality, and nondiscrimination—and "criticalism" founded upon certain key Buddhist tenets such as dependent origination and "discriminating wisdom" (San. *dharma-pravicaya*), but also correlative to the practice of critical rationality exemplified by modern Western thinkers like René Descartes. While criticism—understood primarily in terms of discriminating knowledge—is the foundation of a truly Dharmic mode of being in the world, it is important to note that the goal of Critical Buddhism is very much in line with the traditional understanding of *awakening*: that is to say, "the realization of 'wisdom' (San. *bodhi*) for the practice of 'great compassion' (San. *mahakaruna*)."[17]

From Doctrine to Society

As we have seen, according to the Critical Buddhists, the Mahāyāna Buddhist tradition as a whole, and Zen Buddhism in particular, has, by and large, denied the possibility of talking about truth: "The denigration of language and rational thought implicit in much of the Buddhist tradition has led to an erasure of the critical discrimination of truth that is the heart of Buddhist realization and of social justice."[18] One important issue at stake in this last assertion is the precise relationship between these two things: "Buddhist realization" and "social justice." Are they coextensive? If they are not, what exactly is the relation between Buddhist "truth" and "ethics" and "justice?" Here we are led back, once again, to the case of *Zen at War*—as well as to even earlier attempts within Japanese Buddhism to confront the failures of Buddhist ideas and institutions in the face of social problems, particularly those associated with modernity.

After publishing a monograph on Critical Buddhism in 2011, I became interested in finding a pedigree, as it were, for Critical Buddhism.[19] According to Hakamaya and Matsumoto, their precedents were solitary heroes such as Dōgen, whose work manifested a kind of radical humanism that was quickly lost on his followers (and thus to the Sōtō Zen sect). I discovered, however, that Japan had much more recently experienced several waves of what might be called "critical" Buddhism, some of which were, in fact, more radical, at least politically, than anything proposed by the Critical Buddhists. This research became the basis of my 2017 publication *Against Harmony: Progressive and Radical Buddhism in Modern Japan.*[20] In the following sections, I discuss two movements, in particular, that provide a different analysis of and approach to Buddhist criticism, one that begins with ethics and society and ends with economics and politics.

The New Buddhist Fellowship

The New Buddhist Fellowship (Jpn. Shin Bukkyō Dōshikai 新仏教同志会) which lasted from 1899 to 1915, was an attempt by several dozen young Japanese lay Buddhists to reform or reinvent Buddhism as a trans-sectarian, noninstitutional, and, perhaps most interestingly, *secular* (in the sense of this-worldly and even "materialistic") set of ideas and practices relevant to the just-dawning twentieth century. In July 1900, a journal called *New Buddhism* (Jpn. *Shin Bukkyō* 新仏教) was launched as the new movement's mouthpiece. The first edition of the first volume begins with the group's "manifesto" (Jpn. *sengen* 宣言; lit. declaration). By turns inflammatory, sentimental, and self-consciously poetic, this short piece opens with an apocalyptic call to arms: "Humanity," it begins, "is in a state of decline. Society has been corrupted to its roots, and the rushing water of a great springtide threatens to drown us all, as at the time of the Great Flood. Moreover, religions, which are supposed to give light to darkness and provide solace, have been losing strength year by year." This is immediately followed by a blistering attack on "old Buddhism" (Jpn. *kyū bukkyō* 旧仏教) as being little more than a rotting corpse, its adherents weeping "tears of joy" over their palatial buildings and fine brocades:

> These people [i.e., "old Buddhists"] know how to worship wooden statues and sutras, how to stand before monks at a temple, and how to listen to the sermons. Earnestly holding to the embedded prejudices of their respective sect, they are mutually well versed in worthless matters. They can skillfully mouth the chants, and know how to take the prayer beads and sutras in their hands. Have they not already abandoned the life of faith? If these things make up what is called "Buddhism," then it is an "old Buddhism" that is on the verge of death.[21]

Here, as elsewhere, the New Buddhists borrow from the discourse of Buddhist decadence (Jpn. *daraku bukkyō* 堕落仏教) that first arose with Neo-Confucians of the Edo period (1603–1868) and was adopted by a number of secularists and Shinto nativists in the early years of the Meiji (1868–1912), before being internalized by late–nineteenth-century Buddhist modernists who sought, in different ways, to "cleanse" Japanese Buddhism of its historical accretions, superstitions, and corruptions.[22] That is to say, this line of argument was hardly new with the NBF. And yet, the New Buddhists occasionally pushed the envelope farther, beyond the rather straightforward ("Protestant") critique of Buddhist ritualism, monastic corruption, and materialist hypocrisy.

At the end of the manifesto we find the New Buddhist Fellowship's "Statement of General Principles" (Jpn. *kōryō* 綱領), summarized in the following six points:

1. We regard a sound Buddhist faith (Jpn. *kenzen naru shinkō* 健全なる信仰) as our fundamental principle.

2. We will endeavor to foster sound faith, knowledge, and moral principles in order to bring about fundamental improvements to society.

3. We advocate the free investigation of Buddhism in addition to other religions.

4. We resolve to destroy superstition.

5. We do not accept the necessity of preserving traditional religious institutions and rituals.

6. We believe the government should refrain from favoring religious groups or interfering in religious matters.[23]

As the final point above shows, and as noted above, unlike some other reformers of the day, the New Buddhists were not looking for government support of Buddhism—in fact, they were highly critical of *any* state involvement in religious matters.[24] This was largely based on their analysis of Buddhism during the late Edo (1603–1868) and early Meiji (1868–1912) periods, which, in their estimation, had become corrupted by state support.

As evidence of the changing interpretations given to Buddhist reform in the Meiji period, we might compare the above NBF list of principles with that of the Association of Buddhist Sects (Jpn. Shoshū Dōtoku Kaimei 諸宗同徳会盟; hereafter ABS), a pan-sectarian organization founded in a very different context more than three decades earlier, in the first year of the Meiji period (1868). In that year the ABS pledged to advocate for:

1. The indivisibility of Imperial and Buddhist Law.

2. The study and refutation of Christianity.

3. The cooperation between and perfection of the three Japanese faiths: Shinto, Confucianism, and Buddhism.

4. The study by each sect of its own doctrines and texts.

5. The expurgation of evil habits.

6. The establishment of a new type of school to produce men of ability.

7. The discovery of new ways to use exceptionally qualified priests.

8. The encouragement of popular education.[25]

The differences between these two lists could hardly be starker. Whereas the ABS looked to bring together the modern (imperial) state and Buddhist law, based on the traditional notion of "royal law [together with] Buddha dharma" (Jpn. *ōbō buppō* 王法仏法), the NBF sought to establish separate spheres; where the ABS looked to defeat Christianity, the NBF, while not particularly sympathetic to orthodox Christianity, was in open collaboration with Unitarian thinkers of the day, as well as some Christian socialists; while the ABS sought to unify and harmonize the "three Japanese faiths," the NBF was, if anything, hostile to "syncretism" with traditional religions, which were deemed superstitious and ritually obsessed; where the ABS advocated sectarian study, the NBF was explicitly non or trans-sectarian; where the ABS sought to find ways to "use" priests for the state, the NBF rejected the priestly and monastic traditions, at least as conventionally conceived and practiced. The only possible points of contact lie in the shared emphasis of the two groups on education for society and the expurgation of "evil habits"—though even here the "liberal" NBF would disagree with the ABS as to what, exactly constitutes both a productive education and good moral training. In the following section, I examine some of the doctrinal and philosophical roots for these discrepancies, beginning with the idea of *pantheism* (Jpn. *hanshinron* 汎神論).

According to co-founder Sakaino Kōyō (1871–1933), the NBF fully embraced the "new" aspect of New Buddhism, even as they rejected the charge that the movement is simply a form of Buddhist "liberalism."[26] While New Buddhism is based on a return to foundational Buddhist principles, he argues, such a return will inevitably involve a certain measure of "reform" (Jpn. *kairyō* 改良). As such, he suggests, New Buddhists see no problem in calling their movement "new"—as opposed to "true" or "real."[27] But what, Sakaino goes on to ask, is it that lies at the foundation of this "new" Buddhism? His answer, rather surprisingly, is "pantheism."[28] "We New Buddhists wish to establish Buddhism on the basis of a pantheistic world view. A pantheistic perspective shall be the foundation of Buddhism. Upon this foundation, the Buddhism of the future can be continuously improved and purified. This is what we are calling New Buddhism."[29] For Sakaino, pantheism provides a "this-worldly" and secure foundation for a holistic and inclusive perspective when it comes to the objects or focus of belief.[30] As he puts it: "Standing on a pantheistic foundation, we New Buddhists are a religious organization that seeks freedom of belief."[31] Indeed, we might conclude from these remarks that "pantheism" for Sakaino and the New Buddhists is less an ontological or metaphysical claim than it is a methodological and ethical stance: "We did not arrive at our pantheism by simply jumping on the fast lane to philosophical theory. We believe that pantheism harmonizes nicely with ethics, as well as the latest theories of moral philosophy."[32] And yet, it bears noting that even while aligning their pantheism with modern science and ethics, the New Buddhists were unwilling to fully accept the "pantheistic materialism" (Jpn. *yuibutsuteki hanshinron* 唯物的汎神論) suggested by well-known socialist and occasional *Shin Bukkyō* contributor, Sakai Toshihiko (1871–1933).[33] In response to Sakai's charge of their inconsistency and vagueness on this issue—that is, their refusal to extend their pantheism further toward a more rigorous philosophical materialism—the NBF writers counter that they are merely looking for appropriate ways, in line with twentieth-century scientific thinking, "to express the mysterious workings of matter and mind."[34] This desire to explain the mysterious connection of matter and spirit is one that was picked up later by New Buddhist Takashima Beihō (1875–1949).[35]

In addition to pantheism, "faith" (Jpn. *shinkō* 信仰)) was another matter of great concern for the New Buddhists.[36] Despite their acknowledgment of significant differences between Buddhism and the monotheisms of the West, the New Buddhists followed the scholarly consensus of the day in affirming that "faith" or "belief" must be the foundation of *any* religion. As we have seen, the very first and arguably most significant of their six General Principles states: "We regard a *sound Buddhist faith* as our foundational principle." Thus, it is no surprise to see a number of essays in the pages of *New Buddhism* (*Shin Bukkyō*) dedicated to this general theme. A good example is the third article in the inaugural issue of *Shin Bukkyō*, entitled "Time for a Change of Faith" (Jpn. "*Shinkō itten no ki*" 信仰一転の期), authored by Katō Genchi (1873–1965), who would go on to become professor of religion and Shintō studies at Tokyo Imperial University. Here, following on the heels of earlier Buddhist modernists, Katō begins by denouncing the "worldliness" and "degeneration" of the Buddhist monks and temples of his day, but then goes on to argue, against expectations, that "faith" is a product of religious and social evolution.[37] Thus, while the New Buddhists are adamant that "faith" must remain the foundation for New Buddhism, they are not necessarily calling for a return to the "stabilities" of traditional belief.

> While the root and foundation of religion is of certainty faith, the contents of this faith will depend on the particular period and circumstances. Thus, over time, religions have no choice but to gradually develop and evolve. Therefore it is clear that there will be differences between the faith that was necessary for the establishment of Buddhism as a religion during the ancient period of Śākyamuni, that of the period of Shinran and Nichiren, and that of our own (Meiji) times. . . . As such, when we see people

trying to bring back the old faith of Śākyamuni, Shinran, or Nichiren today in the Meiji period, all we can do is laugh at such a stupid and worthless idea.[38]

As Katō goes on to explain, while the contents of faith today cannot be fully specified, it is also not true that "anything goes." Any faith suitable to the modern period must pass the test of reason and "natural, experiential knowledge." Thus, "reliance on supernatural beings" is ruled out, as is anything that cannot be verified on the basis of information gleaned from our "ordinary, daily experience."[39] Moreover, Katō insists that faith must be directly applicable to "practice" or "projects" (Jpn. *katsudō* 活動 or *jigyō* 事業), thus moving toward the Marxist concept of *praxis*—or, at least away from what we might call a "Protestant" separation between faith and works.

Sakaino clarifies his thinking on the question of "sound faith" in a special issue dedicated to elaborating the founding principles of the NBF published in May 1901. Here Sakaino argues that faith is not *solely* rooted in emotion; if it were, he argues, there would be no way of distinguishing "blind faith" (Jpn. *mōshin* 盲信) from "correct faith" (Jpn. *shōshin* 正信). While faith must surely have a foundation in "refined emotions" (Jpn. *kōshō no kanjō* 交渉の感情), it must also be supported by "clear reason" (Jpn. *meiryō naru risei* 明瞭なる理性).[40] At this point, Sakaino goes on to make the following, rather extraordinary claim: "'To believe in Buddhism' does not mean to blindly obey what is written in Buddhist scriptures. The true essence of Buddhism must be pursued through free investigation. However, New Buddhism does not explain what the essence of Buddhism is. Because we value the free employment of reason, we are unwilling to restrict a person's faith."[41] Here "faith" seems to act as an umbrella term denoting a sincere and enthusiastic commitment to the rational, ethical, and social aspects of New Buddhism; that is, a combination of practical wisdom, personal moral cultivation, and social reform. On one level, especially when contrasted to its perceived lack within "old Buddhism," New Buddhist faith means "sincerity." Elsewhere, however, it becomes clear that for Sakaino and other New Buddhists, "faith" includes a commitment to fundamental Buddhist ethical principles regarding the elimination of suffering.[42] A closer examination of New Buddhist "sound faith" reveals that it comprises the following elements: (1) knowledge; (2) respect for emotions, including poetic feelings; (3) a focus on this world; that is, setting aside transcendence and concerns about the afterlife; (4) pro-active engagement; (5) ethics; and (6) a positive or optimistic outlook.[43] It is, in short, the name for a particular, Buddhist, *style* of living; a commitment to fully investing in the *practice* of living a flourishing life according to generic Buddhist principles.

Finally, as I have indicated, a characteristic feature of the work of the New Buddhists is an unabashed, at times almost Nietzschean, affirmation of "this world" (Jpn. *genseshugi* or *genseishugi* 現世主義). While the modernistic emphasis on free inquiry and a rational, ethical, and scientific outlook were also in evidence among the figures representing the earlier Japanese Buddhist Enlightenment, such as Nakanishi Ushirō (1859–1930), the New Buddhists—at least some of them—took things much farther in this direction, to the point where it could be legitimately asked what was left of "religion" (or "Buddhism") as normally understood. For instance, Nakanishi had contrasted the "materialism" of the "old" Buddhism with the "spiritualism" of the new, and, in similar fashion, the "scholarship" of traditional monastic Buddhism with the "faith" orientation of the new, lay Buddhism. In contrast, the New Buddhists to some extent reverse these positions, so that it is the "old" Buddhism that focuses on "spiritual" matters, while New Buddhism is content with addressing "real," "practical" issues of this life: poverty, hunger, and so on.[44]

Finally, although they began their movement as self-identified "puritans," some NBF members were hesitant to push this idea too far, lest it begin to sound overly severe or pessimistic. Here, again, their "puritanism" was of a different sort than the "passive" and "world-denying" asceticism (Jpn. *kin'yokushugi* 禁欲主義) of the monks and priests. Rather, it denoted a sincere, focused and "pro-active engagement" with the world (Jpn. *sekkyokuteki na katsudō* 積極的な活動), one that was also not averse to seeking "pleasure" (Jpn. *tanoshimi mo motomu* 楽しみも求む).[45] This creates a fascinating tension played out in the pages of *New Buddhism*, between, on the one hand, a renunciative impulse inherited not only from classical Buddhist monasticism but also from nineteenth-century liberal Protestantism and, on the other, an optimistic and this-worldly outlook emerging from Unitarianism, New Thought, Transcendentalism, Nietzsche, and nineteenth-century progressivism.

Despite the fact that they might not have resolved the various problems associated with collapsing conventional distinctions—e.g., between the "secular" and the "religious," and between religion, philosophy, ethics, politics, and society—I believe the New Buddhists should be given credit for putting these categories into question, especially given the tendency among Buddhists past and present to disassociate "awakening" from sociopolitical or "material" concerns. Although the NBF formally disbanded in 1916, their interest in promoting "social Buddhism" was picked up by others in the following decades, as we will see below.

The Youth League for Revitalizing Buddhism

On a rainy afternoon on the fifth day of April 1931, some fifteen years after the demise of the New Buddhist Fellowship, an extraordinary meeting was taking place in a small room on the third floor of the Young Men's Buddhist Association dormitory at Tokyo Imperial University. With some thirty lay Buddhists in attendance, most in their twenties and early thirties, along with four watchful uniformed police officers, Seno'o Girō (1889–1961) inaugurated the Youth League for Revitalizing Buddhism (Jpn. *Shinkō Bukkyō Seinen Dōmei* 新興仏教青年同盟), an experiment in Buddhist social activism that set itself up as a vanguard of socialist protest against poverty, injustice, colonialism and imperialism.

The following are a few highlights from the League's inaugural proclamation, read that afternoon:

> The modern era is one of suffering. Brothers who want to share fellowship are engaged in conflict beyond their control, while the general public is forced to beg for scraps of bread. Whether you run or you fight, the present age is one of chaos and distress. In such an age, what do Buddhists see, and what contributions are they making? Drunk with their own peace of mind, the majority of Buddhists do not see a problem. . . . They say: "Religion is above this; religion values harmony." And yet, the fact is that religion is playing the role of an opiate, imposed upon the people. Unless the righteous indignation of young Buddhists is aroused, nothing will be done about this. The present condition is not one that those of pure heart can endure. . . .
>
> As for us, we cannot help but firmly call for a revitalized Buddhism. . . . Recognizing that most of the current suffering has its origins in the capitalist economic system, a revitalized Buddhism pledges to collaborate with the people to make fundamental reforms in the interest of social welfare. It is a Buddhism for the people—whose aim is to revolutionize the bourgeois Buddhism of the present. . . . While adhering to

necessary logic, the Buddhism in which we believe reveres the
Buddha, who in his practice confirmed the principles of love,
equality, and freedom. . . .

Young Buddhists! Now is the time for us to rise up! Let's
throw all conventions aside at once and return to the Buddha.
And, beginning with our own personal experience of the Buddhist
spirit of love and equality, let's boldly turn to a restructuring of
the capitalist system. Let's make every effort to construct our
ideal Buddhist society![46]

With its relative openness, the Taishō period (1912–1925) had witnessed
a blossoming of Marxism and left-wing activism in Japan—in philosophical,
political, and literary forms. Within this broader wave, the movement most
closely connected to Buddhism was the *Muga-ai* 無我愛 or "Selfless Love"
society, founded by former Shin Buddhist priest Itō Shōshin (1876–1963).
Its mission was to promote and engage in compassionate action toward
the poor and oppressed. Another figure associated with this movement
was economist and writer Kawakami Hajime (1879–1946), author of the
socialist classic *Bimbō monogatari* 貧乏物語 (*Tales of Poverty*, 1916). Despite
these Taishō developments, by the early Shōwa period (1926–1989) tides
had begun to turn decisively against progressive politics, religious or otherwise. By the late 1920s, Buddhist "factory evangelists" began to parrot the
nationalist and imperialist mottos about strength, harmony and unity, while
denouncing "socialist agitators."[47]

It was in this context that Seno'o Girō established the Youth League for
Revitalizing Buddhism, based on the simple but disarming premise that the
capitalist system (and, by extension, the imperialist state) generates suffering
and, as a result, violates the spirit of Buddhism. As with the New Buddhists
of the late Meiji period, Seno'o and the Youth League were fighting a war on
two fronts: against conservative, co-opted Buddhist institutions and so-called
Imperial Way Buddhism, on the one hand, and against secular anti-Buddhist
and antireligious forces on the other. This would require a delicate balance
of apologetics and criticism. The League's Manifesto presents the following
three foundational principles:

1. We resolve to realize the implementation of a Buddha Land
   in this world, based on the highest character of humanity
   as revealed in the teachings of Sākyamuni Buddha and in
   accordance with the principle of brotherly love.

2. We accept that all existing sects, having profaned the Buddhist spirit, exist as mere corpses. We reject these forms, and pledge to enhance Buddhism in the spirit of the new age.

3. We acknowledge that the present capitalist economic system is in contradiction with the spirit of Buddhism and inhibits the social welfare of the general public. We resolve to reform this system in order to implement a more natural society.[48]

Seno'o's Youth League interpreted Buddhism as an atheistic, humanistic and ethical tradition. In this they followed a number of their Buddhist Enlightenment and New Buddhist forebears. Yet while the rejection of preceding and existent forms of Buddhism is also reminiscent of these earlier movements, the language regarding the problems of the capitalist system—and the more explicit emphasis on social justice and material well-being—is new. According to Seno'o, the League was established for three principle reasons, which are largely reflected in the three governing principles mentioned above: (1) to overhaul or replace the decadent Buddhist institutions of the day with a form of Buddhism more suited to the modern age; (2) to put an end to the ugly conflict between Buddhist sects; and (3) to engage in a reconstruction of the capitalist economic system—which, again, is in contradiction to the Buddhist spirit.

Throughout his various writings, Seno'o insists on a proper understanding of the causes and conditions of poverty. Since, he believed, these causes and conditions are both material *and* "spiritual" (or perhaps, emotional/psychic), then naturally the solution to poverty must also, against the secular Marxists, include aspects of the nonmaterial realm.[49] It is worth noting here Seno'o and the League's understanding of Buddhism as being *both* a "religion" (i.e., dealing with nonmaterial issues) *and* "atheistic" (i.e., not relying on belief in God or gods). In point of fact, Seno's atheism is not far removed from the NBF understanding of pantheism; both movements assert that a strict or reductive materialism misses much of importance, while simultaneously noting the "danger" of relying on faith in unseen forces.[50] Thus, both the NBF and Seno'o's Youth League were committed to a "secular" but also "humanistic" form of Buddhism.

Also like the New Buddhists before him, Seno'o strongly denounces the Buddhist establishment for utilizing Buddhist doctrines such as *karma* and the wheel of rebirth as explanations—and *ex post facto* justifications—for social inequalities.[51] Along similar lines, he criticizes the oft-employed Buddhist

expression of "differentiation is equality" (Jpn. *sabetsu soku byōdō* 差別即平
等) as a vague concept that cannot and should not be applied to the social
realm.[52] In addition, Seno'o rejected the metaphysics of harmony—what
Critical Buddhists would later call "topicalism"—as a construct that perpetu-
ates the status quo and thus the suffering entailed by social, economic, and
political structures. It is perhaps more accurate to say that Seno'o came to
see *harmony* and the overarching vision of totality presented in Mahāyāna
thought and works such as the *Lotus Sutra* as a goal to be reached through
historical transformation, including economic and political reforms, rather
than as a given state of things that must simply be recognized and accepted.
In similar fashion, suffering was for Seno'o an existential condition to be
analyzed and eliminated, rather than—as within some East Asian Buddhist
traditions—an illusory concept to be transcended via the dialectics of emptiness or a deeper, meditative realization of Buddha-nature.

In addition to its journal entitled *Under the Banner of Revitalized
Buddhism*, the Youth League held an annual national conference, "Revitalized
Buddhist Youth," where various positions were proclaimed and debated.
For example, at the third conference, held in 1933, the League asserted its
opposition to nationalism, militarism, warfare, and the annexation of Man-
churia; the fourth conference (1934) stated their commitment to building
a "cooperative society," promoting internationalism, and bringing about a
mutually productive unification of all Buddhist sects; while the fifth conference
(1935) announced the League's intent to restructure the capitalist system,
vigorously challenge "reactionary religious sects," and encourage each and
every individual to pursue a state of perfection.[53] Most if not all of these
positions were in conflict with the trends and the views of the political elite
of the times. In fact, they would seem to be framed in a way as to draw
attention to the movement.

In April 1935, at the invitation of Katō Kanjū (1892–1978) and
Takano Minoru (1901–1974), leaders of the National Council of Trade
Unions, Seno'o took up a position as editor of the *Journal of Manual Labor*
(Jpn. *Rōdō zasshi* 労働雑誌). In 1936, he participated in Katō's Convention
of Proletarian Workers—later known as the Proletarian Party of Japan (Jpn.
Nihon Musantō 日本無産等). He also stood as that party's candidate in
the Tokyo municipal elections; although the party campaigned under the
banner of "an anti-fascist and anti-bureaucratic popular front," Seno'o lost
the election.

During this same period, the government began to increase its pressure
against left-wing groups and liberal writers. By 1936 membership in the

Youth League had reached nearly three thousand, and although this made it an object of concern for the government, it was Seno'o's active involvement with the broader left-wing popular front that would lead to his eventual arrest. Under the auspices of the Peace Preservation Act of 1925, Seno'o was arrested on December 7, 1936, and charged with treason, when hundreds of members of all these organizations were rounded up, including Proletarian Party Chairman Katō Kanjū. After five months of relentless interrogation, Seno'o would confess his "crimes" and pledge his loyalty to the emperor in 1937. Sentenced to five years in prison, he was released due to ill health in 1942. After the war, he resumed his work for peace and social justice, though in a much quieter vein.

As with the New Buddhist Fellowship, it is important to examine Seno'o and the Youth League's work in relation to the broader traditions of Buddhist doctrinal interpretation, the Japanese historical tradition of reform and social criticism, and post-1868 movements in Buddhist and Japanese thought (including the Kyoto School, Critical Buddhism, and Engaged Buddhism). Only then can we see the lingering tensions within Buddhist ethics perhaps from the tradition's origins: between the "materialist" desire to create a more just society and the "spiritual" quest for personal libera-tion. For Seno'o Girō, this tension was acutely felt and a central thread in his biography:

> For us, religion is life itself. Society is our concern. That is to say, society is what we are made of. Politics, economics, education, the military as well as the arts and so on, are all subsumed under religion. All aspects of social life must be subject to critique and reform in light of the spirit of the Buddha. Thus aspiring to change society, to know ourselves, to sincerely repent and to simultaneously repay with gratitude the grace [Jpn. *on* 恩] we have received—all these are part of the life of faith. At that level, there is no difference between the movement to better society conducted in faith and the same call to action from those believ-ers in historical materialism, whether socialist or communist.[54]

Conclusion

As with the New Buddhist Fellowship, Seno'o and his fellow Youth League Buddhists saw social activism—and even, in the latter case, economic and political revolution—as inseparable from "spiritual" activity. While this allowed them to engage wholeheartedly in "secular" activities in a way that would have been impossible for monks and priests, it also meant that they had difficulty justifying or explaining why they held onto "Buddhism" at all. Their work was decidedly *not* framed, as John Nelson puts it in speaking of early Japanese precedents for socially active Buddhism, by "a discourse of salvation"—unless salvation is understood in terms of "this-worldly" release. Along these lines, Seno'o certainly, and perhaps the New Buddhists too, would likely not have understood the distinction made by Raoul Birnbaum in his 2009 critique of Engaged Buddhism. Birnbaum argues: "A bodhisattva vow to confront the suffering of others must be coupled with an intention to lead sentient beings to liberation and awakening."[55] For Seno'o, it is *not* the case that social and political activism is a *means* of leading sentient beings to awakening, but rather—echoing Marx's famous remarks on the interdependence of consciousness and material conditions, but also Zen master Dōgen on the unity of theory and practice—the process of liberating the oppressed from suffering is *nothing other than Buddhist awakening*. In other words, from this radical Buddhist perspective, awakening of consciousness (and subsequent liberation from suffering) is a process that emerges from direct engagement with social, economic, and political (structural) transformation. Here we see an extension of the Buddhist logic of interdependence—and dependent origination—to enclose the social, political, and economic spheres.

In his 2013 monograph on recent movements within Japanese Buddhism, Nelson argues that whereas *conventional* Buddhism involves following "well-worn routes emphasizing religious faith and belief, sacred images and icons, the Buddhist precepts or dharma, foundational scriptures, and so forth," *experimental* Buddhism is a "differently focused endeavor to *domesticate* an understanding of Buddhism so that it responds to and privileges the patterns, preferences, and concerns of a person's life."[56] While the latter certainly strikes us as a more "modern" way of practicing religion, the notion of domesticating or "privatizing" Buddhism to fit one's a priori preferences and concerns seems—from a Critical Buddhist perspective—highly problematic, if not dangerous. Neither the New Buddhist Fellowship nor Seno'o's Youth League would opt for either of these choices: while the first reflects the "dead" Buddhism they sought to escape, the second is a form of Buddhism that only serves to perpetuate ego and thus increase inequality and social suffering. The point, after all, is not simply to *interpret* the world of suffering, but to *change* it.

Notes

1. This chapter contains material—revised and redacted—previously published in James Mark Shields, *Critical Buddhism: Engaging with Modern Japanese Buddhist Thought* (London: Ashgate, 2011) and James Mark Shields, *Against Harmony: Progressive and Radical Buddhism in Modern Japan* (London and New York: Oxford University Press, 2017).

2. To cite one example, from an article called "The One Road of Zen and War," published in 1939 by Zen master Daiun Harada Roshi: "[If ordered to] march: tramp, tramp, or shoot: bang, bang. This is the manifestation of the highest Wisdom [of Enlightenment]. The unity of Zen and war of which I speak extends to the furthest reaches of holy way [now under way]" (Brian Victoria, *Zen at War* [New York: Weatherhill, 1997], 137).

3. D. T. Suzuki, *Zen and Japanese Culture* (Princeton: Princeton University Press, 1970), 61.

4. Throughout this essay, Japanese names are presented in accordance with Japanese conventions, i.e., first the family name, then the personal.

5. The ferment reached a peak in the early 1990s, with the publication of Hakamaya Noriaki, *Hongaku shisō hihan* (Tokyo: Daizō Shuppan, 1989), Hakamaya Noriaki, *Hihan Bukkyō* (Tokyo: Daizō Shuppan, 1990), and Matsumoto Shirō, *Zen shisō no hihanteki kenkyū* (Tokyo: Daizō, 1993), and the subsequent session at the American Academy of Religion's 1993 meeting in Washington, DC, entitled "Critical Buddhism: Issues and Responses to a New Methodological Movement," which resulted in the English-language compendium: Jamie Hubbard and Paul L. Swanson, eds., *Pruning the Bodhi Tree: The Storm over Critical Buddhism* (Honolulu: University of Hawai'i Press, 1997).

6. Matsumoto Shirō. "The Meaning of 'Zen,'" in *Pruning the Bodhi Tree: The Storm over Critical Buddhism*, edited by Jamie Hubbard and Paul L. Swanson, 242–50 (Honolulu: University of Hawai'i Press, 1997), 250.

7. Abe Masao, *Zen and Comparative Studies* (Honolulu: University of Hawai'i Press, 1997), 3. The importance of Dōgen to contemporary Japanese Zen studies can hardly be overestimated. In addition to founding the Sōtō sect, Dōgen is generally considered Japan's most significant premodern "philosopher."

8. Paul Swanson, "Why They Say Zen Is Not Buddhism: Recent Japanese Critiques of Buddha-Nature," in *Pruning the Bodhi Tree: The Storm over Critical Buddhism*, edited by Jamie Hubbard and Paul L. Swanson, 3–29 (Honolulu: University of Hawai'i Press, 1997), 27–28.

9. Hakamaya Noriaki, "Critical Philosophy versus Topical Philosophy," in *Pruning the Bodhi Tree: The Storm over Critical Buddhism*, edited by Paul L. Swanson, and Jamie Hubbard, 56–80 (Honolulu: University of Hawai'i Press, 1997), 56.

10. Important to note here is the universal claim of Critical Buddhism: they reject simplistic East-West dichotomies and argue that the battle they are waging lies at the heart of philosophical and religious traditions East and West. As Hakamaya explains in his essay "Critical Philosophy versus Topical Philosophy": "The heart of the intellectual question . . . lies not in the different ways of thought of East and West, but rather in the confrontation between *topica* and *critica*" (58).

11. See Ernesto Grassi, "Critical Philosophy or Topical Philosophy? Meditations on the *De nostri temporis studiorum ratione*," in *Giambattista Vico: An International Symposium*, edited by G. Tagliacozzo and H. V. White (Baltimore: John Hopkins, 1969).

12. Hubbard, Jamie, "Introduction," in *Pruning the Bodhi Tree: The Storm over Critical Buddhism*, edited by Jamie Hubbard and Paul L. Swanson, vii–xxii (Honolulu: University of Hawai'i Press, 1997), vii.

13. See Matsumoto Shirō, "The Doctrine of *Tathāgata-garbha* Is Not Buddhist," in *Pruning the Bodhi Tree: The Storm over Critical Buddhism*, edited by Jamie Hubbard and Paul L. Swanson, 165–73 (Honolulu: University of Hawai'i Press, 1997, 171; Hakamaya, "Critical Philosophy," 56.

14. "Dependent origination" is an idea with deep roots in classical Buddhist texts, and while there are a variety of formulations (and even more interpretations), the basic teaching is that all things and all events arise from a chain of interlocking causes and conditions. More specifically, early Buddhist texts indicate a "12-link chain" of dependent origination that helps explain the origins and persistence of *duḥkha* ("suffering"). The soteriological claim associated with this doctrine is—as stated in the third "Noble Truth"—that eliminating these conditions will lead to liberation from suffering; thus, the goal of all Buddhist practice.

15. Hakamaya ("Critical Philosophy," 64) calls Śākyamuni Buddha "the first such criticalist in India," though he goes on to laud Confucius ("China's Christ") over Laozi and Śākyamuni himself (67), for his superior humanism.

16. Abe, *Zen and Comparative Studies*, 16.

17. Yamaguchi Zuiho, cited in Hubbard, "Introduction," xvi.

18. Hubbard, "Introduction," vii.

19. See Shields, *Critical Buddhism*.

20. See Shields, *Against Harmony*.

21. SB 1, 1 (July 1900), 3; unless otherwise indicated, all translations are mine. The NBF journal, *Shin Bukkyō* (SB), is cited by volume and issue numbers, followed by date of initial publication and page numbers in Akamatsu Tesshin and Fukushima Hirotaka, eds. *Shin Bukkyō*, 4 vols. (Kyoto: Nagata Bunshōdō, 1982).

22. Along with Buddhism, traditional forms of Shintō reverence and folk worship also come under attack in the NBF *sengen*. Though "superstition" is the primary locus of critique, other terms used to describe the "old Buddhism" are "pessimistic" (Jpn. *enseiteki* 厭世的), for its denial of this-worldly happiness, and "imaginary" (Jpn. *kūsōteki* 空想的), for its elaborate cosmology.

23. SB 1, 1 (July 1900), 3.

24. Klautau, Orion. "Against the Ghosts of Recent Past: Meiji Scholarship and the Discourse on Edo-Period Buddhist Decadence," *Japanese Journal of Religious Studies* 35, no. 2 (2008): 263–303.

25. Kishimoto Hideo, *Japanese Religion in the Meiji Era* (Tokyo: Ōbunsha, 1956), 128.

26. SB 2, 9 (August 1901), 325.

27. SB 2, 9 (August 1901), 325.

28. Although neither Sakaino nor other New Buddhists are forthcoming as to their reason for choosing pantheism as a foundation for their New Buddhism, it likely has to do with both the fact that pantheism (and vitalism) played a significant role in late-nineteenth-century European thought and that early Buddhist modernists in Japan (including D. T. Suzuki) had already noted the close correlation between at least some versions of pantheism and traditional Asian cosmologies. Moreover, pantheism in their view provides a "middle way" between theistic religions and materialistic science.

29. SB 2, 9 (August 1901), 325.

30. See in this regard, Gilles Deleuze, *Spinoza: Practical Philosophy* (San Francisco: City Lights, 1988), 122–30; also Najita Tetsuo on pantheism and "freedom" in the work of Andō Shoeki (Najita Tetsuo. "Andō Shōeki—The 'Forgotten Thinker' in Japanese History," in *Learning Places: The Afterlives of Area Studies*, edited by Masao Miyoshi and Harry D. Harootunian, 61–79 (Durham: Duke University Press, 2002), 74.

31. SB 2, 9 (August 1901), 329; for more on pantheism, see SB 1, 5 (November 1900), 140; SB 2, 6 (May 1901), 89–95; SB 2, 12 (November 1901), 386–90; SB 4, 12 (December 1903), 916–19; SB 8, 2 (February 1907), 371–81; SB 8, 7 (July 1907), 454–61. D. T. Suzuki had written on the importance of a pantheistic foundation for contemporary religion as early as 1896, in his *Shin Shūkyōron* (D. T. Suzuki, *Suzuki Daisetsu zenshū*, 23 vols. [Tokyo: Iwanami, 1969), 23, 38). Suzuki argued that pantheism might be conceived as the "positive" or "pro-active" aspect (Jpn. *sekkyokuteki hōmen* 積極的方面) of atheism—or perhaps as a middle way between theism and atheism.

32. SB 8, 2 (February 1907), 381; also see SB 2, 6 (May 1901), 289–95.

33. SB 12, 8 (August 1911), 1313–14.

34. SB 12, 8 (August 1911), 1315–16.

35. See, e.g., Takashima Beihō. *Bukkyō nyūmon—Bukkyō to wa donna mono no ka* (Tokyo: Gakufū shoin, 1956).

36. See Hoshino Seiji, "Reconfiguring Buddhism as a Religion: Nakanishi Ushirō and his Shin Bukkyō," *Japanese Religions* 34, no. 2 (July 2009): 133–54; also see the lead piece of the December 1901 issue for a useful summary of thoughts from various contributors on the "faith question" (Jpn. *shinkō mondai* 信仰問題); SB 2, 13, 398–404.

37. SB 1, 1 (July 1900), 8–9.

38. SB 1, 1 (July 1900), 9.

39. SB 1, 1 (July 1900), 9.

40. In a later work on Buddhist history, frustrated by being unable to reconcile the chronology surrounding the founder of Buddhism's life, Sakaino would go so far as to wonder whether Śākyamuni Buddha might be a "figment of the collective oriental imagination"; see James Edward Ketelaar, *Of Heretics and Martyrs in Meiji Japan: Buddhism and Its Persecution* (Princeton: Princeton University Press, 1990), 73.

41. SB 2, 5 (May 1901), 279–80.

42. See Yoshinaga Shin'ichi, ed., *Kindai Nihon ni okeru chishikijin shūkyō undō no gensetsu kūkan: "Shin Bukkyō" no shisōshi, bunkashiteki kenkyū*, 1–6 (Grants-in-Aid for Scientific Research, no. 20320016, 2011), 30.

43. See, for example, Sakaino's "Confession of Practical Faith" (*Jissai shinkō no hyōhaku*), SB 1, 3 (September 1900), 82–89.

44. According to the results of a survey recorded in the July 1905 edition of *Shin Bukkyō*, more than half of the leading NBF figures expressed their disbelief in any sort of afterlife; see Yoshida Kyūichi, *Nihon kindai bukkyōshi kenkyū* (Tokyo: Yoshikawa kōbunkan, 1992), 331.

45. SB 1, 5 (November 1900), 159; see Yoshida, *Nihon kindai*, 331.

46. Inagaki Masami, *Budda o seoite gaito e: Seno'o Girō to Shinkō Bukkyō Seinen Dōmei* (Tokyo: Iwanami, 1997), 3–6, my translation.

47. Winston Davis, *Japanese Religion and Society: Paradigms of Structure and Change* (Albany: State University of New York Press, 1992), 177.

48. Kashiwahara Yūsen, *Nihon bukkyōshi: kindai* (Tokyo: Yoshikawa kōbunkan, 1990), 214; Hayashi Reihō, *Seno'o Girō to Shinkō Bukkyō Seinen Dōmei: shakaishugi to bukkyō no tachiba* (Tokyo: Hyakkaen, 1976), 26–29; my translation.

49. Seno'o Girō, *Seno'o Girō shūkyō ronshu* (Tokyo: Daizō, 1975), 312–13, 386.

50. Complicating the issue further is the fact that by the late 1920s, Marxist (and Soviet) orthodoxy had become more explicitly antireligious, such that socialists like Seno'o may have felt more pressure to openly avow their "atheist" credentials.

51. Seno'o, *Shūkyō ronshu*, 275.

52. See Inagaki, *Budda o seoite*, 16.

53. Kashiwahara, *Nihon bukkyōshi*, 215.

54. Seno'o, *Shūkyō ronshu*, 253; my translation.

55. Birnbaum, Raoul Birnbaum, "In Search of an Engaged Buddhism," *Religion East and West* 9 (2009): 25–39.

56. John Nelson, *Experimental Buddhism: Innovation and Activism in Contemporary Japan* (Honolulu: University of Hawai'i Press, 2013), 27.

Bibliography

Abe, Masao. *Zen and Comparative Studies*. Honolulu: University of Hawai'i, 1997.

Akamatsu, Tesshin, and Hirotaka Fukushima, eds. *Shin bukkyō* [New Buddhism]. 4 vols. Kyoto: Nagata Bunshōdō, 1982. Cited as SB, by volume and date of original publication.

Birnbaum, Raoul. 2009. "In Search of an Engaged Buddhism." *Religion East and West* 9 (2009): 25–39.

Davis, Winston. *Japanese Religion and Society: Paradigms of Structure and Change.* Albany: State University of New York Press, 1992.

Deleuze, Gilles. *Spinoza: Practical Philosophy.* San Francisco: City Lights, 1988.

Grassi, Ernesto. "Critical Philosophy or Topical Philosophy? Meditations on the *De nostri temporis studiorum ratione.*" In *Giambattista Vico: An International Symposium,* edited by G. Tagliacozzo and H. V. White. Baltimore: John Hopkins University Press, 1969.

Hakamaya, Noriaki. *Hongaku shisō hihan* [Critiques of the doctrine of original enlightenment]. Tokyo: Daizō Shuppan, 1989.

———. *Hihan Bukkyō* [Critical Buddhism]. Tokyo: Daizō Shuppan, 1990.

———. "Critical Philosophy versus Topical Philosophy." In *Pruning the Bodhi Tree: The Storm over Critical Buddhism,* edited by Paul L. Swanson, and Jamie Hubbard, 56–80. Honolulu: University of Hawai'i Press, 1997.

Hayashi, Reihō. *Seno'o Girō to Shinkō Bukkyō Seinen Dōmei: shakaishugi to bukkyō no tachiba* [Seno'o Girō and the Youth League for Revitalizing Buddhism: The Buddhist Socialist Standpoint]. Tokyo: Hyakkaen, 1976.

Heisig, James, and John Maraldo, eds. *Rude Awakenings: Zen, the Kyoto School, and the Question of Nationalism.* Honolulu: University of Hawai'i Press, 1994.

Hoshino, Seiji. "Reconfiguring Buddhism as a Religion: Nakanishi Ushirō and his Shin Bukkyō." *Japanese Religions* 34, no. 2 (July 2009): 133–54.

Hubbard, Jamie. "Introduction." In *Pruning the Bodhi Tree: The Storm over Critical Buddhism,* edited by Jamie Hubbard and Paul L. Swanson, vii–xxii. Honolulu: University of Hawai'i Press, 1997.

Inagaki Masami. *Budda o seoite gaito e: Seno'o Girō to Shinkō Bukkyō Seinen Dōmei* [Taking the Buddha on their backs and going to the streets: Seno'o Girō and the Youth League for Revitalizing Buddhism]. Tokyo: Iwanami, 1997.

Kashiwahara, Yūsen. *Nihon bukkyōshi: kindai* [Japanese Buddhist history: modernity]. Tokyo: Yoshikawa kōbunkan, 1990.

Ketelaar, James Edward. *Of Heretics and Martyrs in Meiji Japan: Buddhism and Its Persecution.* Princeton: Princeton University Press, 1990.

Kishimoto, Hideo. *Japanese Religion in the Meiji Era.* Translated by John F. Howes. Tokyo: Ōbunsha, 1956.

Klautau, Orion. "Against the Ghosts of Recent Past: Meiji Scholarship and the Discourse on Edo-Period Buddhist Decadence." *Japanese Journal of Religious Studies* 35, no. 2 (2008): 263–303.

Matsumoto, Shirō. *Zen shisō no hihanteki kenkyū* [Critical studies on Zen thought]. Tokyo: Daizō, 1993.

———. "The Doctrine of *Tathāgata-garbha* Is Not Buddhist." In *Pruning the Bodhi Tree: The Storm over Critical Buddhism,* edited by Jamie Hubbard and Paul L. Swanson, 165–73. Honolulu: University of Hawai'i Press, 1997.

————. "The Meaning of 'Zen'." In *Pruning the Bodhi Tree: The Storm over Critical Buddhism*, edited by Jamie Hubbard and Paul L. Swanson, 242–50. Honolulu: University of Hawai'i Press, 1997.

Najita Tetsuo. "Andō Shōeki—The 'Forgotten Thinker' in Japanese History." In *Learning Places: The Afterlives of Area Studies*, edited by Masao Miyoshi and Harry D. Harootunian, 61–79. Durham: Duke University Press, 2002.

Nelson, John. *Experimental Buddhism: Innovation and Activism in Contemporary Japan*. Honolulu: University of Hawai'i Press, 2013.

Seno'o, Girō. *Seno'o Girō shūkyō ronshu* [The religious thought of Seno'o Girō]. Tokyo: Daizō, 1975.

Shields, James Mark. *Critical Buddhism: Engaging with Modern Japanese Buddhist Thought*. London: Ashgate, 2011.

————. *Against Harmony: Progressive and Radical Buddhism in Modern Japan*. London and New York: Oxford University, 2017.

Suzuki, D[aisetsu]. T[eitarō]. *Zen and Japanese Culture*. Princeton: Princeton University Press, 1970.

————. *Suzuki Daisetsu Zenshū* (Complete works of Suzuki Daisetsu). 23 vols. Tokyo: Iwanami, 1969. Cited as SDZ, by volume.

Swanson, Paul. "Why They Say Zen Is Not Buddhism: Recent Japanese Critiques of Buddha-Nature." In *Pruning the Bodhi Tree: The Storm over Critical Buddhism*, edited by Jamie Hubbard and Paul L. Swanson, 3–29. Honolulu: University of Hawai'i Press, 1997.

Takashima Beihō. *Bukkyō nyūmon—Bukkyō to wa donna mono no ka* [An introduction to Buddhism: What is Buddhism?]. Tokyo: Gakufū shoin, 1956.

Victoria, Brian. *Zen at War*. New York: Weatherhill, 1997.

Yoshida, Kyūichi. *Nihon kindai bukkyōshi kenkyū* [A study of modern Japanese Buddhist history]. Tokyo: Yoshikawa kōbunkan, 1992.

Yoshinaga, Shin'ichi, ed. *Kindai Nihon ni okeru chishikijin shūkyō undō no gensetsu kūkan: "Shin Bukkyō" no shisōshi, bunkashiteki kenkyū* [The discursive space of an intellectual religious movement in modern Japan: A study of the journal New Buddhism from the viewpoint of the history of culture and thought], 1–6. Grants-in-Aid for Scientific Research, no. 20320016, 2011.

Glossary

Terms are organized alphabetically by their most commonly used English translation, with their equivalents in Sanskrit, Pāli, Chinese, Korean, and Japanese in the adjacent columns. Chinese characters are provided only in the column for the Chinese term unless different characters are used in Japan, in which case the alternative characters are provided after the Japanese term. Chinese terms are Romanized using the current Pinyin system with the older Wade-Giles system in parentheses after the Chinese characters. Korean terms are provided in the current Revised Romanization system with alternative spellings using the older McCune-Reischauer system in parentheses (on those occasions where they differ from RR). Diacritical marks are included for all terms according to the Romanization conventions of each language. Some entries include "N/A" because terms that developed later do not have direct analogues in the earlier traditions (e.g., terms coined in Japan might not have equivalents in the other languages).

English Term	Sanskrit	Pāli	Chinese	Korean	Japanese
action, moral cause and effect	*karma*	*kamma*	*yè* 業 (*yeh*)	*eop* (*ŏp*)	*gō*
aggregate (of craving)	*skandha*	*khandha*	*yùn* 蘊 (*yün*)	*on*	*un*
arhat (enlightened person)	*arhat* or *arhant*	*arahant*	*āluóhàn* 阿羅漢 (*a lo han*)	*arahan*	*arakan*
asceticism	N/A	N/A	N/A	N/A	*kin'yokushugi* 禁欲主義

continued on next page

English Term	Sanskrit	Pāli	Chinese	Korean	Japanese
Association of Buddhist Sects	N/A	N/A	N/A	N/A	*Shoshū Dōtoku Kaimei* 諸宗同徳会盟
awakening (initial insight)	N/A	N/A	*jiàn xìng* 見性 (*chien hsing*)	*gyeonseong* (*kyŏnsŏng*)	*kenshō*
awakening (lasting understanding)	N/A	N/A	*wú* 悟 (*wu*)	*o*	*satori*
blind faith	N/A	N/A	N/A	N/A	*mōshin* 盲信
bodhisattva (one who has vowed to attain buddhahood for the benefit of all sentient beings)	*bodhisattva*	*bodhisatta*	*púsà* 菩薩 (*p'u sa*)	*bosal* (*posal*)	*bosatsu*
Buddha (awakened one)	*Buddha*	*Buddha*	*Fó* 佛 (*fo*)	*Bul* (*Pul*)	仏 *Butsu*
Buddha-nature	*tathāgata-garbha* or *buddha-dhātu*	*tathāgata-garbha* or *buddha-dhātu*	*fóxìng* 佛性 (*fo hsing*)	*bulseong* (*pulsŏng*)	*busshō* 仏性
Buddhist decadence	N/A	N/A	N/A	N/A	*daraku bukkyō* 堕落仏教
compassion	*karuṇā*	*karuṇā*	*cíbēi* 慈悲 (*tz'u pei*)	*jabi* (*chabî*)	*jihi*
consciousness	*vijñāna*	*viññāṇa*	*shí* 識 (*shih*)	*sik* (*shik*)	*shiki*
correct faith	N/A	N/A	N/A	N/A	*shōshin* 正信
craving, thirst	*tṛṣṇā*	*taṇhā*	*tānài* 貪愛 (*t'an ai*)	*tamae* (*t'amae*)	*katsuai* 渇愛
critical Buddhism	N/A	N/A	N/A	N/A	*hihan bukkyō* 批判仏教

English Term	Sanskrit	Pāli	Chinese	Korean	Japanese
cultivation; training	N/A	N/A	*xiūxíng* 修行 (*hsiu hsing*)	*suhaeng*	*shugyō*
degenerate age of the dharma	N/A	N/A	*mòfǎ* 末法 (*mo fa*)	*malbeop* (*malbŏp*)	*mappō*
dependent origination, interdependent arising	*pratītya-samutpāda*	*paṭicca-samuppāda*	*yuánqǐ* 緣起 (*yüan ch'i*)	*yeongi* (*yŏn'gi*)	*engi* 緣起
differentiation is equality	N/A	N/A	N/A	N/A	*sabetsu soku byōdō* 差別即平等
dimension of the dharma	*dharma-dhātu*	*dhamma-dhātu*	*fǎjiè* 法界 (*fa chieh*)	*beopgye* (*pŏpkye*)	*hokkai*
empathetic joy	*muditā*	*muditā*	*xǐ* 喜 (*hsi*)	*hui* (*hŭi*)	*ki*
emptiness	*śūnyatā*	*suññatā*	*kōng* 空 (*k'ung*)	*gong* (*kong*)	*kū*
ethics, morals, right conduct	*śīla*	*sīla*	*jiè* 戒 (*chieh*)	*gye* (*kye*)	*kai*
faith	N/A	N/A	N/A	N/A	*shinkō* 信仰
Faxiang (Buddhist sect)	N/A	N/A	*Fǎxiàng* 法相 (*Fa Hsiang*)	*Beopsang* (*Pŏpsang*)	*Hossō*
Four Noble Truths, Noble Fourfold Truth	*catvāri āryasatyāni*	*cattāri ariyasaccāni*	*sìshèngdì* 四聖諦 (*ssu sheng ti*)	*sa-seong-je* (*sa-sŏng-je*)	*shitai* 四諦
grace	N/A	N/A	N/A	N/A	*on* 恩
Great East Asia Co-Prosperity Sphere	N/A	N/A	N/A	N/A	*Dai Tōa Kyōei Ken* 大東亜共栄圏
heart-mind	N/A	N/A	*xīn* 心 (*hsin*)	*sim*	*shin; kokoro*
Huayan (Buddhist sect)	N/A	N/A	*Huáyán* 華嚴 (*Hua Yen*)	*Hwaeom* (*Hwaŏm*)	*Kegon*
ignorance	*avidyā*	*avijjā*	*wúmíng* 無明 (*wu ming*)	*mumyeong* (*mumyŏng*)	*mumyō*

continued on next page

English Term	Sanskrit	Pāli	Chinese	Korean	Japanese
Imperial Way Zen	N/A	N/A	N/A	N/A	*Dōdō Zen* 皇道禅
impermanence	*anitya*	*anicca*	*wúcháng* 無常 (*wu ch'ang*)	*musang*	*mujō*
judgement and interpretation of Buddhist teachings	N/A	N/A	N/A	N/A	*kyōsō-hanjaku* 競争半弱
just sitting, simply sitting (in meditation)	*utkuṭuka-stha*	*ukkuṭika-stha*	*zhǐ guǎn dǎzuò* 只管打坐 (*chih kuan ta zuò*)	*jigwantajwa* (*chigwant' ajwa*)	*shikantaza*
koan (problem that defies rational solutions)	N/A	N/A	*gōng'àn* 公案 (*kung an*)	*gongan* (*kongan*)	*kōan*
live release (of captive animals)	N/A	N/A	*fàngshēng* 放生 (*fang sheng*)	*bangsaeng* (*pangsaeng*)	*hōjōe* 放生会
loving-kindness	*maitrī*	*mettā*	*cí* 慈 (*tz'u*)	*ja* (*cha*)	*ji* 慈
martial hero (literary and film genre)	N/A	N/A	*wǔxiá* 武俠 (*wu hsia*)	N/A	N/A
meditation	*dhyāna*	*jhāna*	*chán* 禅 (*ch'an*)	*seon* (*sŏn*)	*zen*
meditative concentration/ discipline	*samādhi*	*samādhi*	*sān mèi* 三昧 (*san mei*)	*sammae*	*sanmai*
motivation of a bodhisattva	*bodhicitta*	*bodhicitta*	*pútíxīn* 菩提心 (*p'u t'i hsin*)	*borisim* (*porisim*)	*bodaishin*
New Buddhism	N/A	N/A	N/A	N/A	*Shin Bukkyō* 新仏教
New Buddhist Fellowship	N/A	N/A	N/A	N/A	*Shin Bukkyō Dōshikai* 新仏教同志会

English Term	Sanskrit	Pāli	Chinese	Korean	Japanese
nirvana (extinguishing of karma)	*nirvāṇa*	*nibbana*	*nièpán* 涅槃 (*nieh p'an*)	*yeolban* (*yŏlban*)	*nehan*
no-mind	N/A	N/A	*wúxīn* 無心 (*wu hsin*)	*musim* (*mushim*)	*mushin*
no-self, non-self	*anātman*	*anattā*	*wúwǔ* 無我 (*wu wo*)	*mua*	*muga*
non-violence, non-injury	*ahiṃsā*	*avihiṃsā*	*bù hài* 不害 (*pu hai*)	*bulhae* (*purhae*)	*fugai*
Old Buddhism	N/A	N/A	N/A	N/A	*Kyū Bukkyō* 旧仏教
original enlightenment	N/A	N/A	*běnjué* 本覺 (*pen chüeh*)	*bongak* (*pon'gak*)	*hongaku*
other-power	N/A	N/A	*tālì* 他力 (*t'a li*)	*taryeok* (*t'aryŏk*)	*tariki*
pantheism	N/A	N/A	N/A	N/A	*hanshinron* 汎神論
pantheistic materialism	N/A	N/A	N/A	N/A	*yuibutsuteki hanshinron* 唯物的汎神論
point below the navel (meditative focus)	N/A	N/A	*dantian* 丹田 (*tan t'ien*)	*danjeon* (*tanjŏn*)	*tanden*
praise chant to Amida Buddha	N/A	N/A	*niànfó* 念佛 (*nien fo*)	*yeombul* (*yŏmbul*)	*nembutsu*
Proletarian Party of Japan	N/A	N/A	N/A	N/A	*Nihon Musantō* 日本無産等
Pure Land (Buddhist sect)	N/A	N/A	*Jìngtǔzōng* 淨土宗 (*Ching T'u Tsung*)	*Jeongtojong* (*Chŏngt'ojong*)	*Jōdo Shū*

continued on next page

English Term	Sanskrit	Pāli	Chinese	Korean	Japanese
rebirth (the cycle of rebirth)	*saṃsāra*	*saṃsāra*	*lúnhúi* 輪迴 (*lun hui*)	*yunhoe* (*yunhoe*)	*rinne*
royal law [together with] Buddha dharma	N/A	N/A	N/A	N/A	*ōbō buppō* 王法仏法
Sanlun (Buddhist sect)	N/A	N/A	*Sānlùn* 三論 (*San Lun*)	*Samnon*	*Sanron*
scriptural texts	*sūtra*	*sutta*	*jīng* 經 (*ching*)	*gyeong* (*kyŏng*)	*kyō*
sea-state meditative concentration	*sāgara-mudrā samādhi*	*sāgara-mudrā samādhi*	*hǎi yìn sān mèi* 海印三昧 (*hai yin san mei*)	*haeinsammae*	*kaiin sanmai*
self-power	N/A	N/A	*zìlì* 自力 (*tau li*)	*jaryeok* (*charyŏk*)	*jiriki*
selfless love	N/A	N/A	N/A	N/A	*muga-ai* 無我愛
skillful means, useful means	*upāya*	*upaya*	*fāngbiàn* 方便 (*fang pien*)	*bangpyeon* (*bangp'yŏn*)	*hōben*
special transmission outside the scriptures	N/A	N/A	*jiāo wài bié zhuàn* 教外別傳 (*chiao wai pieh ch'uan*)	*gyooe byeljeon* (*kyooe pyŏlchŏn*)	*kyōge betsuden*
storehouse consciousness	*ālāya-vijñāna*	*ālaya-vijñāna*	*ālàiyēshí* 阿賴耶識 (*a lai yeh shih*)	*aroeyasik* (*aroeyasik*)	*araya-shiki*
suchness	*tathātā*	*tathatā*	*zhēnrú* 真如 (*chen ju*)	*jinyeo* (*chinyŏ*)	*shinnyo*
suffering, sorrow, unsatisfactoriness, stress	*duḥkha*	*dukkha*	*kǔ* 苦 (*k'u*)	*go* (*ko*)	*ku*

English Term	Sanskrit	Pāli	Chinese	Korean	Japanese
symbiosis	N/A	N/A	N/A	N/A	*kyōsei/ tomoiki* 共生
Tales of Poverty	N/A	N/A	N/A	N/A	*Bimbō Monogatari* 貧乏物語
teachings of Buddhism (sometimes refers to phenomeno-logical constituents of reality)	*dharma*	*dhamma*	*fófǎ* 佛法 (*fo fa*)	*bulbeop* (*pulbŏp*)	*buppō* 仏法
techniques of the sword	N/A	N/A	N/A	N/A	*kenjutsu* 劍術
this world	N/A	N/A	N/A	N/A	*gense[i]shugi* 現世主義
three-thousand realms in an instant of thought	N/A	N/A	*yī niàn sān qiān* 一念三千 (*i nien san ch'ien*)	*ilnyeom samcheon* (*ilnyŏm samch'ŏn*)	*ichinen sanzen*
threefold contemplation in a single mind	N/A	N/A	*yīxīn sān guān* 一心三観 (*i hsin san tang*)	*ilsim samgwan* (*ilsim samgwan*)	*isshin sangan*
Tiantai (Buddhist sect)	N/A	N/A	*Tiāntāi* 天台 (*T'ien Tai*)	*Cheontae* (*Ch'ŏnt'ae*)	*Tendai*
unfettered mind; immovable mind	N/A	N/A	N/A	N/A	*fudōshin* 不動心
Way	N/A	N/A	*dào* 道 (tao)	*do* (*to*)	*dō; michi*
way of the sword	N/A	N/A	N/A	N/A	*kendō* 劍道

continued on next page

English Term	Sanskrit	Pāli	Chinese	Korean	Japanese
way of the warrior	N/A	N/A	N/A	N/A	*bushidō* 武士道
wisdom, insight	*prajñā*	*Paññā*	*zhīhuì* 知惠 (*chih hui*)	*jihye* (*chihye*)	*chie*
Youth League for Revitalizing Buddhism	N/A	N/A	N/A	N/A	*Shinkō Bukkyō Seinen Dōmei* 新興仏教青年同盟
Zhenyan (Buddhist sect)	N/A	N/A	*Zhēnyán* 真言 (*Chen Yen*)	N/A	*Shingon*

Contributors

Jesse Butler earned his PhD in philosophy at the University of Oklahoma with specialization in philosophy of mind and epistemology. He currently serves as a full professor in the department of philosophy and religion at the University of Central Arkansas, where he teaches courses on philosophy of mind, self-knowledge, philosophy of language, critical thinking, and philosophy for living. He is the author of *Rethinking Introspection: A Pluralist Approach to the First-Person Perspective* (2013) and has published articles in *Science, Religion and Culture, Journal of Consciousness Studies, Bloomsbury Companion to the Philosophy of Psychiatry* (2019), and other academic outlets. He was a U.S. Fulbright Scholar in 2016/17 at Jinan University in Guangzhou, China, where he taught courses on American philosophy and cross-cultural approaches to self-knowledge. His current research focuses on the cross-cultural epistemic virtue of ecological self-understanding.

Melissa Croteau is professor of film studies and literature and the film program director at California Baptist University. Her research, teaching, and publications center on global cinema, media adaptation, film theory and history, and early modern British literature and culture. She has published essays in *Shakespeare Survey, Cahiers Élisabéthains*, and several edited volumes. Her books include the monographs *Transcendence and Spirituality in Japanese Cinema* and *Re-forming Shakespeare: Adaptations and Appropriations of the Bard in Millennial Film and Popular Culture* and the co-edited volume *Apocalyptic Shakespeare: Essays on Visions of Chaos and Revelation in Recent Film Adaptations*. She currently is working on a book for Bloomsbury on Shakespeare and film theory.

Peter D. Hershock is director of the Asian Studies Development Program and coordinator of the Humane AI Initiative at the East-West Center in

Honolulu and was a Berggruen Institute China Center fellow from 2017–18. His philosophical work makes use of Buddhist conceptual resources to address contemporary issues of global concern. He has authored or edited more than a dozen books on Buddhism, Asian philosophy, and contemporary issues, including: *Reinventing the Wheel: A Buddhist Response to the Information Age* (1999); *Buddhism in the Public Sphere: Reorienting Global Interdependence* (2006); *Valuing Diversity: Buddhist Reflection on Realizing a More Equitable Global Future* (2012); *Public Zen, Personal Zen: A Buddhist Introduction* (2014); *Philosophies of Place: An Intercultural Conversation* (edited, 2020); *Human Beings or Human Becomings? A Conversation with Confucianism on the Concept of Person* (edited, 2021); and *Buddhism and Intelligent Technology: Toward a More Humane Future* (2021).

Jesús Ilundáin-Agurruza is professor and chair of the philosophy department at Linfield College (Oregon). Former president of the International Association for the Philosophy of Sport, his areas of expertise include phenomenology, philosophy of mind, comparative philosophy, and aesthetics. He has published *Holism and the Cultivation of Excellence: Skillful Striving* (2016), dozens of articles in journals such as *Journal of the Philosophy of Sport Phenomenology and the Cognitive Sciences,* and *Sports, Ethics, and Philosophy,* as well as many book chapters on comparative philosophy, martial arts, and sports. His current research is concerned with a comparative examination of expertise in high performance situations. An avid cyclist, swimmer, and budding freediver, he also enjoys sparring with his steel longsword.

Sujung Kim is associate professor of religious studies at DePauw University. She received her PhD in East Asian languages and cultures from Columbia University in 2014. Her chief research field is Japanese Buddhism of the medieval period with a focus on transcultural interactions between Japanese and Korean Buddhism. Her first book, *Shinra Myōjin and Buddhist Networks of the East Asian "Mediterranean"* (2019) is one of the first book-length studies that deal with the Buddhist interactions between Japan and Korea in the premodern period. She has published several journal articles and chapters in volumes such as *The Sea and the Sacred in Japan* (2018) and *New Perspectives in Modern Korean Buddhism* (forthcoming). She is currently working on a book project, *Korean Magical Medicine: Buddhist Healing Talismans in Chosŏn Korea.*

Sarah Mattice is a professor in the department of philosophy and religious studies at the University of North Florida. She specializes in comparative and

East Asian philosophy, and often teaches courses on Chinese and Japanese philosophy and on Buddhism. Her books include *Exploring the* Heart Sutra (2021) and *Metaphor and Metaphilosophy: Philosophy as Combat, Play, and Aesthetic Experience* (2014). In addition, she regularly publishes on feminist, Ruist/Confucian, and Daoist philosophies.

James McRae earned his PhD in comparative philosophy at the University of Hawai'i at Mānoa with specializations in Japanese philosophy and ethics. He currently serves as professor of Asian philosophy and religion and chair of the department of classics, philosophy, and religious studies at Westminster College in Fulton, Missouri. He regularly teaches courses on Buddhism, Asian thought, applied ethics, and critical thinking. His publications include *Japanese Environmental Philosophy* (with J. Baird Callicott, 2017), *Environmental Philosophy in Asian Traditions of Thought* (with J. Baird Callicott, 2014), and *The Philosophy of Ang Lee* (with Robert Arp and Adam Barkman, 2013).

Elizabeth Schiltz received her BA from Ohio Wesleyan University, and her PhD from Duke University. She has the good fortune to hold the Purna, Rao, Raju Chair of East-West Philosophy in the department of philosophy at the College of Wooster, in Wooster, Ohio. Her publications include "Two Chariots: Moral Psychology in Plato's *Phaedrus* and the *Kaṭha Upanishad*," in *Philosophy East and West*, "How to Teach Comparative Philosophy" in *Teaching Philosophy*, and " 'The Vessel of Knowledge' that Stole Our Hearts," in the *Good Place and Philosophy*.

Robert H. Scott is associate professor of philosophy at University of North Georgia, specializing in phenomenology, environmental philosophy, ethics, and comparative philosophy. He has served as president and is a member of the executive board of the Georgia Philosophical Society and is co-editor of *The Significance of Indeterminacy: Perspectives from Asian and Continental Philosophy* (with Gregory Moss, 2019) and *Freedom and Society: Essays on Autonomy, Identity, and Political Freedom* (with Yi Deng, Creighton Rosental, and Rosalind Simson, 2021).

James Mark Shields is professor of comparative humanities and Asian thought and was inaugural director of the Humanities Center at Bucknell University (Lewisburg, PA). Educated at McGill University (Canada), the University of Cambridge (UK), and Kyoto University (Japan), he conducts research on modern Buddhist thought, Japanese philosophy, comparative ethics, and philosophy of religion. He is author of *Critical Buddhism: Engaging with Modern Japanese Buddhist Thought* (2011), *Against Harmony: Progressive and Radical Buddhism in Modern Japan* (2017), and co-editor of *Teaching Buddhism in the West: From the Wheel to the Web* (Routledge, 2003), *Buddhist Responses to Globalization* (2014), and *The Oxford Handbook of Buddhist Ethics* (2018).

Mark Wells is an assistant teaching professor at Northeastern University in Boston, Massachusetts, where he teaches courses on the ethics of healthcare, technology, and the environment. He earned his PhD in philosophy from Bowling Green State University. His publications include "Race, Romantic Attraction and Dating" (with Megan Mitchell, *Ethical Theory and Moral Practice*, 2018), "Markets with Some Limits" (*Journal of Value Inquiry*, 2017), and "Liberty for Corvids" (with Scott Simmons and Diana Klimas, *Public Affairs Quarterly*, 2017).

George Wrisley earned his PhD in philosophy at the University of Iowa, specializing in the philosophy of language and metaphysics. At Georgia State University he earned an MA in philosophy, specializing in Wittgenstein. He has since gone on to focus his research on metaphilosophy, and his long-standing interests in Nietzsche, Buddhism, and Zen, particularly Dōgen's Sōtō Zen; one interest has been to bring Nietzsche's work on suffering and a passionate affirmation of life into conversation with Dōgen's Zen. His publications include "The Nietzschean Bodhisattva—Passionately Navigating Indeterminacy" in *The Significance of Indeterminacy: Perspectives from Asian and Continental Philosophy* (ed. Robert H. Scott and Gregory S. Moss, 2019), "Wherefore the Failure of Private Ostension?" in the *Australasian Journal of Philosophy* (2011), and "The Role of Compassion in Actualizing Dōgen's Zen," in *Japan Studies Review* (2021).

Zhang Xin earned her PhD in comparative literature at Peking University with a specialization in Western Christian literature. She is currently an associate professor at Beijing Normal University and the deputy director of the Center for the Study of Christian Literature and Arts at BNU. Her teaching and publications focus on Christian literature from ancient to present. Her books include the monograph *Jesus as Mirror: The Figure of Jesus in Western Novels in the 20th Century* and *The British Catholic Novels in the 20th Century*. She is working on a project on "Hagiographies in Late Antiquity."

Index